FIVE
ILLUMINATED
MANUSCRIPTS
OF
GIANGALEAZZO VISCONTI

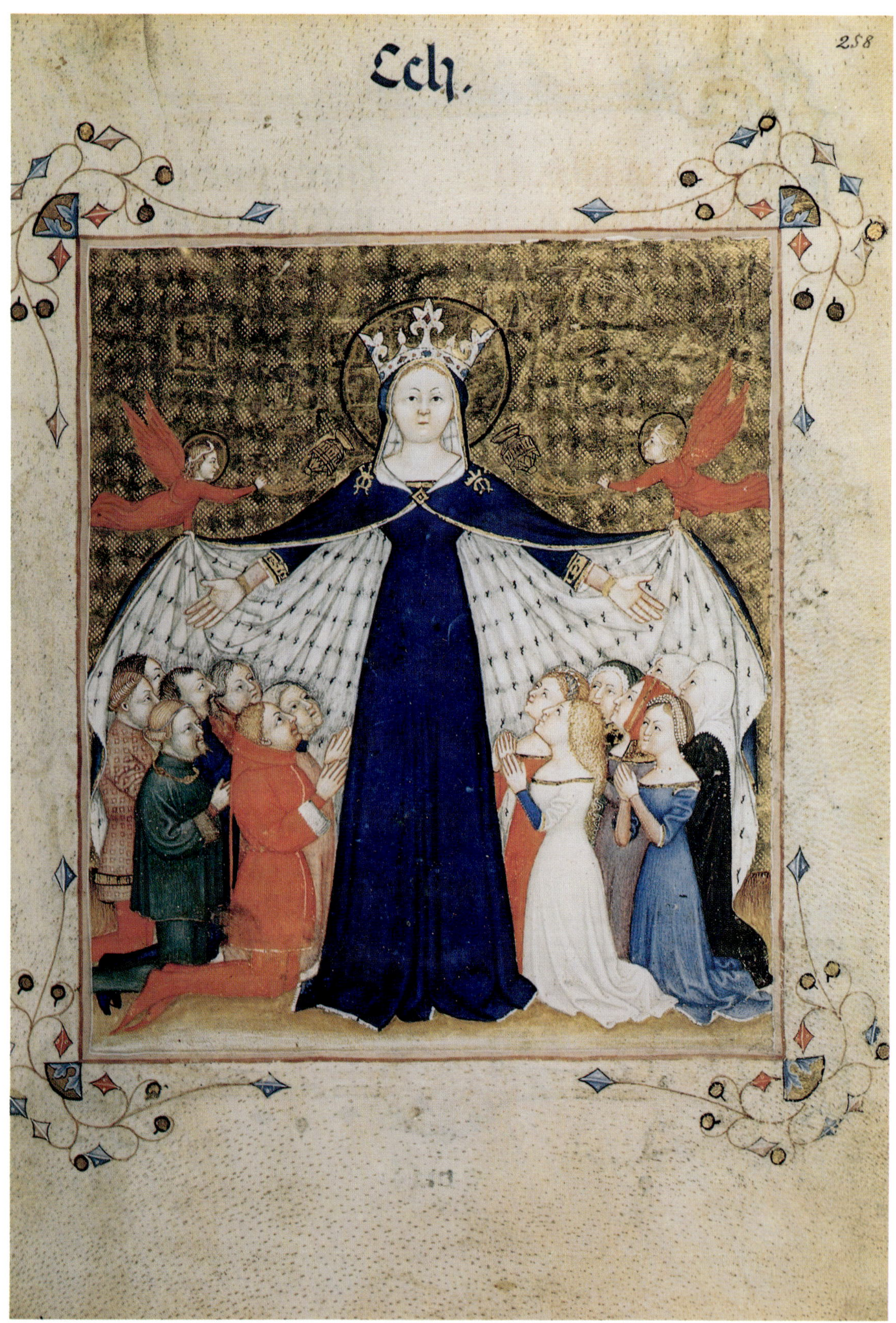

FIVE
ILLUMINATED MANUSCRIPTS
OF
GIANGALEAZZO VISCONTI

EDITH W. KIRSCH

Published for
COLLEGE ART ASSOCIATION
by
The Pennsylvania State University Press
University Park and London
1991

Monographs on the Fine Arts
sponsored by
COLLEGE ART ASSOCIATION
Volume XLVI
Editors, Isabelle Hyman and Lucy Freeman Sandler

Library of Congress Cataloging-in-Publication Data

Kirsch, Edith W.
     Five illuminated manuscripts of Giangaleazzo Visconti /
Edith W. Kirsch.

        p.   cm.—(Monographs on the fine arts ; 46)
     Includes bibliographical references.
     ISBN 0-271-00700-1
     1. Illumination of books and manuscripts, Italian.
2. Illumination of books and manuscripts, Gothic—Italy.
3. Visconti, Gian Galeazzo—Art patronage.   4. Art patronage—Italy—
Milan.   I. College Art Association.   II. Title.
III. Series.
ND3159.K57   1991
745.6′7′09452109023—dc20   90-30593

It is the policy of The Pennsylvania State University Press to use acid-free paper for the first printing of
all clothbound books. Publications on uncoated stock satisfy the minimum requirements of American
National Standard for Information Sciences—Permanence of Paper for Printed Library Materials, ANSI
239.48–1984.

Frontispiece: Lombard, c. 1380, Giangaleazzo and Caterina Visconti with courtiers worship the Madonna of Mercy.
Paris, Bibl. nat., Lat. 757, fol. 258

To R.W.J. and N.B.J.

CONTENTS

LIST OF ILLUSTRATIONS

Photographic Credits

Art Bulletin: 101. The Beinecke Rare Book and Manuscript Library, Yale University, New Haven: 37, 61. Bayerische Staatsbibliothek, Munich: 6–8. Biblioteca Capitolare di Sant'Ambrogio, Milan: 3, 4, 48, 93, 94, 96, 98. Biblioteca Estense, Modena: 89. Biblioteca nazionale, Florence: 29, 39–41, 46, 47, 53, 59, 60, 63–67, 70–73, 75–77, 85–88, 90–92, 107. Biblioteca Trivulziana, Milan: 78–84. Biblioteca Vaticana, Rome: 99, 102. Bibliothèque nationale, Paris: frontispiece, 1, 9–20, 22–24, 26–28, 30–35, 38, 42–45, 49–52, 54–57, 95, 97, 103, 105. D'A.J.D. Boulton, University of Notre Dame, Indiana: 36. By permission of the Trustees of the British Library, London: 100. Trustees of the British Museum, London: 104. Cassa di Risparmio delle Provincie Lombarde, Milan: 21. Hirmer, Munich: 106. Curia Vescovile, Mantua: 25. The Librarian, Glasgow University Library: 62. Institut de France—Musée Jacquemart-André, Paris: 58. Bild-Archiv der Österreichischen Nationalbibliothek, Vienna: 74. Studio Fotografico Perotti, Milan: 2, 5. Richelli, Verona: 69. By permission of the Trustees of the Wallace Collection, London: 68.

ACKNOWLEDGMENTS

For support and encouragement in the writing of this book, I owe thanks to many institutions and individuals. This study grows out of a Princeton University Ph.D. dissertation on the Psalter-Hours of Giangaleazzo Visconti, begun under the supervision of the late Professor Millard Meiss and supported by a Samuel H. Kress Foundation Fellowship to the Kunsthistorisches Institut and a Leopold Schepp Foundation Fellowship to Villa I Tatti, Florence. The monograph was written during several summers at the Institute for Advanced Study, Princeton. I have benefited also from the scholarly hospitality of the Marquand Library and the Scheide Library at Princeton University, as well as the Biblioteca Ambrosiana and the Istituto per la Storia dell'Arte Lombarda in Milan. I am grateful to all the libraries that allowed me to examine manuscripts in their collections; for this privilege I am especially thankful to the Biblioteca capitolare di Sant'Ambrogio, Milan; the Biblioteca nazionale, Florence; and the Bibliothèque nationale, Paris. The Colorado College, through divisional research funds and the Harold E. Berg endowment, granted me both time and financial support toward completing this project.

I am indebted to friends and colleagues who have read all or parts of the monograph and who have been a constant source of knowledge as well as encouragement: Professor George Bauer and Professor Linda Freeman Bauer (first both alphabetically and in terms of the magnitude of my debt to them); Dr. Sabine Eiche; Professor Christian Habicht; Dr. Adelaide Bennett Hagens; Professor Irving Lavin; Professor Marilyn Aronberg Lavin; the late Professor Otto Neugebauer, for sharing knowledge of astronomical matters, but even more for his sustained interest in my work; and the co-editors of this series, Professors Isabelle Hyman and Lucy Freeman Sandler, the latter not only for exigent editing but also for lending the monograph her expertise as a manuscript scholar. Professor D'A. J. D. Boulton kindly permitted me to reproduce Figures 6.2 and 6.5 from his book *The Knights of the Crown*. Professors Gloria and Irwin Merker improved my reading of Latin texts. Dr. Gerd Grasshoff wrote the computer program that produced the genealogical table. I thank also manuscript editor Cherene Holland at Penn State Press. Mrs. Carol Erickson, Mrs. Dee Fischer, and Mrs. Valerie Nowak provided excellent secretarial assistance.

I

THE TWELVE LOMBARD CAESARS

I̲T is doubtless happenstance that the number of Visconti lords who ruled Milan and its dominions between 1277 and 1447 corresponds to the number of Roman emperors—twelve—whose biographies were recounted in the second century by Suetonius. It is not fortuitous, however, that the similarity was perceived and emphasized by the Viscontis themselves and by their contemporaries.[1] The most ambitious and probably the most clever Visconti ruler of Milan was Giangaleazzo, Count of Virtues, co-lord of Milan and its dominions from 1378 to 1385, sole lord from 1385 to 1395, and first Duke of Milan

---

1. The twelve Visconti lords of Milan and the years of their rule were: Ottone (1277–78, 1282–95); Matteo I (1287–1302, 1311–22); Galeazzo I (1322–28); Azzo (1329–39); Giovanni (1339–54); Luchino (1339–49); Matteo II (1354–55); Bernabò (1354–85); Galeazzo II (1354–78); Giangaleazzo (1378–1402); Giovanni Maria (1402–12); Filippo Maria (1412–47).

The presentation copy of an Italian translation of Suetonius commissioned by Filippo Maria Visconti was completed in 1431 and is now Paris, Bibl. nat., It. 131 (Paris, 1984, no. 128). The Master of the Vitae Imperatorum takes his name from his illuminations in this manuscript. An illuminated copy of Suetonius in Latin, written by the scribe Milanus Burrus, dated 1433, and also associated with the circle of the Master of the Vitae Imperatorum, is Princeton University Library, Kane 44, in which the original arms have been overpainted. On this, see D. Miner, "The Manuscripts in the Grenville Kane Collection," *Princeton University Library Chronicle,* XI, 1949–50, 37–44; and J. Wilson, "The Iconography of the Kane Suetonius," *Princeton University Library Chronicle,* XIX, 1957–58, 34–45. Another Suetonius written by the same scribe, dated 1443, and likewise illuminated in the style of the Master of the Vitae Imperatorum, is Cambridge, Fitzwilliam Museum, McClean 162. For additional copies of the Latin text in the Visconti library, see Pellegrin, 1955, A178, 363–65.

Filippo Maria's secretary, Pier Candido Decembrio, wrote a biography of Filippo Maria, *Vita Philippi Mariae tertii Ligurum ducis,* which appeared first in manuscript in 1447 and was widely diffused in this form. The first printed edition was published in Milan in 1625 (Decembrio, ed. Bartolini, 41). On Milanus Burrus, see E. Pellegrin, "Bibliothèques d'humanistes lombards de la cour des Visconti Sforza," *Bibliothèque d'humanisme et de Renaissance,* XVII, 1955, 218–45.

from 1395 to his death in 1402. In this study I shall propose that a group of manuscripts commissioned by Giangaleazzo (and, in one instance, by his immediate family) reflects not only his dynastic concerns but also the development of his inclination to express these concerns through works of art establishing both his heroism *all'antica* and his Christian piety.[2]

In his discussion of the fourteenth-century princes of Italy, Jacob Burckhardt wrote that in Giangaleazzo Visconti "that passion for the colossal which was common to most of the despots shows itself on the largest scale."[3] One expression of Giangaleazzo's passion for the colossal was his enormous library. Whereas most of the large aristocratic libraries of Italy, including those of Ferrara, Mantua, Urbino, and Florence, were collected during the fifteenth century, Giangaleazzo's was one of the two greatest manuscript collections of the fourteenth century, on a par with that of his brother-in-law Charles V of France.[4] Like another of his French bibliophile brothers-in-law, Jean, Duke of Berry, Giangaleazzo was not always scrupulous in his means of acquisition.[5] Important segments of his library were confiscated from the lords of Verona and Padua after the Visconti conquest of those cities in 1387 and 1388, respectively, and yet a third major collection was appropriated from Giangaleazzo's secretary and counselor, Pasquino Capelli, when the latter was executed for treason in 1398.[6]

This study will examine five manuscripts that previously have not been perceived as a group. They warrant consideration of this kind because, as a group, they document one of Giangaleazzo's most innovative activities as a manuscript collector—his practice of commissioning lavish illuminated manuscripts to commemorate major dynastic events. In

2. The centuries-old perception of Giangaleazzo as the most unprincipled of fourteenth-century despots yielded in the early twentieth century to a somewhat romanticized Risorgimento view of him as a would-be unifier of Italy cut off by an untimely death. Giangaleazzo did in fact expand his dominions well beyond the Po Valley, even into Tuscany, and at the time of his death posed a serious threat to the independence of Florence. It was with this Milanese despot in mind that Machiavelli wrote: "E cosi la morte fu sempre più amica a' Fiorentini che niuno altro amico, e più potente a salvargli che alcuna loro virtù" (*Istorie fiorentine*, III, 29, in N. Machiavelli, *Tutte le opere*, ed. M. Martelli, Florence, 1971, 715) [Thus, death was always more of a friend to the Florentines than any other friend, and did more to save them than did any of their virtues]. Daniel Bueno de Mesquita, Giangaleazzo's most authoritative modern biographer, emphasizes his extraordinary diplomatic and administrative abilities, leaving open the question of the Duke's desire to become a monarch (310ff.).

3. *The Civilization of the Renaissance in Italy*, ed. B. Nelson and C. Trinkaus, New York, 1958, I, 32.

4. The first inventory of the Visconti library, made in 1426 at the direction of Giangaleazzo's son, Filippo Maria, included 988 volumes, most of which had probably entered the collection by the time of Giangaleazzo's death in 1402 (Pellegrin, 1955, 41–52). The testamentary inventory of 1380 of the library of Charles V includes 917 volumes, although it has been estimated that manuscripts not inventoried because they were kept in residences outside Paris would have brought the total size of this collection to about 1,000 volumes. See L. Delisle, *Le Cabinet des manuscrits de la Bibliothèque impériale*, I, 1863, 21f., III, 1881, 114ff.; and Paris, Bibliothèque nationale, *La Librairie de Charles V*, Paris, 1968, 45.

5. On the Duke of Berry's habits as a manuscript collector, including the characterization of him as "a kind of ambulance-chaser" where illuminated manuscripts were concerned, see Meiss, 1967, 290f.

6. Pellegrin, 1955, 44, 47. No fewer than thirty-three manuscripts in the Carrara library had belonged to Petrarch (Pellegrin, 45).

their richness and in the extraordinary verisimilitude and historical specificity of their decoration, these manuscripts document the self-image of a prince who chose to record his unprecedented accomplishments in unprecedented fashion. Like his politics, however, Giangaleazzo's patronage of the arts was shaped by the practices of his ancestors, and his accomplishments as a patron are best understood in the context of family tradition.

Azzo, lord of Milan from 1328 to 1339, was the greatest Visconti Maecenas of the first half of the fourteenth century. He is the earliest Visconti to be named in a manuscript, Godfrey da Viterbo's *Liber Pantheon*, written in 1331 and dedicated to Azzo by the Milanese scribe and notary, Johannes de Nuxigia. As noted by François Avril, the illumination by one of the two anonymous hands in this manuscript is one of the earliest testimonies in Lombard book painting to the new monumental style of Giotto and his followers.[7] Around 1335, Azzo invited Giotto himself to Milan to adorn his splendid new palace. Here, in a large room, was a painting of pagan warriors, among them Hercules, Hector, Aeneas, and Attila. Only two Christian princes were included among this company: Charlemagne and Azzo Visconti. Creighton Gilbert has shown that in all probability this was the *Triumph of Fame* (*Vana Gloria*) that Giotto is recorded as having painted in fresco for Azzo in 1335. Moreover, Gilbert has demonstrated that the appearance of Giotto's lost work may be reconstructed through illuminations of the same subject in three manuscripts of Petrarch's *De viris illustribus*, two of them confiscated by Giangaleazzo, together with the rest of Francesco da Carrara's library, in 1388 (Fig. 1).[8] Irving Lavin has observed that if Gilbert's reconstruction is correct, Giotto must be credited with having invented in Azzo's palace the tradition of monumental grisaille for the representation of worthies of antiquity and of Renaissance princes who wished to identify themselves with these worthies.[9]

Azzo must have known also the classical tradition of equestrian portraiture. A gilded bronze equestrian statue of an emperor was brought to Pavia from Ravenna in the late Middle Ages. In 1315, during the rule of Matteo il Grande, the monument was moved to Milan. It was returned to Pavia in 1335, where it remained until its destruction by the French in 1796.[10] The early fourteenth-century Milanese chronicler Galvano Fiamma recounts that the bell tower of the winter cathedral of Milan, Santa Maria Maggiore, reconstructed by Azzo, was adorned with insignia of the principal gates of the city, of the

7. Paris, 1984, no. 78.

8. C. Gilbert, "The Fresco by Giotto in Milan," *Arte lombarda*, nos. 47/48, 1977, 31–72. Gilbert's article contains a comprehensive bibliography on the subject. The two Petrarch manuscripts expropriated by Giangaleazzo from Francesco da Carrara are now in the Bibliothèque nationale in Paris (Lat. 6069 F and Lat. 6069 I), having been confiscated by Louis XII in 1499. On these manuscripts, see Paris, 1984, nos. 73 and 74. A contemporary description of Azzo's palace appears in Galvano Fiamma's *Opusculum de rebus gestis ab Azone, Luchino, et Johanne Vicecomitibus ab anno MCCCXXVIII usque ad annum MCCCXLII, RIS*, XII, pt. 4, 1011f.

9. Professor Lavin is preparing a study of this tradition for publication. He kindly communicated his observation on Giotto to me during several stimulating discussions of Visconti patronage.

10. G. Bovini, "Le vicende del 'Regisole' statua equestre ravennate," *Felix Ravenna*, LXXXVII, 1963, 138–54.

church itself, of the empire, and of the Visconti family; on the side facing the summer cathedral, Santa Tecla, was a gilded equestrian representation of Azzo.[11]

Giotto was not the only Tuscan artist invited to Milan by Azzo, who also summoned to the city the Pisan sculptor Giovanni di Balduccio, already renowned elsewhere in Italy. Balduccio's best-known project in Milan is the great tomb of Saint Peter Martyr, carved between 1335 and 1339, in the church of Sant'Eustorgio. Conceived as a pendant to the tomb of Saint Dominic himself in the church of San Domenico in Bologna, the monument was in large part paid for by Archbishop Giovanni Visconti, uncle of Azzo (and, together with his brother Luchino, successor to Azzo as lord of Milan), who is represented in the upper part of the tomb in adoration of the Virgin and Child.[12]

In addition to the tomb of Peter Martyr, Balduccio and his shop carved a number of statues for the gates of the Milanese city walls that were rebuilt by Azzo. Thirteenth-century chroniclers record an inscription in the Porta Romana of the Milanese walls, referring to Milan as "Roma secunda," worthy of the homage of all, a notion reiterated on the tomb carved by Balduccio for Azzo, probably between 1342 and 1346.[13]

Although Azzo's tomb was dismembered, displaced, and in part lost during the seventeenth and eighteenth centuries, parts of it, including the recumbent effigy and the sarcophagus of Azzo, have since the nineteenth century again been visible in their original location, the apse of Azzo's palace chapel, originally dedicated to the Immaculate Conception, but rededicated in the fifteenth century to San Gottardo.[14] Along the sides of Azzo's sarcophagus, ten kneeling personifications of cities subject to Milan (Bobbio, Novara, Bergamo, Vercelli, Como, Brescia, Cremona, Piacenza, Asti, and Lodi) are presented by their patron saints to Saint Ambrose, patron of Milan, who stands at the center of the sarcophagus, holding the standard of Milan, before a cloth of honor supported by two angels (Fig. 2). Directly above, two angels hold a cloth of honor behind the recumbent effigy of Azzo. On the console that supports the sarcophagus, directly beneath Saint Ambrose, is the Visconti viper.

In a tradition that seems to have originated with Paolo Giovio in his lives of the Visconti lords of Milan, first published in 1549, the two figures seated at either side of the dominating figure of Saint Ambrose and within the protective ambience of his cloth of honor have been identified as Azzo, presumably as he appeared in 1329 (and hence beardless), and Ludwig of Bavaria, by whom he was invested imperial vicar of Milan in that year.[15] If this is true, the relief on Azzo's sarcophagus provides a direct precedent for

11. Dell'Acqua, 133.

12. Ibid., 142–44.

13. As noted in the paper by Peter Seiler, "Das Grabmal des Azzo Visconti in San Gottardo in Mailand," presented at the conference Scultura e monumento sepolcrale del Tardo Medioevo a Roma e in Italia, Rome, 1985. The proceedings of the conference, sponsored by the Accademia austriaca delle Scienze in Rome and by the Istituto dell'Enciclopedia Italiana, will be published. Dr. Seiler has kindly allowed me to refer here to his findings.

14. Dell'Acqua, 144. Implausibilities in the present reconstruction of the tomb noted by both Dell'Acqua and Seiler are not relevant to the present discussion.

15. P. Giovio, *Vita duodecim Vicecomitum Mediolani Principum*, Paris, 1549, 127.

the investiture page of 1395 in Giangaleazzo Visconti's Coronation Missal, which shows Giangaleazzo seated beside Benesio Cumsinich, the imperial emissary who invested him with the dukedom of Milan (Fig. 3). Cumsinich and Giangaleazzo are flanked by their respective standards. A group of bishops stands in front of them, and clusters of citizens pay homage at either side.[16]

In 1928 Giuseppe Gerola and more recently Peter Seiler have questioned the traditional identification of the two seated figures on the sarcophagus as Azzo Visconti and Ludwig of Bavaria.[17] Seiler proposes that they represent instead personifications of Milan (at the left) and the common good (at the right). Regardless of the precise identity of the seated figures, however, the hieratic, allegorical representation of subject territories paying homage to their liege is a rare early Renaissance revival of Roman imperial imagery that points ahead in composition, as in spirit, to the grandiose investiture page of the Coronation Missal.

Seiler suggests that on Azzo's sarcophagus Saint Ambrose appears not only as patron of Milan but also as a symbol of Visconti political legitimacy, because shortly before Azzo's death in 1339, the miraculous intervention of Saint Ambrose at the Battle of Parabiago enabled Luchino Visconti to defeat the forces of Lodrisio Visconti, a seditious member of the family. The patronage of Saint Ambrose and the legitimacy of Visconti power are linked again in the Coronation Missal of 1395, where a mass for the victory at Parabiago precedes the mass for Giangaleazzo's investiture as Duke of Milan, and a miniature on folio 200, showing the investiture of Ambrose as bishop of Milan (Fig. 4), echoes the coronation miniature on folio 8 (Fig. 3).[18]

In 1354 Azzo's cousins Bernabò, Galeazzo II, and Matteo II succeeded to the lordship of Milan. Matteo died mysteriously within the first year of the shared signory, but Bernabò and Galeazzo II (Giangaleazzo's father) lived long and flourished also as patrons of art. Bernabò is perhaps best remembered for the monumental equestrian sculpture of himself, carved by the Lombard master, Bonino da Campione, which as early as 1363 stood in the apse of Bernabò's parish church, San Giovanni in Conca, where it probably towered above the high altar (Fig. 5).[19]

---

16. On the Coronation Missal, see pages 69–74 below. The imagery of Azzo's tomb is also related to that of the frontispiece of an approximately contemporary manuscript (c. 1344), Paris, Bibl. nat., Lat. 6467 (Luca de Manellis, *Compendium moralis philosophiae*), made for Luchino Visconti's illegitimate son, Bruzio, governor of Bologna from 1354 to 1356. On folio 1 of this manuscript (Pellegrin, 1969, pl. 92), six cities subject to Milan are represented (as actual walled cities, not personifications) in each lateral margin, while a representation of Milan appears in the upper margin. On this manuscript (A132 in the Visconti inventory of 1426) and on other manuscripts that belonged to Bruzio, an

active collector, see Pellegrin, 1955, 41; 1969, 27; and Kirsch, 1981, 164ff.

17. G. Gerola, "Le figurazioni araldiche nel mausoleo di Azzone Visconti," *Rendiconti del Reale Istituto Lombardo di Scienze e Lettere*, LXI, 1928, 98ff.; Seiler, as cited in note 13 above.

18. On the Mass of Parabiago in the Coronation Missal, see chapter IV, note 4.

19. Baroni, 1944, 110–15, and 1955, 808–9; Dell'Acqua, 161f. The sarcophagus on which it now stands in the Castello Sforzesco was probably carved by Bonino da Campione and assistants about the time of Bernabò's death in 1385.

Recently, Costanzo Baroni has numbered this work "tra i grandi sconosciuti della nostra storia dell'arte . . . una tra le più forti realizzazioni della plastica italiana del Trecento!"[20] Both the size and the verisimilitude of the sculpture, which was originally polychromed and gilded, stupefied Bernabò's contemporaries. Pietro Azario, a contemporary chronicler, marveled also that horse and rider were carved from one piece of stone. Indeed this work is among the earliest monumental equestrian portraits carved from one piece of marble since antiquity.[21]

In his youth Galeazzo II Visconti was described by Petrarch as "il più bello fra i più delicati giovani milanesi,"[22] but around 1360, though only forty years old, Giangaleazzo's father was afflicted with an increasingly painful illness that hindered his ability to walk, to stand, or even to sleep. He sought relief from his illness through absorption in two great building projects: the castle of Porta Giovia in Milan (parts of which are incorporated in the present Castello Sforzesco) and the celebrated Castello that still survives in Pavia, to which he and his family moved in 1365.[23]

Galeazzo's grandiose building projects may have been stimulated by his close association with several of the most powerful European monarchs of his time. He was the first Visconti lord to arrange marriages between his children and theirs. When the family moved to Pavia, Galeazzo's only son, Giangaleazzo, then fourteen years old, brought with him his wife of five years, Isabelle of Valois, daughter of Jean le Bon of France. From Galeazzo's castle in Milan, his only other child, Violante, was married in 1368 to Lionel, Duke of Clarence, son of Edward III of England.[24] Galeazzo was closely involved also with the third great sovereign of mid-fourteenth-century Europe, Emperor Charles IV, from whom the Viscontis held their fiefdom, and with whom they shared their boundless admiration for Petrarch. In 1355, after receiving the Iron Crown of Lombardy in Sant'Ambrogio, Charles knighted the four-year-old Giangaleazzo, and on 22 January 1360 he conferred upon Galeazzo and his male descendants the title of Imperial Vicar of Pavia.[25]

When Galeazzo began building his castle in Pavia in 1360, he may have done so in emulation of the Emperor, whose great castle at Karlstein, near Prague, was by then almost complete.[26] Giangaleazzo seems to have followed a similar pattern in the 1390s, when he established the Certosa of Pavia as a burial site for his family, only several years

---

20. "One of the great unrecognized [works] in our history of art . . . among the strongest accomplishments in Italian Trecento sculpture" (Baroni, 1944, 111).

21. Azario is cited by Baroni, 1944, 120 n. 58. On monumental sculpture carved from one piece of marble, see also I. Lavin, "The Sculptor's 'Last Will and Testament,' " *Allen Memorial Art Museum Bulletin*, xxxv, nos. 1–2, 1977–78, 4–39 (20ff.).

22. ". . . the most handsome amongst the most refined Milanese youth" (Bellonci, 52).

23. Bellonci, 53; Bueno de Mesquita, 9, 11; Muir, 61.

24. Bueno de Mesquita, 12; Corio, I, 818ff.

25. Bueno de Mesquita, 10; Beltrami, 1896, 20f. Construction on the castle in Pavia began on 27 March 1360 (ibid., 21f.).

26. The most comprehensive study of the Castello at Pavia is that of Magenta, 1896. The construction of Karlstein began in 1348 and ended in 1367, but much of the work was finished by 1357. See Stejskal, 101ff.

after his Burgundian brother-in-law, Philippe le Hardi, had founded the Chartreuse of Champmol as a mausoleum for his family.[27]

The castles at both Karlstein and Pavia were unusual for their time in combining battlemented exteriors with interiors more appropriate to palaces than to fortresses. The notorious dungeon at Pavia (the *lunga dimora*) was complemented on the upper floors of the castle by great halls, airy rooms with large windows, and wide balconies overlooking gardens and a vast park. Neither Charles nor Galeazzo spared effort or expense in decorating the interior of their palaces, employing imported as well as local artists for this purpose.[28]

Whereas the castle at Karlstein consisted of several buildings constructed around a series of chapels, Galeazzo's could boast only one chapel within the building.[29] Like those of Charles IV, however, Galeazzo's chapel contained an important collection of relics, including several of Christ's Passion.[30] One may surmise that, like Charles, Galeazzo prized his relics of Christ both through piety and through recognition that they linked imperial with divine majesty, underscoring the emperor's role (and by extension the role of his vassals) as Christ's vicar on earth.[31] A strong sense of symbolic identification with the Emperor was expressed visually in the next generation, when Charles's son, Wenceslaus IV, proclaimed Giangaleazzo Duke of Milan. As we shall see below, Giangaleazzo was invested on this occasion not merely with a ducal coronet, but with a small version of the imperial crown, reputedly worth 200,000 crowns of currency.[32]

Like Charles IV, Galeazzo vigorously promoted learning as well as art. Petrarch, who

27. The decision to build a Carthusian monastery at Pavia received the approval of the order in 1394, but the foundation stones were not laid until 1396, a year after Giangaleazzo's investiture as Duke. According to Corio (I, 908f.), Giangaleazzo's decision to endow a Carthusian monastery fulfilled a vow made by his wife, Caterina, during a pregnancy in 1390. Caterina, however, had envisioned a foundation for the customary twelve Carthusians, whereas Giangaleazzo doubled the number to twenty-four, as Philippe had done at Champmol (Beltrami, 1896, 28f., 31, 52; on the Chartreuse at Champmol, begun in 1377 and dedicated in 1388, see P. Vaughan, *Philip the Bold,* Cambridge [Mass.], 1962, 202–7).

On the importance of Stefano Macone (Caterina Visconti's confessor and the first prior of the Certosa of Pavia) in the planning of the Certosa and especially in its dedication to Santa Maria delle Grazie, see Beltrami, 1896, 36, and D. Sant'Ambrogio, "Sull'iconografia della Vergine nella Certosa de Pavia," *Rivista di scienze storiche,* I, no. 2, 1904, 288ff. On the building of the Certosa, see also J. Ackerman, "The Certosa of Pavia and the Renaissance in Milan," *Marsyas,* v, 1947–49, 23–27.

28. On the decoration of the interior at Karlstein, including the contribution of Tommaso da Modena, see

Stejskal, 106–33 passim. Among the local artists employed by Galeazzo for the pictorial decoration of the Castello in Pavia was a certain Martino Lucini "eccellentissimo," as well as the Bolognese painters Andrea de' Bartoli and Jacopino and Pietro de' Papazoni. In May 1366 Galeazzo wrote to Guido Gonzaga in Mantua, stating his intention to paint the entire interior of the castle and asking Gonzaga to send to Pavia "tutti i pittori" of Mantua to help carry out the work (Dell'Acqua, 151). See also Magenta, I, pt. 1, 76–79; Welch, 1989.

29. No trace remains of a second chapel, near the castle of Pavia, suppressed in 1783. During the Spanish domination of the city, it bore the inscription "Esta capilla es del Real Castillo di Pavia" (Magenta, I, pt. 1, 80 n. 3).

30. On Charles's relics, see Stejskal, 80, 122. On the relics at the Castello of Pavia, see Magenta, I, pt. 1, 79f., and J. Gualla, *Sanctuarium Papie,* Pavia, 1505, 89ff.

31. On Charles's linkage of the royal majesty with the cult of Christ's relics, see K. Stejskal, "The Ideological Design of Karlstejn Castle and Its Pictorial Decoration," in *Gothic Mural Painting in Bohemia and Moravia, 1300–1378,* ed. V. Dvoráková et al., London, 1964, 51–65.

32. See page 70 and Fig. 3.

had come to Milan in 1353 at the invitation of Matteo II, remained at the Visconti court for an additional seven years under the sovereignty of Galeazzo.[33] In 1368, though then living in Padua, Petrarch is mentioned as one of the honored guests at the marriage of Violante to Lionel of Clarence.[34] A generation later, between 1400 and 1402, Giangaleazzo invited to Pavia the most distinguished female author of her time, Christine de Pizan, who, around 1400, had dedicated to his son-in-law, Louis of Orléans, her *Epistre d'Othea*.[35] In 1348 Charles established a university in Prague; in 1361 Galeazzo refounded the university in Pavia.[36] The patron of both universities was Saint Catherine of Alexandria. The *studium* reestablished by his father was also actively supported by Giangaleazzo, who in the late fourteenth century brought there such distinguished scholars as Giovanni Dondi of Padua.[37]

In a tower of the Castello in Pavia, Galeazzo II installed the library which, during the reign of his son, was to become one of the glories of Europe.[38] Of the 988 manuscripts included in the earliest surviving inventory of the Visconti library, ordered by Filippo Maria in 1426, the majority appear to have originated in Italy in the second half of the fourteenth century.[39] Galeazzo II himself can be securely associated with only one manuscript in the inventory of 1426, a Mass of Saint Bernard, in which he is portrayed in adoration of the Virgin and Child.[40]

Giangaleazzo's mother, Blanche of Savoy, is, on the other hand, better documented as a collector of manuscripts. It is possible that a group of forty-two French manuscripts in the inventory of 1426 entered the Visconti library between her arrival in Milan in 1350 as the wife of Galeazzo II and her death in 1387. Her son Giangaleazzo gave her a copy of Brunetto Latini's *Trésor,* and she is recorded as having purchased Parisian Books of Hours for herself and her daughter-in-law Isabelle in 1366.[41] Another of her Books of Hours, extensively illuminated by Giovanni di Benedetto da Como (now in Munich, Staatsbibliothek, Cod. Lat. 23215), was certainly known to Giangaleazzo, who seems to have shared many of his mother's devotional interests.[42]

33. E. Wilkins, *Petrarch's Eight Years in Milan, 1353–1361,* Cambridge (Mass.), 1958; and idem, *Life of Petrarch,* Chicago, 1961, 129–79.

34. Wilkins, 1958, 216; Muir, 224f.

35. King Henry IV of England also invited Christine to his court. She chose, however, to remain at the court of Charles VI in France. On these invitations, see Christine's autobiography, *Lavision-Christine,* ed. M. L. Towner, Washington, D.C., 1932, 165f.

36. Stejskal, 232; Bueno de Mesquita, 42.

37. Bueno de Mesquita, 182f.; Magenta, I, pt. I, 219, 247.

38. Magenta, I, pt. I, 79; Pellegrin, 1955, 42.

39. Pellegrin, 1955, 50.

40. Pellegrin identified the kneeling figure in Lat. 1142 as Galeazzo ("Portraits de Galéas II Visconti, seigneur de Milan [† 1378]," *Scriptorium,* VIII, 1954,

113– 15). See also Paris, 1984, no. 81. The inventory of 1426 lists not only the Office of Saint Bernard now in Paris (Pellegrin, 1955, A273) but also ten other volumes devoted entirely or in part to the writings of Saint Bernard (Pellegrin, 1955, A262–69, A524, A702).

41. The *Trésor* is now Bibl. nat., Fr. 1110 (Pellegrin, 1955, 42; 1969, 90f.). On Blanche's purchase of manuscripts in Paris, see Magenta, I, pt. I, 113.

42. On Cod. Lat. 23215, see Milan, 1958, no. 65; see also pages 15, 25, 25 note 40, 45, and 49; and Kirsch, 1981, 247–57. Blanche's prayerbook is generally dated before 1378 (the year of her husband's death) because while his arms appear with hers (the cross of Savoy) in many of the miniatures, a prayer for him was inserted on folio 212, at the end of the Office of the Dead.

Four full-page miniatures illustrating the story of the Magi in Blanche's Munich Hours (two of them devoted to the Journey of the Three Kings) in all likelihood reflect a Milanese cult of the Magi.[43] At an unknown time before 1158, the bones of the Magi were deposited in the Milanese church of Sant'Eustorgio.[44] After the capture of the relics by Frederick Barbarossa in 1162 and their translation to Cologne in 1164, the cult of the Magi in Milan gained ever greater importance. It must have inspired the exceptionally early and elaborate pageant of the Magi, established by Azzo and Archbishop Giovanni Visconti to celebrate the Feast of the Epiphany in 1336 and carried on by their successors.[45]

Additional relics of the Magi linked the cult to Giangaleazzo's family in Pavia. Such relics existed in the Castello built by Galeazzo II; in the Franciscan monastery of Santa Chiara, founded in 1380 by Blanche, and, beginning with her, the burial place of all the women in the Visconti family; and in the Cistercian convent of San Cristoforo.[46] In 1374 the Pavian nobleman Melchiorre Cani founded a hospital dedicated to the Magi, to which Blanche granted special privileges in 1378, very likely the approximate date also of the Book of Hours in Munich.[47]

Giangaleazzo himself enriched the pageant of the Magi with an annual gift of twenty-five ducats, and he also presented a marble altar to the chapel of the Magi in Sant'Eustorgio.[48] The importance of the Magi to Giangaleazzo is most vividly apparent in the massive central panel of the monumental triptych of hippopotamus-tooth ivory that he commissioned from the Embriachi workshop around 1396 for the Certosa of Pavia, probably for the high altar, in front of which his tomb was to stand. The left wing of this triptych contained eighteen plaques recounting the life of the Virgin, while the right wing contained an equal number of plaques narrating the life of Christ. The central panel presented in no fewer than twenty-six plaques the story of the Magi.[49]

Blanche's Munich Hours is noteworthy also for a full-page miniature on folio 226v showing Blanche and others praying to an enthroned Christ (Fig. 6). Clothed in a red

43. The most recent and fullest account of the cult of the Magi in Milan and of Visconti participation in it is H. Hofmann, *Die Heiligen Drei Könige* (Rheinisches Archiv, 94), Bonn, 1975, 75–95, 218–26, and passim.

44. Hofmann, 75ff.

45. The procession, which began at the Porta Romana and ended at Sant'Eustorgio, is described by Galvano Fiamma (as in note 8), 1017f. See also Hatfield, 112f.

46. Hofmann, 264 n. 227.

47. Ibid., 260ff.

48. Ibid., 230 n. 105. A document of 1588 refers to the Chapel of the Three Magi as the Visconti Chapel (ibid., 219).

49. On the use of hippopotamus ivory by the Embriachis for the Certosa triptych, as well as for two coffrets also originally from the Certosa but now in the Metropolitan Museum of Art, see J. von Schlosser, "Der Werkstatt der Embriachi in Venedig," *Jahrbuch der Kunsthistorischen Sammlungen des Allerhöchsten Kaiserhauses*, XX, 1899, 233f., and D. D. Egbert, "North Italian Gothic Ivories in the Museo Cristiano of the Vatican Library," *Art Studies*, VII, 1929, 174, who states, "Bone, rather than ivory, was by all odds the more favored material in North Italy."

For the compelling hypothesis that Giangaleazzo commissioned this triptych to commemorate his investiture as Duke of Milan in 1395, see Trexler, 169–71, and Merlini, 139–54. On the association of Magi liturgy and ceremony with German royal coronations in the fourteenth and fifteenth centuries, see Hofmann, 141ff.

gown and heavy gold belt, Blanche kneels in the foreground of the miniature. A man directly beside her, the only other person in the miniature who also wears a gold belt, closely resembles Giangaleazzo as he appears in the Psalter-Hours in Florence (Figs. 41, 46, 47) and also, it will be suggested below, in Lat. 757. A prayer inserted near the end of the manuscript (folios 241 and 241v), which names specifically only Blanche herself and Giangaleazzo, supports the identification as her son of the male figure in the Munich miniature.[50]

Blanche, who died in 1387, bequeathed to the convent of Santa Chiara 40,000 florins and a portrait of herself as a Clarissan that was valued at 300 gold florins.[51] In so doing, she seems to have established yet another precedent for her son, who stipulated in his will that his viscera be buried in the sanctuary of Saint Anthony in Vienne, and that an effigy of himself as an Antonine friar be installed beside the tomb of the saint.[52]

Two passages in Pier Candido Decembrio's biography of Filippo Maria Visconti underscore the importance of portraiture in the Visconti dynasty, as well as an awareness of this importance in the eyes and minds of their contemporaries. In chapter L of his *Vita* of Filippo Maria ("Suo aspetto e sua conformazione fisica"), Decembrio emphasizes, presumably because it was so unusual, the Duke's unwillingness to be portrayed (perhaps because of the "imponente corporatura, magari eccessiva" mentioned in the same chapter). It was despite this aversion to portraiture, writes Decembrio, that the great Pisanello, with marvelous skill, made of Filippo Maria a likeness that seems to breathe.[53] In an earlier chapter (XL), on his affection for his parents and brothers ("Del suo affetto verso i genitori e i fratelli"), Decembrio adduces as evidence of Filippo Maria's love for and loyalty to his brother Giovanni Maria the fact that among his most treasured possessions was a portrait of his brother by the most celebrated Lombard painter of the time, Michelino da Besozzo.[54]

What we know of Visconti portraiture indicates that the family as a whole provides a notable exception to the recent assertion that although before the fifteenth century there are instances of portraiture, "l'uso dei ritratti per esaltare o un fatto storico . . . o la personalità e la posizione sociale delle persone . . . è novità del Quattrocento."[55] In many

50. F. Boll, "Photographische Einzelaufnahmen aus den Schätzen der K. Hof-und-Staats-Bibliothek in München," *Centralblatt für Bibliothekswesen*, XIX, 1902, 229–48, suggested (239) that the second prayer may also have been inserted after 1386 (by which date both of Blanche's daughters—neither named in the prayer—were dead) and before her own death in 1387.

51. Osio, I, pt. 2, 261.

52. Corio, II, 969. Corio's *Historia di Milano* was first published in Milan in 1503. The will of 1402 published by Osio does not mention the image of Giangaleazzo as an Antonine friar, but stipulates that he is to be buried

"juxta arcam beatissimi Antonii patroni sui" (321) [near the altar of his patron, the most blessed Anthony]. The Duke also endowed a chapel of Saint Anthony in Pavia (Osio, 337).

53. Ed. Bartolini, 98.

54. Ibid., 81.

55. [The use of portraiture to exalt either an historical fact . . . or the personality or the social position of persons . . . is a novelty of the fifteenth century] (M. L. Eiko Wakayama, "Iconografia ritrattistica negli affreschi a Castiglione Olona," *Arte lombarda*, no. 36, 1972, 87).

ways, including their attitude toward portraiture, the Viscontis were a *novità* of the Trecento, and in this respect as in others Giangaleazzo was the most exceptional member of an exceptional family.

Although far from exhaustive, the preceding survey of Visconti patronage before Giangaleazzo suggests a pattern in which art served, often on a grand scale, to express secular power, piety, and dynastic concerns. As a patron of art, Giangaleazzo epitomized and built upon the practices of his ancestors. In so doing he became one of the most active European patrons of art in the last quarter of the fourteenth century, involved with the rebuilding of the Cathedral of Milan and responsible also, perhaps to a greater extent than has been recognized, with not only the founding but also the final appearance of the Certosa of Pavia.

As a group, the five manuscripts to be examined here afford a view of the governing principles of Giangaleazzo's patronage that may be useful also in assessing his role in shaping monuments grander in scale though perhaps not in conception or beauty. The five manuscripts grouped in this study have never before been considered together. Not even those three in the group unequivocally associated with Giangaleazzo—the Psalter-Hours in Florence (Biblioteca nazionale, Banco Rari 397 [BR] and Landau-Finaly 22 [LF]), the Coronation Missal in Milan (Chapter Library of Sant'Ambrogio, Lat. 6), and the Eulogy-Genealogy in Paris (Bibliothèque nationale, Lat. 5888)—have been considered as a distinctive unit, textually, structurally, iconographically, and stylistically related; yet to consider even these three manuscripts together is to understand each of them more fully. I propose, furthermore, to add to this nucleus of three books two Hours-Missals in Paris (Bibliothèque nationale, Lat. 757 and Smith-Lesouëf 22) that elucidate, and in turn are elucidated by, the others.

My grouping of the five manuscripts rests on the premise that Giangaleazzo Visconti's patronage of manuscripts was marked by certain characteristic features: execution of the work by exceptionally gifted scribes and illuminators, unusual fullness and richness of both text and illumination, unusual combinations of texts, unusual conjunctions of text and image, and iconographical manipulation of miniatures and borders to fit certain historical circumstances and to express particular devotions. Not all these characteristics occur in all the manuscripts, but they do occur, in various combinations and with striking frequency, above all in the richest and most complex of the manuscripts, the Psalter-Hours in Florence, which, on the one hand, elucidates the Hours-Missals in Paris and, on the other, points ahead to the Coronation Missal and the Eulogy-Genealogy.

As the earliest manuscripts in the group, the Hours-Missals, Lat. 757 and Smith-Lesouëf 22, are the most problematic. Here those traits that were to become characteristic are introduced tentatively and developed cautiously. For example, the systematic insertion of monograms and emblems in the margins of Lat. 757 occurs only in the last third of the manuscript. Nonetheless, the bravura effects evident in the other manuscripts are already present in the Paris Hours-Missals. Furthermore, unusual features of the Paris manuscripts, which resisted clarification so long as the books were studied in isolation, are explained when the two works are considered as characteristic products of Visconti patronage. Though the nature of the evidence for Lat. 757 and Smith-Lesouëf 22 is more circumstantial than it is for the other manuscripts with which they are here grouped, they are included in the conviction that they contribute to a consistent picture of the patronage of the leading collector of illuminated manuscripts in late fourteenth-century Italy.

II

THE PRELUDE

Lat. 757

EVEN before the manuscript is opened, the most immediately striking quality of Paris, Bibliothèque nationale, Lat. 757 is its bulk. Bound in unprepossessing modern gray leather, the manuscript contains 452 parchment leaves that measure approximately 265 by 207 millimeters. Few if any other private devotional texts of the fourteenth or fifteenth century attain such dimensions, needed in this instance to accommodate an exceptionally extensive text as well as an unusually full pictorial program that includes seventy-three full-page miniatures. A complete list of texts and miniatures is included in the Catalogue. The text may be summarized as follows:

> Table of Contents, folios 1–3v
> Easter Tables for 1380–1520, folios 4v–5
> Table of Lunar and Solar Conjunctions for 1395–1400, folios 6–9v
> Franciscan Calendar, folios 10v–22
> Votive Offices for the Days of the Week, Use of Rome, folios 25–56
> Franciscan Office of the Virgin, Use of Rome, folios 58–108v
> Seven Joys of the Virgin, folios 110–112
> Office of the Dead, Use of Rome, folios 115v–146
> Penitential Psalms, folios 148–154v
> Franciscan Litanies, folios 156–161

Office of the Passion, folios 163–184
Passion Readings from the Four Gospels, folios 186–224
Prayer of Saint Augustine ("Dulcissime Yesu Christe . . ."), folios 225–227
Votive Masses for the Days of the Week, folios 230–261
Ordinary of the Mass, folios 263–282v
Proper of Time and Proper of Saints, folios 284–366
Common of Saints, folios 367v–383
Office of Saint John the Baptist, folios 383v–396
Office of Saint Nicholas of Bari, folios 396v–410
Office of Saint Anthony Abbot, folios 410v–424
Office of Saint Catherine of Alexandria, folios 424v–434
Obsecro Te and Other Prayers, folios 434v–439
Conclusion of the Missal: Prayers and Blessings, folios 440–450v

The extraordinary scope of the text of Lat. 757 is clear from the preceding list. Rarely if ever do votive offices for the days of the week occur in Books of Hours of the fourteenth and fifteenth centuries. Equally anomalous is the addition of an extensive Missal to a full Book of Hours, as well as the inclusion near the end of the Missal of four offices of saints, which more properly belong to a Book of Hours.[1]

Like the text of Lat. 757, its copious illumination is anomalous in several ways. Uniquely, to my knowledge, the votive offices for the days of the week are here illustrated by a Creation cycle.[2] The Office of the Virgin is illustrated by Passion scenes (unusual but not unprecedented), probably chosen in this instance because most of the Infancy scenes and episodes from the life of the Virgin conventional to this office were to be represented in the Missal.[3] Probably for similar reasons the Flagellation (folio 254v) rather than the Crucifixion illustrates the Friday Mass for the Cross. The Crucifixion is represented twice

1. Leroquais (1927, I, 1) describes the combination of Hours and Missal in Lat. 757 and Smith-Lesouëf as "assez rare." Salmon cites only one fourteenth-century example, Chigi. D V 71, of 1330 (1971, no. 459).

Even in the fifteenth century, when the practice of combining Hours with a Missal became more common, normally only a few masses were included (for example, Salmon, 1971, nos. 428, 430, 432, 440, 443, 452). Only the Duke of Berry provides an exception. His *Très Belles Heures de Notre-Dame*, the earliest part of which Meiss dates to 1380–85, contains masses for the Temporale, from Advent to Pentecost, as well as a Sanctorale and five votive masses: one for the dead, one for the Holy Cross, one for the Virgin, and two for Saint Andrew, Berry's patron (Meiss, 1967, chap. VI and 337ff.). L. M. J. Delaissé proposes that in this instance the Duke of Berry decided to combine a Book of Hours with a Missal that had been written for someone else, introduc-

ing his portrait into each and changing the original arms in the Missal. Delaissé adds, however, that this "entreprise prétentieuse fut abandonnée," and that part or all of the manuscript was given to Berry's librarian, Robinet d'Estampes (1963, 123–24, 134, 139; also Meiss, 1967, 337–39). An enterprise that proved too pretentious even for the Duke of Berry was congenial to the owner of Lat. 757, which contains fifty-three masses, more also than the number in Berry's fifteenth-century Books of Hours: the *Très Riches Heures*, which contains twenty-two masses, and the *Belles Heures*, which contains only eight (Meiss, 1974, 318–20, 334).

2. A Creation cycle also anomalously illustrates the Office of the Virgin in Giangaleazzo Visconti's Psalter-Hours now in Florence. See chapter III, 55–58 and passim.

3. For examples of Passion cycles in the Office of the Virgin, see Wieck, 66–71.

elsewhere in the manuscript: at None in the Office of the Virgin (folio 82) and at the Canon of the Mass (folio 276v). Unconventional also is the illustration of the Penitential Psalms and the Litanies, respectively, by the Procession with the Ark of the Covenant (folio 147) and the Procession of Gregory the Great (folio 155).[4] Including as it does Creation scenes from the Old Testament, cycles of the Infancy, Ministry, and Passion of Christ, Evangelist portraits, scenes from the Acts of the Apostles, and a multitude of representations drawn from the lives of saints, the idiosyncratic pictorial program of Lat. 757 constitutes a compact pictorial encyclopedia of Christian history.

The richness of the pictorial embellishment of Lat. 757 extends beyond its seventy-three full-page miniatures. The manuscript also contains 135 historiated or otherwise decorated initials five lines high at the beginning of major textual subdivisions such as the canonical hours. Numerous gilded or painted two-line and one-line initials appear throughout the text at the opening of lesser textual subdivisions, such as versicles and responses. Roman numerals painted in red and blue in the center of the top margin of each recto are also original.[5] In addition, the borders of many of the text pages in Lat. 757 are richly decorated. All pages containing major textual subdivisions are framed by florid acanthus arabesques of blue, green, red, and rose. Often, like the five-line initials, the arabesques are set against heavy burnished gold backgrounds. Many of the frames open out at the corners into medallion-like shapes filled with a variety of motifs, including plant forms, birds, dogs, and human figures. Beginning on folio 335, the opening of the Mass for Pentecost, a monogram and an emblem appear frequently in the corner openings, as, for example, in Figure 9 and elsewhere in the borders. These will be discussed below (pages 19–24).

The anonymous principal illuminator of Lat. 757 was both versatile and innovative. His modernity is evident in a comparison of his style with that of Giovanni di Benedetto da Como, the illustrator of Blanche of Savoy's Book of Hours of around 1378, to whose work the Master of Lat. 757 is nevertheless clearly indebted.[6] The Crucifixion on folio 82 in Lat. 757 (Fig. 10), for example, although it includes many more figures and is conceived on a larger scale, is related in facial and body types, as in drapery, to the corresponding miniature on folio 156v in Blanche's manuscript (Fig. 8). Yet as the comparison

4. In both the *Belles Heures* and the *Très Riches Heures*, the Limbourgs also placed the Procession of Saint Gregory at the opening of the Litanies (Meiss, 1974, 119ff. and figs. 575, 576, 641).

5. Because the modern arabic numeration in the upper-right corner of each recto includes the table of contents and lunar tables (both without roman numerals), all the roman numbers are seven lower than the arabic. Leroquais (1927 and 1943) transposes the roman numbers to arabic; consequently, the folio numbers cited by him are also seven lower than those used here.

6. Even the decorative scheme of Lat. 757 reflects the illuminator's debt to Giovanni di Benedetto da Como. In Lat. 757, as in the Hours of Blanche of Savoy, a full-page miniature, generally blank on the reverse, is paired with an historiated initial to introduce each major text. The border designs of acanthus scrolls, decorative loops, and gold bars in Lat. 757 are also derived from the Munich manuscript, as are the decorations at the corners of full-page miniatures (see, for example, Figs. 6, 7, 10, 33). On the Hours of Blanche of Savoy, see chapter I, pages 8–10; also pages 20, 25 note 40, 45, and 49 below.

shows, the Master of Lat. 757 was far more influenced than Blanche's illuminator by the courtly manners and fashions that, beginning with Blanche's arrival in Milan in 1350 and increasingly throughout the rest of the fourteenth century, reached Lombardy from France, and were received with special enthusiasm in Galeazzo's court at Pavia.

Such monumental compositions as Saint Ursula with her Companions on folio 380 and the Madonna of Mercy on folio 258 (Figs. 11, 51) might readily be transposed to the walls of a church, and the style of the master of Lat. 757 has in fact been associated with several fresco cycles of the late fourteenth century near Milan.[7] He seems to have preferred large-scale figures. Indeed, on folio 114v, in the Obsequies of a Bishop (probably Saint Martin of Tours), a subject requiring both a complex architectural setting and a large number of figures, the Master of Lat. 757 was forced to paint the figures on an unaccustomed small scale (Fig. 12), so that they are somewhat cramped and overwhelmed by their environment.[8]

One of the miniatures by the principal assistant of the Master of Lat. 757, in its sister manuscript, Smith-Lesouëf 22, may indicate that his shop even furnished designs for sculpture. Pilate in the scene of Christ before Pilate on folio 34v in Smith-Lesouëf 22 (Fig. 20), is the twin, even in such small details as his meringue-peak cap, of the corresponding figure in the marble dossal with a Crucifixion and eight Passion scenes (Fig. 21) on the high altar of Sant'Eustorgio, which, according to tradition, was given to the church at an unknown date by Giangaleazzo Visconti.[9]

In Lat. 757 the principal assistant painted the Creation cycle beginning on folio 24 and ending on folio 53 (Figs. 13–18) and the Transfiguration on folio 309 (Fig. 19), and he participated also in the illumination of several other miniatures, for example, Christ before Pilate on folio 72v, the Last Judgment on folio 162, and the Crucifixion on folio 276v. The style of this master, who was entirely responsible for the fourteenth-century illumination of Smith-Lesouëf 22, is distinguished from that of the Master of Lat. 757 through greater delicacy of design, more fluid and more decorative handling of line, and a

7. For the suggestion that the style of the Master of Lat. 757 is related to fresco painting, see Toesca, 1966, 134f.; Salmi, 1955a, 868; Matalon, 388f. The Master of Lat. 757 played a major role also in the illumination of at least two other luxury manuscripts: a Lancelot and a *Tacuinum Sanitatis*, both in the Bibliothèque nationale, Paris: Fr. 343 (Paris, 1984, no. 84) and Nouv. acq. lat. 1673 (Paris, 1984, no. 86).

8. The bishop saint who presides at the funeral on folio 114v is probably Ambrose. In his *De virtutibus s. Martini* 1, 5, Gregory of Tours describes the miraculous presence of Saint Ambrose at the funeral of Saint Martin. For Gregory's text, its incorporation into a Carolingian life of Saint Ambrose, and depictions of the funeral of Saint Martin that include Saint Ambrose, see Courcelle, 106f., 171, 175, 180, 191, 207. In Italy, representations of Saint Ambrose at the funeral of Saint

Martin are for the most part local to the basilica of Sant'Ambrogio in Milan, where the scene occurs in the ninth-century altar frontal, the tenth-century apse mosaics, and the choir stalls of the fifteenth century. Simone Martini's fresco in the Saint Martin Chapel in the Lower Church at Assisi is a notable example of this kind of depiction outside Milan (Courcelle, 236).

9. For the dossal, see Dell'Acqua, 177.

A far less gifted assistant than the Master of Smith-Lesouëf 22 was responsible for at least parts of the Feeding of the Multitude on folio 315v and the Entry into Jerusalem on folio 322. It will be suggested below (pages 72–74) that Anovelo da Imbonate, illuminator of Giangaleazzo's Coronation Missal, had direct knowledge of, and may also have contributed to, the illumination of Lat. 757.

softer, lighter palette. In contrast to the miniatures of the Master of Lat. 757, which evoke monumental painting, those by the Master of Smith-Lesouëf 22 reflect more strongly the influence of French book illumination.

Smith-Lesouëf 22

Whereas armorials show that in the first half of the sixteenth century Lat. 757 belonged to the Regin family from whose collection it entered the royal library, the provenance of Smith-Lesouëf 22 can be traced back only to 1913, when it entered the Bibliothèque nationale as part of the Smith-Lesouëf donation.[10] Nonetheless, the manuscripts are clearly related—textually, iconographically, stylistically, and heraldically.

In Smith-Lesouëf 22, as in Lat. 757, a Book of Hours is combined with a Missal. In text, as in pictorial content and in format, however, Smith-Lesouëf 22 is a reduced version of its sister manuscript. Its 378 parchment leaves, measuring approximately 160 by 120 millimeters, contain only ten masses, compared to forty-four in the larger manuscript. The Office of the Passion is omitted, as are offices for saints. Smith-Lesouëf 22 contains only twenty-one full-page miniatures, and some of these, as we shall see below, probably did not belong to the original plan of the manuscript. As in Lat. 757, Passion scenes illustrate the Office of the Virgin.

Left incomplete in the fourteenth century, the illumination of Smith-Lesouëf 22 was completed in the fifteenth. The decorative scheme of the manuscript, however, was established in the first campaign of illumination and, for the most part, followed in the second. The basic scheme is that of Lat. 757: full-page miniatures, followed by historiated initials, introduce each of the principal texts, and painted frames fill the borders of all pages containing large historiated initials.[11] Painted initials, one or two lines high, introduce subsidiary divisions of the text. As in Lat. 757, the frames in Smith-Lesouëf 22 are constructed of gilded bars onto which interlace patterns and acanthus are painted. In Smith-Lesouëf 22, however, rinceaux of grape leaves and tendrils, derived from French illumination, are added to the framework (Figs. 22, 43). Similar sprays of foliage adorn the borders on folios with full-page miniatures. The monogram and emblem that appear in the margins of Lat. 757, beginning with folio 335, recur regularly throughout the margins of the fourteenth-century portion of Smith-Lesouëf 22.[12] Finally, blue and red roman numeration of the fourteenth century, like that in Lat. 757, appears in the upper

10. Paris, 1984, no. 85. Complete bibliography appears below in the Catalogue.

11. Unlike most of their counterparts in Lat. 757, the full-page miniatures in Smith-Lesouëf 22 are not blank on the reverse.

12. The monogram and emblem appear nowhere on leaves painted entirely in the fifteenth century.

borders of the rectos in Smith-Lesouëf 22. This numeration was continued in the fifteenth century, sometimes in purple and gold. There are errors in the fourteenth-century
numbers in the eighteenth quire, folios 113–19 (from which a leaf, probably blank, has
been excised); otherwise the roman numbers correspond to the modern arabic numbers in
the upper-right corners of all the leaves.

Many of the fifteenth-century miniatures in Smith-Lesouëf 22 fill spaces at the ends
of texts (which often coincide with the ends of quires), where there is no reason to
believe that miniatures were originally intended. There are no half-page fourteenth-
century miniatures anywhere in the manuscript, and on all those pages painted with
half-page miniatures in the fifteenth century, the border decoration also dates from the
fifteenth century, further indication that no miniatures were planned for these pages in
the first campaign of illumination. In two half-page miniatures in the Office of the
Virgin—the Adoration of the Magi at the end of Terce on folio 44v (Fig. 24) and the
Annunciation to the Shepherds on folio 56v at the conclusion of Vespers—Infancy
scenes are arbitrarily introduced into the midst of a Passion cycle. (These scenes would
not be appropriate to the Hours at which they are introduced even if there were an
Infancy cycle in Smith-Lesouëf 22.) On folio 212, at the end of the masses, a half-page
miniature of Christ in the House of Mary and Martha is no doubt entirely the invention
of the fifteenth-century illuminator, since none of the preceding masses is illustrated
with a narrative scene.

Whereas all the half-page miniatures in Smith-Lesouëf 22 seem to have been planned
only in the fifteenth century, several full-page miniatures completed in the fifteenth
century were evidently begun in the earlier campaign of illumination. The latter include
the Crucifixion on folio 45 and the Descent from the Cross on folio 48v, both closely
related to their counterparts in Lat. 757, but badly flaked and apparently touched up and
completed in the fifteenth century. Other full-page miniatures appear to have been
painted entirely in the fifteenth century but on fourteenth-century designs: the Crucifixion on folio 168v, at the Canon of the Mass; a noble couple (their faces repainted)
presented by Saints Anthony Abbot and Catherine of Alexandria to the Man of Sorrows
on folio 285v (Fig. 23), at the opening of the Passion readings from the Gospels; the
Baptism of Saint Augustine on folio 213, illustrating the prayer of Saint Augustine; and
the badly damaged (perhaps defaced) Funeral of a Nobleman on folio 223, at the opening
of the Office of the Dead. Still other full-page miniatures painted entirely in the fifteenth
century are linked to the fourteenth-century campaign through their subject and their
position in the manuscript. The Admonition to Adam and Eve on folio 89, at the
beginning of the daily votive offices, may have been planned in the fourteenth century as
a sequel to the Creation cycle that illustrates the same offices in Lat. 757. The Baptism of
Christ that precedes the first of the blessings—for holy water—on folio 348v is the same
subject that introduces this section in Lat. 757.

Armorials

The emblem that constitutes the primary evidence for the original ownership of Lat. 757 by Giangaleazzo Visconti is the radiant gold sun enclosing a white dove against a blue sky, worn as a pendant by the nobleman who kneels before the Madonna and Child on folio 109v, at the opening of the Seven Joys of the Virgin (Fig. 26). A dove against a blue sky and radiant sun was the personal emblem of Giangaleazzo Visconti, said to have been devised for him by Petrarch on the occasion of his first marriage, in 1360, at the age of nine, to Isabelle of Valois, who, as part of her dowry, brought Giangaleazzo the county of Vertus, in Champagne, together with the title Count of Virtues. A sentiment appropriate to this title—the motto "a buon droyt" (sometimes "a bon droit")—occasionally accompanies the *sol-cum-columba* motif, which figures prominently in the Florence Psalter-Hours (Fig. 41), the Coronation Missal (Fig. 3), and the Eulogy-Genealogy (Fig. 30), all three indubitably associated with Giangaleazzo.[13]

In his *Canzon morale fatta per la divisa del conte di Virtù* of about 1389, the Visconti court poet Giovanni di Vannozzo explicates the emblem as follows: the radiant sun represents Giangaleazzo's power, reaching out to all; the dove symbolizes humility and chastity; the azure background denotes serenity. Each component, however, carries a second meaning: the sky evokes heaven, "loco del padre," the sun is Christ, and the dove the Holy Ghost.[14] The bold full-page miniature at the opening of the Mass of the Holy Ghost on folio 241v in Lat. 757 (Fig. 42) would have served aptly also as a frontispiece to Vannozzo's *Canzon*.[15] In the miniature on folio 109v the Trinitarian significance of the

13. Petrarch claims to have suggested the device in a letter cited in *Storia di Milano*, v, 891. The device is described in the letter as "turturem cum brevi notula *a bon droit* radiantis solis in medio" [a turtle dove with a short notation "a bon droit" in the middle of a radiant sun]. It is attributed to Petrarch also at the beginning of the poem by Giovanni di Vannozzo cited in note 14 below.

14. Vannozzo's poem is published in *Le rime di Francesco di Vannozzo*, ed. A. Medin, Bologna, 1928, 3–14. A bust-length representation of God the Father holding the orb of the universe, with the dove of the Holy Spirit and an enormous radiating sun beneath him, dominates the central window of the apse of the Cathedral of Milan. For the identification of this window motif with Giangaleazzo, see *Annali*, I, 249. As we shall see below (note 73), the carved boss at the keystone of the ribbing in the apse reiterates the theme of the Trinity.

15. A smaller but similar representation of the Holy Dove fills the initial that introduces the Tuesday Office of the Holy Ghost on folio 104 in Smith-Lesouëf 22,

where it is accompanied by a knot and a monogram in the border (Fig. 43). A dove in a radiant sun quite exceptionally occupies the central panel of a triptych on the altar in the concluding miniature of the same manuscript, the Purification of the Virgin, on folio 359 (Fig. 44). The fifteenth-century illuminator of this leaf gives the dove additional unwonted prominence by placing four of these birds, rather than the customary two, in the basket held by Joseph.

Outside of Lat. 757, no Mass or Office of the Holy Ghost known to me is introduced by a full-page depiction of the Holy Spirit, alone, against a brilliant sun and a vast blue sky. If a full page is allotted to such a miniature, the subject represented is usually Pentecost or the Preaching of the Apostles. Although it is true that the rays behind the sun in Lat. 757 are straight, while the Visconti sun is normally depicted with undulating rays, the latter often emits both (for example, Figs. 30, 41). The dove that serves as both the Holy Spirit and an emblem of Giangaleazzo in Banco Rari 397 emerges from a blue sky amidst straight rays (Fig. 46—see also page 20).

nobleman's badge is underscored by the dove in the gable of the Madonna's throne, the radiant sun behind the Christ child, and the fiery seraphim and other angels in the upper part of the miniature, whose presence implies that the Madonna's throne is situated in the "loco del padre."

The Count of Virtues' veneration of both the Holy Spirit and the Trinity is amply documented. In his will he stipulated the completion of a church dedicated to the Holy Ghost already begun under his auspices in Pavia, and he bequeathed a chapel to the Trinity in Verona.[16] Moreover, the first of three portraits of Giangaleazzo in the Psalter-Hours in Florence appears in the *bas-de-page* of BR 105, a page devoted to the Trinity, where a dove descending from a radiant sun in the upper margin without doubt serves both as the Holy Spirit and as an emblem of the Count of Virtues. From this page Giangaleazzo gazes at the *Annunciation* on the facing leaf, BR 104v (Fig. 46). Here too the Trinity is accorded special prominence. Although the naked Christ child appears in addition to the more customary combination of God the Father and the Holy Spirit in at least one earlier Lombard version of this event, on folio 68v in the Hours of Blanche of Savoy, the dazzling Trinitarian apparition directed at the Virgin in Blanche's son Giangaleazzo's Psalter-Hours conspicuously relates this miniature to the depiction of the Trinity on the facing page.[17] Furthermore, in the same manuscript, an offset on BR 150 discloses that an excised leaf, which contained the opening of the hymn to the Trinity, *Gloria in Excelsis*, was also adorned by a *bas-de-page* portrait of Giangaleazzo.[18] As Duke of Milan, Giangaleazzo is linked to the Trinity also on folio 1 of the Paris Eulogy, where the Christ child himself (completely nude as in the miniature of the nobleman with the Madonna and Child in Lat. 757) crowns Giangaleazzo (Figs. 30, 97); in the upper borders of this page, the dove-in-sun device is flanked by four prophets, gesticulating toward Giangaleazzo and holding scrolls proclaiming that his throne was the sun and his goodness like that of the dove. Here, on an even grander scale than in Lat. 757, the heavenly setting of the miniature bespeaks the realm and hence the immanent presence of God the Father.

A monogram consisting of interlaced initials and an emblem that has been described previously as consisting of two interlocking circles or rings (Figs. 9, 22) are the most recurrent emblematic decoration in both Lat. 757 and Smith-Lesouëf 22.[19] Like the sun-in-dove pendant worn by the nobleman on folio 109v, the monogram and emblem belong

---

16. Osio, 337. The will is undated. Osio dates it to 1397, Bueno de Mesquita (258 n. 3) to 1402.

17. On the Hours of Blanche of Savoy, see also chapter I, pages 8, 10; note 40 and pages 45, 49 below. On the motif of the Christ child in the Annunciation, see Robb, 524f. Robb associates the motif with the *Lignum Vitae* of Saint Bonaventure. Franciscan use may have dictated its appearance in Lat. 757.

18. The offset also reveals the presence of hunting birds in the lateral margins of the lost leaf, as on BR

105. When the missing leaf was excised from the manuscript is unknown. A rubric on the last line of BR 149v, *Canticum Simeonis p̄phete*, shows that the recto of the missing leaf contained the third evangelical canticle, *Nunc dimittis*, which was perhaps illustrated by the Presentation of the Christ Child in the Temple.

19. The emblem was described by Toesca as "due cerchi intrecciati" (1966, 131 n. 2). Leroquais (1927, 1, 4) characterized it as "deux anneaux entrelacés."

without doubt to the original decoration of these manuscripts. In Lat. 757 these devices appear not only in the margins and in illuminated initials; like the pendant on folio 109v (Fig. 26), they also constitute an integral part of some of the full-page miniatures. The emblem occurs first in the background of the Procession with the Ark of the Covenant on folio 147, at the opening of the Penitential Psalms, and the monogram appears first as background patterning in the Transfiguration on folio 309 (Fig. 19), which illustrates the Mass for the second Sunday in Lent. Both emblem and monogram, however, begin to occur regularly in Lat. 757 only on folio 335, often paired with one another in the borders of the leaves they adorn. In Smith-Lesouëf 22, they occur from the very beginning of the manuscript.

On the page for the Mass of Saint Nicholas in Lat. 757, on folio 364, both the monogram and the emblem are presented by a woman whose gown is patterned with the monogram (Fig. 9). Even in such small details as the shape of her headdress, this woman evokes the later figure who displays Giangaleazzo Visconti's armorials—a shield charged with a viper and a viper-crested tilting helmet—in a copy of Cicero's *De natura deorum* written and partially illuminated in Bologna around 1370–80 but probably embellished for Giangaleazzo around 1400 (Fig. 28).[20] The monogram in the left hand of the figure on folio 364 has been variously read as *BE*, *FB*, *SB*, and *BV*.[21] Recently, Kay Sutton has suggested that the monogram may be simply an *A*, but has concluded that both the monogram and the emblem "remain cryptic."[22] The monogram seems to me quite clearly to be an interlaced G and V, for Giangaleazzo Visconti, or perhaps for Galeazzo Visconti, the name Giangaleazzo seems to have preferred between 1378, the year of his father's death, and a point much later in his life, probably after he rose to the dukedom in 1395, when once again he was called Giangaleazzo.[23] Acorns and stylized oak leaves in the monogram on folio 364 and elsewhere may also allude to Giangaleazzo. The oak, a time-honored symbol of strength, appears frequently as his emblem in the Florence Psalter-Hours (Fig. 29). It figures also in the Coronation scene of the Missal of 1395 (Fig. 3) and in the genealogy of 1403, where oak leaves frame the portrait medallions (Figs. 31, 32).[24]

The emblem in the right hand of the woman in Lat. 757 cannot be the interlocking circles or rings that it has been said to represent.[25] As two small protruding ends clearly

20. Paris, Bibl. nat., Lat. 6340 (Paris, 1984, no. 91).

21. Toesca read the initials as *BE* (1966, 131 n. 2). Leroquais suggested *SB* or *FB* (1927, I, 7; 1943, 13). E. Berti Toesca (28) also read them as *BE*, for Bernabò Visconti. L. Cogliati Arano (1970a, 410) interpreted the monogram as *BV*, signifying both Beatrice Regina della Scala and her husband Bernabò.

If the monogram is, as I believe, *GV*, it may also be read as an interlaced *G*, *V*, and *C*, if the *C* is read as coextensive with the *G*, but without the crossbar. In that event, the monogram would allude not only to Giangaleazzo but also to his wife Caterina.

22. Sutton, 1982, 93 and note 5.

23. Giovanni de Muzio, *Chronicon Placentinum*, *RIS*, XVI, 443–633 (557). See also G. Giulini, V, 580f; Riboldi and Seregni, 104–17, esp. 212. Giangaleazzo is still called "Galeaz" in the prayer that includes his name in the Psalter-Hours in Florence (LF 9v).

24. On the oak and acorns as symbols of strength, see J. C. Cooper, *An Illustrated Encyclopedia of Traditional Symbols*, London, 1978, 121; and J. Hall, *Dictionary of Subjects and Symbols in Art*, New York, 1979, 9 (s.v. Ages of the World).

25. See note 19 above.

indicate, this emblem is in fact a knot. Joseph Krása has shown that the omnipresent slipknots in the manuscripts of Wenceslaus IV were multivalent christological and imperial symbols that also stood for the bond of love between Wenceslaus and his wife Sophia.[26] I would suggest that the knots in the Paris Hours-Missals likewise signify several concerns of their owners, and that one of these was marriage.

From antiquity to our own time, knots have signified marriage, and in ancient Rome they came to symbolize the chastity of brides.[27] It is not fortuitous that in Lat. 757 the knot is given its most explicitly emblematic setting on the page for the mass of Saint Nicholas, guardian of the chastity of nubile maidens. (A full-page miniature of Nicholas providing dowries for three impoverished women who might otherwise have been condemned to prostitution introduces his mass on folio 363v.) In the lower border of folio 404, at Terce in the Office of Saint Nicholas, a monkey, symbol of lust, is controlled by a ball and chain, presumably under the influence of two flanking knots and a chaste woman in the initial above (Fig. 33). The woman is one of several who appear, only in this office, holding reddish-yellow balls that may allude to Saint Nicholas's gift.

Knots, accompanied by interlaced initials, commonly symbolized marriage in late medieval and Renaissance painting. Often, as in the lower border of a page from the fifteenth-century *Livre des échecs amoureux* of Antoine Rollin and Marie d'Ailly (Fig. 35), the initials were themselves interlaced with a three-looped lovers' knot. In the right border of the same page, however, the initials *A* and *M*, interlaced only with one another, are paired with knots (in this case knotted dogs' leashes), as in Lat. 757.[28] The object held by the heraldic figure on the page for the Mass of Saint Nicholas reappears as gold patterning on the white gown of one of Saint Ursula's companions on folio 380, in the miniature that introduces the Mass for Several Virgins (Fig. 11). If Lat. 757 was made for Giangaleazzo, the young woman whose gown is adorned with gold knots probably represents his bride of 1380, Caterina Visconti (it is even possible that the small book tucked under her arm refers to the smaller version of Lat. 757, Smith-Lesouëf 22). Caterina links arms with a woman gowned in deep blue-black, embroidered with Giangaleazzo's principal emblem as Count of Virtues, white doves (here embroidered in pearls) springing from flamelike rays. It seems reasonable to suggest that she represents Isabelle, Giangaleazzo's first wife, through whom he acquired the county of Vertus in Champagne, with which the

---

26. Krása, 1971, 99–101. A slip-knotted cloth, like that of Wenceslaus, became a device of Giangaleazzo's son, Filippo Maria.

27. On the symbolism of knots in antiquity, A. Pauly and G. Wissowa, *Paulys Real-Encyclopädie der Classischen Altertumswissenschaft*, XVII, 1, Stuttgart, 1936, 803f., 808 (s.v. *Nodus*); C. Daremberg and E. Saglio, *Dictionnaire des antiquités grecques et romains*, IV, 1, Paris, 1977, 88 (s.v. *Nodus*). Marriage was symbolized in antiquity by the knot of Hercules (also called a love-knot). For examples,

see B. Segall, *Katalog der Goldschmiede-Arbeiten (Museum Benaki, Athen)*, Athens, 1938, 32ff., nos. 29, 30, and many others.

In Italian, the word *nodo* signified a marriage bond at least as early as the fourteenth century and was used as such by Petrarch (*Vocabolario degli Accademici della Crusca*, XI, 178 §xxxv).

28. Paris, Bibl. nat., Fr. 9197, folio 202. On this manuscript, see M. B. Freeman, *The Unicorn Tapestries*, New York, 1976, 167 and fig. 209.

dove-and-sun emblem is associated.[29] The Duke did after all direct in his will that effigies of each of his wives be placed at the sides of his tomb in the Certosa of Pavia.[30] In the miniature on folio 380, Saint Ursula herself wears a gown embellished with crescent moons, a reiteration of the theme of chastity.

In his recent study of European monarchical orders of knighthood, Jonathan Boulton traces the transmission of the princely passion for the display of para-heraldic personal devices (badges and devices adopted in addition to, rather than instead of, heraldic arms, with which they were often paired) from its probable point of origin at the court of Edward III of England in the 1330s, through France, and finally, around 1350, to Italy, where the practice, not surprisingly, took firmest hold at the court of Giangaleazzo's father, Galeazzo II Visconti.[31] Often associated with tournaments, especially in England and France, para-heraldic devices were also employed by monarchical orders of knighthood, defined by Boulton as orders distinguished by the permanent attachment of their presidential offices to the crowns of their princely founders.[32] The first such device in Italy was the knot of Hercules (or love-knot) of the Company of the Holy Spirit of Right Desire, informally known as the Company or Order of the Knot, established in 1353 by Louis of Taranto, King of Naples.[33] Although the Hercules knot is more complex than the knot in the Paris Hours-Missals, yet another device of the Order of the Knot—a dove against a radiant sun—is remarkably similar to the personal device of Giangaleazzo discussed above (Fig. 36).

With the death of Louis of Taranto in 1362, the Order of the Knot ceased to exist. The love-knot, however, soon reappeared as part of the device of the Order of the Collar established in Avignon in 1364 by Giangaleazzo's uncle, Count Amadeus VI of Savoy, whose sister, Blanche, had married Galeazzo II Visconti in 1350.[34] The device of this order was a collar from which hung a circlet of three love-knots. At about the same time that the order was founded, the love-knot became the personal badge of Amadeus himself, and is thus one of the earliest-known para-heraldic badges not symbolic of membership in an organized order.

Galeazzo II was introduced to the fashion for para-heraldry by his Savoyard brother-in-law and was doubtlessly exposed to it also through the English and French royal emissaries who visited his court, first in Milan and then in Pavia, to arrange marriages between members of the English and French royal families and Galeazzo's children. A company even older than the Order of the Collar, the Order of the Black Swan, had been founded

<hr>

29. See page 19 above.

30. Corio, ii, 969.

31. Boulton, 1987. I have also benefited from reading a paper, now in press, presented by Boulton at a conference held in April 1988 at the University of Notre Dame: *Art and Politics in Late Medieval and Early Renaissance Italy: 1250–1500*. In his paper of 1988, Boulton points out that the heirs of Galeazzo II Visconti adopted at least twenty-two distinct devices—more than any other dynasty either in Italy or elsewhere in Europe.

32. Boulton, 1987, xviif.

33. Ibid., 211–40; M. Keen, *Chivalry*, New Haven, 1984, 192 and fig. 43. The original copy of the statutes of this order is now Paris, Bibl. nat., Fr. 4274, included in the catalogue of 1984 as no. 61.

34. Boulton, 1987, 249–70; idem, 1988.

by Amadeus on the occasion of the marriage of Blanche and Galeazzo in 1350, and Galeazzo was among the founding members of this society.[35] Eighteen years later, at the banquet given by Galeazzo to celebrate the marriage of his daughter Violante to Lionel Duke of Clarence, Galeazzo is said to have distributed buttons bearing the *divisa dell'acqua e del fuoco*, a ragged diagonal staff, burning at its lower end and supporting at its upper end two pails of water suspended from a rope.[36] It seems not unreasonable to suppose that Giangaleazzo Visconti, in his turn, would have welcomed the burgeoning practice of para-heraldry, associated in his family with marriages.

As we have seen above, a knot was one of the emblems of the Order of the Holy Spirit founded by Louis of Taranto in 1353. That a knot might symbolize the Trinity as well as the Holy Spirit is clear in one of various miniatures associated with the Trinity in the Rothschild Canticles of the early fourteenth century in which the Dove of the Holy Spirit constitutes part of a knot that loops around to enclose the other two persons of the Trinity, all three set against a sunlike radiance (Fig. 37).[37] As also noted above, Giangaleazzo's personal emblem was conflated with the Dove of the Holy Spirit in the Florence Psalter-Hours. In Lat. 757 and Smith-Lesouëf 22, the knot may likewise have served as a multivalent signifier, appropriate in this instance to a specific occasion— Giangaleazzo's marriage to Caterina—and expressing as well his lifelong devotion to both the Holy Ghost and the Trinity.[38]

In addition to the monogram GV, Lat. 757 has a second pair of initials—*B* and *E*—not intertwined, but displayed separately on folios 58, 115v, and 410v, flanking shields of the Regin family, sixteenth-century owners of the manuscript. Although the shields are

35. Boulton, 1987, 250f.

36. Giulini, *Memorie*, v, 597. This device continued to be used by Giangaleazzo and his children and was adopted also by the Sforza dukes of Milan.

37. New Haven, Yale, no. 29, and Hamburger, 1987.

38. Both the knot and the monogram in Lat. 757 and Smith-Lesouëf 22 are linked to Giangaleazzo through association also with other emblematic devices in the borders of both Hours-Missals. In the Calendar pages of Smith-Lesouëf 22, the knot and the monogram appear in the borders of some of the pages (January and April, while the borders of others (February, June, and August) are adorned by acorns. In the Office of Saint Nicholas on folio 406v in Lat. 757, the monogram and knot (the latter outlined but not completed) are paired with a pug dog (Fig. 38) related to the hunting dogs and dogs as ruler symbols that populate the pages of Giangaleazzo's Psalter-Hours in Florence (Fig. 39). Though not a recurrent emblem in either manuscript, the short-legged crested bird in the lower margin of folio

55 in Lat. 757 (Fig. 34) also finds a counterpart in the first volume of the Psalter-Hours, in the margins of the last leaf (folio 151), where the bird is almost certainly a para-heraldic device (Fig. 40).

As noted by Sutton (1982, 93 n. 5), an emblem similar to the knot in the Paris Hours-Missals appears on the frontispieces of two manuscripts written and illuminated in France during the last decades of the fourteenth century: The Hague, Royal Library, MS 71.A.16–18 (Pierre Bersuire's translation of Livy), and Brussels, Bibl. Royale, MS 9091 (a French translation of Seneca's letters to Lucilius). In the Livy, the knot is paired with the sixteenth-century arms of Philip of Cleves, painted over erasures; in the Seneca they occur with what seems to be a contemporary initial A. For the French manuscripts, see A. Byvanck, *Les principaux manuscrits à peintures de la Bibliothèque Royale des Pays-Bas et du Musée Meermanno-Westreenianum à la Haye*, SFRMP, Paris, 1924, no. 9; and C. Gaspar and F. Lyna, *Les principaux manuscrits à peintures de la Bibliothèque Royale de Belgique*, SFRMP, I, Paris, 1937, 356–58.

certainly sixteenth-century additions, Kay Sutton has proposed that the flanking initials are original and refer to the original owner of Lat. 757, whom she identifies as Bertrando de' Rossi, from sometime after 1385 a councillor to Giangaleazzo Visconti. (She does not deny the presence of Visconti emblems in the manuscript or the relation between Smith-Lesouëf 22 and Lat. 757.)[39] Since the connection between Giangaleazzo and Bertrando began in 1385, Sutton dates Lat. 757 after that year. She suggests further that Smith-Lesouëf 22 was made around 1394, when Bertrando visited France on an embassy for Giangaleazzo, and proposes that this visit accounts for the French influence in the decoration of the manuscript as well as the Bruges saints in its otherwise North Italian calendar.[40]

39. The arms of Annet Regin, papal protonotary and precentor of the Cathedral of Clermont in 1528–29, appear on folio 9v, at the conclusion of the tables of lunar and solar conjunctions, and the arms of his brother, Julien, were painted on folio 4, preceding the Easter tables. The Regin shield, a gold crowned pomegranate on a field of azure, was added beneath the portrait of a nobleman worshipping the Madonna that introduces the Seven Joys of the Virgin on folio 109v (Fig. 26). It was also painted onto the cope of the saint performing mass on folio 329, perhaps as an allusion to the eccelesiastical dignity of Annet Regin. The shield charged with a pomegranate appears in the *bas-de-page* on nine other leaves, all of them associated with the beginning of a text: Office of the Virgin, folio 58 (where the Regin shield appears not only in the *bas-de-page* but also in the illuminated initial that introduces the text—Fig. 27); Office of the Dead, folio 115v; Penitential Psalms, folio 148; Office of the Passion, folio 163; Mass for Saint Francis, folio 361; Mass for a Confessor Bishop, folio 375; Office of Saint Nicholas of Bari, folio 396v; Office of Saint Anthony Abbot, folio 410v; Office of Saint Catherine of Alexandria, folio 424v.

In the initial on folio 58 the Regin shield is surmounted by a crowned, visored helmet crested with the head and neck of a swan. Because the arms of the de' Rossi family of Parma consisted of a silver lion rampant on azure surmounted by a helmet crested with a swan's neck and head, Sutton (1982) concluded that the initials on folios 58 and 115v (she does not mention folio 410v) must be those of Bertrando, a courtier of Bernabò Visconti, who shifted his loyalty to Giangaleazzo after the coup of 1385. Sutton's assertion that the sixteenth-century illuminator who inserted the Regin pomegranate over an earlier heraldic device throughout Lat. 757 simply overlooked two (actually three) instances is not entirely accurate. On all three folios, the pomegranate does in fact appear between the initials *B* and *E*. Why the Regin illuminator should have left earlier initials while painting over the original charge of the shield (presumably the rampant lion of the de' Rossis) is not at all clear and at least allows for the possibility that the swan crest and initials *BE* did not exist when the Regin family introduced its armorials in the manuscript.

Sutton proposes that the nobleman who worships the Madonna on folio 109v in Lat. 757 is Bertrando de' Rossi and that he wears Giangaleazzo's dove-in-sun emblem as a badge of office. In support of her identification, she cites as a parallel an unidentified liveried swordbearer whose scarlet robe is patterned with gold radiant suns and banderoles in the Coronation Missal of 1395 (Fig. 3). Her comparison between the pendant worn as an isolated mark of identification by the owner of the manuscript in Lat. 757, on the one hand, and, on the other, radiant suns and banderoles (no doves) worn by a swordbearer on a page ablaze with the armorials and devices of the Duke of Milan at the most important ceremonial event of his life is not persuasive.

40. Both Sutton (1982, 93f.) and F. Avril (Paris, 1984, 99) infer that because the borders in Smith-Lesouëf 22 show greater French influence than those in Lat. 757, Smith-Lesouëf 22 must be dated to the 1390s, when this influence was most apparent in Lombard illumination. Many undated Lombard manuscripts of this period, however, show French influence in their borders, including several associated with the illuminator Pietro da Pavia and Giangaleazzo's chancellor, Pasquino dei Capelli. The Pliny illuminated by Pietro for Capelli in 1389 already has borders in the French style (Milan, Bibl. Ambrosiana, MS E 24 Inf.—Cogliati Arano, 1970a, 415). French manuscripts were available to Lombard illuminators from the time of the arrival of Blanche of Savoy in Lombardy in 1350.

While the borders of Smith-Lesouëf 22 resemble those in the Baldus de Ubaldis presented to Giangaleazzo in 1393, they are not, as Sutton and Avril propose, identical with them. Though the leaves in Smith-Lesouëf 22 are considerably smaller than those in

Sutton did not observe, however, that the initials *B* and *E* are no more original than the Regin arms. On both folios 58 (Fig. 27) and 115v, the uneven quality of the maroon ground on which the gold letters are painted indicates that the pigment was applied to an abraded surface, where earlier identifying symbols had been erased. Furthermore, the gold initials themselves are conspicuously more rubbed than any of the other gold letters that occur throughout the manuscript (for example, the *G* on the horse of Saint George and on the chest of the saint himself on folio 327v, or the monogram *MV* on the cloth of honor behind the Virgin in the Annunciation on folio 302v). Some of the maroon pigment as well as the green that outlines both the initial on folio 58 and the quatrefoil in which the initials appear on folio 115v has also flaked—additional evidence that both colors were painted on a rough surface. The avocado green that outlines the armorials on these pages appears nowhere else in the manuscript. The third instance of the letters *BE* also occurs within a quatrefoil, in the lower margin of folio 410v. There, the quatrefoil, which is outlined in a deep forest green, overlaps the decorative bands of gold at either side, another indication that it was added later. Finally, one of the most serious difficulties with Sutton's hypothesis is that neither the swan helmet nor the initials *BE* occur anywhere in Smith-Lesouëf 22, where there has been no tampering with the original armorials.

In sum, the dove-in-sun pendant points to the original ownership of Lat. 757 by Giangaleazzo Visconti, and the monogram and knot in both Lat. 757 and Smith-Lesouëf 22 indicate that these manuscripts were made around 1380 to commemorate Gianga-leazzo's marriage to Caterina Visconti. A date as early as 1380 would explain why a ubiquitous Visconti device—the viper (*biscia*)—omnipresent in other manuscripts illumi-nated for Giangaleazzo Visconti, especially the Psalter-Hours in Florence (Figs. 29, 41), is not yet found in these Hours-Missals. Among the numerous emblems of the Viscontis, the viper is the most closely associated with the commune of Milan.[41] When upon the death of his father Galeazzo II in 1378, the twenty-seven-year-old Giangaleazzo became co-ruler with his uncle Bernabò of Milan and its dominions, the young nephew, with his uncle's approval, for seven years confined his political activities to Pavia and to

---

the Baldus, the rinceaux in the former are larger, freer, and less rectilinear than those in the Baldus. The crimping of the grape leaves in the manuscript of 1393, for example, is far more detailed than in Smith-Lesouëf 22. The Baldus de Ubaldis is now Paris, Bibl. nat., Lat. 11727 (Paris, 1984, 90).

Several of the saints local to Bruges in the Calendar of Smith-Lesouëf 22 also occur in the Hours of Gian-galeazzo's mother, Blanche of Savoy: David (1 March), Remigius (1 October), Dionysius (9 October), and Leon-ard (6 November).

41. E. Galli suggests that a serpent was first dis-played on a Milanese standard during the Crusade of 1096 and that its selection as an emblem of the city

was inspired by the presence in Milan since 1002 of the brazen serpent of Moses. The bronze serpent still stands upon a column in the nave of Sant'Ambrogio, opposite its typological counterpart, a cross. Both are included in the miniature of Giangaleazzo's ducal investiture painted by Anovelo da Imbonate in the Coronation Missal still belonging to Sant'Ambrogio (Fig. 3).

Tradition holds that Ottone Visconti, returning vic-torious from the First Crusade, obtained the privilege for himself and his descendants of employing the viper as a personal device, with the addition of a red infidel in its mouth. By the fourteenth century, the Florentine chronicler Giovanni Villani referred to this creature simply as "un uomo rosso" in the mouth of the viper (Galli, 372).

Piedmont, expressing fear of even visiting the city of Milan.[42] In other matters as well, the Count of Virtues remained submissive to his powerful and, by all accounts, brutal uncle, and acceded willingly to the marriage Bernabò planned for him with his daughter, Caterina. If the pious nephew commemorated this marriage with two lavish manuscripts, he might deliberately have refrained from embellishing such books with his father-in-law's viper, symbol of dominion over Milan. The *biscia* was proudly displayed on Bernabò's armor in the enormous equestrian statue (Fig. 5) in the apse of San Giovanni in Conca, the very church in which Giangaleazzo and Caterina were married. Only in 1385 did Giangaleazzo seize all power from his uncle and make the viper his own. For these reasons, in his marriage books of about 1380 the viper would have had no place.[43]

After Giangaleazzo's imprisonment of his uncle Bernabò in 1385, and Bernabò's death in the same year, chroniclers condemned the Count of Virtues for what they regarded as feigned or at least exaggerated piety, designed to conceal his political ambition during the period of co-rule with his uncle. The Anonymous Florentine, for example, wrote: "Egli fece vista d'essere ingesuato e cattolico uomo più di dieci anni, e faceasi dire due or tre messe per mattina, e udiale in apparenza assai divotamente, e andava a' perdoni e alle perdonanze, e communicavasi ispesso, e dicea molti ofici ecclesiatichi . . ."[44] The chroniclers Galeazzo and Bartolomeo Gatari report: "[Giangaleazzo] simullò esser diventà catolico e relizioxo . . . e tuto se de' a contenplacione, orazione, degiunii e astinenzie . . . tegnando senpre sego dí e notte in camera e ala tavolla quando manziava frati e religiosi, i quali con sego celebrasono lo divino oficio."[45] To the young Count of Virtues, given to well-publicized piety, rarely without clergymen near him, hearing mass two or three times a day, Lat. 757 would have been useful, for himself or for his chaplain.

Computational Tables

If Lat. 757 and Smith-Lesouëf 22 were made for Giangaleazzo and Caterina Visconti on the occasion of their marriage in 1380, the manuscripts must have been illuminated

---

42. Muir, 67–87; Bueno de Mesquita, 10–32.

43. The author of the *Lamento di Bernabò Visconti*, composed soon after Bernabò's demise, refers to him as the "dragone" and to Giangaleazzo as the "splendor dal ciel" by whom "quel dragon subito fu conquixo." For this passage, see Romano, 609. On the statue of Bernabò, see page 5 above.

44. *Cronica volgare di Anonimo Fiorentino dall'anno 1385 al 1409, RIS, N.S.,* xxvii, pt. 2, 281 [For more than ten years he (Giangaleazzo) pretended to be a thoroughly devout Catholic, having masses said two or three times each morning, apparently hearing them very

devoutly; and he went to confession and to ceremonies of absolution; and he took communion often and said many religious offices].

45. *Cronaca carrarese, RIS, N.S.,* xvii, pt. 1, 232 [(Giangaleazzo) pretended to have become a pious Catholic . . . and devoted himself entirely to contemplation, prayer, fasts, and abstinences . . . always having with him, day and night, in his room and at table when he ate, friars and ecclesiastics, who also celebrated the divine office with him]. Acerbic observations concerning Giangaleazzo's piety occur also in Corio, 1, 878. See also Bueno de Mesquita, 22ff.

around that date. The opening date in the Easter tables of both Hours-Missals is indeed 1380. Sutton suggests, however, that in neither manuscript does the first date in the Easter tables correspond to the date in which the manuscript was made, and that in fact the manuscripts are separated by about eight years.[46] My own examination of the Easter computations, however, indicates that in both books they were written in 1380, probably by the same scribe.

It is true, as Sutton proposes, that because the registers in the Easter tables of Lat. 757 are organized by decade, the scribe was compelled to begin the first register with 1380 in order to provide the necessary information for any years during this decade. However, in Smith-Lesouëf 22, the scribe was under no such compulsion since the tables are organized by lustrum rather than by decade (Fig. 45). If Smith-Lesouëf 22 were as late as Sutton believes, the tables could have begun with 1385, or even 1390. Yet they begin with 1380, like those in Lat. 757. Consequently, their starting date seems to offer valid evidence for the execution of the two books for Giangaleazzo and Caterina Visconti on the occasion of their marriage in the year 1380.

Giangaleazzo's ownership of Lat. 757 would also account for the tables of solar and lunar conjunctions and oppositions beginning with 1395 on folios 6–9v. Written on a quire inserted in the manuscript after its roman numeration, these tables may have been added in that year, at the time the Count of Virtues became the Duke of Milan. Contemporary accounts document Giangaleazzo's dread of solar eclipses (especially understandable in view of the sun's role as one of his principal emblems), and he very probably would have regarded tables indicating the possibility of such events as aids in promoting an auspicious ducal reign.[47]

Portraits and Visconti Saints

As noted above, Sutton has inferred that the nobleman portrayed both on folio 109v in Lat. 757 and on folio 15 in Smith-Lesouëf 22 (Figs. 26, 49) must be Bertrando de' Rossi, of whom no other portraits survive.[48] Arguing against Sutton that the miniature in Lat. 757 still represents Giangaleazzo Visconti and that its counterpart in Smith-Lesouëf 22 probably originally represented him, Michael Zaccaria has proposed that both miniatures have been repainted.[49] While the area around the back and shoulder of

46. Sutton, 1982, 93.

47. See, for example, the dispatch of a Gonzaga emissary cited by Bueno de Mesquita, 38. A solar eclipse occurred in Milan in 1389 (*Annales Mediolanensis, RIS,* XVI, 638).

48. Sutton, 1982, 1983; see also note 39 above.

49. Zaccaria, 160f.

the nobleman in the Smith-Lesouëf miniature has surely been repainted, it is difficult to see with certainty whether the face itself is also a repainting; I see no evidence of repainting in the face of the donor in Lat. 757. I do, however, agree with Zaccaria that it closely resembles unequivocal portraits of Giangaleazzo. The three surviving representations of the Count of Virtues in the Florence Psalter-Hours share several characteristics with the portrait in Lat. 757: reddish hair sharply receding from a sloping brow, dark eyes, a straight nose, and full lips sometimes set in a quasi-smile (Figs. 41, 46, 47). Similar features characterize also the nobleman portrayed beside Blanche of Savoy in her Book of Hours now in Munich (Fig. 6). As suggested above, this figure may also represent Giangaleazzo, as he appeared before 1378. In two of the three depictions in Florence, Giangaleazzo, like the nobleman in both Hours-Missals, wears a scarlet tunic and cowl.

Portraits of Giangaleazzo in the Coronation Missal of 1395 (Figs. 3, 48) and the Eulogy-Genealogy of 1403 (Figs. 32, 97) show that he did not always wear a beard and moustache such as those in the Hours-Missals. In the Coronation Missal his two-pointed goatee is shorter than its counterpart in Banco Rari 397, whereas in the Eulogy-Genealogy he wears a short beard but no moustache. It is possible that, like his brother-in-law, Jean de Berry, whose hirsute appendages also varied, Giangaleazzo at times wore neither a beard nor a moustache.[50]

The attributes of the Madonna on folio 109v in Lat. 757 (Fig. 26) also connect the manuscript with Giangaleazzo Visconti. The sun behind the Christ child in this miniature is associated not only with the infant Savior but also, in conjunction with the silver crescent moon on the step of the throne, with the Virgin as the Woman of the Apocalypse, "clothed with the sun" and with the moon "under her feet" (Revelation 12:1). Petrus de Castelletto, the Augustinian friar who composed Giangaleazzo's eulogy, constructed it around yet another attribute of the Woman of the Apocalypse. The Duke of Milan and Count of Virtues, whose ensign in life had been the rays of the sun, said Petrus, would in death receive a radiant crown terminating in twelve stars, each representing one of his virtues; this crown, moreover, would be none other than that described in Revelation 12:1 as belonging to the Woman of the Apocalypse.[51]

The Woman of the Apocalypse, especially when associated with the Trinity, expressed the immaculacy of the Virgin long before her immaculacy became dogma.[52] Azzo Visconti seems to have established a pattern followed by his descendants when, in 1335, he dedicated his palace chapel to the Immaculate Conception of the Virgin and staffed the chapel with Franciscans, who in the fourteenth century actively promoted the cult of the

---

50. The much-portrayed Duke of Berry was also represented as clean-shaven in some portraits and with a beard and/or moustache of varying lengths and shapes in others (Meiss, 1967, 80–82).

51. *RIS*, XVI, 1039.
52. Levi D'Ancona, 1957, 55f.

Virgin Immaculate.[53] That the Franciscans continued to celebrate the feast of the Conception of the Virgin in the Visconti chapel is clear from a supplication of 1403 from them to Giangaleazzo's widow, Caterina, requesting permission to move the celebration from the palace chapel to the church of San Francesco.[54]

An image of the owner of a manuscript worshipping the Madonna as the Woman of the Apocalypse at an identical point in the text recurs in the Boucicaut Hours, illuminated for the Maréchal de Boucicaut around 1405–8, probably in Genoa.[55] At the opening of the Seven Joys of the Virgin, the Maréchal and his wife, like Giangaleazzo Visconti, are represented in adoration of the Madonna as the Woman of the Sun. As we shall see below, the Maréchal had close ties with Giangaleazzo, and it is very likely also that the illuminator of his Hours knew and was influenced by Lat. 757.[56]

The nobleman on folio 15 in Smith-Lesouëf 22 (Fig. 49) is presented to the Madonna by a crowned female saint, a hermit saint (probably Anthony Abbot) and Saint Christopher. While the only attribute of the female saint is her crown, it seems likely that she is Catherine of Alexandria, who, like Anthony Abbot, is one of only four saints to whom masses are dedicated in the manuscript. Unlike the enthroned Madonna in Lat. 757, the Virgin in Smith-Lesouëf 22 is a Madonna of Humility, perhaps deemed more suitable for a woman's prayerbook. The theme of chastity is introduced through the conspicuous bit of fencing in the lower left of the miniature, an allusion to Mary as the *hortus conclusus*. The presence of Saint Catherine and the Madonna of Humility, as well as the emphasis upon chastity, is entirely appropriate for a manuscript intended as a gift from Giangaleazzo to Caterina on the occasion of their marriage. One of the many forms of assistance for which Saint Christopher was invoked was protection against sudden death. To Giangaleazzo, whose first wife had died in childbirth when she was twenty-three, this invocation would have been particularly meaningful.

The circle composed by the thumb and forefinger of the Madonna and of Saint Catherine in the Smith-Lesouëf miniature seems to be more than a simple gesture of discourse. A similar gesture is made by Gabriel in the Annunciation on folio 84 (Fig. 50), and it recurs frequently in both Paris manuscripts, often in a situation that clearly highlights Trinitarian dogma (for example, Fig. 19). In the context of numerous pointed Trinitarian allusions in both Paris manuscripts, the gesture of the circle may affirm the unending goodness and all-encompassing unity of the triune God, as it does also on folio

53. Sevesi, 327–33; Alberzoni, 67–70. The Feast of the Conception of the Virgin (8 December) is included in the Calendars of both Lat. 757 and Smith-Lesouëf 22.

54. Caterina granted the privilege and decreed support for it. Francesco Sforza renewed her decree in 1450 (Sevesi, 327–33; Alberzoni, 67f.).

55. Meiss, 1968, 21 and fig. 12. The sun with undulating rays behind the Madonna in the Boucicaut miniature, as well as the conspicuous display of the Marshal's armorials here and throughout the Boucicaut Hours, connects the manuscript also to Giangaleazzo's Psalter-Hours.

56. Page 37.

105 of Banco Rari 397, where one of the persons of the Trinity himself makes this gesture (Fig. 46).[57]

It has not previously been observed that the owner of Lat. 757, again clad in scarlet trimmed with white fur, reappears in the miniature that introduces the Saturday Mass of the Blessed Virgin Mary on folio 258 (Frontispiece, Fig. 51). Here, with other noblemen, he kneels at the right of the Madonna of Mercy. In a parallel position, at the left of the Madonna, is a woman distinguished from those behind her by her white gown and unbound hair, a symbol of maidenhood. The implication that this is a portrait of Giangaleazzo and Caterina Visconti on the occasion of their marriage in 1380 is reinforced by the miniature on folio 176 of the Coronation Missal (Fig. 48), in which Giangaleazzo, now in ducal regalia, and Caterina, likewise accompanied by nobles and ladies, also worship the Madonna of Mercy, who here, as in Lat. 757, is adored by angels.[58]

A portrait of the original owner of Smith-Lesouëf 22, together with his wife, may have been intended in the miniature of a man and woman venerating the Man of Sorrows on folio 285v at the opening of the Passion reading from Matthew (Fig. 23). The original appearance of the donors has certainly been altered (perhaps twice, because the entire miniature seems to have been painted in the fifteenth century, possibly on a fourteenth-century design). The patron saints are Anthony Abbot and Catherine, both of whom probably appear also in the presentation portrait on folio 15 (Fig. 49).[59]

The Fifteenth-Century Illuminators of Smith-Lesouëf 22

Assuming that Smith-Lesouëf 22 was indeed painted for Caterina Visconti on the occasion of her marriage, why it should have remained incomplete in the fourteenth century is an important and vexing question for which there is no apparent answer. However, the eventual completion of the manuscript in the following century may at least suggest that it was in the hands of Caterina's granddaughter, Bianca Maria Sforza, in the early 1460s. As has been observed, the fifteenth-century portion of Smith-Lesouëf 22 was painted in

57. On circles as symbols of the unity and perfection of the Trinity, see *Lexikon der christlichen Ikonographie*, 1, 1968, 528 (s.v. *Dreifaltigkeit*). The Sforzas adopted as one of their emblems three interlocking rings.

58. The young woman reaching to take the child from Mary in the Nativity on folio 283v (Fig. 52) has conspicuously long, flowing hair. She wears a green gown patterned with a pale blue monogram that, though rubbed, appears to be CA. Here, as in other instances (e.g., the imperial portraits in Lat. 5888—see page 83 below), Paduan painting of the last third of the four-

teenth century may have set a precedent followed by Lombard illuminators. For the suggestion that Fina Buzzacarina, wife of Francesco da Carrara, appears with her three daughters in the Birth of the Baptist in the Baptistery of Padua (Bettini, pl. 20), see Kirsch, 1981, 241ff. n. 43.

59. Pentimenti are visible in the painting of both donors, especially in the heads on folio 285v. The tarnished silver monogram on the bodice and right sleeve of the praying man in the miniature is difficult to read. It may consist of an interlaced G and M.

the style of Belbello da Pavia, the illuminator who, among others, completed the Florence Psalter-Hours for Filippo Maria Visconti, around 1428–30.[60] Belbello himself was responsible for one, possibly two, miniatures in Smith-Lesouëf 22, while most of the remainder were by an anonymous master with whom he had some association during the 1460s.[61] Both were involved in a Book of Hours, now in Geneva, illuminated between 1460 and 1470 for a member of the Birago family, who had close ties to the Sforzas.[62] Again the two participated, Belbello for the second time, in the illumination of a Missal for Barbara of Brandenburg, Duchess of Mantua, about 1460–62.[63] The style of Belbello's one sure miniature in Smith-Lesouëf 22, the Adoration of the Magi on folio 44v (Fig. 24), is particularly close to his work in the late phase of the Mantua Missal (Fig. 25). The personae of the Smith-Lesouëf Adoration share with their counterparts in this part of the Missal (and with Belbello's figures in the Birago Hours) an intensity inversely proportional to the subtlety of artistic means used to produce them. From beneath beetling brows they exchange fervid glances. Their gestures are histrionic. Their draperies are swollen to enormous but hollow volumes. All of Belbello's resources are now at the service of high-pitched drama, in which there is little room for the jewel-like precision and flowing elegance of his work in the Visconti Psalter-Hours (Fig. 73) and in the Bible he illuminated for Nicolò d'Este before 1434.[64]

In view of the coincidence of style and date, it seems permissible to speculate that when in October 1462 the Pavian humanist Giorgio Valagussa wrote to Bianca Maria Sforza, daughter of Filippo Maria and granddaughter of Caterina, requesting work for Belbello, she gave him Smith-Lesouëf 22 to complete.[65] Then in straitened circumstances, Belbello had expressed to Valagussa his willingness, in exchange for room, board, and clothes, to illuminate a Book of Hours or any other kind of book. It would have been natural for Bianca Maria to employ Belbello, who had so dazzlingly helped to complete

60. Alexander and de la Mare, 149f.; Cogliati Arano, 1970a, 410; idem, 1970b. For the date of Belbello's illumination in the Florence Psalter-Hours, see Meiss and Kirsch, 1972, 27f.; Cadei, 1976, 43–56.

61. Belbello surely painted the Adoration of the Magi on folio 44v (Fig. 24). Alexander and de la Mare (149 n. 6) suggest that he was responsible also for the Annunciation to the Shepherds on folio 56v, but the quality of this miniature is markedly inferior to that of the Adoration.

62. Alexander and de la Mare, 147–50. The miniature by Belbello in the Birago Hours, a Raising of Lazarus on folio 125, is reproduced by Alexander and de la Mare as pl. LXVIII, fig. a. On the Birago Hours, see also London, Sotheby's, 1985.

63. Barbara's Missal is now in the Curia Vescovile, Mantua. For this manuscript and for the most recent examination of Belbello's career, see Cadei, 1984. On

the two campaigns of illumination by Belbello, see Pacchioni, 368–70; Kirsch, 1975, 68 n. 1; and Cadei, 1984, 179–94.

Like the late paintings in the Mantua Missal, the Adoration in Smith-Lesouëf 22 is framed by a colored band striped in white and outlined by a band of gold. In the miniatures belonging to Belbello's first phase of activity in the Mantua Missal, c. 1447–50, the colored framing bands intersect upon the outer band of gold.

64. Vatican Library, Barb. Lat. 613. The *terminus ante quem* was established by J. Hermann, "Zur Geschichte der Miniaturmalerei am Hofe der Este in Ferrara," *Jahrbuch der Kunsthistorisches Sammlungen des Allerhöchsten Kaiserhauses*, XXI, 1900, 247.

65. For the most accurate transcription of Valagussa's letter, see G. Resta, *Giorgio Valagussa*, 1964, 32 n. 1. On Belbello's last years, see Mariani Canova, 38–64; Kirsch, 1975, 66–74.

the Psalter-Hours that had belonged to her grandfather and then to her father, to do
likewise for an unfinished Hours-Missal inherited from her grandmother.

The Trinitarian Subtext

If the pictorial program of Lat. 757 as a whole constitutes a compendium of Christian
history, several of its pictorial sequences constitute an intrinsic Trinitarian subtext that
both localizes the manuscript to Milan and strengthens its connection to Giangaleazzo.
The Creation cycle that illustrates the votive daily offices at the beginning of Lat. 757
(Figs. 13–18) is the first instance of the Trinitarian focus in the manuscript. Leroquais
wrote of his sequence that "elle ne se rattache à aucun des éléments du recueil et donne
l'impression d'un hors-d'oeuvre."[66] The Creation sequence that illustrates the Office of
the Virgin in Giangaleazzo's Psalter-Hours in Florence (Figs. 60, 73, 75, 92) likewise
gives the impression of an "hors-d'oeuvre" and may have been suggested by the cycle in
Lat. 757.[67] Although there is no textual basis in either manuscript for the inclusion of a
Creation sequence, its appearance in these manuscripts may have been suggested by the
coincidence of the number seven in the cycle of Creation on the one hand, and in the
weekly cycle of votive offices and the hours for the recitation of daily offices on the other.
The particular iconography of the cycle in Lat. 757, however, may be inspired by the
Hexameron of Saint Ambrose, a series of sermons on the Creation preached by the bishop
and patron of Milan, probably during Holy Week in 387.[68]

In the *Hexameron*, as in virtually all his preaching and writings, Ambrose expounds the
dogma of the Trinity, defending it against any hint of the Arian heresy that God and
Christ are not of one substance. He insists upon the Creator as the Trinity. In the first
homily of the *Hexameron*, for example, he writes that "the operation of the Holy Trinity
clearly shines forth in the constitution of the world . . . 'In the beginning God created
heaven and earth,' that is, God created it in Christ or the Son of God had, as God,
created it or God created it through the Son, since 'all things were made through him and
without him was made nothing that was made' (John 1.3). There was still to come the
plenitude of the operation in the Spirit, as it is written: 'By the word of the Lord the
heavens were established and all the power of them by the spirit of his mouth' (Ps.
32.6)."[69]

---

66. Leroquais, 1927, I, LVII. [It is not related to any of
the (other) elements of the collection (of miniatures) and
gives the impression of being an hors-d'oeuvre.]

67. The Florence Psalter-Hours also contains seven
Creation miniatures, on LF 19, 26, 30, 34, 37v, 41,
46v, and 47. A ring of zodiacal signs in the Creation of

Sun, Moon, and Stars in the Psalter-Hours (LF 37v)
links the cycle in that manuscript to Lat. 757. In other
respects, however, the iconography of the two sequences is different.

68. Saint Ambrose, *Hexameron*, ed. Savage, VI.

69. Ibid., 32.

The inclusion of a brilliant, radiant sun in the miniature on folio 37 of Lat. 757, the Separation of Land from Water and the Creation of Plants and Trees (Fig. 15), accords well with Saint Ambrose's strict exegesis of the third day of Creation. In the fifth homily for this day, Ambrose denounces the "foolish speech" of men who are troubled because in Genesis plants and trees precede the creation of the sun (on the fourth day), which must have been essential to the germination of seeds in the earth.[70] The only sun, both necessary and present on the third day, argues Ambrose, is the Son of God who, Ambrose stresses in his exegesis of the fourth day, is of course the creator of the earthly sun. Given the widespread Christian equation of Christ with the sun, as exemplified in Vannozzo's explication of Giangaleazzo's *sol-cum-columba* device, may we interpret the proleptic sun on folio 37 as Christ? How then may we explain the white sphere imposed on the outer blue rim of the evolving world in the first two miniatures of the cycle, the Lord above the Deep on folio 24 (Fig. 13) and the Creation of the Firmament on folio 28 (Fig. 14)?

In the first of these miniatures (Fig. 13), the white-haired and bearded Creator, holding the sphere of the universe, is depicted in a radiant mandorla surrounded by seraphim. He hovers in an immense golden *primum mobile* above the world, which is still dark and void. In the second miniature of the sequence (Fig. 14), the world has been separated from the empyrean, and the Creator descends to complete his work. The upper part of his mandorla, in the shape of a curved triangle, frames the upper part of his body, almost as a second halo. Beginning with the third day of Creation on folio 37 (Tuesday Office of the Holy Spirit—Fig. 15), this form emits golden rays. Beginning with the second day of the cycle (Creation of the Firmament—Fig. 14), the Creator's nimbus is inscribed with a form that at first glance may be read as a cross, but which in fact consists of a triangular arrangement of the letters *PAT* (with the *P* at the top and the *A* and *T* at the sides).

By the fourteenth century, triangles had long been symbols of the Trinity, and the unusual triangular forms in the Creation cycle of Lat. 757 probably signify this mystery.[71] With its enormous golden outer rim, not yet separated from the universe to be created by God, the first miniature in the sequence (Fig. 13) probably alludes not only to the light to be created for mortals but also to preexisting divine light (suggested too by the bright red angels who appear only in this miniature), as well as the ineffable unity of the Trinity, both of which, according to Ambrose, and after him Augustine, were inapprehensible to man.[72] Only on the second day of Creation is the gold circle of heaven separated from the universe (Fig. 14). On that day too the Creator begins his descent to the world of his

70. Ibid., 129.

71. On triangles as symbols of the Trinity, see *Lexikon der christlichen Ikonographie*, 1, 1968, 531 (s.v. *Dreifaltigkeit*). I am grateful to Professor Karlfried Froehlich for an enlightening discussion of the theological concepts reflected in the Creation cycle of Lat. 757.

72. Saint Ambrose, Second Homily for the First Day of Creation, chap. 9 (ed. Savage, 38f.); Saint Augustine, *On the Trinity*, Bk. 1, in *The Nicene and Post-Nicene Fathers*, ed. P. Schaff, iii, New York, 1877, 17f.

making. Beginning only with the third day does he completely leave behind him the curved, radiating triangle that appears in all the subsequent miniatures (Fig. 15). The Creator's nimbus is probably inscribed *PAT*[er] rather than *P*[ater], *F*[ilius], *S*[piritus] (the inscription that begins to appear in the fifteenth century in Trinitarian halos, often triangular in shape), in order to distinguish God the Father from the other two persons of the Trinity: the sun as Christ (present as a white sphere of divine light on the first two days, but "activated" only on the third, to make a liturgical point) and the radiant triangle as the Holy Spirit of God, which, Ambrose repeatedly reminds us, moved over the waters and caused all things to be created.[73] If this interpretation is correct, the Creation cycle in Lat. 757 is a distinctively Ambrosian visual expression of the dogma of the Trinity as Creator, analogous to but quite different from Neapolitan cycles of the mid-fourteenth century that show the Creator with two faces, and either winged or with a dove perched on his shoulder.[74] The conclusion that the Creation cycle in Lat. 757 makes an innovative pictorial statement about the Trinity is reinforced by the first miniature in the Missal (that is, in a parallel position with the Creation cycle, which appears at the beginning of the Book of Hours). This miniature, on folio 229v, introduces the Sunday Mass of the Trinity with a representation of the triune God as three identical persons (Fig. 54). As early as the twelfth-century *Hortus Deliciarum* of Herrad of Hohenbourg, this form of the Trinity was linked with the Creation.[75]

The theme of the Trinity is carried through in the two full-page miniatures that follow the representation on folio 229v. In the depiction of the Man of Sorrows on folio 237, at the beginning of the Mass for the Dead, two identical smaller heads flank the head of the dead Christ (Fig. 55). The miniature on folio 241v, which introduces the Mass of the Holy Spirit (Fig. 42), is probably also Trinitarian, with blue sky as the "loco del padre," the sun as Christ, and the dove as the Holy Spirit.

Trinitarian dogma also shaped a third sequence of miniatures, the Circumcision on folio 291v, which illustrates the Mass of the Circumcision for 1 January, and the Adoration of the Magi on folio 293v, which introduces the Mass for Epiphany on 6 January (Figs. 56, 57). An ostrich egg above the altar in the former may now be added to the group of ostrich eggs suspended above altars published by Millard Meiss, to which Isa

73. For example, *Hexameron*, ed. Savage, 32f., where Ambrose distinguishes the Spirit of God from air by identifying it as part of the divine radiance opposed to the "darkness of forces which are contrary to it."

Triangular Trinitarian halos, sometimes inscribed, appear early in the fifteenth century in Lombardy. A very early example is the triangular nimbus of the Deity in the large gilded copper boss that was executed by Beltramino de Zuttis on a design of Jacopino da Tradate between 1416 and 1425 for the keystone of the vaulting in the apse of Milan Cathedral (P. Airaghi, "Schedula per Beltramino de Zottis [o Zuttis] da Rho," in *Il Duomo*

di Milano, ed. M. L. Gatti Perer, Milan, 1969, I, 106–10, fig. 1).

A triangular nimbus inscribed *PFS* appears in the upper border of the Ascension page (folio 204v) by Gerolamo da Cremona in the Missal of Barbara of Brandenburg (*Mantova. Le arti*, II, Mantua, 1961, fig. 297).

74. Heimann, 1938, who gives further bibliography concerning the Neapolitan Bibles (48f. n. 4; 49 nn. 1f.).

75. Heimann, 46–48. Also Herrad of Hohenbourg, *Hortus Deliciarum*, ed. R. Green et al., 2 vols., London, 1979, I, 91; II, pl. 3.

Ragusa has added another early Lombard example.[76] Citing as textual sources the Bestiary and William Durandus's *Rationis divinorum officiorum,* Meiss and Ragusa have argued persuasively that in a number of paintings dating from the fourteenth through the sixteenth century large eggs suspended in churches are in fact ostrich eggs, symbolic of the virgin birth of Christ, as well as his death and resurrection.[77] In the touching miniature on folio 291v, the Christ child, beneath an ostrich egg, reluctantly leaves the hands of his troubled earthly father, Joseph, to accept the destiny that the rite of circumcision prefigures, while a master of theology at the left makes the circular gesture that in the Paris Hours-Missals seems to signify the mystery of the Trinity, celebrated also in the Adoration miniature that follows the Circumcision.

The special and enduring devotion to the cult of the Magi by the Viscontis as a family and by Giangaleazzo in particular, discussed in chapter I, is confirmed in the Adoration miniature by an emblem that is also linked to the Trinity.[78] In the miniature on folio 293v (Fig. 57), the second Magus wears as a badge the device of the owner of Lat. 757 and Smith-Lesouëf 22—a gold knot.[79] This knot, which is set into a radiance fashioned of pearls, two of which mark its ends, most closely resembles its counterpart within a scalloped frame studded with white dots in the lower-left margin of folio 364 in Lat. 757, where both the knot and the monogram are heraldically presented (Fig. 9). If, as I have suggested above, the knot in Lat. 757 is both a symbol of the Trinity and a personal device of Giangaleazzo Visconti, its presence in the Adoration miniature would, on the one hand, underscore the Trinitarian significance of the Epiphany, and, on the other, refer to Giangaleazzo, devoted both to the cult of the Magi and to the Trinity. In response to the expression of his recognition of the Trinity, the crowned Virgin of Humility seated before him yet once more makes the circular gesture. She, in turn, is related to the crowned Madonna of Humility in the donor miniature of Smith-Lesouëf 22, who makes the same gesture (Fig. 49).

That the badge worn by the Magus on folio 293v alludes specifically to Giangaleazzo Visconti is also suggested by the Adoration of the Magi in the Boucicaut Hours, where a reference to an actual person is introduced in a parallel fashion (Fig. 58). Instead of the badge with its knot, the second Magus here wears a stubby stick that has been identified by Meiss as the *bâton noueux,* the symbol of the Armagnac faction of the French royal family led by Louis d'Orléans. Proposing that the Boucicaut miniature was a memorial to the Maréchal de Boucicaut's friend Louis, who had been assassinated in November 1407,

76. Meiss, 1976 (incorporating material published originally in 1954); Ragusa, 1971.

77. Meiss, 1976, 107–10; Ragusa, 438f.

78. Visconti devotion to the Magi is discussed on page 9 above.

79. For knots as attributes of pagan kings and wise men during the Middle Ages, see Krása, 100.

The Epiphany miniature in Lat. 757 is an early,

though not unprecedented, instance of the patron of a work of art identifying himself with a Magus. K. Weitzmann has published a thirteenth-century Venetian icon in which one of the Magi is a portrait of a Mongol general who claimed to be descended from a Magus ("Icon Painting in the Crusader Kingdom," *Dumbarton Oaks Papers,* xx, 1966, 49–83, esp. 63 and fig. 23).

Meiss dated the manuscript to 1405–8, when Boucicaut was governor of Genoa.[80] Of particular interest in our context is the fact that Louis was the son-in-law of Giangaleazzo, through his marriage in 1387 to Valentina, the Count of Virtues' daughter by his first wife, Isabelle of Valois. The Marshal himself, furthermore, was directly associated with the Duke of Milan and other members of his family. In 1401 Boucicaut personally brought to Giangaleazzo the acceptance of Charles VI to the Duke's proposal of a marriage between Giovanni Maria, Giangaleazzo's older son, and one of the daughters of the French king. In 1403, during the period of factional strife that followed Giangaleazzo's death, the Marshal assisted his widow, Caterina.[81] It is understandable and even probable that Boucicaut, who may well have known the large Paris Hours-Missal, should have decided to honor his friend Louis d'Orléans in a manner analogous to a celebration of that friend's illustrious father-in-law in Lat. 757.[82]

80. Meiss, 1968, 10f., 132.

81. Jarry, 258f., 290.

82. As noted above, page 30, the motif of the donor venerating the Woman of the Sun at the opening of the Seven Joys of the Virgin in Lat. 757 recurs in the Boucicaut Hours. The indebtedness of the Boucicaut Master to Lombard illumination has been suggested by Meiss, 1968, 128, 131. This matter warrants further study. I would propose here that the Boucicaut Master may have adopted from the Florence Psalter-Hours the practice of glazing metallic pigment with other colors (for example, in the miniature of Saint Michael in the Boucicaut Hours—Meiss, 1968, fig. 2), and from Lat. 757 the combination of brilliant blue sky and radiant sun (for example, the Flight into Egypt in the Boucicaut Hours—Meiss, 1968, fig. 35).

III

THE PSALTER-HOURS IN FLORENCE

THERE is no doubt that the patron who commissioned the Psalter-Hours in Florence (Banco Rari 397 and Landau-Finaly 22) was Giangaleazzo Visconti. He is named twice in the second volume of the manuscript (on LF 9v and LF 22), and his armorials appear throughout both volumes. The date of the Psalter-Hours is undocumented; however, the structure, iconography, and style of the manuscript, as well as evidence concerning its scribe and illuminator, all point to the period around 1388, the year of the birth of the first child of Giangaleazzo and Caterina Visconti—a son, Giovanni Maria, who was to become the second Duke of Milan. Thus, the Florence Psalter-Hours may be understood as a sequel to the Paris Hours-Missals, which, as suggested in chapter II, commemorated the marriage of Giangaleazzo and Caterina. In text as in image, the anomalous characteristics of Lat. 757 and Smith-Lesouëf 22 are developed in Giangaleazzo's Psalter-Hours.

Structure, Format, and Provenance

Like Lat. 757 and its smaller version, Smith-Lesouëf 22, the two-volume Psalter-Hours in Florence is characterized by unusual fullness of text and lavishness of decoration. The Florence manuscript is further related to the Paris Hours-Missals by an eccentric pictorial program that evokes the earlier manuscripts. The anomalies as well as the high quality of all three manuscripts bespeak a patron who favored exceptionally grandiose objects of piety, shaped to express his particular concerns. The Psalter-Hours in Florence demonstrates unequivocally that Giangaleazzo Visconti was such a patron.

The prayerbook in Florence lacks the Calendar, Pericopes, Suffrages, and other prayers, all or some of which are occasionally found in luxurious Books of Hours. In other respects, however, its text is unusually full.[1] Abbreviations common to Hours of the Virgin are here written out in full, and so too are the Propers for Advent of this office. The Hours of the Virgin and of the Dead are supplemented by offices for the Holy Ghost, the Passion, and the Cross.[2] The most expansive aspect of the Visconti prayerbook, however, is the complete ferial Psalter (including canticles, hymns, and creeds) that precedes the Hours. Although fairly common earlier, full Psalter-Hours were exceptional by the late fourteenth century. A complete Psalter combined with as many offices as those in the Visconti Hours would in any period have been a rarity.[3]

An exceptionally full pictorial program complements the text of the Florence Psalter-Hours. As in the Paris Hours-Missals, principal texts are introduced by a full-page miniature paired with an historiated initial. Texts that elsewhere are unilluminated are adorned in the Visconti Hours with historiated initials. Psalter illustration, for example, usually concludes with Psalm 109, but the Visconti manuscript contains eleven additional psalm illustrations. As a result of this kind of pictorial expansiveness, the Psalter-Hours contains thirty-eight full-page or nearly full-page miniatures and ninety historiated initials. Many of the historiated initials occur on folios that include, in addition, only one line of large, ornamental script or only a few text lines of normal size; in these instances, they are almost as large and often as prominent as the full-page miniatures (Fig. 67). The total number of miniatures—128—is rarely matched in other prayerbooks.[4]

Border decoration conceived with infinite imagination further enriches the manuscript. Thus, for example, on BR 150v Augustus and the Ara Coeli in the left margin and the Magi beholding the Infant in a star at the right both involve figures gazing upward at the Christ child, much as the disciples within the *P* of the Pater Noster look up to Christ during the Sermon on the Mount (Fig. 40). On BR 108v, which introduces Psalm 114, celestial music-making putti (noteworthy forerunners of the classically inspired music-making angels of the Florentine Quattrocento) accompany the psalmist within the initial; the lower border, alive with trees, fish, birds, rabbits, and a variety of human dwellings

1. See the Catalogue for the contents of both volumes.

2. On the contents of Books of Hours, see Leroquais, 1927, I, i–lxxxv; Plummer, 32, 45–51; Wieck, 27f.

3. On the origin and structure of the ferial (or liturgical) Psalter, see Leroquais, 1940–41, I, li–lxii. Leroquais (lixf.) lists twelve Psalter-Hours of the fourteenth century and twenty of the fifteenth century. None of the Psalter-Hours published by him contains as many offices as the Visconti Hours. Salmon, 1971, lists only five Psalter-Hours of the fifteenth century: nos. 430, 466, 477, 559, 564 (a Psalter with only the Office of the Virgin); and only two of the fourteenth century: nos. 480 (with only a partial Book of Hours) and 597 (with a nonliturgical Psalter).

4. For comparable extravagance one must turn to the prayerbooks of the greatest bibliophile of the late fourteenth century, Jean, Duke of Berry. His *Petites Heures* (Paris, Bibl. nat., Lat. 18014) contains 119 miniatures and his *Belles Heures* (New York, The Cloisters) 156 (Meiss, 1967, 335–37; 1974, 333f.).

(the latter perhaps an expression of the architectural interests of the illuminator), illustrates the last verse of the psalm: "I will please the Lord in the land of the living" (Fig. 59). Personifications of Justice and Temperance presenting Visconti tilting helmets in the lateral margins of the same folio are only two among a multitude of devices of the Count of Virtues that inhabit the borders of his Psalter-Hours. Yet other borders are notable for innovative portraits and nature studies (for example, Fig. 47).

Size, script, and content indicate that the two volumes of the Florence prayerbook were planned as a unit. Though all the leaves have been trimmed, they are approximately the same size; each full text page in both volumes contains twenty-one lines occupying the same amount of space on all pages; and the script of both parts, with only minor exceptions, appears to be uniform.[5] The first three textual components of Landau-Finaly 22 (Athanasian Creed, Penitential Psalms, and Litany of the Saints) properly belong to the group of prayers at the conclusion of the Psalter that constitutes the first volume (Banco Rari 397). A second set of Penitential Psalms and Litany following the Office of the Dead in the Book of Hours underscores the redundancy of the first set. On the other hand, the presence on conjugate leaves (LF 9 and 15, LF 10 and 14) of parts of the first Litany and parts of the Hours of the Virgin suggests that the first Litany (and hence probably the entire Psalter) was also originally intended to be bound with the Book of Hours.

The pictorial life of the Virgin that begins in the Psalter and ends in the Hours also indicates that the two volumes were planned as a unit. Because the Annunciation appears in the Psalter (BR 104v), it does not occur in its customary position at the beginning of the Office of the Virgin; the latter text is introduced instead by the Visitation and the Nativity (LF 10v, 11). As we shall see below, the Old Testament sequences, ending with I Kings 1–3, that follow the Creation cycle in the Hours are thematically related to the narrative of Anna and Joachim at the opening of the Psalter. For all these reasons, there can be little doubt that Banco Rari 397 and Landau-Finaly 22 were planned as one book.[6]

5. The leaves in Banco Rari 397 measure 247 by 175 mm; those in Landau-Finaly 22 are 250 by 179 mm.

Professor Julian Brown, who examined the manuscript in 1972, concurred with P. Toesca's judgment (1951, IV) that the script is by one hand. At the end of the Office of the Dead on LF 109 appears the signature "Frater Amadeus s(ub)s(cript)us" [Brother Amadeus, signed]. On Frater Amadeus, see page 43f. below.

LF 13, which lacks a conjugate leaf, as well as LF 33 and 38, which are conjugate with one another, appear to me to have been written in a different hand. With the exception of these leaves, all the border decoration and small initials through LF 55v were illuminated during the fourteenth century, whereas the corresponding illumination on LF 13, 33, and 38 was carried out during the fifteenth-century campaign of Belbello da Pavia and his

associates. There is no break in the text, however, and it is not clear why these pages should have been rewritten.

6. Had Banco Rari 397 and Landau-Finaly 22 been bound as one volume, the resulting prayerbook would have contained 319 leaves, including the leaf excised from Banco Rari 397. This would have made a thick manuscript, but contrary to the assertion of Cadei (1984, 43), it would not have been destined to fall apart whenever opened. There are precedents for such bulk. The Book of Hours illuminated by the Master of the Brussels Initials that is now in the Cleveland Museum of Art, for example, contains 332 leaves. Its pages, measuring 200 by 140 mm, are even smaller than those of the Visconti Hours (approximately 250 by 179 mm), rendering it proportionately even thicker than the combined Visconti Psalter-Hours would have been. On the format

Nonetheless, examination of the sewing holes of the two volumes suggests that they were in fact never bound together.[7] Early separation of the prayerbook into its present two parts probably resulted from the failure of Giovannino dei Grassi's workshop to complete the decoration of the manuscript. Their painting, which ends on LF 54, is sporadic even in the early gatherings of Landau-Finaly 22, and the fifteenth-century intervention of Belbello da Pavia is apparent even on LF 1.[8] On the other hand, Belbello's presence is nowhere evident in Banco Rari 397. In all probability, then, the gatherings that now constitute Banco Rari 397, entirely painted by the dei Grassi workshop and useful by themselves as an almost complete and hence independent Psalter, were bound before the illumination of the rest of the manuscript was carried out.[9]

Neither Banco Rari 397 nor Landau-Finaly 22 appears in any of the three inventories (made in 1426, 1459, and 1469) of the Visconti and Sforza libraries. Inasmuch as these inventories do include other Psalters and Books of Hours, the absence of the manuscripts now in Florence probably reflects their use in private rooms or chapels.

Banco Rari 397 entered the Biblioteca nazionale from the collection of Duke Uberto Visconti di Modrone in 1969. When Toesca published his study of Lombard painting in 1912, the manuscript already belonged to the Viscontis di Modrone, a collateral branch of the Visconti family. Princess Giulia Rospigliosi (*née* Visconti di Modrone) believes that the manuscript may have been bought in the nineteenth century by her grandfather, Raimondo, whose historical interests prompted him to acquire other objects connected with his family, including the *tarocchi* painted for Filippo Maria Visconti and now in the Beinecke Library at Yale University (Fig. 61).[10]

Although the association has not previously been observed, it seems likely that Landau-Finaly 22 is the costly "ofitiolo" belonging to Filippo Maria Visconti that was found at the time of his death, along with other valuables, in the *monitione* of his castle in Milan, having been put there for safekeeping during one of the periods of political turmoil that characterized the Duke's last years. The Book of Hours is described as follows in a letter of 1447 to Bianca Maria Sforza (Filippo Maria's daughter) from the group of Milanese noblemen who salvaged the Duke's valuables from the arms storeroom in 1447, shortly before the sack of the castle and the proclamation of the Ambrosian Republic: "Li

---

and dimensions of the Cleveland Hours, see Meiss, 1967, 323. The Missal-Hours in Paris (Bibl. nat., Lat. 757), discussed in chapter II above, contains 452 leaves measuring 265 by 207 mm.

7. The author made this examination with the assistance of conservators Anthony Cains and Barbara Giuffrida when the manuscripts were unbound in 1971.

8. See note 58 below.

9. Early division of the manuscript into its present two parts is suggested also by the absence on the last page of Banco Rari 397 (BR 151v) of either a rubric denoting the Athanasian Creed that begins on LF 1 (all the other hymns and canticles as well as the Apostles' Creed are rubricated) or a catchword linking the final gathering of Banco Rari with the first in Landau-Finaly (catchwords appear at the end of all the other gatherings of both manuscripts). Neither rubric nor catchword is visible even through ultraviolet light.

10. Giulia Visconti di Modrone Rospigliosi kindly discussed with me the history of her family's collection. The Visconti di Modrone tarot cards are now at Yale University in the Cary Collection of Playing Cards, No. ITA 109 (New Haven, Yale, no. 51).

era l'ofitiolo del prefato Signore in una imagina de coyro [*cuojo*] rosso il quale era coperto de veluto cremisi con le serature fate in modo de fazoli il quale costò ducati duemila secondo pyu volte sodi [si udì] da persona digna de fede."[11] The "fazoli" in the clasps were probably in the form of the knotted imperial headband (*capitergium*), which appears also as an armorial device of Filippo Maria on LF 85v. The binding described in the letter may have been the "velvet wrapper" type, in which a book bound in leather—in this instance stamped with a picture ("imagina")—was covered with red velvet for protection. Landau-Finaly 22 now has a modern red velvet binding; preserved inside the front cover, however, is an old, threadbare piece of red velvet.[12] The present clasps of the manuscript are bifurcated pennants beneath a cardinal's hat, the device of Ludovico Calini, a Brescian elevated to the purple in 1766 by Pope Clement XIII.[13] An unpublished catalogue of manuscripts belonging to Giulio Cesare Rospigliosi-Pallavicini, Duke of Zagarolo, compiled in 1851, discloses that the second volume of the Psalter-Hours then belonged to him. Beside the description of Landau-Finaly 22, a penciled note in a later hand indicates the sale of the manuscript to "Landau (Firenza) nel 1902, Lire 55,000." "Landau" was Baron Horace Landau, the banker and bibliophile whose large collection of manuscripts included also the Pucellian Psalter of Bonne of Luxembourg, now at the Cloisters in New York.[14] In 1945 Landau's great-nephew, Baron Horace Finaly, bequeathed the *ofitiolo* to the *Comune* of Florence, which keeps it on deposit in the Biblioteca nazionale, thus reuniting two volumes that have been separated since at least the fifteenth century.

The Scribe

The signature of Frater Amadeus in Giangaleazzo's Psalter-Hours is in itself evidence of his distinction as a scribe.[15] The excellence of Amadeus's script is, however, evident not

11. [There (in the arms storeroom) was the Book of Hours of the above-mentioned Lord in a (stamped) leather binding, covered with crimson velvet, and with clasps in the shape of knotted cloth which, according to many trustworthy persons, cost two thousand ducats.] The Italian transcription is that of L. Beltrami, *Il castello di Milano*, Milan, 1894, 48. Beltrami publishes the entire letter, which is now in Paris, Bibl. nat., It. 1584, fols. 281–282.

12. On the velvet wrapper type, see Baltimore, Walters Art Gallery, *The History of Bookbinding 525–1950 A.D.*, 1957, no. 118. Banco Rari 397 is bound in modern red leather.

13. See, in the Vatican Library, *Cardinalium S.R.E. Imagines*, Ex. calcografia Rev. Camerae Apostolicae, n.d., III, 103. Calini's probable ownership of Landau-Finaly 22 has not previously been noted.

14. The Rospigliosi catalogue is now in the Vatican Library, Lat. 13534; the description of Landau-Finaly 22 occurs on folio 22. Professor Margaret Murata brought my attention to this manuscript. On the Cloisters manuscript, see the exhibition catalogue, Paris, Galeries nationales du Grand Palais, *Fastes du Gothique*, Paris, 1981, no. 267.

15. The only other Lombard instance of a signed Book of Hours known to me is now in Modena, Bibl. Estense, Lat. 862, which was written and signed in 1383 by Albertolus de Porcellis, master of a writing school in Milan, who contributed to Jean Lebègue's compendium of recipes for scribes and illuminators. On this manuscript, see Milan, 1958, no. 66; Cogliati Arano, 1970a, 413f. On Lebègue, see Meiss, 1967, 64. On Frater Amadeus, whose identity remains enigmatic, see Bénédictins du Bouveret, *Colophons des manuscrits occidentaux des origines au XVIᵉ siècle*, 1, Fribourg, 1965, nos. 485f.

only in the Visconti prayerbook but also in a copy of Boethius's *De Consolatione Philosophiae* now in the Hunterian Collection, Glasgow (MS 374).[16] The Glasgow manuscript is especially noteworthy for a leaf of sample script preceding the text of Boethius (Fig. 62). The recto of this leaf contains sample alphabets as well as excerpts from prayers in various kinds and sizes of writing. Beneath this virtuoso display, Amadeus signed the page, perhaps with a touch of false modesty belied by the splendid opening *E* of the statement: "Ego enim sum minimus omnium scriptorum fr. Amadeus subscriptus." In burnished gold letters that compose part of the frame in the lower border of the page are the name of the owner of the manuscript and a date: "Istud opus est Gregorii de ianua MCCCLXXXV."[17] The influence of Amadeus's script (perhaps also his hand) is apparent in the illumination of the Florence Psalter-Hours. Striking even among the wealth of innovative borders in Banco Rari 397 are those in which the burnished gold letters of Giangaleazzo's motto, "a buon droyt," constitute a frame (Figs. 63, 64). Pen flourishes also figure conspicuously in the decoration of many leaves of the Visconti manuscript, for example, BR 1 (Fig. 65). Only the greater spontaneity of some of the flourishing in the Psalter-Hours (for example, on BR 36—Fig. 63), at variance with the stricter control of the sample page in the Boethius, diminishes the possibility that Frater Amadeus himself executed the pen designs in the prayerbook.

The Illuminator

The principal illuminator of the Psalter-Hours in Florence was Giovannino dei Grassi. Beginning with Toesca's reintegration of Giovannino's *oeuvre* in 1912, his exceptional merits as an illuminator have been universally acknowledged.[18] Giovannino's activity as an artist, however, was not limited to manuscript illumination. He is first documented on 21 October 1389, when he received payment from the Fabbrica of the Duomo of Milan for a banner of Saint Gall given by the Count of Virtues for the high altar of the Cathedral.[19] Subsequently, Giovannino was entrusted with a wide range of projects by

16. University of Glasgow, Library, 1987, no. 71 and frontispiece.

17. [For I, brother Amadeus, the least of all scribes, have signed (this work); This work belongs to Gregory of Genoa 1385.] On the writing samples in the Hunterian Boethius, see B. Wolpe, "Florilegium Alphabeticum: Alphabets in Medieval Manuscripts," in *Calligraphy and Palaeography: Essays Presented to Alfred Fairbank on His 70th Birthday*, ed. A. S. Osley, London, 1965, 72f. The Gregory of Genoa who owned Frater Amadeus's Boethius has not been identified.

18. Ed. 1966, 136–50. For subsequent examinations of individual works or for surveys of Giovannino's art, see Toesca, 1951b, iv–vi; Salmi, 1955b, 767–72; Arslan, 58–66; Cadei, 1969, 77–88; 1970, 17–36; 1976, 18–42; 1984, 41–78; Cogliati Arano, 1970a, 405–8; Meiss and Kirsch, 1972; A. Romanini, "Architettura," in *Il Duomo di Milano*, 2 vols., Milan, 1973, 1, 97–232. Giovannino's border decorations are discussed by Treuherz, 79ff.

19. *Annali*, app. 1, 100. The feast day of Saint Gall is 16 October. On 18 October 1390 Giovannino was paid for restoration of a banner (probably the same one

the Fabbrica, for which he executed various kinds of paintings, designed sculpture and stained glass, and participated in architectural planning. In 1391 he became an *ingegnere* of the Cathedral.[20] In July 1398 the Fabbrica paid the expenses of his funeral.[21]

Giovannino's maturity as an artist in the Visconti Psalter-Hours is attested both by the quality of his own work and by the presence of workshop assistance in the manuscript. His early career remains a mystery, although he appears to have emerged from a circle of illuminators active at the Visconti court in the 1370s, including the illuminator of the Hours of Blanche of Savoy, Giovanni di Benedetto da Como.[22] It is possible that like Giovanni di Benedetto, who stated in the prayerbook of Blanche of Savoy that he had both painted and set it in order, Giovannino was not only the illuminator but also the coordinator, perhaps even the planner, of the Florence Psalter-Hours.[23] If so, he followed the example of his predecessor in the distinctive layout of Giangaleazzo's prayerbook. The practice of introducing each principal textual division by both a full-page miniature and an historiated initial, normally facing each other, could have been suggested either by Blanche's Hours or by Lat. 757. Only in the Munich and Florence manuscripts, however, are the borders graded for the convenience of the user: all four borders are decorated on text pages containing the beginning of prayers, while only the upper, left, and lower borders are embellished on pages containing only smaller textual units, such as versicles and responses. The delicacy of Giovannino's style is also more closely related to the manner of Giovanni di Benedetto da Como than to the monumentality of the style of the Master of Lat. 757.

Piety, Dynastic Ambition, and the Iconography of the Manuscript

Giangaleazzo Visconti's presence in his Psalter-Hours is most emphatic in his portraits and in the relentless display of his armorials throughout the manuscript. Not so readily apparent is the extent to which the Count of Virtues' dynastic ambition, often insepara-

---

mentioned in the document of 1389) bearing an image of Saint Gall as well as the insignia of Giangaleazzo and the commune of Milan (*Annali,* app. 1, 142). The second notice of payment identifies the banner as a gift of the Count in honor of his own birthday, 15 October. On Giangaleazzo's special devotion to Saint Gall, see also note 36 below.

20. *Annali,* app. 1, 184f. In 1396 Giovannino was consulted in connection with the building of the Certosa of Pavia (Beltrami, 1896, 52f.).

21. *Annali,* app. 1, 187.

22. Giovanni di Benedetto da Como himself may have introduced Giovannino dei Grassi, as a fellow townsman, to the circle of illuminators employed by the Viscontis. A statement in the *Annali* of 1391 that Giovannino resided in the parish of San Tommaso in Terramara, near the Porta Comacina of Milan, led Toesca (1966, 136) to surmise that Giovannino also came from Como. Salmi, 1955b, 767, also accepts this possibility.

23. On the flyleaf (fol. 1v) of Blanche's manuscript, Giovanni di Benedetto wrote: "Iohanes filius maḡri benedicti de cumis me pinxit et ordinavit. Ora voce pia pro me Virgo Maria" [Giovanni, son of master Benedetto of Como painted me and set me in order. Pray for me with pious speech, Virgin Mary].

ble from his religious devotions, dictated the iconography of the manuscript as a whole as well as many of its pictorial details.

On 5 May 1385 Giangaleazzo executed the audacious coup d'état that earned him a prominent, albeit notorious, place in European history.[24] Accompanied by the enormous bodyguard that had over a period of years come to signal his timidity, the Count of Virtues set out on a pilgrimage to the Madonna del Monte at Varese. He made known his wish to pay homage to his uncle en route but expressed fear of entering the walls of Milan, thus luring Bernabò outside the city. There Bernabò and two of his sons were ambushed and imprisoned. Bernabò died in the fortress of Trezzo in December of the same year. Giangaleazzo Visconti had become sole ruler of Milan.

Almost immediately, the Count of Virtues embarked upon an unremitting program of territorial expansion, complemented by skillful administrative reforms, that brought under Milan's dominion the cities of Mantua, Verona, Vicenza, Padua, and Bologna in the North, and, south of the Appenines, Pisa, Siena, and Perugia. At the time of his unexpected death in 1402 at the age of fifty-one, the lord of Milan even threatened the independence of Florence.[25]

Soon after the coup of 1385, the Count of Virtues' aspirations to a greater and more lasting title became apparent. After Verona capitulated in 1387, he spoke of his ambition to assume the status of "Re de' Lombardi." In 1389 a Florentine ambassador reported that Giangaleazzo had been soliciting from Urban VI in Rome, "a just title for that which he holds, the more easily to make himself king."[26] Nor did the Count hesitate to exploit the papal schism in his quest for a hereditary title, turning to the Clementist faction in France when his appeal to Urban failed. Finally, frustrated by the papacy, Giangaleazzo directed his efforts, successfully, to the empire. On 11 May 1395 Wenceslaus, King of the Romans, in return for the sum of 100,000 florins, conferred upon Giangaleazzo the hereditary title Duke of Milan.[27]

After the death of his son Azzone in 1381, however, Giangaleazzo lacked the male heir crucial to the fulfillment of his dynastic hopes. In progeny, Giangaleazzo had been vastly outnumbered by Bernabò, who is reported by the fifteenth-century Milanese historian Bernardino Corio to have fathered at least fifteen legitimate and twenty illegitimate children.[28] For his offspring Bernabò arranged a network of politically expedient marriages throughout Europe, including the alliance between Giangaleazzo and Caterina in 1380 and the betrothal of Azzone to Bernabò's daughter Elisabetta in the same year.

With his sole remaining child, Valentina (who, like Azzone, was the offspring of Giangaleazzo's first marriage), the Count also played the politico-matrimonial game of his

---

24. Giangaleazzo's coup is the most recent event mentioned in Chaucer's *Canterbury Tales* (*The Monk's Tale*). See the edition of N. Coghill, Baltimore, 1958, 217 and the note on 512f. (where, however, Bernabò is mistakenly called "Duke").

25. See the comment of Machiavelli cited in chapter I, note 2.
26. Bueno de Mesquita, 171.
27. Ibid., 64–66, 173.
28. Corio, I, 883.

time, scoring a spectacular triumph in 1386 when he arranged a marriage between her and Louis d'Orléans, brother of King Charles VI of France. The cost, however, was enormous: a dowry of 450,000 francs, and—ultimately a far greater sacrifice—agreement that Valentina and her descendants were to inherit all Giangaleazzo's dominions if he died without an heir.[29]

When Giangaleazzo ratified the marriage contract between Louis and Valentina in April 1387, the stipulation regarding the inheritance of his domains must have been a serious concern. His marriage of seven years to Caterina had so far been childless. But by the time of the actual marriage of Louis and Valentina, in August 1389, extinction of the male line of the Viscontis had been rendered less probable by the birth of a son, Giovanni Maria, to Giangaleazzo and Caterina. The child was born in 1388, on 7 September, the eve of the feast of the Nativity of the Virgin.[30]

Almost immediately after the birth of Giovanni Maria, the Great Council of Milan swore fealty to him as Giangaleazzo's heir. The feast of the Virgin's nativity was thenceforth to be celebrated with special ceremonies and oblations in her church in Abbiategrasso, the country town in which the child had been born. In Milan itself, the eve of the Virgin's birth was decreed an annual holiday, to be marked by votive offerings and processions of the guilds from the city gates to the basilica of Santa Maria Maggiore, then in an early stage of transformation to the present cathedral of Milan.[31] An even more remarkable expression of gratitude for the birth of a Visconti heir was the subsequent and apparently unprecedented dedication of the new cathedral to Santa Maria Nascente—a dedication that, if not directly owing to Giangaleazzo, would indubitably have pleased him.[32]

29. On the basis of this agreement, Valentina's grandson, King Louis XII of France, invaded Milan in 1499, initiating the fall of the Sforza dynasty (Chamberlin, 90f.). The Visconti male line had ended with Giangaleazzo's son Filippo Maria, whose only child—an illegitimate daughter, Bianca Maria—married Francesco Sforza. For an account of the negotiations concerning Valentina's marriage to Louis d'Orléans, see Jarry, 28–43.

30. An unusually long period—more than two years—elapsed between the ratification of the contract and the actual marriage of Louis and Valentina. The delay resulted in part from Giangaleazzo's need to raise additional funds for Valentina's dowry, after spending on wars against Verona and Padua money initially intended for this purpose (Cognasso, 521–56; also Muir, 214).

The question of inheritance, however, may also have contributed to the postponement. After the birth of Giovanni Maria, Giangaleazzo obtained from Charles VI a declaration, signed 2 December 1388, canceling the stipulation in the marriage contract concerning the absence of Visconti heirs (Cognasso, 551).

31. Magenta, I, pt. 1, 183; Cattaneo, 64.

32. In 1577 Carlo Borromeo dedicated the Cathedral of Milan to Santa Maria Nascente. (An inscription of 1645 on the facade of the building—*Mariae Nascenti*—records this dedication.) Although any earlier dedication of the Duomo to Santa Maria Nascente appears to be undocumented, most of the early guides associate this dedication with Giangaleazzo. See, for example, P. Morigi, *Il Duomo di Milano*, 1597, 2: "E [Giangaleazzo] volse che questa Chiesa [the Duomo] fosse dedicata alla sempre Gloriosa Madre di Dio, Maria Vergine, sotto il titolo della sua felicissima al mōdo Natività. Votādosi alla benedetta Madre de gratia di porre nome Maria à tutti i suoi figliuoli" [And (Giangaleazzo) wished that this church (the Cathedral) be dedicated to the eternally glorious Mother of God, the Virgin Mary, under the title of her most fortunate birth into the world. Vowing to the blessed Mother of grace to give the name Maria to all his children]. Martin V consecrated the high altar of the new cathedral in 1418, but the annals of the Fabbrica as well as other contemporary records state only that it was dedicated to the Virgin (*Annali*, app. I, 219, and app. II,

The name of Giangaleazzo's newborn son, Giovanni Maria, also honored the Virgin. Concerning this name, Corio explained that the Count of Virtues had vowed to dedicate to the Virgin any sons born to him.[33] And indeed Giangaleazzo's next legitimate son, Filippo Maria, was also named after the Virgin; so too was an illegitimate son, Gabriele Maria.[34] The "abundantissima fonte di gratia" was again honored on 27 August 1396, when Giangaleazzo (by then Duke of Milan), Giovanni Maria, Gabriele Maria, and Francesco Barbavara, acting as surrogate for the four-year-old Filippo Maria, each laid a foundation stone for the Certosa of Pavia, the Duke's great personal architectural project, dedicated to Santa Maria delle Grazie.[35]

The Visconti Psalter-Hours now in Florence constitutes yet another aspect of Giangaleazzo's fulfillment of his vow to the Virgin. The Count of Virtues' particular veneration of the Virgin, emphasizing the feast of her birth, not only explains the exceptional prominence accorded Mary and her parents in the manuscript but enriches the meaning of

28; Corio, II, 1058–59). Cattaneo (63f.) asserts, but without documentation, that both the earlier cathedral, Santa Maria Maggiore, and its successor were originally dedicated to Santa Maria Assunta in Cielo, but that the dedication to Santa Maria Nascente became associated with the original dedication after the birth of Giovanni Maria.

Churches dedicated to the birth of the Virgin are rare and seem for the most part to be confined to Milan. Three such churches are mentioned by C. Ponzoni, *Le chiese de Milano*, Milan, 1930: Santa Maria Nascente di Capodisotto, originally built in 1304 but completely restored in 1658 (376); Santa Maria Nascente in Casoretto, built in 1401 (140f.); and Santa Maria Nascente in Lampugnano (338f.). The latter was built and dedicated by a monsignor of the cathedral of Milan, who wished to repeat the dedication of the Duomo. C. Huelsen, *Le chiese di Roma nel Medio Evo*, Florence, 1927, contains no reference to Roman churches bearing this dedication. M. Armellini, *Le chiese di Roma del secolo IV al XIX*, 2 vols., Rome, 1942, mentions only one: a seventeenth-century chapel of the Ceni Bolognetti family, dedicated to the Natività di Maria Santissima (II, 1063).

Recent scholarship has tended to minimize Giangaleazzo's patronage of the Cathedral of Milan and to view the building program as primarily a communal achievement within an otherwise signorial domain (see, for example, P. Mezzanotte, "Il Duomo," in *Storia di Milano*, Milan, VI, 1955, 859–931 [861–63, 866f.]; and J. Larner, *Culture and Society in Italy 1290–1490*, London, 1971, 257–63). The *Annali* of the Fabbrica, however, point

repeatedly to Giangaleazzo's direct involvement in the building campaign. Larner himself admits that "Giangaleazzo did much for the building. He provided funds of 500 florins a month, gave exemptions, privileges, and exclusive use of the Candoglia quarries to the Fabbrica, and secured help from the Pope" (257). By 1399 donations to the cathedral by members of Giangaleazzo's immediate family (including a gift by Giovanni Maria of 160 imperial lire on his second birthday) amounted to 12,416 imperial lire (Mezzanotte, 866). On the association of Giangaleazzo with the principal motif of the apse window of the Cathedral, see *Annali*, I, 249.

33. "Al septimo di septembre in Abiate Giovanne Galeazo hebbe da Catelina, sua mugliere, uno figliolo a baptesmo nominato Giovanne Maria, a la quale abundantissima fonte di gratia s'era invotato, potendo havere figlioli, insignirli dil suo celebratissimo nome e per questo a gli altri descendenti fu dato il secundo nome di Maria" (Corio, I, 899) [On the seventh of September in Abiate, Giovanni Galeazzo had by his wife Caterina a son baptized Giovanni Maria, (Giangaleazzo) having vowed to the most abundant source of grace that if he were able to have sons he would give them her most celebrated name, and for this reason this celebrated name became the second name of his other descendants (sons), and for this reason also other descendants (of Giangaleazzo) were given Maria as a second name].

34. Gabriele Maria was later legitimized by Wenceslaus, and inherited Crema and Pisa by the terms of Giangaleazzo's will (Corio, II, 968; Chamberlin, 219).

35. Beltrami, 1896, 59–62; Chamberlin, 175.

many of its individual scenes as well. It also elucidates the themes of creation and procreation that permeate the Psalter-Hours.[36]

The pictorial sequence that precedes the Psalter in Banco Rari 397 and continues on BR 22v and BR 35v consists of six full-page miniatures representing a total of ten episodes from the life of the Virgin's parents before her birth (Figs. 63, 65–67, 70). Absent from the canonical New Testament, Anna and Joachim play an important role in apocryphal accounts of Mary's life: the second-century Protoevangelium of James and the tenth-century Pseudo-Matthew. From these, many details were incorporated into Jacopo de Voragine's *Golden Legend* of the thirteenth century, the literary source of innumerable late medieval and Renaissance pictorial narratives.[37]

Episodes from the life of the Virgin's parents had appeared in earlier prayerbooks, including the Hours of Blanche of Savoy, in which the Office of the Virgin is illuminated with a cycle of her life.[38] In none of the earlier cycles, however, is the narrative so densely illustrated. In Giangaleazzo's Psalter-Hours, the cycle of Mary's life that begins with the prefatory full-page miniatures continues in the body of the Psalter, where each major division of the text is introduced not only by an historiated initial showing David engaged in activities conventional to Psalter illustration but also by a full-page miniature belonging to the narrative of the Virgin. The last of these pairs occurs on BR 104v–105 (Psalm 109), where the first of four border portraits of the Count (one of them now excised—see page 20 above) is introduced beneath a representation of the Trinity and opposite the Annunciation (Fig. 46). In the Office of the Virgin in Landau-Finaly 22, eight additional

36. Another instance of Giangaleazzo's expression of religious gratitude for a personal triumph occurred shortly after Giovanni Maria's birth. On 23 November 1388, following an arduous five-month military campaign (preceded by an even longer period of the kind of ingenious political maneuvering for which the Count of Virtues was renowned), Padua fell to Milan. Immediately, Giangaleazzo undertook special observance of two holy days that had occurred during the siege: the feast of Santa Maria della Neve on 5 August and that of San Gallo on 16 October (Giulini, v, 733–37). The *Annali* of the Fabbrica report that on the initiative of Giangaleazzo, Santa Maria della Neve was to be honored by special solemnities on 5 August in the Metropolitan church of Santa Tecla (under the authority of the Fabbrica), and a chapel to San Gallo was to be constructed in Santa Maria Maggiore itself (*Annali, I,* 23ff. [document of 1 April 1389]). For the banner of San Gallo to be hung over the high altar of the Cathedral, see page 44 above. In his will Giangaleazzo endowed a church honoring the Virgin of the Snow in Rome (Osio, 336).

37. For a survey of apocryphal accounts of the life

of the Virgin and their reflection in the visual arts, see J. Lafontaine-Dosogne, *Iconographie de l'enfance de la Vierge dans l'Empire Byzantin et en Occident,* 2 vols., Brussels, 1964–65 (vol. II for Western art), and G. Schiller, *Ikonographie der christlichen Kunst,* IV, pt. 2 (s.v. *Maria*), Gütersloh, 1980, 38–54, for Western cycles.

On extended cycles of the life of the Virgin as a vehicle for the expression of Immaculist belief, see Levi D'Ancona, 1957, 18. As noted above (p. 29f.), the Viscontis promoted the cult of the Virgin Immaculate throughout the fourteenth century.

38. In Blanche's manuscript the Office of the Virgin contains five full-page miniatures of the life of the Virgin's parents: Expulsion of Joachim from the Temple (Prime, fol. 26v), Meeting at the Golden Gate (None, fol. 33v), Birth of the Virgin (Vespers, fol. 37v), Joachim's Return to the Sheepfold (Terce, fol. 39v), and Annunciation to Joachim (Sext, fol. 44v). The incorrect sequence of hours in this office results from the misplacement of the quire containing the illustrations for None and Vespers (fols. 31–38) in the present binding of the manuscript.

scenes, beginning with the Visitation and ending with the Coronation of the Virgin, conclude the story begun on BR 1.[39]

The Marriage of Anna and Joachim on BR 1 (Fig. 65) is accorded unusual prominence in the Psalter-Hours, where it introduces the manuscript as well as the extraordinary Marian cycle. Whereas Visconti emblems are restricted to the borders on all other pages containing narrative episodes in the cycle, the only device on BR 1—a radiant sun, the personal emblem of Giangaleazzo, never used before him by a Visconti—is incorporated into the scene itself, where it adorns the hanging beyond the wedding group. The position of this emblem suggests that the Marriage of Anna and Joachim refers also to the wedding of Giangaleazzo Visconti and his cousin Caterina, an implication sustained not only by other aspects of the miniature on BR 1 but also by the entire Marian sequence of the Psalter.

Compelling similarities exist between the face of the young Joachim on BR 1 and the three surviving portraits of Giangaleazzo in the lower borders of BR 105, 115, and 128 (Figs. 46, 47, 41). All four depictions represent a handsome man with reddish hair, cut and combed in approximately the same way, a wide, sloping brow, straight nose, moustache, and double goatee. Yet another element in the miniature on BR 1 suggests a parallel with the marriage of Giangaleazzo and Caterina. Although children are sometimes present in the depictions of the Marriage of the Virgin, from which the composition of the Marriage of Anna and Joachim is derived, those on BR 1, similarly dressed, as brother and sister might be, probably represent Giangaleazzo's son and daughter by his first marriage: Azzone and Valentina, who were eleven and ten years old when their father remarried in 1380.

Long before the illumination of the Visconti Psalter-Hours, precedents existed for pictorial identification of a patron with a holy figure.[40] An example close in time to Giangaleazzo occurs in a Bible of Robert of Anjou, illuminated in Naples between 1328 and 1334. Here Robert is represented as Ecclesiastes, and Solomon too is clothed as an Angevin king.[41] Nonetheless, identification of patron and saint was not common in Western painting at the time of the Visconti Hours, and what ambiguity there may be in

<hr>

39. As in Banco Rari 397, the miniatures in the pictorial life of the Virgin in Landau-Finaly 22 are distinguished from all others by segmented frames (Fig. 60, etc.). The only exception in either volume is BR 22v (Fig. 70), where the Annunciation to Anna and the Meeting at the Golden Gate are framed by a rectangular green band embellished with gold pseudo-arabic script.

40. A notable early instance is the sixth-century apse mosaic in Saint Catherine's monastery on Mount Sinai, where the beardless and imperially crowned bust of David (who is normally bearded in Byzantine art) alludes to Justinian. See K. Weitzmann, in G. H. Forsyth, K. Weitz-

mann et al., *The Monastery of Saint Catherine at Mount Sinai: The Church and Fortress of Justinian*, Ann Arbor, 1973, 15. For identification of later Byzantine emperors with the prophet David, see H. Steger, *David Rex et Propheta*, Nuremberg, 1961, 107ff., and H. Buchthal, "The Exaltation of David," *Journal of the Warburg and Courtauld Institutes*, XXXVII, 1974, 330–33.

41. Malines, Bibl. du Grand Séminaire, MS 1. See F. Avril, "Trois manuscrits napolitains des collections de Charles V et de Jean de Berry," *Bibliothèque de l'Ecole des chartes*, CXXVII, 1969, 291–328 (317 n. 2 and 321).

the representation of Joachim as Giangaleazzo may reflect a degree of reticence on the part of the patron, the illuminator, or both.

That the Marriage of Anna and Joachim on BR 1 (Fig. 65) was understood by Giangaleazzo and Caterina Visconti's great-grandson, Galeazzo Maria Sforza, as a representation of his great-grandparents' wedding is almost certainly proved by a manuscript painted for Galeazzo Maria in 1476 by Cristoforo de' Predis. At the beginning of a long pictorial narrative that opens with the story of the Virgin's parents and ends with eschatological subjects, both the betrothal and marriage of Anna and Joachim are depicted among an array of Galeazzo Maria's devices, including the fleur-de-lys worn both by Galeazzo Maria in a portrait now in the Uffizi and by Joachim in the Turin wedding miniature.[42]

The analogy established on the first page of the Visconti Hours between Joachim and Anna on the one hand and Giangaleazzo and Caterina on the other is developed in the following pages of the introductory Psalter cycle. In the miniature on BR 1v depicting their distribution of alms, the aged Anna and Joachim stand in front of their palace (Fig. 66) rather than the table that is more common in representations of this scene—for example, in the fourteenth-century fresco at Solaro, near Milan.[43] In the imposing structure on BR 1v the illuminator may have intended a reference to the Castello of Pavia. The display of Giangaleazzo's armorials is expanded on this folio with the introduction in the borders of the viper and the dove, further linking Giangaleazzo to Joachim.

The facing page, BR 2 (Fig. 66), depicts an event rarely represented: Anna and Joachim vowing to dedicate their offspring to the service of the Lord.[44] This unusual episode evokes the similar pledge made by the Count of Virtues and reported by Corio.[45] The second scene in this miniature, the Expulsion of Joachim from the Temple, which probably also alludes to the Visconti family, will be discussed below in the context of the date of the Psalter-Hours.

In the next pair of facing pages the focus shifts from Joachim, depicted in the Wilderness on BR 2v, to David on BR 3 (Fig. 67), where the text of the Psalter begins. Both

---

42. Kirsch, 1981, figs. 69–71. The Turin manuscript is Biblioteca Reale, Var. 124 (Milan, 1958, no. 344, and Cipriani, 1959, 74). As in the instance of Giangaleazzo in the Psalter-Hours, the identification of Galeazzo Maria with Joachim in the Turin manuscript is implied through setting and armorials. Galeazzo Maria acquired the fleur-de-lys as an emblem through his marriage in 1468 to Bona of Savoy, sister-in-law to the King of France.

Around 1477, Cristoforo de' Predis painted a miniature portraying Galeazzo Maria Sforza as David in an initial illustrating Psalm 24 (Fig. 68—London, Wallace Collection, M342; see M. Jacobsen, "A Sforza Miniature by Cristoforo da Preda," *Burlington Magazine*, cxvi, 1974, 91–96). Here the extravagant array of armorials clearly evokes the Psalter-Hours, and the very outline of the initial, an architectural structure inhabited by putti, is a transposition into a late fifteenth-century idiom of forms in the Visconti Hours (cf. BR 108v—Fig. 59). On the identification of Giangaleazzo Visconti with David in the Visconti Hours, see page 52 below.

43. Matalon, 386–88.

44. The episode is not included among the categories of Lafontaine-Dosogne or of Schiller (both as in note 37).

45. Note 33 above.

formally and thematically, these leaves constitute a diptych, carrying forward the analogy
between Joachim and Giangaleazzo as progenitors of long-desired children, and at the
same time introducing a parallel between Giangaleazzo and David. At the right of the
miniature on BR 2v an angel announces to Joachim that Anna will bear a daughter to be
named Mary, who will herself give birth to the Son of God. Psalm 1, which begins on BR
3, celebrates all men who have "not walked in the counsel of the ungodly, nor stood in
the way of sinners." In Giangaleazzo's manuscript, the Psalm also serves as a gloss on the
destiny of Joachim in particular, who, like the virtuous man of Psalm 1, "shall be like a
tree which is planted near the running waters, which shall bring forth its fruit in due
season." In the facing miniature, Joachim, portrayed beside an abundance of trees planted
near running waters, learns from the angel that his wife will not remain barren: "For God
indeed punishes not nature, but sin; and therefore, when He closes a womb, it is only that
He may later open it more wondrously, and that all may know that what is born thereof is
not the fruit of lust, but of the divine munificence."[46] The apple-laden tree beside the
home of Anna and Joachim, who are portrayed on BR 35v giving thanks for their child
(Fig. 63), develops still farther the metaphor of the fruitful tree in Psalm 1. Composi-
tional similarities between Joachim and the angel on BR 2v and David and the Lord on
the facing folio underscore the parallel between BR 2v and BR 3 (Fig. 67). Color also
links the two pages. Fresh green, orange, and mauve acanthus stemming from the spine of
the *B* on BR 3 (the pigment in the upper stem has been extensively washed away)
reiterate hues prominent on BR 2v.

The confrontation of these pages, however, involves not only Joachim and David but
also the patron for whom the miniatures were painted. On BR 2v, references to
Giangaleazzo are embodied in the four lively cheetahs in the borders of the page.[47]
Allusions to the Count of Virtues are even more striking on the facing page. Although by
the late fourteenth century there existed a venerable tradition for adorning the first of the
Psalms with a portrait of David, Giovannino's treatment of the motif on BR 3 is spectacu-
larly original. Not even considerable staining obscures the brilliance of the burnished gold
sun, glazed in red, against which David is depicted. The sun, moreover, is only the
dominant note on a page ablaze with Giangaleazzo's emblems. Viper shields hang in the
niches of the initial and are suspended also from the necks of three damaged lions who
rest on its uppermost parapet. Additional viper escutcheons are set within clouds surrounded by angels in the borders, and in two corner roundels they are poised between a
pair of Visconti tilting helmets, one surmounted by a viper and the other by a sphere of
blue and gold feathers. In the opposite corners, white doves appear in the center of two
more suns.

46. Voragine, ed. 1969, reading for 8 September,
Nativity of the Virgin.

47. Tethered cheetahs appear also among a series of
personal emblems in the Coronation Missal of 1395
(Fig. 3). Cheetahs undoubtedly flourished also in the
park at Pavia, among innumerable hunting animals kept
there for the Viscontis, whose passion for hunting is well
known (Magenta, I, pt. 1, 119ff., 341f.).

With characteristic tact and gaiety, Giovannino introduces on this first page of text in the manuscript a border consisting mainly of words—*a buon droyt*—the French motto of Giangaleazzo, associated with his French title, Count of Virtues. Fleurs-de-lys in the borders as well as in the initial on BR 3 also allude to Giangaleazzo's French connection.[48] All these armorials, emphasizing especially Giangaleazzo's role as Count of Virtues, identify him also as the virtuous man honored by the psalmist. Joachim had prayed for a child, whom he pledged to the service of the Lord. Giangaleazzo had made a similar vow with regard to his sons. The message is clear: Giangaleazzo, like Joachim, is a virtuous man. He too is worthy of the divine gift of progeny.

On BR 35v (Fig. 63) procreation is further emphasized on the page facing the opening of Psalm 38. Here, again uncommonly, Joachim and Anna give thanks twice, first at an altar and then at their bedside, for the child promised them by the Lord. In harmony with the apple-laden tree within the miniature, the borders of this page also celebrate fruitfulness. Two peacocks in the lower corners sit in brooding pens, and a hoopoe perches in the upper margin. The hoopoe, according to the Bestiary, looks after and comforts its parents when they grow old.[49] Giangaleazzo is emblematically present in the *bas-de-page*, where yet another pair of peacocks is heraldically disposed with stylized radiant oak leaves. On the facing page, the motto "a buon droyt" figures prominently together with fleurs-de-lys in the right border and in the initial *D*, which introduces Psalm 38.

In the Visconti Psalter-Hours as in the *Golden Legend*, the fulfillment of the angel's prophecy to Joachim and Anna—the Incarnation of Christ—concludes the narrative of the early life of the Virgin; and in his prayerbook, the Count of Virtues is personally involved with this episode also. The borders surrounding the Annunciation on BR 104v (Fig. 46) are once again embellished with Giangaleazzo's radiant suns and viper shields. Moreover, as we have seen, the diptych constituted by BR 104v and 105 includes the first portrait of Giangaleazzo in the manuscript, in a context designed to express his devotion to the Trinity.

In order to emphasize the dual role of the dove on BR 105 as both Holy Spirit and emblem of Giangaleazzo, it is displaced from its expected position within the miniature to the upper border, where it corresponds to the Count's portrait in the lower border and to the emblematic hunting birds and oak leaves in the lateral margins.[50] This displacement involves a striking inversion of the arrangement on BR 1 (Fig. 65), the opening page of the Marian cycle, where the Visconti sun is placed as a personal reference *within* the miniature of the Marriage of Anna and Joachim, rather than in the borders, where it might be expected. Thus BR 1 and BR 105 not only mark the beginning and culmination of the cycle of the early life of the Virgin but may also be understood as brackets around a dynastic statement to which Giangaleazzo's portrait serves as a period. Through its association of the Count of Virtues with Joachim and David, the major pictorial cycle of the

48. On the motto, see chapter II, note 13.
49. *The Bestiary*, ed. White, 131f.

50. A dove and a portrait of Giangaleazzo are similarly positioned on BR 128 (Fig. 41).

Florence Psalter-Hours implies divine sanction of the rule of Giangaleazzo and his progeny. In this respect the Florence manuscript anticipates by about fifteen years the funeral
oration of 1403, which begins with a depiction of the Duke of Milan crowned by Christ,
King of Heaven (Fig. 30), and concludes with a pictorial demonstration of the Duke's
descent from Jupiter, king of pagan gods (Figs. 31, 32).

The boldness that led the Count of Virtues to associate himself with Joachim and
David is evident also in the *bas-de-page* portraits of the Psalter-Hours. Other patrons of
illuminated manuscripts, most notably the Duke of Berry, had been portrayed in their
prayerbooks. Berry, however, was always shown in adoration of the Deity or the Madonna, or at least in the company of holy figures, whereas Giangaleazzo's portraits are
independent. The frame of his portrait on BR 105 (Fig. 46) is also novel. Painstakingly
painted to resemble an architectural trefoil, it evokes the simulated architectural
quatrefoils that frame the busts of Roman emperors painted by Altichiero in the 1360s in
the loggia of the palace of Can Signorio in Verona, which in 1387 had fallen to
Giangaleazzo (Fig. 69).[51] The transformation of the quatrefoil into a trefoil on BR 105
probably reflects the patron's devotion to the Trinity, which constitutes the principal
theme of BR 104v–105.[52] While the emperors of Verona are painted in grisaille (and in
strict profile), Giangaleazzo is shown in the full colors of life, and in movement, as
though to emphasize his living presence and importance.

Among manuscripts of the late fourteenth century, only those of Jean de Berry rival the
Psalter-Hours in its extravagant display of armorials. In none of Berry's books, however,
do his devices enjoy the divine favor bestowed on Giangaleazzo's emblems in Banco Rari
397. Nowhere in Berry's manuscripts do angels display his armorials as they do Giangaleazzo's in the Psalter-Hours (Fig. 70), where they share this privilege with the Cardinal
Virtues, themselves recruited as emblems of the Count (Fig. 59). Nor do any of Berry's
armorials harbor the kind of visual pun embodied in the dove on BR 105 (Fig. 46).

The theme of fertility introduced in the prefatory pictorial cycle resounds throughout
Banco Rari 397. On BR 22v rabbits adorn the lower margin of the page that depicts the
Annunciation to Anna and the Meeting at the Golden Gate (Fig. 70). For less apparent
reasons these prolific creatures migrate into the facing miniature of David pointing to his
eyes. Rabbits again populate borders on BR 112v and 124v (Fig. 71). Giangaleazzo's
armorials (shields, pennants, tilting helmets, oak leaves, vipers) also abound on these
leaves.[53] Rabbits scamper on the ground before Elizabeth's house in the miniature of the
Magnificat on BR 147v (Fig. 72), where the image of Mary holding the infant Baptist
alludes to a tradition of the Virgin caring for the infant Saint John that is also evident in
Lat. 757.[54]

---

51. Bueno de Mesquita, 76f. On the emperors, now
in the Museo di Castelvecchio, see Mellini, 29–32.

52. See page 20 above.

53. For an alternative hypothesis regarding BR 124v,
with which I cannot agree, see Levi D'Ancona, 1978.

54. Mary swaddles the infant Baptist on folio 337v
of Lat. 757. For the tradition of Mary assisting at the
birth of the infant Baptist, see M. A. Lavin, "Giovannino Battista: A Study in Renaissance Religious
Symbolism," *Art Bulletin*, xxxvii, 1955, 85–101; and

Themes of procreation and of virtue rewarded by fecundity also shaped the pictorial content of the second volume of the Psalter-Hours, Landau-Finaly 22. Here, the unprecedented illustration of the Hours with an Old Testament cycle begins with seven pages devoted to God's creation of the universe. Whereas in Lat. 757 the number of Creation miniatures—seven—corresponds to the number of daily votive offices, in Landau-Finaly 22 the same number of Creation miniatures corresponds to the Hours in the Office of the Virgin. In Florence, the Creation miniatures are paired with Infancy scenes, a continuation of the Marian cycle of the Psalter.[55] The Creation cycle in Landau-Finaly 22 carries the theme into the second volume of Giangaleazzo's Psalter-Hours. As noted above, in both Lat. 757 and Landau-Finaly 22, the miniatures depicting the Creation of Sun, Moon, and Stars include zodiacal signs in the fixed ring of the firmament (Figs. 16, 73).[56] Despite parallels with Lat. 757 and other North Italian Creation cycles, however, Giovannino's sequence in Landau-Finaly 22 is a series of unprecedented pages, in which historiated initials and borders are orchestrated into a joyous pictorial hymn to Creation.

Like the first miniature of David in Banco Rari 397 (Fig. 67), the first Creation scene in Landau-Finaly 22, on folio 19 (Fig. 60), is set against a brilliant Visconti sun, again emphatically linking the patron with the subject portrayed. The oak, another emblem of Giangaleazzo, also figures prominently in the miniature: on an oak branch painted over an earlier architectural design (pentimenti of the original towers are still visible), a bird seated in a nest of oak leaves hatches its own small creation. Seven flies, a moth, and a beetle scattered in the margins of LF 19 seem to celebrate the creative powers of the illuminator himself. Like the oversized flies that torment Joachim's cows on BR 2v (Fig. 67), the insects on LF 19 may have been painted in emulation of the artists of antiquity who excelled in *trompe l'oeil*. Their skills were reported and admired by Pliny, whose *Natural History* was being transcribed and illuminated in Pavia for Giangaleazzo's chancellor, Pasquino dei Capelli, perhaps simultaneously with the production of Giangaleazzo's Psalter-Hours. Both Giangaleazzo and Giovannino may have known the content of its chapters on classical art.[57]

In scope, the most impressive image in the Landau-Finaly Creation series is the Creation of Astral Bodies on LF 37v, painted in the fifteenth century by Belbello da Pavia, but, like many miniatures in the first seven gatherings of Landau-Finaly 22, very probably executed over a dei Grassi design (Fig. 73).[58] This is strongly suggested by the décolleté,

---

"Giovannino Battista: A Supplement," *Art Bulletin*, XLIII, 1961, 319–26.

The women playing catch within acanthus fronds in the initial on BR 147v are related to figures in the Office of Saint Nicholas in Lat. 757 (for example, Fig. 33). The context of their appearance in Lat. 757 (page 22 above) suggests an association with chastity that may also be implied in the Florence miniature.

55. On the Creation cycle in Lat. 757, see pages 33–35.

56. Chapter II, note 67.

57. Pasquino Capelli's Pliny, illuminated by Pietro da Pavia, is dated 1389. The manuscript is now in Milan, Bibl. Ambrosiana, MS E 24 inf. (Pellegrin, 1969, 16f.; Cogliati Arano, 1970a, 415).

58. Within these quires the dei Grassis began but did not finish the painting of a number of leaves that were subsequently completed by Belbello and others. These include LF 18, 29v, 37, 47, and 50v. Belbello's intervention is apparent even on LF 1, in the punched and squared gold leaf behind the initial; in each compart-

high-waisted, full-sleeved costumes of the women, which resemble those in Giovannino's Bergamo sketchbook.[59] In a synthesis that in its encyclopedic quality evokes monumental art, Giovannino combined on LF 37v a Ptolemaic representation of the universe in the historiated initial (a series of concentric circles of the four elements, illumined by sun, moon, and stars, with the signs of the zodiac on its rim) with a series of personified planets in the right margin, belonging to a tradition of scientific illustration associated with the thirteenth-century cosmological treatise composed by Michael Scot, astrologer of Emperor Frederick II. The cosmology of the page is completed in the right and lower margins by personifications of the four seasons.[60]

Giovannino's skill in depicting the universe may have been known to the Fabbrica of the Duomo, which paid him on 17 September 1396 for a "mapamundum de carbone vel alio colore" in the North sacristy of the cathedral.[61] Certainly the representation of the universe on LF 37v is more correct than its counterpart in Lat. 757 (Fig. 16), where fire is erroneously represented as the third rather than the fourth and outermost ring of the elements, and where the zodiacal signs are almost entirely out of sequence and sometimes

ment a four-petaled flower is painted in gold emulsion against the burnished ground. This design, not found in any of the miniatures completely executed by the dei Grassis, was favored by Belbello (for example, LF 90v, 99, 102).

59. *Taccuino di disegni. Codice della Biblioteca civica di Bergamo*, Milan, 1961. See also Cadei, 1970.

60. Ptolemy's scheme of the universe, of the first century B.C., persisted in scientific imagery during the Middle Ages (*Enciclopedia dell'arte antica, classica e orientale*, IV, 1280). A well-known medieval example occurs in the ninth-century Ptolemy, Vat. Lib., Gr. 1291, fol. 9 (ibid., color plate following 1046). In the Ptolemaic scheme (in contrast to the Visconti miniature), the seven planetary spheres are represented as rings concentric with the circles of the elements.

Assimilation of the Ptolemaic form into the context of Christian Creation iconography seems to have occurred in Italy during the fourteenth century. An example of the early fourteenth century in North Italy is the panel depicting thirty biblical episodes from Creation through the Last Judgment now in the Museo di Castelvecchio, Verona (E. Sandberg Vavalà, "A Chapter in Fourteenth Century Iconography: Verona," *Art Bulletin*, XI, 1929, 376–412 [381 and fig. 1], where the panel is attributed to the workshop of Turone). Two Paduan examples close in time to the Visconti miniature are the Creation fresco of the 1370s by Giusto de' Menabuoi in the dome of the Paduan Baptistery (see Bettini, passim, and pl. 8) and a miniature in the Paduan Bible of the

late fourteenth century that has been attributed to the circle of Jacopo Avanzi (G. Folena and G. L. Mellini, *Bibbia istoriata padovana della fine del Trecento*, Venice, 1962, xxxii–xxxvii and pl. 1).

Another Paduan fresco cycle, even earlier than Giusto's, probably also belongs to this group. Near the bottom of the scene of Joseph before the Pharaoh in an extensive but now fragmentary Old Testament cycle painted by Guariento in the chapel of the Carrarese palace (now the Sala dell'Accademia Patavina di Scienze, Lettere e Arti), there seems to be a partially surviving representation of the universe, consisting of concentric planetary rings with a zodiac at the outermost rim. This fragment, which has not previously been observed, may have belonged to a Creation scene beneath the Joseph episode (the narrative proceeds from lower to upper registers). F. Flores d'Arcais, *Guariento*, Venice, 1965, 70, dates the frescoes between 1345 and 1357.

On the personified seasons in antiquity, see G. Hanfmann, *The Season Sarcophagus in Dumbarton Oaks*, 2 vols., Cambridge (Mass.), 1951 (II, no. 33 for Autumn as a vintage scene, and no. 16 for Winter as a bearded man warming himself at a fire). Such types also persisted into the Middle Ages (see R. van Marle, *L'iconographie de l'art profane au Moyen-Âge et à la Renaissance*, 2 vols., The Hague, 1931–32, I, 373ff.; II, 318ff.).

On the Michael Scot tradition, see note 64 below.

61. *Annali*, I, 168 [a map of the world in charcoal or some other color]. This work is apparently lost.

quite distorted.[62] In contrast, the zodiacal signs on LF 37v appear in proper order and are, for the most part, paragons of iconographical detail and accuracy. Virgo, for example, holds both a spray of grain and a less common attribute, a caduceus, to show that she is one of Mercury's houses.[63] The planets on LF 37v, which correspond with extraordinary precision to scientific images found in earlier fourteenth-century Bohemian manuscripts of the cosmology of Michael Scot (Fig. 74), are stacked above one another (unlike their Bohemian counterparts), in astronomically correct order, so that Mercury, represented as the lowest, may be understood as the innermost of the planets, while Saturn, the highest in the stack, is thereby designated as outermost.[64]

Where deviations from the norm do occur on LF 37v, they may be associated with the particular inclinations of Giovannino dei Grassi and his patron. The red ring of fire in the historiated initial is transformed to a ring of red Gothic architecture incorporating two radiant Visconti doves. The sun in the uppermost zone of the initial is likewise of the radiant, undulating Visconti variety, and a Visconti oak leaf emerges from the red architectural forms that extend into the left margin. The small angels who dive into and swoop out of the newly brightened firmament are likewise a dei Grassi idea (compare LF 26— Fig. 75), as is also the nest on which Spring perches.

The diptych on LF 11v and 12 (at Matins of the Office of the Virgin) represents the Fall of the Rebel Angels, the event that precipitated the Creation of the world (Fig. 53). An enormous pair of silver keys identifies the Creator on LF 11v as the Deity of Revelation 1:18, who keeps the keys of death and of hell. He is surrounded by a heavenly court of loyal angels and by the three Theological and four Cardinal Virtues (as elsewhere in this manuscript symbols of the Count of Virtues). In the lower margin, Humility, the root of all other virtues, reads from a book supported on her left knee and, with her right hand, makes the gesture identified with the Trinity on BR 105 (Fig. 46) and throughout both Hours-Missals in Paris (Figs. 19, 49, 56).[65] Thus the Creator of Giangaleazzo's Psalter-

62. The Twins, for example, are preceded by an extremely odd Crab, and followed in turn by Scorpio, Leo, and Sagittarius; Pisces, which should come between Aries and Sagittarius, instead precedes the Crab.

63. Aries, however, seems to have been provided with a cross of the Lamb of the Apocalypse—compare the lower border on LF 163.

64. For Michael Scot, see Saxl, 1927, 15–19, and III, pt. 1, xxxv–xliii; C. H. Haskins, *Studies in the History of Medieval Science*, Cambridge (Mass.), 1927, 272–98; Seznec, 156–60; L. Thorndike, *Michael Scot*, London, 1965, 1–21, 40–59.

The planetary deities reproduced here in Figure 74 are in Vienna, Nationalbibliothek, Cod. 2378, fol. 12v. On this manuscript, see Saxl, 1927, II, 99–103. An additional Bohemian example is the Astronomical Codex of the Kings of Bohemia, now in Bernkastel-Cues,

Library of the Hospital of Saint Nicholas, Cus. 207, fols. 115v–116 (Stejskal, 225 and fig. 25). An inscription on folio 1 of the Vienna manuscript states that the book belonged to Nicholas, a canon of Prague Cathedral. The illustrations of the Munich manuscript, though comparatively crude in execution, correspond morphologically, even in minute details, to the more elegant personifications in the Visconti manuscript. In the figures of both Saturn and Mars, for example, the number and variety of weapons, as well as their placement, are almost identical. Such numerous and precise correspondences of detail raise the possibility that the immediate source of the Visconti personifications was a scientific text.

65. On Humility as the root of other virtues, see Meiss, 1951, 153, fig. 162.

Hours in Florence is linked with the Trinitarian Creator of Lat. 757. On LF 12, Satan and his cohorts, unredeemed by virtues (Visconti or otherwise), are driven from heaven by military angels. The splendid leaflike architectural forms in the margins of this folio clearly indicate a dei Grassi design beneath the painting of Belbello.[66] The complex interweaving of Genesis and Infancy scenes in the Psalter-Hours culminates in a typological confrontation of the Coronation of the Virgin and Original Sin on folios 50v and 51 (Fig. 77).

Although direct evidence of dei Grassi participation in the illumination of Landau-Finaly 22 is not apparent beyond LF 54 (The Lord Reproaching Adam and Eve—Fig. 87), spaces left by Frater Amadeus for miniatures beyond this point in the Hours almost surely indicate that a continuation of the Old Testament cycle was planned in the fourteenth century. The copiousness of an illustrative program in which the traditional Infancy cycle is supplemented not only by an unusually extensive narrative of the life of the Virgin but also by an anomalous Old Testament cycle is consistent with the taste of the patron for whom Lat. 757 was designed. Indeed, the Marian and Old Testament cycles in the Psalter-Hours may be seen as complementing the already extensive pictorial repertory of the Missal-Hours.

The Old Testament sequences that follow the Genesis cycle in Landau-Finaly 22 sustain the theme of procreation established in Banco Rari 397. In the *Golden Legend* the angel of the Annunciation to Joachim catechizes him as follows: "Did not Sara, the first mother of your race, bear the shame of barrenness until her ninetieth year, and yet bear Isaac, to whom was promised the blessing of all nations? Did not Rachel also long remain barren, and yet beget Joseph, who was ruler of all Egypt? Who was stronger than Samson or holier than Samuel? Yet both of these were the sons of barren mothers!"[67] All four worthies mentioned by the angel are prominent in the Old Testament picture story that follows the Creation scenes in the Florence Hours.

Particularly interesting in this connection is the pride of place given to the story of Samuel at the conclusion of Landau-Finaly 22. Like the Virgin, Samuel was dedicated by his parents to the service of the Lord. The last narrative miniature in the Old Testament sequence represents Samuel called by the Lord (LF 166—Fig. 76). In the borders personifications of Justice and Fortitude display the Visconti tilting helmets familiar from Banco Rari 397. Not even the armor and the Walkyrean proportions of the maidens on LF 166 obscure their origins in the more delicate personifications of Justice and Temperance in corresponding positions on BR 108v (Fig. 59). The paint is thinner than customary in these figures, especially in their rose-colored gowns and in the sky-blue linings of their

66. For similar forms in the Beroldo painted by Giovannino's son, Salomone dei Grassi, see Figure 80.

The thick application of pigment throughout Landau-Finaly 22 suggests that dei Grassi designs may have continued even beyond the first eight quires of Landau-Finaly 22. Examination by infrared reflectography would

be useful, as it might reveal fourteenth-century drawings beneath the fifteenth-century illumination. Such drawings would be helpful also in defining the precise contribution of Belbello da Pavia and the other illuminators who completed Landau-Finaly 22 for Filippo Maria Visconti.

67. Voragine, ed. 1969, 522.

helmets. The fluid drawing of these fabrics is also close to the manner of the dei Grassis, particularly in the looping squiggles of the Virtues' sleeves, which also evoke the figures on BR 108v. The sphere of feathers surmounting the tilting helmet held by Fortitude on LF 166 was drawn with small circles around its circumference, coinciding with those on BR 108v, though the circles remain unpainted in Landau-Finaly 22. The obvious stylistic quotations from BR 108v on LF 166 reinforce the thematic evidence that the illuminator of the latter was following a pictorial program established by his fourteenth-century predecessors, and that the story of Samuel was part of the original plan of the Visconti Hours, to which the linked themes of piety and fertility are central.

Date and Style

References to Giangaleazzo on LF 9v and LF 122 as Count of Virtues rather than Duke of Milan, as well as the absence of any ducal armorials in the fourteenth-century portion of the Psalter-Hours, indicate a *terminus ante quem* of 1395, the year of Giangaleazzo's investiture as Duke. An incorrect assumption that the date inscribed at the base of the temple on BR 2 (Fig. 66) refers to the date the manuscript was illuminated, and hence must provide a *terminus post quem,* has led to the equally incorrect reading of this date as 1370. The Z-like form of the third digit in this number is identified as a two by Cappelli, who offers several examples of precisely this form in the fourteenth and fifteenth centuries.[68] The reading of this digit as a two has recently been confirmed by several scholars, among them Professor Ugo Procacci, who examined BR 2 through ultraviolet light and concluded that the date on the temple is and always has been 1320.[69] Nonetheless, art historians have tended with increasing dogmatism, unsupported by evidence, to interpret the date as 1370.[70]

In view of the personal aspect of the imagery throughout the Psalter-Hours, initiated

68. A. Cappelli, *Dizionario di abbreviature latine ed italiane,* 6th ed., Milan, 1973, 423f.

69. Professor Procacci kindly made his examination of the date in the manuscript at my request. I am also indebted to the Milanese archivists Dr. Andreina Bazzi and Professor Alfio Rosario Natale, who, on the basis of a photograph of BR 2, concur with Procacci's reading.

The digit Z, written almost exactly as on BR 2, appears twice, in the date 1227, on folio 6 in the Mass of Parabiago in the Coronation Missal in Milan. The date has been corrected in the margin to 1337, the actual date of the battle that this mass commemorates.

70. Toesca, 1951b, xiii n. 5, allowed the possibilities of 1380 or 1370 (in that order) but excluded 1320. Arslan (60) accepted 1370 as plausible and suggested

that the miniature may have been painted at that date. Subsequent scholars (Cogliati Arano, 1970a, 405; Cadei, 1976, 19; idem, 1984, 42; Bollati, 221 n. 2) assert without qualification that the date at the base of the temple is 1370 and that the illumination was begun in that year. None of these authors, however, offers an analogue or any other evidence, paleographic or otherwise, to support this reading of the date.

Cadei's insistence on reading the date on BR 2 as 1370, combined with his conclusion that Giovannino alone illuminated all of Banco Rari 397, has led him to the unpersuasive deduction that Giovannino took nineteen years to paint the thirty-seven miniatures in Banco Rari 397 (1976, 32f.; 1984, 76).

and particularly stressed in the cycle of Anna and Joachim, to which BR 2 belongs, it seems reasonable to propose that the date 1320 in this context had personal, perhaps dynastic significance to Giangaleazzo Visconti. The position of the date near the base of the temple suggests that it may reproduce an inscription on the foundation stone of an actual church sponsored by the Viscontis, a possibility consonant with Giangaleazzo's role as patron of the two major ecclesiastic building programs of his time in Lombardy—the Duomo of Milan and the Certosa of Pavia. If this is so, however, the building to which the miniature refers has eluded identification.

A second hypothesis may also merit consideration. The decision to place the date 1320 on the temple from which Joachim is expelled rather than any of the other numerous buildings in the cycle of Anna and Joachim may have been rooted in Giangaleazzo's wish to commemorate a crucial event in the career of his illustrious great-grandfather, Matteo I, il Grande, the first Visconti to obtain the title of Imperial Vicar as well as hereditary rights to the lordship of Milan.[71] The greatest obstacle to the fulfillment of Matteo's political ambitions was the papacy, with which he engaged in a long and sometimes violent struggle. The most bitter events in this controversy took place between 1318 and 1322, and included a papal interdict of Milan as well as the excommunication and trial for heresy and sorcery of Matteo, who in 1322 abdicated as lord of Milan in favor of his son Galeazzo I. The climax of the struggle occurred in 1320, when Pope John XXII appointed Bertrand de Guesclin Vicar of Milan and sent an army led by Philip of Valois to drive the Viscontis from the city.[72] Although the invasion failed, Giangaleazzo would have remembered 1320 as a year of extraordinary menace to the dynastic fortunes of his family. Precisely because an analogue to Joachim's expulsion was lacking in his own life, except insofar as the demise of his family had been threatened through the extinction of his line, Giangaleazzo may have directed the illuminator of BR 2 to inscribe the year 1320 on the temple. By so doing, he strengthened the parallel between his own ancestry and that of Christ, which we have seen to be central to the iconography of the Visconti Hours.

If, as seems highly probable, the date on the temple of BR 2 is not 1370 and does not signify the year in which illumination of the manuscript was begun, evidence for a *terminus post quem* must be sought elsewhere. It has been suggested above that the extended cycle of the Virgin's early life in Banco Rari 397 fulfills a vow made by Giangaleazzo to dedicate his male offspring to the Virgin.[73] Neither Corio nor any of the later historians who mention this vow indicate when it was made. The urgency of Giangaleazzo's need for a son, however, became acute only after the death in 1381 of the sole surviving son of his first marriage. It is probable also that the exigency that precipi-

---

71. Bueno de Mesquita, 3f. On the similarities between Giangaleazzo's political ambition and Matteo's, see Giulini, v, 103.

72. Giulini, v, 100–103. The entire account of the year 1320 in the early fifteenth-century *Annales Mediolanensis* is concerned with this invasion (*RIS*, xvi, 698f.).

73. Page 48.

tated his pledge to the Virgin became more pressing after at least several years of a childless second marriage. The terms of the marriage contract of 1387 between Valentina Visconti and Louis d'Orléans further intensified Giangaleazzo's need for an heir. These circumstances suggest that the vow was made, and hence the manuscript painted, after 1381 and probably toward 1388.

Evidence within the manuscript itself may provide an even more precise *terminus post quem*. The two most prominent armorials in the Visconti Hours are the radiant sun and the viper. As noted above, Giangaleazzo seems to have deliberately avoided using the viper as his personal emblem until the coup d'état of 1385, in which he seized all power from his uncle Bernabò and became sole ruler of Milan.[74] Only after that date could the dreaded Visconti serpent have figured so conspicuously in a manuscript made for the Count of Virtues. Moreover, a date of 1385 to 1388 accords with what is known of both the scribe and the illuminator of the Visconti Hours. The signed sample page by Amadeus in Glasgow is dated 1385 (Fig. 62). The earliest surviving document that mentions Giovannino dei Grassi, payment for a banner on 21 October 1389, links him to Giangaleazzo Visconti soon after 1388.[75] It is possible that, like the construction of the Duomo, begun in 1386, the decision to commission the Visconti Hours anticipated the realization of Giangaleazzo's prayers for a son;[76] nonetheless, the coincidence of the birth of the long-awaited heir, Giovanni Maria, with the eve of the feast of the Nativity of the Virgin in 1388 strongly suggests that the extraordinary Marian cycle in the Visconti Hours may have been a celebration of that birth as well as a fulfillment of the Count of Virtues' vow. In either case, the beginning of the Psalter-Hours would be firmly situated between 1385 and 1388.

As we have seen, it has been generally agreed that the absence of Giangaleazzo's ducal insignia throughout both Banco Rari 397 and Landau-Finaly 22 provides a *terminus ante quem* of 1395 for the dei Grassi portion of the Psalter-Hours. However, Antonio Cadei, who, as noted above, dates the beginning of the manuscript to 1370, also argues that the fourteenth-century portion of Landau-Finaly 22 was painted entirely by Giovannino's son Salomone after 1398 and perhaps as late as 1402, the year of Giangaleazzo's death and the

74. Page 26f.

75. On Amadeus, see page 43f. above; on the banner, see note 19 above.

76. Whereas the presence of the viper in the Visconti Hours clearly indicates a date after 1385, the absence of yet another armorial may suggest a date before 1387. In the marriage contract between Valentina and Louis, signed by emissaries of the principals on 27 January 1387, and ratified by Giangaleazzo himself in April of that year, Louis' brother, Charles VI, accorded Giangaleazzo the privilege of quartering his arms with those of France (Jarry, 30–32). Although in the Visconti Hours Giangaleazzo employed stylized fleurs-de-lys in conjunction with the title Count of Virtues acquired through his own marriage to Isabelle of Valois in 1360 (Fig. 67), nowhere in the prayerbook is the viper quartered with fleurs-de-lys. The Count may, however, have felt some constraint about accepting the royal privilege before the actual marriage of Valentina and Louis in 1389 (Jarry, 49). In any event, the only surviving instances in which Giangaleazzo did quarter the viper with the fleurs-de-lys occurred after his investiture as Duke of Milan in 1395, and then usually in conjunction with arms bearing the imperial eagle. See, for example, the Coronation Missal of 1395 (Fig. 3) and a Bible given to the Certosa (Milan, Bibl. Braidense, AE xiv, 24; Milan, 1958, no. 76).

last year in which Salomone is documented.[77] Cadei's hypothesis is based on a stylistic comparison between the Visconti Psalter-Hours and the only manuscript documented as a dei Grassi work, the Beroldo (Milan, Biblioteca Trivulziana, MS 2262), which takes its name from the twelfth-century compiler of the Milanese liturgy, the *Ordo et caerimonie Ecclesiae Ambrosianae Mediolanensis*. In 1396 the Fabbrica of the new cathedral, on which construction had begun approximately ten years earlier, engaged the scribe Andriolo dei Medici di Novate to copy an older manuscript of this text. In August 1398, approximately one month after Giovannino's death, his son Salomone received payment from the Fabbrica for the decoration of this manuscript.[78]

Through comparison of the Psalter-Hours with the Beroldo, Cadei arrives at two conclusions: first, that Giovannino himself painted extensively in the Beroldo, and, second, that the work in the Beroldo (1396–98) must have preceded the dei Grassi contributions to Landau-Finaly 22, which therefore cannot contain painting by the hand of Giovannino, who died in 1398. Both conclusions are erroneous. Giovannino almost certainly did not execute any of the illumination in the Beroldo, and though Salomone, who collaborated with his father in both Banco Rari 397 and Landau-Finaly 22, played a larger role in the latter, Giovannino continued to work alongside his son in Landau-Finaly 22, even though an interval of several years seems to have separated the two parts of the Psalter-Hours.

Both documentary and stylistic evidence belie the hypothesis that Giovannino painted in the Beroldo. The record of payment for the manuscript indicates that though the Fabbrica was honoring a schedule of costs computed by the father in his capacity as head of the family and senior employee of the Duomo, the work was carried out by the son.[79] In no way does the document suggest that Giovannino personally participated in the illumination of the Beroldo. Furthermore, beginning with its first folio (Fig. 78), and consistently throughout the manuscript, the illumination of the Beroldo itself reveals an artistic personality distinct from Giovannino's. Dominated by a proclivity for ornamentation that governs not only the overall composition of folio 1 but also its individual components, the result lacks the clarity, balance, and restraint so characteristic of Giovannino.[80]

77. Cadei, 1976, 19–42; 1984, 60–76.

78. *Annali*, app. 1, 243 (13 August 1398). On the relationship between the Beroldo and Giovannino's designs for the Cathedral of Milan, see M. L. Gatti Perer, "Appunti per l'attribuzione di un disegno della Raccolta Ferrari: Giovannino dei Grassi e il Duomo di Milano," *Arte lombarda*, x, no. 1, 1965, 49–64; Cadei, 1969.

79. The document reads: "Salomon filius q. magistri Johannis de Grassis, pro *ejus* remuneratione et solutione infradictarum litterum, per *eum* aminiatarum et ornatarum . . . ad computa infradicta data in scriptis *per* dictum q. magistrum Johanninum, qui decessit die 5 jullii . . . et *per* dictum Salomonem ejus filium videlicet ameniaturae et ornaturae litterarum" (*Annali*, app. 1.,

243 n. 24, italics mine). [Salomone, son of the late master Giovanni dei Grassi, for his recompense and payment for the letters mentioned below, colored and decorated by him . . . to the accounts mentioned below given in writing by the late said master Giovanni, who died on the fifth day of July . . . namely for the coloring and ornamentation of the letters by the said Salomone his son]. Toesca (1966, 142) interprets the document as I do.

80. For Toesca's original opinion that Giovannino himself did not paint in the Beroldo, see "Di alcuni miniatori lombardi della fine del Trecento," *L'arte*, x, 1907, 184–96 (190–94). In 1912 (ed. 1966, 141–43) Toesca maintained his earlier opinion that Giovannino

Figures are jammed uneasily into a cluttered architectural framework (compare Saints Ambrose and Augustine in the *Te Deum* initial with their counterparts in Landau-Finaly 22 and Banco Rari 397—Figs. 85, 29); architectural elements are multiplied to become a parody of corresponding forms in Giovannino's work (compare the structure in which the baptism takes place in the *bas-de-page* of the Beroldo with the temple in BR 2—Fig. 66); figures in the representation of the Baptism are related to the architecture in that scene through a medley of borrowings from BR 1 (Fig. 65, women peering over a parapet), BR 2 (Fig. 66, a figure looming against a dark interior), and BR 108 (Fig. 59, a person emerging through an opening onto a ledge).

The border decoration of folio 1 in the Beroldo is also an unrestrained melange of motifs borrowed from the Psalter-Hours: scintillating gold droplets of various sizes and shapes; acanthus, here given a vigorously undulating, lumpy appearance; five-petaled flowers with gold centers and sepals; oak leaves and acorns, here irrationally associated with clusters of grapes (contrast the grapevines twining around an oak on BR 124v—Fig. 71). A Madonna in a Visconti-like sun in the right border is venerated by David and a little winged soul in the outline of the *B* in the second text column, but the initial and the object of devotion are so far apart that their relationship is not easily grasped. Unlike Giovannino's, the angels who flutter about the Trinity in the upper border of the Beroldo are all sharp points and angles. Their wings are enormous, the contours of their drapery spiny, and their hair a bizarre exaggeration of Giovannino's occasional loose strands (Fig. 65).

There is surely, as Cadei points out, a relationship between certain architectural motifs in the Beroldo (consoles topped by tabernacles [Fig. 79], bifore windows employed as uprights in initials [Fig. 83], curved and twisted tracery [Fig. 80], and corresponding forms on some leaves of Landau-Finaly 22 [Figs. 53, 73, 87]) that are lacking in Banco Rari 397. This relationship is to be explained by a disruption in the execution of the two parts of the Psalter-Hours, which is suggested also by orthographical and technical differences. In Banco Rari 397, the motto of Giangaleazzo is consistently "a buon droyt" or "a droyt" (Figs. 63, 67), while in Landau-Finaly 22 the final word is uniformly spelled "droit" (Fig. 29). While the color of the underpaint beneath the gold leaf in Banco Rari 397 is always gray, in Landau-Finaly 22 it is orange.[81] None of these discrepancies, however, implies, as Cadei suggests, that Banco Rari 397 was painted entirely by Giovannino or that Landau-Finaly 22 was painted after the Beroldo (and hence after the death of Giovannino). In

directed but did not actively participate in the illumination of the Beroldo. He allowed the possibility that Giovannino's hand might be present in a few figures, such as the Saint Ambrose on folio 215 (Fig. 80), but concluded that even these are less elegant than those in the Bergamo sketchbook, and therefore probably by Salomone (142f.). Cipriani saw the opening page of the Beroldo as characterized by a "horror vacui" (Milan, 1958, 33). For an extended discussion of Cadei's views on the relationship between the Psalter-Hours and the Beroldo, see Kirsch, 1981, 276–91.

81. For example, gray underpaint is visible beneath the abraded gold-leaf background of the miniature on BR 22v, while orange appears above God the Father's shoulder on LF 51.

fact, there is strong evidence not only that Salomone participated in the painting of
Banco Rari 397 but also that Giovannino was active in planning and even in painting the
fourteenth-century portion of Landau-Finaly 22.

Some of the weaker passages in Banco Rari 397 can be associated with Giovannino's
son. For example, the feeble dove in the upper margin of BR 128 (Fig. 41) resembles the
bird in the lower border of folio 14v in the Beroldo (Fig. 81). Despite the presence of a
portrait of Giangaleazzo in the *bas-de-page* of BR 128, the borders as a whole are exiguous
and inadequate as a frame for the page. Within the initial on this leaf, David's head is
disproportionately large, recalling the megacephalic figures of Saints Ambrose and Augustine on folio 1 of the Beroldo.[82]

Salomone participated also in the painting of some of the most beautiful leaves in
Banco Rari 397. The deep blue in the Madonna's mantle on BR 104v (Fig 46), for
instance, is unparalleled in Giovannino's miniatures, but the same shade of blue is used
for the column in the right margin of LF 19 (Fig. 60), in which Salomone also collaborated.[83] Moreover, this column is modeled with the same kind of heavy stippling used by
the painter of the Virgin's gown on BR 104v. The pink that is combined with the blue in
the gown is very close to the pink of the column in the left border of LF 19.

Salomone's participation becomes more evident toward the end of Banco Rari 397, for
example in the representation of Zachariah on BR 146v (Fig. 91). One of the prophet's
arms is awkwardly articulated, and the sleeves of his gown ripple in cascades of superficial
curves. He is swathed in a thinly painted mantle that abounds in bucket folds and
flourishes. The drapery of Saint Ambrose on folio 215 of the Beroldo (Fig. 80) is similar.
The scroll on BR 146v enjoys a prominence more characteristic of Salomone's work than
of his father's (compare folios 1 and 5 in the Beroldo—Figs. 78, 84), and the heavy,
vigorously undulating acanthus in the borders of BR 146v is also consistent with Salomone's taste as reflected in the Beroldo (Fig. 82).

82. Meiss also doubted that BR 128 was autograph;
he ascribed it to the "workshop of Giovannino" (1974,
464 n. 424). The weak border on BR 128 is only one of
several in the latter part of Banco Rari 397 that seem
unlikely to have come from the hand of Giovannino.
Some of them, such as the borders of BR 132 and 136,
are heavier and stiffer than their predecessors. Others,
such as BR 146v (Fig. 91) and 148v, bespeak either a
lapse or a poverty of imagination. Heaviness, dryness,
and dullness characterize also some of the borders at the
beginning of Landau-Finaly 22 (LF 1 and the towers on
LF 19—Figs. 90, 60). Salomone may have been in some
measure responsible for all of them.

The weakest miniature in the Psalter Hours, the
Virgin Visited by Angels in the Temple (BR 76—Fig.
88), was probably executed by neither Giovannino nor
Salomone. A close parallel to the flaccid bodies, sum-

marily executed faces, and balding heads in this miniature exists in the Assumption of the Virgin in a Milanese prayerbook of the 1390s in Modena (Biblioteca
Estense, Lat. 842—Fig. 89). On the Modena manuscript, which was executed by an illuminator who
emerged from the circle of Giovannino, see Milan,
1958, no. 88; Cipriani, 1959, 53; Cogliati Arano,
1970a, 414f.

That Giovannino employed assistants other than
Salomone is clear from the *Annali* of the Duomo. The
services of an assistant are specified in his appointment
as engineer of the Cathedral on 18 July 1391 (1, 51,
183). On 3 October 1395 Giovannino's brother Porrino
was hired to assist him in various tasks for the Fabbrica
(1, 150).

83. On LF 19, see also page 65 below.

It is equally apparent that Giovannino was active in painting as well as planning the opening quires of Landau-Finaly 22, although beginning with the second quire, Salomone's role increases, especially in the borders. Giovannino did not, however, entrust even the borders in Landau-Finaly 22 entirely to his son. The glowing autumnal bouquets of oak leaves in the margins of LF 17 (Fig. 29) bear the stamp of his originality, and he may also have conceived and in part executed the personifications of Prudence and Justice seated on enormous oak leaves in the *bas-de-page* of this leaf. Pentimenti in the figure of Prudence, however, as well as the corkscrew curls of Justice and the elaborate scrolls held by both personifications, suggest the intervention in this part of the page of Salomone, whose probable authorship of the doves in the upper border has been noted above.

Pentimenti at the sides of the upper border of LF 19 (Fig. 60) may indicate that in this instance Giovannino altered a design by Salomone. Drawings of turrets and crenellations, painted over in white, are visible above the nesting bird and the inscribed book at the left and right of the upper zones of the page, and also to the right of the falcon perched on the stem of the initial *D*. Whereas the latter may indicate simply a decision to shift to the right the church finally painted at the juncture of the initial with its stem, the other two changes are substantive and related to the theme of the miniature: the bird at the left is engaged in creation, while the open book at the right is inscribed with the words of Genesis describing the making of heaven and earth. These components of the borders as well as the initial itself are distinctly superior to the remainder of the marginal decoration and may have been painted by Giovannino. The outline of the *D*, set against a radiant sun that lends particular importance to this opening scene of Creation, is filled with a variety of carefully painted architecture, plants, animals, and pious hermits. Within the initial, the Lord, whose costume is quite different from the belted-peplum type favored by Salomone (compare LF 26—Fig. 75), hovers in a deep blue firmament, graded to bluish white, picked out with angels' heads toward the top, and merging with bluish-white waves below. It is impossible to believe that the same hand that painted this initial also executed the dry, hard towers in the lateral margins and the animals in the *bas-de-page*. The contrast between the stags in the lower margin and those painted by Giovannino himself on BR 115 (Fig. 47) is particularly striking. All four specimens on LF 19 (Fig. 60) were copied either directly from those on BR 115 or from the same models, but whereas Giovannino's stags are composed in a lifelike, complex grouping (including a doe omitted in his son's copy), Salomone's are as isolated as their poses are arbitrary. His hard outlines are a sorry substitute for the lightness of Giovannino's touch, and within the heavy contours, rather large areas of alternating white and brown pigment replace the unpainted parchment and hairlike brushstrokes used to model Giovannino's agile creatures.

Meiss commented at length on the qualities of LF 30 (Fig. 92) that identify it as the work of Giovannino. He observed, for example, that the aquatic theme of the miniature is carried out by the canteen-bearing figures in the outline of the initial and by the rippling ornamental band between the lines of text beneath it.[84] The theme of water extends also to the *bas-de-page,* where three hermits engage in lively discourse beside a pond. The exquisite, grisaille-like landscape, clearly related to the hillside on BR 2v (Fig. 67), is softer, lighter, and more variegated than its counterpart in the lower border of LF 19 (Fig. 60). Giovannino provides each of his creatures with a local habitation: a shed for the beehive at the upper left, lean-tos for the hermits in the trees and for an ox in the *bas-de-page,* and an appropriately secular dwelling for the temptress who approaches the holy man in the lower margin. With regard to the golden trees at the sides of the page, filled with architectural fantasies set in enamel-like flowers that put forth golden "stamens," Meiss wrote: "Irrational as these structures may be, they are realized with so wonderful a taste and tact that we delight in their imaginativeness without doubting their probability."[85] Yet, even on this splendid page there are signs of Salomone's collaboration with his father: the scroll that seems to grow out of God the Father's hand, the elaboration of the hermits' drapery, and the ringlets of the temptress undeniably evoke Salomone. The page as a whole, however, is characterized by a sense of decorum lacking in the Beroldo. The rippling scroll and drapery contours are harmonious with the meandering bodies of water, and the disheveled hair of the would-be seductress is appropriate to her role.

Giovannino's hand may be present even in the last two miniatures painted by the dei Grassis in Landau-Finaly 22. Characteristic of his fantasy is the initial *E* of LF 51 (Fig. 77), constructed of acanthus fronds, which reappear not only in the borders but also within the miniature to conceal the sinners' nudity. Within the initial, the Garden of Eden is filled with flowers and fruit trees painted with careful attention to minutiae. Here too there is another touch of distinctively Giovanninesque caprice: the verdancy of the setting is incorporated also into the bodies of Adam and Eve, who in their innocence did indeed belong to the fabric of Paradise. If Giovannino did participate in the illumination of Landau-Finaly 22, the work cannot have been carried out in 1399–1400, after his death.

Although Cadei has argued that Salomone's work in the Beroldo preceded his illumination in the Visconti Psalter-Hours, I would propose the reverse. The mannerisms, the lack of organic structure, and the penchant for the overdone that characterize Salomone's contributions to the Visconti manuscript are carried to greater extremes in the Beroldo. As we have seen, even the first page of the Beroldo (Fig. 78) is a pastiche of motifs borrowed from the Psalter-Hours. Finally, the absence of Giangaleazzo's ducal armorials throughout the fourteenth-century portion of the Psalter-Hours renders highly unlikely any possibility that it was illuminated after 1395. The Psalter-Hours itself is ample proof that the Count of Virtues neglected no opportunity of proclaiming his rank. It would seem reasonable to suppose that Giovannino's illumination in Giangaleazzo's Psalter-

---

84. In Meiss and Kirsch, 18f.   85. Ibid., 18.

Hours was disrupted, though not halted, when he became engineer of the Duomo in 1391.[86]

In summary, I propose the following sequence and attributions for the painting of the Visconti Hours. Giovannino dei Grassi began illuminating the manuscript after 1385, when Giangaleazzo Visconti became the sole ruler of Milan, and probably around 1388 in connection with the birth of Giangaleazzo's son, Giovanni Maria. From the onset, Giovannino seems to have employed assistants. This is suggested, for example, on BR 35v and 36 by cursory repetition of motifs from other miniatures and by generally coarser execution, especially of the faces on those leaves. BR 76 is markedly inferior to other pages in the Psalter and seems to have been painted neither by Giovannino nor by Salomone.

Around 1391, when Giovannino was appointed engineer of the cathedral, work on the manuscript was disrupted. Several years later, probably toward 1395, illumination of the manuscript was resumed. Giovannino retained an active, supervisory role but assigned a large share of the work to his son. While Salomone's presence is indicated in some of the miniatures in the latter part of Banco Rari 397 (BR 104v, 105, 128, 146v), his participation in this portion of the manuscript is evident primarily in the borders (BR 128, 132, 136, 146v, 147v, 148v). In Landau-Finaly 22 Salomone's hand is present in even a larger share of the borders (LF 1, 10v, 17, 18, 25v, 26, 29, 29v, 40v), and even near the beginning of this volume it becomes increasingly apparent in the miniatures themselves (LF 26, 40v). He seems to have shared with Giovannino the execution of some of the finest pages in this section of the book (LF 19, 30, 51, 54), though his own inclinations toward more florid decoration are subject here to the restraint of his father. In addition, many of the leaves completed in the fifteenth century by Belbello da Pavia and his collaborators appear to have been designed and in some instances partly painted by Salomone (LF 11v, 12, 29, 37v, 50v). Salomone's illumination of the Beroldo between 1396 and 1398 is derived from both Banco Rari 397 and Landau-Finaly 22. For unknown reasons the illumination of the Psalter-Hours, which had advanced into the section now known as Landau-Finaly 22, was disrupted again in or before 1395. Perhaps the break occurred in 1395, when the Duke's attention turned to another project, the illumination of his Coronation Missal.

86. His appointment to this position stipulated full-time service: "che [Giovannino] però abbia a lavorare continuamente per la fabbrica" (*Annali*, I, 51) [that (Giovannino), however, be required to work continuously for the Fabbrica]. It seems improbable, however, that an employee of Giovaninno's stature would not have been permitted to work for the Duke. In 1396, for example, he acted as consultant for the planning of the Certosa (Beltrami, 1896, 52f.).

On 15 June 1399 the Fabbrica deducted one florin per month from Salomone's monthly salary of four florins so that he might work one week each month for the Duke (I, 196). An entry of September 1400 states that Salomone spent one week a month engaged in book illumination for the Duchess (app. I, 256). Cadei (1976, 20; 1984, 43) infers that these documents prove that Salomone was painting in the Visconti Hours during 1399–1400, but the nature of his work for the Duchess in 1399 is unspecified, and the Duke, not the Duchess, owned the Visconti Hours.

IV

AFTER THE DUKEDOM

The Coronation Missal

O N 11 May 1395 Wenceslaus IV, King of the Romans, signed the diploma conferring upon Giangaleazzo the title of Duke of Milan.[1] The ceremony in which the imperial representative, Benesio Cumsinich, invested Giangaleazzo with the insignia of his dukedom did not, however, occur until Sunday, 5 September, of that year. It seems not improbable that the Count himself chose the latter date for his ducal investiture because it was the Sunday closest to 7 September, the eve of the feast of the Nativity of the Virgin, which had been declared a Milanese holiday following the birth on 7 September 1388 of Giangaleazzo's much-desired heir, Giovanni Maria.[2] The festivities indeed continued for four days, according to the account of the investiture and associated events in a letter written five days after the ceremony by the Milanese Giorgio Azanelli to his friend Andreolo Arese, one of the Count's secretaries, then absent from Milan.[3]

Azanelli recounts that late in the morning of 5 September the Count of Virtues, accompanied by a vast number of ambassadors and courtiers, as well as musicians and other entertainers, proceeded from the Visconti castle at Porta Giovia to the square in front of Sant'Ambrogio. There, a large wooden platform, draped in scarlet and covered by a gold

---

1. See page 46 above.

2. See page 47 above. The dukedom was announced on 4 January 1395, when Giangaleazzo ordered his arms to be displayed with the imperial eagle (Valeri, 248). For the suggestion that this announcement was timed to

coincide with timed to coincide with the Epiphany celebrations in Milan, see Trexler, 169f. n. 156.

3. *Annales Mediolanensis, RIS,* xvi, 821–26. The account is amplified by Corio, ii, 928–31.

and scarlet brocaded canopy, had been constructed for the principals in the ceremony. Surrounding the dais was a palisade to keep back the throngs who filled the square, where armed knights and soldiers kept order. Awaiting Giangaleazzo on the podium was the imperial lieutenant Benesio Cumsinich, who seated the Count beside himself, as the prelates, courtiers, and ambassadors took their assigned places. The imperial diploma of investiture was read. After the reading, Giangaleazzo knelt to receive from Cumsinich the ducal cape and a jeweled crown in the shape of a biretta, the crown valued at 200,000 florins. The multitude of prelates (including thirteen bishops) in the ducal enclosure then sang hymns. Pietro Filargo, bishop of Novara (later Pope Alexander V) and principal negotiator in Giangaleazzo's pursuit of the dukedom, then delivered a speech in fulsome praise of the Duke. Mass was said, and the company moved on to a banquet at the communal palace of Milan.

The remarkable fidelity with which the events described in Azanelli's letter are depicted in the Missal presented by Giangaleazzo to the basilica of Sant'Ambrogio indicates that the illuminator, Anovelo da Imbonate, like Azanelli, probably witnessed the events himself. Most of the Missal was written about 1370, but important pictorial and textual additions were made at the time of Giangaleazzo's coronation.[4] In the framed tableau that dominates folio 8 (Fig. 3), historical precision and the flavor of miniature-*cum*-souvenir are more pronounced than in any of Giangaleazzo's earlier manuscripts. Into a relatively small rectangle (12.5 by 15.6 cm), Anovelo crammed as many details as possible. In accordance with the minutiae of Azanelli's description, even the steps leading up to the dais are draped in scarlet, and the platform itself is covered with cloth embroidered in reddish-gold. Also in conformity with Azanelli's account, a picket fence surrounds the central structure, but the hardware (painted in silver) that secures it from the multitudes outside is one of several details in the painting not mentioned by Azanelli that must be credited either to Anovelo's observation or to his imagination.[5] The pygmylike figures within the palisade include watchful soldiers who gaze attentively outward, while many of

4. The Coronation Missal is now in Milan, Chapter Library, Lat. 6. For its contents, see the Catalogue.

There is no reason to believe that Anovelo knew Azanelli's letter, although a copy of the letter, in a hand of the late fifteenth or early sixteenth century, has been bound into the Coronation Missal (fols. 4–5), as part of a quire (fols. 1–6), containing also a genealogy of the Viscontis in a fourteenth-century hand (fols. 2–4) and a mass (fol. 6) in commemoration of the victory at Parabiago in 1337, when Azzo Visconti, with the miraculous intervention of Saint Ambrose himself, subdued an invading army led by Lodrisio Visconti. On this battle, see Corio, I, 739f. Also added at a later date to the end of the Missal are an ordo for the coronation of the King of the Romans, a ceremony that normally took place in Sant'Ambrogio, additional masses, and a copy, dated 1431, of privileges granted the canons of Sant'Ambrogio

by Sigismund, King of the Romans. The additions at the beginning and end of the manuscript suggest that after its presentation to the church by Giangaleazzo, the Missal came to be regarded as a compendium of imperial ritual focused on the mother church of the city.

5. Anovelo's representation of the dais accords with the description in Azanelli's letter of a "decorum quadratum tribunal, undique lignamine rotundo vallatum" (*RIS*, XVI, 822) [a handsome square raised platform surrounded by wooden posts]. In 1503 Corio, perhaps inspired by the imperial flavor of Azanelli's account of the proceedings, described the structure as "uno grandissimo tribunale di legname rotondo et a gradi, concavato a modo de Culiseo" (II, 929) [a very great round wooden platform with steps, concave in the manner of the Colosseum].

the others—presumably invited guests—crane their necks to gaze at the crowd of dignitaries on the dais. To the left of the podium, two oak trees (a personal emblem of Giangaleazzo, but here probably symbolic of the strength of both leaders) enhance the outdoor setting established by the fence and the grass on which it stands. Several groups of spectators mentioned by Azanelli are also represented. These include ecclesiastics, a Franciscan (perhaps because the Bishop of Novara himself belonged to this order), and three groups on horseback: nobles at the left, knights and musicians at the right. Beyond the pale, in the lower corners, Anovelo portrayed on a smaller scale but in a lively variety of poses a variegated throng of observers.

Giangaleazzo and Cumsinich, flanked by their standards—the imperial eagle for the lieutenant, the viper quartered with fleurs-de-lys for the Count of Virtues—tower over the others on the platform. In his zeal for comprehensiveness Anovelo depicts simultaneously a number of events. As one of Cumsinich's associates reads the imperial diploma, from which hangs a golden seal, the Bishop of Novara ticks off the new Duke's virtues, while musicians sound their trumpets and beat their drums at the right. On the platform a notary dictates the proceedings to a scribe.

Still other moments are represented in the illuminated initial below. In the upper half of the initial, the notary continues his dictation as Cumsinich places on Giangaleazzo's head a crown of markedly imperial appearance.[6] The ducal capelet is already in place. As in the miniature above, a Bohemian knight, at the left, and Giangaleazzo's courtier, Ottone de Mandello, at the right, both mentioned by Azanelli, hold, respectively, the imperial standard and the standard of the Count of Virtues. Also included from the miniature above is Giangaleazzo's swordbearer (not mentioned in Azanelli's letter), wearing a scarlet coat embroidered with Giangaleazzo's sun and with banderoles that probably allude to the motto associated with the device of the sun, *a bon droit*.

In the lower half of the initial, encompassed by the three groups emphasized by Azanelli—clergy, knights, and nobles—stands an altar prepared for mass, its gold and jeweled frontal painted in such detail that one may read in the upper tier a Deesis flanked by an Annunciation and, in the lower band, Passion scenes beginning with the Way to Calvary and ending with the Resurrection.[7] Within architectural openings in the acanthus outline of the initial are the brazen serpent and its typological counterpart, a jeweled cross, that still today flank the nave of Sant'Ambrogio.

Anovelo filled the borders of this impressive page with a panoply of Giangaleazzo's

6. One source reports that Giangaleazzo announced his intention of giving the crown to the two young sons of Francesco Novello of Padua (Chamberlin, 166), but to my knowledge it does not survive. C. M. Ady reports that Ludovico Sforza pawned the ducal crown and jewels to help finance the war against Louis XII in 1499–1500 (*A History of Milan under the Sforza*, New York and London, 1907, 182).

7. So particularized is the detail in Anovelo's miniature that the discrepancy in subject matter between the golden altar in the Missal and the Carolingian/ Romanesque altar now in the church raises the question of whether its appearance was different in the fourteenth century. On restorations and reconstructions of the altar, see A. K. Porter, *Lombard Architecture*, II, New Haven, 547f., 574, 575. See also Courcelle, 169–79.

armorials. In the upper border and in the lateral margins the illuminator four times painted the radiant dove against an azure background with a banderole inscribed "a bon droit." In the upper lateral margins, cheetahs are tethered to fruitful trees, both familiar from Giangaleazzo's Psalter-Hours in Florence; and in the lower border the Count's tilting helmets, also present in the Florence manuscript, flank the imperial shield and the viper quartered with fleurs-de-lys.[8]

The investiture leaf is the first of several contributions to the Missal by Anovelo and an associate. They also painted eleven illuminated initials on other leaves, as well as a large Christ in Majesty and a full-page Crucifixion.[9] The theme that occasioned the illumination of the Sant'Ambrogio Missal resounds in several of its illuminated initials. The largest of these, depicting the investiture of Ambrose as archbishop of Milan (Fig. 4), evokes the representation on folio 8. Anovelo represented the moment when the miter is placed on Ambrose's head, an echo of the coronation of Giangaleazzo on folio 8. Ambrose too is seated upon a draped and canopied throne, and the investiture is witnessed by a large group of clergy and laymen, some of whom strain to look up at the enthroned archbishop. The prominence of the entire leaf is enhanced by acanthus ornament in all four margins. In the lower border, the shield of the viper quartered with fleurs-de-lys emphasizes the connection between the two investitures, thus implying sanction of Giangaleazzo's rule through association with the city's most important bishop, though the ceremony for Saint Ambrose depicted in the Missal is modest in comparison with the Duke's.

Wearing a scarlet robe and his ducal cape and biretta, Giangaleazzo, together with the Duchess, also wearing scarlet, worships the Madonna of Mercy, at the opening of the mass for Giangaleazzo on folio 176 (Fig. 48). Here Anovelo evokes the miniature on folio 258 in Lat. 757, at the opening of the Saturday Mass of the Virgin Mary (Fig. 51), which, I have proposed above, represents Giangaleazzo and Caterina, with their noble attendants, as they appeared at the time of their marriage in 1380.[10] Like the Duke and the Duchess, the Madonna in Anovelo's miniature appears older than her counterpart in Lat.

8. In his letter, Azanelli refers to Giangaleazzo's standard simply as "quartilata," and this term has been understood to refer to the viper quartered with the eagle. See, for example, E. Verga, *Storia della vita milanese*, Milan, 1931, 126. What Anovelo painted on this page, however, twice as a standard and once on the shield in the lower border, is the viper quartered with fleurs-de-lys, an armorial bearing that Giangaleazzo apparently began to use only around the time of his investiture as Duke. An additional stimulus to its use in 1395 may have been the ratification of a new treaty of alliance with France late in 1394, after which, according to Corio (I, 925), Giangaleazzo decreed that all public buildings in his domain display the viper quartered with the arms of France.

9. See the Catalogue for a list of miniatures in the Missal. Cogliati Arano (1970a, 420f.) has pointed out that the Crucifixion on folio 156v was probably painted by an associate of Anovelo. Nonetheless, even in this miniature, in keeping with the spirit of the ducal investiture, Saint John, perhaps as Giangaleazzo's namesake, is provided with a coronet (Fig. 98).

On the occasion of his investiture, Giangaleazzo may have chosen to expand an already existing Missal because it had special significance for the Visconti family or the canons of Sant'Ambrogio, or both; or he may have done so because there was insufficient time to write and illuminate a Missal before his coronation.

10. Page 31.

757. Although she is heavier and coarser, Anovelo's Madonna is nonetheless clearly related to her predecessor by body type, drapery, and details of costume, including her crown. Like the Madonna in Lat. 757, Anovelo's is attended by angels. Giangaleazzo and Caterina also closely resemble their counterparts in the Hours-Missal. In this miniature and throughout the Coronation Missal, Anovelo's forms (for example, the shape of the Madonna's body) and his faces, characterized by small arcs of eyebrows, pudgy noses, and prominent chins, are so similar to those of the Master of Lat. 757 as to indicate that Anovelo emerged from the shop that produced the large Missal-Hours.

Other similarities also point to Anovelo's firsthand knowledge of Lat. 757. After his work on the Coronation Missal, large roman folio numbers were placed in the upper margin, the same position that roman numerals occupy in Lat. 757 and Smith-Lesouëf 22. In the initial that introduces the Vigil of Saint Martin on folio 177 of the Coronation Missal, Saint Ambrose presides at the funeral of the French saint, as he does also in the miniature on folio 114v, at the beginning of the Office of the Dead, in Lat. 757 (Figs. 93, 12).[11] In the Baptism of Saint Augustine that illustrates the Vigil of Saint Ambrose on folio 193 in the Coronation Missal (Fig. 94), Augustine wears the same unusual non-ecclesiastical costume—a scarlet hooded cloak lined in ermine—as in the corresponding scene that introduces the Prayer of Saint Augustine on folio 224v in Lat. 757 (Fig. 95).

Anovelo signed his work at the end of the preface to the Canon of the Mass, beneath his miniature of the Lord in Majesty and above the armorials of the new Duke (Fig. 96). Here too his debts to the Master of Lat. 757 are apparent—in the foliate forms at the corners of the frame (cf. Fig. 95), the acanthus borders, the tessellated background of the miniature, and the figure of the Deity himself. Anovelo borrowed from even earlier sources, in Bolognese and Paduan art, the somewhat retardataire outlining of the haloes (red for the Evangelist symbols and dotted white on black for God the Father). In the eagle of Saint John, Anovelo also adopted the Bolognese practice of giving the animal symbols human torsos.[12] The lion and the ox, on the other hand, have the bodies of animals, their tails constituting an upended ogee arch that reinforces the flourish in the margin that frames the illuminator's signature.

Anovelo's Evangelist symbols are certainly not outstanding examples of the animal representations for which Lombard illuminators of the fourteenth century are renowned. Nor, indeed, despite his extraordinary attention to detail and the sumptuousness of his painting in the Coronation Missal, is Anovelo an artist of the stature of the Master of Lat. 757, Giovannino dei Grassi, or Michelino da Besozzo. It is possible that Giangaleazzo

11. The miniature of Saint Ambrose at the Funeral of Saint Martin in the Coronation Missal may now be added to a group of such representations centered on the Basilica of Sant'Ambrogio (chapter II, note 8 above).

12. For example, the Book of Hours of 1349 in Kremsmünster, Stiftsbibliothek, Cim. 4, fol. 10v, reproduced in Schmidt, 1973, fig. 110. For additional icono-graphic and stylistic connections between the Kremsmünster Hours and other manuscripts of Giangaleazzo Visconti, see Kirsch, 1981, chaps. III and IV, passim. An earlier Lombard use of the hybrid Bolognese type occurs in the Missal of Archbishop Roberto Visconti, dated 1354 (Cogliati Arano, 1970a, fig. 120).

entrusted Anovelo with such a major commission as the Coronation Missal at least in part because of his association with the Master of Lat. 757, whom he may even have assisted in the painting of the earlier Missal.

The genealogy of the Visconti family on folios 2–4 in the Coronation Missal links this manuscript to Lat. 5888, the last manuscript in the group considered in this study. Although written on the first three leaves of a quire of six that contains also later material (an early sixteenth-century copy of Azanelli's letter and the text of a mass for the victory at Parabiago), both the script and the small decorated initials of the genealogy, which is entitled *Prohemium missalis,* belong to the campaign of 1395. Thus the genealogy in the Missal probably predates the Paris manuscript of 1403 by about eight years. The prologue to the genealogy in the Missal emphasizes the magnificence and stresses the authenticity of the lineage claimed by the family.[13] As we shall see below, in the funeral oration, which is based on twelve virtues ascribed to Giangaleazzo, it is the tenth, Magnificence, that occasions Pietro de Castelletto's recitation of the Duke's ancestry. Castelletto like-wise asserts the accuracy of the genealogy.

The lineage recited by Pietro is fuller than that in the Missal, including a greater number of putative Visconti ancestors in antiquity, but omitting Giangaleazzo's uncles, Matteo and Bernabò, who are included in the Missal. In both genealogies some members of the family (not always the same in both) receive fuller descriptions than others. Occasionally the language of the descriptions in both manuscripts is identical. It is therefore possible that both genealogies were drawn from a common and fuller source. The special emphasis upon the Duke's ancestry in Lat. 5888, which concludes with a twelve-page pictorial genealogy organized by Pietro and illuminated by Michelino da Besozzo, suggests that both Pietro and Michelino conceived of their manuscript, which begins with a splendid image of the Duke being crowned in heaven by the Christ child (Fig. 30), as a pendant to the Missal, which represents his coronation on earth.

The Eulogy-Genealogy

On 3 September 1402, little more than two months after he had conquered Bologna— with Perugia, Siena, Lucca, and Pisa already under his control and Florence threatened by his forces—Giangaleazzo Visconti unexpectedly died at the age of fifty-one at Melegnano, one of his hunting lodges near Milan.[14] On 20 October 1402 Giangaleazzo's

13. "Quorum genologia pro ut ī nonullis autenticis libris et eidmeis antiqissimis se in hoc concordantibus veraciter repitur" (fol. 2) [whose genealogy is ascertained truthfully by some legally valid books and also very ancient sources, themselves agreeing in this].

14. On Giangaleazzo's last weeks, see Bueno de Mesquita (293–98), who proposes that the delay in actually attacking Florence resulted from a financial crisis brought on by the Duke's overtaxation of his dominions. He suggests that the legend of the Duke's ordering a crown and robes in 1402 to be ready for his royal coronation as soon as Florence had fallen may be

funeral rites were performed in the Cathedral of Milan, with "pompi stupendissimi" equal in splendor to the ceremonies that had marked his investiture as Duke seven years earlier.[15] Among the thousands who participated in the funeral, which lasted fourteen hours, were numerous members of all branches of the Visconti family, representatives of all the Duke's dominions, all the princes of Italy who were his allies, a vast array of ecclesiastics, led by Franciscans, and more than two thousand paid mourners, the bodices of whose mourning costumes (also paid for by the ducal treasury) were adorned with the arms of the duchy of Milan and the county of Pavia.[16] Indeed, the Duke's armorials were omnipresent throughout the events; and his bier, like the throne of his ducal investiture, was covered with a canopy of gold.

After services in the Cathedral, the entire party proceeded to the nearby Great Hall, where they were joined by other "innumerabilis Populus," inside and out, to hear Master Petrus de Castelletto, of the Order of Augustinian Hermits, deliver a eulogy.[17] Although he is mentioned in art-historical literature solely as the author of Giangaleazzo's funeral oration, Petrus had also written a life of Petrarch.[18] As Castelletto acknowledges in the preface to his *Vita Francisci Petrarca*, it is almost identical with Boccaccio's biography of the great humanist;[19] however, in an age when imitation was not only the sincerest form of flattery but also evidence of erudition and authority, this fact probably did not diminish Frater Petrus's reputation as a man of learning.

A copy of Petrus's eulogy of Giangaleazzo was subsequently illuminated by Michelino da Besozzo (Paris, Bibliothèque nationale, Lat. 5888). To this copy Petrus appended a genealogy of the Viscontis, also composed by him and dated 26 January 1403. This too was illuminated by Michelino, probably at the same time that he illuminated the oration.[20]

---

true. The commune of Pavia did record in that year that Giangaleazzo was held to be "not unworthy of the crown of all Italy." Bueno de Mesquita argues further that Giangaleazzo probably planned at least to obtain the iron crown of Lombardy from Wenceslaus, in return for assisting the latter in obtaining the imperial crown in Rome (310). Wenceslaus in fact remained only King and never became Emperor of the Romans.

15. Corio, II, 977–80; *RIS*, XVI, 1023–50.

16. Corio, II, 976–77.

17. *RIS*, XVI, 1036; Petrus is called "Magister" on folios 1 and 7 of Lat. 5888. For the text of the sermon, see *RIS*, XVI, 1038–50.

18. A. De Meijer, "Bibliographie historique de l'ordre de Saint Augustin, 1870–1974," *Augustiniana*, XXVIII, 1978, 274; A. Perini, *Bibliographia Augustiniana*, Florence, I, 1929, 212. Perini, following the error of F. Argelati, *Bibliotheca Scriptorem Mediolanensum*, I, pt. 2, Milan, 1745, 341, also attributes to Castelletto an eclogue to Francesco Sforza that is now Paris, Bibl. nat.,

Lat. 8382. The author of this eclogue is Ioannis Stephani Cotte, whose name, monogram, and arms appear on folio 1.

19. Edition of A. Solerti, in *Storia letteraria d'Italia*, IV, app., Milan, 1904–5, 267. Petrarch had ties to Castelletto's church, San Pietro in Ciel d'Oro in Pavia, which contains both the tomb of Saint Augustine and the remains of Boethius. Petrarch stated in his will that if he died in Pavia he wished to be buried in that church. See T. Mommsen, *Petrarch's Testament*, Ithaca, 1957, 17f., 75.

20. A second version of Petrus's genealogy, illuminated in the style of Michelino, is now in London, British Library, Add. 26814. This manuscript has been severely damaged by fire, and the remains of its parchment leaves have been pasted onto paper. The London manuscript differs from its Paris counterpart in that it includes, in addition to the genealogical line leading directly to Giangaleazzo and his sons, collateral members of the family, beginning with Uberto (brother of Matteo I). This expansion of the genealogy suggests that

By the time he was selected to illuminate Fra Pietro's funeral sermon, Michelino and his work must have been known both to the learned friar and to the Duke's family, for whom the manuscript was made.[21] Michelino is first recorded in 1388, when he was painting frescoes of the life of Saint Augustine in the cloister of the Augustinian church of San Pietro in Ciel d'Oro, the foundation to which Petrus de Castelletto belonged.[22] In 1402–3 Michelino is recorded as painting frescoes in the Visconti palace in Pavia.[23] His illumination of the funeral oration is the work of a mature master, worthy of his contemporaries' praise of him as *pictor summus*.[24]

Much as the coronation page in the Sant'Ambrogio Missal faithfully records the events it commemorates, so too is the frontispiece of the funeral oration closely related both to the event and to the text it illustrates (Fig. 30). In the *H* of the first word of his oration, "Heu" [Alas], the orator, Fra Pietro, is represented addressing his brother Augustinians. With the subtle handling of color that is one of the characteristics of his genius, Michelino enhances the mournful aspect of the black-robed Augustinians with a deep yet immensely rich blue hanging set within an enclosure of brighter royal blue (the outline of the letter *H*), which suggests simultaneously an ecclesiastical interior (pitched roof with tiles picked out in gold) and the notion of speech (pseudo-arabic gold script); the entire composition is set against a rectangle of glittering burnished gold. Royal blue and gold also dominate the principal scene above (Fig. 97), which illustrates the crux of Fra Pietro's eulogy, his assertion that the Count of Virtues would receive in heaven the twelve-pointed crown of the Madonna of the Apocalypse, each of its points symbolizing one of his virtues. The splendor of the heavenly court, at which seraphs, cherubs, armorial-bearing military angels, and personifications of the Duke's virtues witness his coronation, is irradiated not only by gold but also by the scarlet of the seraphs, which is repeated also in Giangaleazzo's ducal regalia, in the homunculus devoured by the viper in one of the Duke's tilting helmets, and in the plumage of the other. The Virtues, all wearing delicate crowns that echo the principal crowns of the Virgin and Giangaleazzo, are framed at one side by the luminous salmon tint of Charity's gown behind the Duke and at the other by the pearl gray of Mercy. Directly behind these figures, the green robe of Temperance and the blue of Humility establish a tone that resounds in the blue and green raiment of the angel-pages who hold the Duke's standards and helmets.

In keeping with the emphasis on Giangaleazzo's armorials in the funeral ceremonies, the angels in the miniature display all his principal emblems: the imperial eagle by itself, the eagle quartered with the *biscia*, the *biscia* alone, the three eagles of the County of Pavia, and the *biscia* quartered with fleurs-de-lys. Before the silver in the armorials and in

---

the London copy was made for a member of a collateral branch of the family. Medallions for additional portraits of collateral members of the family on folio 8, the last in the manuscript, were never completed. On Add. 26814, see also page 80.

21. Of the five manuscripts considered in this study, only Lat. 5888 was in the Visconti Library at the time of the inventory of 1426 (Pellegrin, 1955, A938).

22. Castelfranchi Vegas, 1975, 102 n. 18.

23. Schilling, 68 n. 5.

24. *Annali*, i, 261.

the angels' wings tarnished, the display must have been even more dazzling than it is today.

As in the Coronation Missal (Fig. 3), the borders of the funeral oration provided the illuminator with even further opportunity to present the Duke's arms. So brilliantly did Michelino exploit this occasion that Anovelo's borders by comparison appear somewhat brash and heavy. Once again, Giangaleazzo's earliest and most personal emblem, the dove in a radiant sun, is given a prominent position, in this case at the center of both the upper and lower borders. Surrounding these emblems, scroll-bearing prophets in all four borders alternate with the viper shield (again dulled through tarnishing of the silver) within burnished gold quatrefoils. In harmony with the miniature, two of the prophets, possibly Solomon and David, also wear gold crowns. Like those of their turbaned and bareheaded brethren, their scrolls, inscribed alternately with red and blue ink, underscore the extraordinary cooperation between scribe and illuminator on this page.[25] The beauty of this leaf alone is sufficient to explain why Giovanni Alcherio, an agent of the Duke of Berry who collected recipes for ink as well as paint, and who especially prized good formulas for mixing lapis lazuli, was moved, when he met Michelino in Venice in 1410, to call him the most excellent painter of all the painters of the world.[26]

The scrolls of the four prophets in the upper border allude to the dove-in-sun device that they flank. They read: "Tronus eius sicut sol," "Bene ille sicut turturus," "sub ipso erunt radiix solis," and "refulgent radius solis."[27] The scrolls of the twelve other prophets refer to the same virtues of the Duke that are personified within the miniature. Even in the context of the banderolemania of the era in which Michelino worked, his scrolls are designed with a special resilience and grace consonant with his distinctively fluid style. This is even more true of the flamelike, seemingly wind-tossed leaves that interweave the prophets with the armorials. Even the lone acanthus in the historiated initial seems to flutter in a breeze that sweeps through the borders, and the upright stroke at the left of the H, like the gold leaf beneath it, also undulates with the rhythm of the borders.[28]

Michelino created on the opening page of the funeral oration a *summa* of themes and visual forms central to the earlier manuscripts considered above. The Woman of the Apocalypse and her conspicuously nude child, to whom the patron paid homage in Lat. 757 and Smith-Lesouëf 22, here bestow upon the Duke his ultimate glory.[29] The seven

---

25. The coordination of the blue ink with the royal blue pigment in the illumination is still striking. The original red ink, now faded, would probably have reinforced the scarlet in the miniatures.

26. ". . . pictor excellentissimus inter omnes pictores mundi" (Milan, 1958, 53).

27. [His throne (is) just as the sun; he is good just as the turtle dove; under him will be the rays of the sun; the rays of the sun gleam.]

28. Another aspect of the appreciation for sinuous line expressed in Michelino's scrolls and leaves is the slouching stance of his Virtues. Their sloping shoulders and the forward thrust of their heads and abdomens are an early statement of the canon of feminine beauty that found great favor especially in Northern Europe—for example, in the work of the Boucicaut Master, and later with the generation of Jan van Eyck.

29. The Madonna in the funeral oration is identified by the text as the Woman of the Sun. She is also radiant in the manner of this type of Virgin.

virtues of the Count, so prominent in his Psalter-Hours, have here been augmented to twelve, and the angels who bear the Duke's arms and serve as his pages have also migrated from that manuscript. In the Eulogy as in the Missal of 1395, a host of onlookers witness the Duke's coronation (Figs. 3, 97).

The tenth of the twelve virtues that constitute the rhetorical framework of Fra Pietro's sermon is Magnificence, and his entire discourse on this virtue is devoted to the lineage of the Viscontis. At the outset of this part of his oration, Castelletto asserts that there are some who, like dogs baying at the moon ("ut canes ad Lunam"), would deny that Giangaleazzo and his two surviving sons were directly descended from Aeneas, the son of Venus and Anchises. In claiming descent from the ancient house of Troy, as in so many other aspects of their lives, the Viscontis followed the precedent of their royal French and English relatives. The fabricators of these genealogies multiplied the descendants of King Priam by inventing persons who do not exist in the classical sources. Thus Francio, the putative son of Hector, was said to have founded France, while Brutus, a fabricated great-grandson of Aeneas and great-grand-nephew of Priam, was claimed as the first king of Britain. The Viscontis traced their stock through an invented grandson of Aeneas and son of Ascanius, Anglus, founder of the city of Angleria (present-day Angera, on Lake Maggiore), and the Visconti lords of Milan always styled themselves also as lords of that city, site of the oldest of their fortresses. Anglus was probably brought into the genealogy as an eponym of the city he was supposed to have founded.[30]

Like the genealogy of the Viscontis in the Coronation Missal, Castelletto's begins with Anchises and Venus, followed by Aeneas, Ascanius, Anglus, and Anglus Junior. From this point, however, the genealogist in the Missal moves directly to Uberto Visconti, who in 384 acquired land in Milan by driving serpents from the Porta Nova of that city.[31] Fra Pietro, on the other hand, includes before Uberto nineteen other lords, all of whom he identifies as King of Angleria and Milan ("Rex Angleriae & Mediolini"), placing several of them chronologically in conjunction with Roman rulers. Thus, for example, Astatius ruled at the time Numa Pompilius reigned in Rome, and Lucius of Angleria flourished at the time of the wars between Pompey and Caesar. Castelletto's genealogy includes also many more Viscontis of the Middle Ages, among them "Agistulphus Rex Langobardorum, qui maximam familiaritatem habuit cum Pippino Rege Francorum" and his son Desiderius, "novissimus Rex Langobardorum, qui claruit Anno Domini DCCVI. victoriarum felicissimus, inter quas de CCC. millibus Saracenorum Romam & Castrum de Vico, in quo Pap Adrianus & Rex Carolus Magnus dicti Regis cognatus obsessi erant."[32]

---

30. On Anglus, see G. F. Hill, *Pisanello*, London and New York, 1905, 125 n. ·

31. Milan, Bibl. capitolare di Sant'Ambrogio, Lat. 6, fol. 2.

32. *RIS*, XVI, 1047 [Agistulph King of the Lombards, who had the greatest familiarity with Pepin, King of the Franks] and Desiderius, [the last King of the Lombards, who was famous in A.D. 706 (*sic*); most fortunate in his victories, among which one over 300,000 Saracens at Rome and the castle of Vico, in which Pope Adrian and King Charlemagne, a relative of the said King, had been besieged].

The extensive genealogy in the funeral oration, underscoring as it does the links between the Viscontis and Roman emperors at every major point in European history, emphasized the strength of the family at a precarious moment. Giangaleazzo's counselors and his widow, Caterina, must have known that Giovanni Maria, the unpromising fourteen-year-old who had succeeded to the dukedom, possessed neither the intelligence nor the will to maintain the vastly expanded state that had been created by his father. In fact, soon after Giangaleazzo's death, unity vanished, and the cities conquered by Giangaleazzo quickly regained their independence from Milan. Political disorder prevailed until the assassination of Giovanni Maria in 1412. At that time, Giangaleazzo's younger son, Filippo Maria, succeeded to the dukedom and began to rebuild the state. The pomp of Giangaleazzo's funeral, including the eulogy, may have been part of an effort to shore up the dukedom against impending disaster, and the pictorial genealogy of Lat. 5888, like the funeral oration itself, is rich in classical allusions that emphasize both the legitimacy and the continuity of Visconti rule.[33]

The pictorial genealogy (Figs. 31, 32) occupies twelve pages (folios 7–12v) of Lat. 5888. Like the eulogy, it begins with a rubric identifying the author:

> Introduction of the genealogy from which descends the house of the Viscontis, among whom there were many princes, and, of the same house, the Duke of Milan, Giangaleazzo, with his immediate posterity in the direct line. Arranged by Master Petrus de Castelletto of the Order of the Hermits of Saint Augustine, of the church of the Blessed Augustine in Pavia, as appears below, 26 January 1403, in praise of the most illustrious Duke.[34]

For the pictorial genealogy, Fra Pietro selected only sixty-one family members, including Anchises, Venus, and Venus's father, Jupiter. From the beginning (Fig. 31), Fra Pietro composed for each portrayal a brief inscription (related, as we shall see below, to the *tituli* of ancient Roman as well as earlier Italian art), identifying the person depicted and stating the most salient facts about him. The execution of the genealogy was left to the very capable hands of Michelino and the scribe who collaborated with him also on folio 1 of the manuscript.

The pictorial form of the Visconti genealogy seems to be unprecedented in, though not unrelated to, earlier family trees. Rooted in the marriage of Venus and Anchises at the top of folio 7, the Visconti family tree conforms to the concept of *direct* descent ("per lineam rectam") emphasized in Castelletto's introduction, but in doing so it inverts the normal

---

33. Bellonci, 86.

34. [Exordium geonologie (*sic*) a qua descendit domus vicecomitus et eiusdem domus Dux Mediolani Iohanes Galeas cum suis posteris per lineam rectam dimissis collateralibus inter quos maximi fuere principes.

Ordinate per Magistrum Petrum de Castelletto ordinis heremitarum Sancti Augustini. Sacri loci beati Augustini de papia. Ut infra patet mcccciii. die xxvi. mensis Ianuarii. Ad laudes dicti illustrissimi Ducis] (Lat. 5888, fol. 7).

direction of a tree's growth. In this respect, the Visconti tree is related to the consanguinity trees that from the mid-thirteenth century onward appeared in numerous illuminated manuscripts of canon law, most of them produced in Bologna, such as the consanguinity tree in the *Decretals of Gregory IX*, now in the Vatican Library (Pal. Lat. 629), written and illuminated in the first half of the fourteenth century (Fig. 99). Gerhart Ladner has shown that consanguinity trees, which were designed to represent graphically those degrees of blood relationship that prohibited marriage without ecclesiastical dispensation, were in turn derived from the geometric diagrams found in early medieval manuscripts and intended to illustrate family relations for purposes of inheritance according to Roman civil law.[35] These diagrams, which were called *stemmata*, were not trees in the vegetative sense, but as Ladner points out, their shape evoked the shape of a tree with its branches.[36]

Michelino's genealogy of the Viscontis, in which Giangaleazzo's direct ancestors and progeny are depicted in disks, appears to have been adapted from the trunk of a tree of consanguinity such as that in the Vatican manuscript, where the direct line descends from great-great-grandfather to great-great-grandson. Sisters and brothers and their progeny, included in the tree of consanguinity, were purposefully omitted from the Paris copy of the Visconti genealogy. Giangaleazzo would no doubt have approved of the absence from his genealogy of his uncle Bernabò and the latter's countless, troublesome offspring.[37] On the other hand, the inclusion of collateral members of the family in the London version (Fig. 100), also produced in Michelino's workshop, probably for a collateral branch of the family, confirms the structural relationship of both Visconti manuscripts with trees of consanguinity.[38]

The form of the roundels in the Visconti genealogy, however, differs conspicuously from the simply inscribed disks of consanguinity trees, and is to my knowledge unprecedented. Onto the trunk of a consanguinity tree, Fra Pietro and Michelino grafted a novel genealogy, linking the Viscontis to the dawn of Roman history as emphatically as possible. In so doing, they acted with knowledge of and earned a place in a tradition of North Italian antiquarianism rooted in the early Trecento humanism of Verona and richly

---

35. "Medieval and Modern Understanding of Symbolism: A Comparison," *Speculum*, LIV, 1979, 223–56 (242–44). On vegetative symbolism of various kinds as an expression of the Renaissance concept of "rinascita," see two further studies by Ladner: "Vegetation Symbolism and the Concept of Renaissance," in *De artibus opuscula XL: Essays in Honor of Erwin Panofsky*, ed. M. Meiss, New York, 1961, I, 303–22; and "Terms and Ideas of Renewal," in *Renaissance and Renewal in the Twelfth Century*, ed. R. L. Benson and G. Constable, Cambridge (Mass.), 1982, 1–33.

36. Ladner, 1979 (as in note 35), 244.

37. With the exception of Venus, the genealogy excludes women, even Giangaleazzo's daughter Valentina and her children by Louis d'Orléans (who, as we have seen above, posed a special threat to Giangaleazzo's dynastic ambitions).

38. For the London genealogy, see note 20 above. As stated there, the collateral relatives included in the London manuscript begin with Uberto Visconti, brother of Matteo I. The first open revolt against Giovanni Maria in Milan was led by Antonio and Francesco Visconti, grandsons of Uberto (Bellonci, 90). It is possible that the London copy was in fact begun for one of these brothers.

nourished by the protracted residence at the courts of North Italy of the greatest humanist of the Trecento, Petrarch.[39]

The flamelike roots of the Visconti family tree at the top of folio 7 in the Paris manuscript (Fig. 31) form a roundel within which Jupiter joins his daughter Venus in marriage with Anchises, underscoring the Visconti claim to descent, through Venus, from the king of the gods himself.[40] The family's descent from Jupiter is emphasized also by the oak leaves with golden acorns that frame the roundels throughout the genealogy.[41] Full color is reserved for the root of the Visconti tree and for the most important modern component of its trunk, Giangaleazzo, who is portrayed in regal purple on folio 12v (Fig. 32). Beginning with Aeneas, all the other representations are painted in grisaille against a burnished gold background. All the portraits are bust-length profiles, facing alternatively left and right, with the exception of the last page, on which Giangaleazzo's grandfather (Stefano) and father, Giangaleazzo himself, and his two surviving sons all face right.

The arrangement of the concluding page may have been dictated by a reluctance to portray the living Duke, Giovanni Maria, facing left, as a strict sequence of alternation would have prescribed. The configuration used also makes the two living Viscontis, as well as those closest in living memory, literally forward-looking, and creates a special bond of unity among them. A similar wish to express the continuity of Visconti rule probably explains the placement of Giangaleazzo's sons in a direct line of descent rather than as brothers. Neither Fra Pietro nor Michelino could have known in 1403 that

39. T. Mommsen, 95–116; R. Weiss, esp. 30–58; Schmitt, 167–218.

40. In the marriage scene, Jupiter assists Anchises in placing an enormous ring on the index finger of Venus's right hand. Rings are also prominent in the only two surviving panels by Michelino, both of which represent marriages—the Marriage of the Virgin in the Metropolitan Museum of Art and the Mystic Marriage of Saint Catherine in the Pinacoteca, Siena. The particular attention paid to rings in these paintings has led Eisler, 12, to suggest that Michelino may have been trained as a goldsmith.

It is a striking fact, which should probably be seen in conjunction with other visual expressions of their dynastic concerns, that beginning with Giangaleazzo the Viscontis demonstrated an unparalleled predilection for pictorially recording their own marriages or betrothals. As suggested in chapter II, the miniature of the patron and his bride on folio 258 in Lat. 757 may be the first wedding portrait in the series (Fig. 51). BR 1 in the Psalter-Hours may be the second (Fig. 65). The group also includes a representation of Filippo Maria and Marie of Savoy on a tarot card (Yale University, Beinecke Library, Cary Collection of Playing Cards, No. ITA 109 [Fig. 61]) and a portrait of Francesco Sforza and Filippo Maria's daughter, Bianca Maria Visconti, in a miniature in Cremona (Archivio parocchiale di S. Sigismondo, Atto di donazione, reproduced in *Visconti a Milano*, fig. 204). The tradition was carried on by Galeazzo Maria Sforza, whose marriage to Bona of Savoy in 1468 was represented in 1476 by Cristoforo de' Predis in Turin, Bibl. reale, ms. Var. 124, fols. 1v, 2v, where the bridal couple, as in Banco Rari 397, are depicted as Anna and Joachim (reproduced in Kirsch, 1981, figs. 70, 71; see also page 51 above).

41. Michelino's awareness of the oak not only as the tree of Jupiter but also as the tree of the Golden Age is suggested by the golden acorns in the genealogy. See also chapter II, note 24. As we have seen above, the oak also plays an emblematic role in Giangaleazzo's Psalter-Hours in Florence (Fig. 29) and in the miniature of Giangaleazzo's investiture as Duke on folio 1 of the Coronation Missal (Fig. 3). Within the coronation miniature on folio 1 of Lat. 5888 (Fig. 97), the lowest military angel in the group of three at the right holds a tarnished silver standard painted with green remains of what seems to have been a tree, perhaps an oak, on a hill. The botanical continuity of the Visconti family oak "tree" in the funeral oration is suggested by small green stems beneath the last scroll on each page and above the first medallion on the next.

Filippo Maria would in fact succeed his brother or that the male line of the Viscontis would die out with Filippo Maria, despite the hopeful spray of leaves and acorns painted by Michelino at the end of the family oak tree.

The most striking and most classical quality of the Visconti portrait medallions is their resemblance to ancient coins. The size of the medallions, about 2.7 centimeters in diameter, approximates that of Roman aurei—probably a deliberate choice of the illuminator, inasmuch as wide margins at either side of the roundels (about 7.5 cm on one side and 9.2 cm on the other) indicate that had he wished to do so Michelino could have made the medallions considerably larger. The brilliant gold background of the portraits also evokes ancient coins, while the grisaille of the busts themselves not only emulates relief sculpture but also belongs to a Renaissance pictorial tradition of representing the worthies of antiquity in a technique that evokes ancient sculpture.[42]

Michelino was not the first Renaissance artist to be inspired by ancient coins. As early as 1310 the Veronese humanist Giovanni Mansionario wrote, and illustrated with copies of Roman coins, the *Historia imperialis*, a series of biographies of Roman emperors (Fig. 102). Both the script and the portraits in Mansionario's drawings are characterized by a somewhat stiff, dry quality foreign to Roman coins. Nonetheless, as Roberto Weiss has shown, they are important because in these drawings, apparently for the first time, an Italian scholar gives visual expression to his antiquarian interests.[43]

In 1390, doubtless under the influence of Petrarch, who had spent the last four years of his life at the court of the Carraras in Padua, Francesco Novello da Carrara issued four medals *all'antica*, representing himself and his father, to commemorate the expulsion of the usurping Viscontis from his city. These medals are generally acknowledged to be the first of their kind in the Renaissance.[44] Modern accounts of the early Renaissance antiquarian fascination with classical medals and coins normally begin with Mansionario, proceed to the Carrara medals (and a small group closely related to them), and then to the medals Pisanello began producing about 1438, skipping over Michelino's genealogy of 1403.[45]

Yet Michelino's painted coins, though less literal as copies than Mansionario's draw-

---

42. As noted in chapter I, page 3, this practice seems to have originated with Giotto in a lost fresco of the triumph of fame painted around 1335 in the palace of Azzo Visconti (Fig. 1). On the manuscript versions of Giotto's fresco, see also Mommsen, 106 and n. 84, who transmits the suggestion of Schlosser (185, 189 n. 4) that the frescoes painted under Petrarch's supervision between 1367 and 1379 in the Sala Virorum Illustrium in the Carrara Palace in Padua were also in grisaille. On the Paris manuscripts, Lat. 6069 F and Lat. 6069 I, both of which have been associated with the circle of Altichiero, see Paris, 1984, nos. 73 and 74. The grisaille in Lat. 6069 F is echoed in a *Thebaid* of Statius attributed to Altichiero's associate, Jacopo Avanzo (Mellini, pl. opp. 104).

43. Weiss, 22–24.

44. On the Carrara medals, see Hill, 1, 3; Weiss, 53f., and Schmitt, 168f. Although neither Giangaleazzo nor any of his predecessors struck coins or medals *all'antica*, Fra Pietro and Michelino would surely have known the Carrara medals. It has been pointed out above (page 54) that Giovannino dei Grassi may have based one of his *bas-de-page* portraits of Giangaleazzo in the Florence Psalter-Hours on the frescoed cycle of imperial portraits also painted by Altichiero in the loggia of Can Signorio in Verona.

45. Cf. Hill, 1, 1ff.; Weiss; and Schmitt, who adds to the group a mid-fourteenth-century illustrated collection of works by Suetonius, Livy, and Sallust (Fermo, Bibl. Comunale, MS 81).

ings, are even at first glance more classical in feeling (Figs. 31, 32, 102). Closer examination discloses a specific affinity between Michelino's portraits and antiquity—an affinity apparently unprecedented in earlier surviving works and much imitated in later ones. For his depictions of the fabricated classical ancestors of the Viscontis, Michelino used ancient coins as models. The bearded Anglus, purported son of Ascanius, is probably based on a Hadrianic coin (Figs. 103, 104). Anglus's son, Anglus Junior (Fig. 105), slighter and clean-shaven, apparently to designate his junior status, is based on an Augustan medal of the early, softly modeled type (Fig. 106).[46] The similarities between Giangaleazzo's heraldic devices and Roman coins may have prompted the use of such coins as models for the genealogy. The oak leaves that encircle the medallions in the genealogy evoke the *corona civica* sometimes worn by the emperor on imperial coins and sometimes displayed as a wreath either framing the portrait bust or on the reverse of such coins. The crowns worn by the Viscontis in the Paris genealogy evoke the radiate crowns of Roman emperors that express the concept of the emperor as *sol invictus*—a concept entirely consonant with the inscriptions identifying Giangaleazzo and his rule with the sun on folio 1 of the eulogy.[47]

Rather than inscribing their medallions in the Roman fashion, the designers of the Visconti genealogy inscribed the names of those portrayed above the roundels and amplified the names with *tituli* beneath the medallions. But even in this apparent departure from classical custom, Fra Pietro and Michelino followed what they believed to be classical precedents. In 1952 Theodore Mommsen demonstrated that between 1367 and 1374 the Sala Virorum Illustrium was frescoed in the palace of Francesco il Vecchio da Carrara under the direct supervision of Petrarch, as a visual pendant to the latter's *De viris illustribus*.[48] Around 1500, under unknown circumstances, almost all the Trecento murals in the Carrara palace were lost; but Mommsen further demonstrated that the present decoration of the hall, begun in 1539 or 1540, closely followed the layout of the Trecento cycle, which surely would have been known to both Fra Pietro and Michelino.[49] The format was as follows: between fictive pairs of columns, full-length representations of one or more Roman heroes were painted. Beneath each representation, the hero's name was inscribed above a narrative depiction of one of his exploits. Beneath the narrative scene was a *titulus* inscribed on a painted scroll (Fig. 101). The similarities with the Visconti genealogy are apparent.

---

46. On the Hadrianic and Augustan coins, see J. P. C. Kent, *Roman Coins*, New York, 1978, no. 281 (Hadrian) and no. 127 (Augustus).

47. For Augustus wearing the *corona civica*, see C. H. V. Sutherland and C. M. Kraay, *Catalogue of Coins of the Roman Empire in the Ashmolean Museum*, Pt. 1, Oxford, 1975, no. 22 (a coin of 25–17 B.C.); for portraits framed by oak wreaths, see ibid, nos. 324, 325 (denarii of uncertain date). For the radiate crown, see the dupondius of Tiberius of about A.D. 25, in Kent, no. 150. The radiate crown was used by Altichiero in his Veronese frescoes of the 1360s (Fig. 69). I am grateful to Jean Baptiste Giard and to Patricia Erhard Mottahedeh for generously sharing with me their observations concerning the relationship between the Visconti portraits and antique coins.

48. Mommsen, 95–116.

49. Ibid., 102ff.

But the Visconti genealogy is related to antiquity more directly than through the intermediacy of Petrarch. It was a Roman practice to inscribe *tituli* at the base of family portrait busts.[50] Furthermore, Pliny writes in Book 35 of his *Natural History* (of which, as we have seen, a splendid copy dated 1389 was illuminated in Pavia) that the Romans also painted stemmas. In a dense and somewhat obscure discussion of various kinds of ancestor portraits, Pliny states that "the pedigrees too were traced in a spread of lines running near the several painted portraits."[51] We cannot be certain whether Pliny is here referring to actual painted portraits or to polychromed sculpture between which lines of relationship were drawn. We can be quite certain, however, that yet another statement in Book 35 was known to Pietro and Michelino. Pliny writes that, through the use of ancestor portraits, "always when some member of [a clan] passed away the entire company of his house . . . was present."[52] By appending a pictorial genealogy, redolent with classical allusions, to Giangaleazzo's funeral oration, the creators of Lat. 5888 provided the Duke of Milan with similar support.

Other, mightier patrons of art than Giangaleazzo Visconti commissioned pictorial genealogies in the fourteenth century. Around 1300, a genealogical roll was made, in which the English kings, down to Edward I, are shown as seated figures in roundels forming a "tree" descending from five rows of large medallions containing a pictorial history of the founding of Britain by Brutus.[53] Before 1343, an Angevin genealogy was painted in the Bible now in Malines, made for Robert of Anjou, King of Naples.[54] A mural stemma of the Luxembourg dynasty was painted for Emperor Charles IV between 1351 and 1355 in his castle at Karlstein.[55] In all these cycles, however, the ancient ancestors of the families were represented either in three-quarter or full-length, seated on Gothic thrones and dressed as Gothic monarchs. The disjunction between classical form and classical content articulated by Panofsky had not yet been bridged in these works, as it was to be half a century later in the Visconti manuscript.[56]

Michelino's genealogy of the Viscontis may have inspired the genealogy, which likewise grows from top to bottom, in the borders of LF 57v, the first page in the Florence

50. On Roman *tituli*, see C. Daremberg and E. Saglio, *Dictionnaire des antiquités grecques et romains*, II, pt. I, Paris, 1892, 585, s.v. *elogia*.

51. Pliny, *Natural History*, ed. H. Rackham, IX, Cambridge (Mass.) and London, 1952, 265. Pliny writes, ". . . stemmata vero lineis discurrebant ad imagines pictas" (ed. Rackham, 264). On the illuminated Pliny, which is now in Milan, Bibl. Ambrosiana, MS E 24 inf., see page 25 note 40 above.

52. Ed. Rackham (as in note 51), 265.

53. Professor Lucy Freeman Sandler brought my attention to the genealogical roll, which is now in the Bodleian Library, Bodl. Rolls 3. See W. H. Monroe, "Two Medieval Genealogical Roll-Chronicles in the Bodleian Library," *Bodleian Library Record*, X, 1981,

215–21. Monroe (219f.) proposes that the roll was compiled as evidence in support of the claim of Edward I to dominion over Scotland.

54. On the Angevin genealogy, see O. Pujmanova, "Malířství doby Karlovy a Neapol," *Umění*, XXVII, 1979, 30–57 (fig. 1 on p. 30). For the suggestion that the Malines Bible also provides a precedent for the identification of a Christian ruler with sages of the Old Testament, see page 50 above.

55. For the most recent study of the Karlstein genealogy, including references to the earlier literature, see K. Stejskal, "Die Rekonstruction des Luxemburger Stammbaums auf Karlstein," *Umění*, XXVII, 1978, 535–63.

56. E. Panofsky, *Renaissance and Renascences in Western Art*, New York, 1969, 82ff.

Psalter-Hours to be painted entirely for Filippo Maria. On this and the facing page, LF 58 (Fig. 107), the rather heavy-handed illuminator whom Cadei calls the Genesis Master boldly declares Filippo Maria's ownership of the book begun for Giangaleazzo.[57] Recalling trees of consanguinity that spring from the hands of Adam, the acanthus roundels of the genealogy on LF 57v stem from an historiated initial depicting Adam's transference of blame to Eve.[58] With Michelino's genealogy as a precedent, it is perhaps possible to identify the persons portrayed in the foliate roundels on LF 57v. The highest-ranking ancestor on this leaf, Venus—identifiable by the now-tarnished silver "pillbox" and veiled headdress, which is probably a form of the *polos* worn by this goddess in antiquity— occupies the roundel that grows directly out of the initial. Her husband, Anchises, is represented below, wreathed with roses (sacred to Venus), probably to identify him as her bridegroom. The figure below Anchises in the left border is evidently a female, because her hair is entwined with a ribbon and she wears a hat, which in the genealogy on LF 57 v is apparently reserved for females. This woman may be Hippodameia, the daughter of Anchises and Venus, "whom her father and queenly mother heartily loved in their hall, for that she excelled all maidens of her years in comeliness, and in handiwork, and in wisdom."[59]

The more illustrious child of this union, Aeneas, appears alone in the upper border, a place of honor appropriate to the founder of Italy. The portrait of Aeneas is paired with the even larger representation, in the lower border, of Filippo Maria, who, like Aeneas, is encircled by blue and pink. In the upper-right border, with a veiled head, is Lavinia, Aeneas's wife, gazing at his mother, directly opposite her in the left border, and framed, like Venus, in green and orange-red acanthus. Beneath Lavinia is either her son by Aeneas, Ascanius, or their grandson, Anglus Senior, crowned in laurel. The beardless youth beneath him is probably Anglus Junior. Thus, Filippo Maria, in the lower border, is flanked by a young man and a young woman, both descended from the marriage of Venus to Anchises. The figures in the lower corners may also allude to Filippo Maria's parents, Giangaleazzo and Caterina, who were first cousins (and hence, like Hippodameia and Anglus, collateral members of the same family), who needed a papal dispensation for their marriage. The male and female cousins in the lower corners of trees of consanguinity (Fig. 99) are also suggested by this image. Like Filippo Maria, the young woman and man at either side of him are also shown in three-quarter view, in contrast to the strict profile views of the other figures in the genealogy.

The representation of Filippo Maria is the largest on the page. Set within blue and pink clouds against a golden radiance, it is clearly intended as a parallel to the portrait of his

---

57. Cadei, 1976, 48f.; 1984, 89–93.

58. For a tree of consanguinity springing from Adam's hands, see Ladner, 1979 (as in note 35), fig. 17. The acanthus roundels on LF 57v also evoke the acanthus foliage in Figure 99.

59. *Iliad*, XIII, 429ff. (trans. A. T. Murray, II, London, 1924).

father on BR 115 (Fig. 47). Whereas in the earlier representation, however, Giangaleazzo is bareheaded, Filippo Maria on LF 57v wears a wreath of roses, like the figure we have identified as Anchises. If the rose-wreath is to be understood as an emblem of a bridegroom, Filippo Maria's portrait on this leaf would provide a date for the beginning of his completion of his father's prayerbook—1427, when he married Marie of Savoy, who was in turn descended from the family of Filippo Maria's grandmother, Blanche of Savoy.[60] In that case, Filippo Maria might have been following yet another precedent set by his father: the commissioning of an illuminated prayerbook to commemorate his marriage.

Having established the lineage of Filippo Maria Visconti on folio 57v, the illuminator embellished the borders of the facing folio with an equally emphatic display of his armorials. The emblem devised for Giangaleazzo and inherited by his sons, the dove with the motto *a bon droit,* which is here set in aedicules also evocative of the first part of the manuscript, is the dominant motif in the lateral margins. Viper shields are suspended from branches in the outline of the historiated initial. In the lower margin, a putto, wearing only a gold cape, triumphs over a lion, an allusion to the power of the Duke, who is portrayed in the lower margin of the facing folio. Additional doves, set against blue within a radiant sun, are strewn in all the borders, together with roses, perhaps again a reference to the wedding of the present Count of Virtues. It is striking that among the vast repertory of plant forms that adorn the margins of Banco Rari 397 roses never appear, whereas they continue to appear in many margins of Landau-Finaly 22, for example, LF 68, 131v, 150v, 155, and 166.

The tenth gathering of Landau-Finaly 22 also begins (on LF 72) with a conspicuous array of Filippo Maria's armorials. This leaf emphasizes the military prowess of the Duke of Milan, who is here identified not with his putative classical ancestors but with the Old Testament patriarch, Noah, saving the animals from the flood.

The genealogy created by Petrus de Castelletto and Michelino da Besozzo in Lat. 5888 concludes in a classical mode a manuscript begun in a Christian key. In the opening miniature, the King of Heaven himself confers Christian legitimacy upon Giangaleazzo (Figs. 30, 97), and by implication upon his dynasty, while the genealogy at the end (Figs. 31, 32) confers secular legitimacy upon them by tracing the family back to the founder of Italy, and through him even to the king of pagan gods. During the fifteenth century a keen concern for both Christian authority and a pagan pedigree increasingly obsessed the noble families of Europe, especially those of Italy. Its exquisite visual expression of this dual concern at the dawn of the century places Lat. 5888 among the most innovative as well as the most beautiful manuscripts of its time. Like the other manuscripts made for Giangaleazzo Visconti that have been the subject of this study, it is in all senses an exceptional work of art.

60. This date would accord with the date suggested
for stylistic and other reasons by Kirsch, in Meiss and
Kirsch, 27f.

CATALOGUE

Florence, Biblioteca nazionale
Banco Rari 397 and **Landau-Finaly 22**

Psalter-Hours for the Use of Rome

Banco Rari 397

247 by 175 mm, 151 folios
21 long lines
c. 1388–91, c. 1394–95   Figs. 39–41, 46, 47, 59, 63–67, 70–72, 85, 86, 88, 91

COLLATION: 1^8–18^8 (1–144), 19^7 (145–151, conjugate of 147 is lacking).

11 full-page miniatures, 26 historiated initials 10 or more lines high. Historiated or otherwise illuminated initials 3 lines high at the beginning of each secondary textual division, such as hymns and psalms within offices. Illuminated initials 1 line high at the beginning of each subsidiary verse or other line of text. Many illuminated line endings and illuminated bands between lines of text on pages with illuminated initials 10 lines or more high. Four borders decorated at the beginning of principal texts. Upper, lower, and left borders with foliate decoration on a rectilinear staff on all pages with initials 3 lines high. Armorials, devices, and motto of Giangaleazzo Visconti in almost all decorated borders.

PSALMS 1–150, except Psalm 143, which is lacking (fols. 3–144v), preceded by 4 full-page miniatures: Marriage of Anna and Joachim (fol. 1); Charity of Anna and Joachim (fol. 1v); Anna and Joachim Pray at an Altar, Expulsion of Joachim from the Temple (fol. 2); Joachim Mourns in the Wilderness, Annunciation to Joachim (fol. 2v). Sunday, Matins, Psalm 1, initial, David Playing Psaltery (fol. 3), Psalm 21, initial, David and Angels Bearing Symbols of the Passion (fol. 18); Monday, Matins, Psalm 26, full-page

Annunciation to Anna, Meeting at the Golden Gate, borders with Visconti arms and rabbits (fol. 22v), initial, David Pointing to His Eye (fol. 23); Tuesday, Matins, Psalm 38, full-page Thanksgiving of Anna and Joachim, borders with peacocks and hoopoe (fol. 35v), initial, David Pointing to His Mouth (fol. 36); Wednesday, Matins, Psalm 52, full-page Birth of the Virgin, borders with Visconti arms, stags, falcons (fol. 48), initial, David and the Fool (fol. 48v); Thursday, Matins, Psalm 68, full-page Presentation of the Virgin in the Temple, borders with evangelist symbols (fol. 60v), initial, David in the Water (fol. 61); Friday, Matins, Psalm 80, full-page Virgin Visited by Angels in the Temple (fol. 76), initial, David and Courtiers Playing Musical Instruments (fol. 76v); Saturday, Matins, Psalm 97, full-page Marriage of the Virgin (fol. 90), initial, Courtiers Singing (fol. 90v); Sunday, Vespers, Psalm 109, full-page Annunciation (fol. 104v), initial, Trinity, portrait of Giangaleazzo Visconti in *bas-de-page,* dove of Holy Spirit and falcons in other borders (fol. 105); Monday, Vespers, Psalm 114, initial, David in Prayer, landscape in *bas-de-page,* Justice and Temperance holding Visconti tilting helmets in lateral borders, music-making angels in upper border (fol. 108v), Prime, Psalm 118.1, initial, David Addressing a Group of Men (fol. 111), Terce, Psalm 118.33, David in Prayer (fol. 112v), Sext, Psalm 118.81, initial, David Addressed by the Lord, portrait of Giangaleazzo Visconti in *bas-de-page,* hunting dogs and stags in lateral borders (fol. 115), None, Psalm 118.129, initial, David and the Creator (fol. 117v); Tuesday, Vespers, Psalm 121, initial, David and Music-Making Noblemen (fol. 120v); Wednesday, Vespers, Psalm 126, initial, David Supervises Construction of a Palace (fol. 122v); Thursday, Vespers, Psalm 131, initial, David in Prayer, rabbit hutch in *bas-de-page,* oaks and Visconti arms in other borders (fol. 124v); Friday, Vespers, Psalm 137, initial, Kneeling David Addressed by the Lord, portrait of Giangaleazzo Visconti in *bas-de-page,* arms and devices in other borders (fol. 128); Saturday, Vespers, Psalm 143, initial, David and Goliath (fol. 132), Lauds, Psalm 148, initial, David and Nobles Exalt the Creations of the Lord (fol. 136).

Canticles, hymns, creeds, each preceded by an illuminated initial 10 or more lines high: Canticle of the Three Hebrews, Three Hebrews in the Fiery Furnace, borders with Moses Receiving Law, Baptism of Christ, Visconti armorials (fol. 145); Canticle of Zacharias, Zachiaras (fol. 146v); *Magnificat,* Virgin with Sts. Elizabeth and the Infant John the Baptist (fol. 147v); *Te Deum,* Sts. Ambrose and Augustine (fol. 148v); *Pater Noster,* Sermon on the Mount, borders with Ara Coeli, Magi See Star, Visconti armorials (fol. 150v); Apostles' Creed, Apostles (fol. 151).

Provenance: Giangaleazzo Visconti; Duke Uberto Visconti di Modrone, from whom the manuscript was acquired by the Biblioteca nazionale, Florence, 1969.

Literature: Mongeri, 1885, 350; Toesca, 1912, ed. 1966, 143–46, figs. 157–167; D'Ancona, 1925, 23; Toesca, 1951a, 854; idem, 1951b, iii and passim; Samek Ludovici,

1953, 212–13; Salmi, 1955b, 771, 772; idem, 1956, 42; Cipriani, in Milan, 1958, 32, 76; Arslan, 1963, 60ff.; Cadei, 1970, 18, 22, fig. 7; Cogliati Arano, 1970a, 405–7, figs. 137–61; Meiss and Kirsch, 1972; Treuherz, 1972, 80–82, fig. 51; Cadei, 1976, 18–42, figs. 4–5, 14–21, 24–26, 31; Kirsch, 1981, passim; Cadei, 1984, 41–78; Bollati, 1987, 211–24, figs. 1, 2, 17, 21.

Landau-Finaly 22

250 by 179 mm, 167 folios
21 long lines
c. 1394–95, c. 1428–30 Figs. 29, 53, 60, 73, 75–77, 87, 90, 92, 107

COLLATION: 1^8 (1–8), 2^7 (9–15, fol. 13, inserted on a stub, appears never to have had a conjugate), 3^8–13^8 (16–103), 14^6 (104–109), 15^8–16^8 (110–125), 17^2 (126–127), 18^8–20^8 (128–151), 21^4 (152–155), 22^8 (156–163), 23^4 (164–167).

20 full-page miniatures (rubrics included within the frame on fols. 11, 40v; 1 line of text and rubric within the frame of fol. 25v; rubric above the frame on fols. 80, 80v); 6 miniatures 8 or more lines high, on fols. 10v, 18, 29, 84v, 90v, 95, 117v; 52 historiated initials approximately or precisely as wide as the text line and between 13 and 19 lines high, and 12 illustrated initials approximately half the width of a text line and between 8 and 17 lines high (fols. 59v, 89, 123v, 124v, 142, 146, 147v, 149, 150v, 153, 157v, 166v). Decorative scheme of pages without either miniatures or large historiated initials the same as in Banco Rari 397. Armorials, devices, and motto of Filippo Maria Visconti, as well as those of Giangaleazzo Visconti, in many of the decorated borders. Fourteenth-century painting is not evident after fol. 54.

ATHANASIAN CREED (fols. 1–3), initial, Bishop Addresses the Faithful (fol. 1; 14th-century initial upon burnished gold punched and painted with gold emulsion in the 15th century).

SEVEN PENITENTIAL PSALMS, abbreviated (fols. 3v–4). LITANY (fols. 4v–10v), preceded by 14th-century initial, Lord in Majesty with Saints and Angels, and angels with Visconti arms in borders (fol. 4v); followed by 14th-century miniature 15 lines high, Visitation (fol. 10v).

OFFICE OF THE VIRGIN (fols. 11–56): Matins: preceded by 14th-century full-page Nativity, 15th-century Annunciation to Shepherds in borders (fol. 11); 15th-century initial and borders on 14th-century designs, Lord in Majesty with Theological Virtues, Cardinal

Virtues and Humility (fol. 11v), and Fall of the Rebel Angels (fol. 12); 14th-century initial, Sts. Ambrose and Augustine, and 14th-century borders with Prudence, Temperance, oaks, and Visconti armorials, preceding *Te Deum* (fol. 17); 15th-century Annunciation to Shepherds 11 lines high, at conclusion of Matins (fol. 18). Lauds: full-page miniature, 15th-century on 14th-century design, Adoration of the Magi (fol. 18v); initial, 14th-century, Creation of Heaven and Earth (fol. 19). Prime: preceded by 14th-century full-page Flight into Egypt (fol. 25v) and 14th-century initial, Separation of Firmament from Waters (fol. 26), and followed by 14th-century Massacre of Innocents 11 lines high, painted around explicit (fol. 29). Terce: preceded by full-page Massacre of the Innocents, partially painted in the 14th century, completed in the 15th (fol. 29v); 14th-century initial, Separation of Land from Water, and 14th-century borders with hermits, trees, beehive, animals (fol. 30). Sext: preceded by 15th-century full-page Annunciation of the Death of the Virgin (fol. 33v) and 14th-century initial, Creation of Trees and Plants (fol. 34). None: preceded by full-page Death of the Virgin, and borders with St. George, the Dragon, and the Princess, both begun in the 14th century and completed in the 15th (fol. 37); initial, Creation of Sun, Moon, and Stars, 15th-century on a 14th-century design (fol. 37v). Vespers: preceded by 14th-century full-page Obsequies of the Virgin (fol. 40v), and 15th-century full-page Creation of the Birds (fol. 41). Compline: preceded by initial, Creation of Eve, and borders with animals and angels holding Visconti shields, begun in the 14th century and completed in the 15th (fol. 46v); initial and borders, Creator in Majesty with Choirs of Angels, begun in the 14th century and completed in the 15th (fol. 47). Psalms for Tuesday and Friday preceded by full-page initial, Coronation of the Virgin, and borders with Sts. Catherine of Alexandria, John the Baptist, Barnabas, and Ambrose, Visconti arms and devices, all begun in the 14th century and completed in the 15th (fol. 50v); 14th-century initial, Original Sin, and 14th-century borders with kings and emperors (fol. 51). Psalms for Wednesday and Saturday preceded by 14th-century initial, Adam and Eve Reproached by the Lord (fol. 54).

OFFICE OF THE VIRGIN FOR ADVENT (fols. 57–78): Matins: initial, Adam Blames Eve, borders with Visconti genealogy and portrait of Filippo Maria Visconti in *bas-de-page* (fol. 57v); initial, Eve Blames Serpent, borders with nude infant slaying lion, Visconti devices, roses (fol. 58); initial preceding first lesson, Annunciation (fol. 59v). Lauds: initial, Expulsion from Paradise (fol. 61v). Prime: initial, Adam and Eve Delve, borders with King David, Sts. George and Christopher (fol. 64). Terce: initial, Sacrifice of Cain and Abel, borders with Evangelist symbols and Visconti devices (fol. 66). Sext: initial, Cain Slays Abel (fol. 68). None: initial, Lamech Slays Cain (fol. 70). Vespers: Noah Guides Animals into the Ark, borders with arms and initials of Filippo Maria Visconti (fol. 72). Compline: initial, Sacrifice of Isaac (fol. 74); initial, Isaac Blesses Jacob (fol. 74v).

THREE FULL-PAGE MINIATURES UNASSOCIATED WITH TEXT: Joseph, His Brothers, and the Ishmaelites (fol. 78v), Joseph and Potiphar's Wife (fol. 79), Joseph Blesses His Family (fol. 79v).

OFFICE OF THE DEAD (fols. 80v–109): Vespers: preceded by full-page Baptism of Christ (fol. 80), initial, Moses Placed in Nile and Moses Returned by Pharaoh's Daughter (fol. 80v); first lesson preceded by miniature 16 lines high of Moses Slaying an Egyptian (fol. 84v), full-page Moses and the Burning Bush (fol. 85), and initial, Rod of Moses Changed to a Serpent (fol. 85v); first lesson preceded by initial, Meeting of Moses and Aaron (fol. 89); Second Nocturn preceded by miniature 17 lines high, Miracle of the Rods (fol. 90v) and initial, Plague of Hail (fol. 91), and followed by miniature 11 lines high, Plague of the Firstborn (fol. 95); Third Nocturn preceded by initial, Israelites Leave Egypt (fol. 95v), seventh lesson preceded by initial, Crossing of the Red Sea (fol. 99); Lauds preceded by full-page Pharaoh's Army Drowned (fol. 101v) and initial, Moses Receives the Ten Commandments (fol. 102).

SEVEN PENITENTIAL PSALMS, in full (fols. 110–117v) preceded by full-page Adoration of the Golden Calf (fol. 109v) and initial, Punishment of Korah (fol. 110); LITANY (fols. 117v–126) preceded by miniature 10 lines high, Moses Strikes the Rock (fol. 117v) and initial, Israelites Smitten by a Serpent (fol. 118); Psalm 69 preceded by initial, Brazen Serpent (fol. 123v); prayer preceded by initial, Balaam Opposed by an Angel (fol. 124v).

LITTLE OFFICE OF THE HOLY GHOST (fols. 126v–135): Matins, preceded by three full-page miniatures: Balak Receives Balaam (fol. 126v), Balaam Speaks with God (fol. 127), Balaam Blesses Israel (fol. 127v), and initials, Moses Sees the Promised Land (fol. 128) and Death of Moses (fol. 128v); each remaining hour preceded by 1 initial: Prime, Spies before Jericho (fol. 129v); Terce, Spies of Jericho Hidden (fol. 130v); Sext, Spies of Jericho Escape (fol. 131v); None, Fall of Jericho (fol. 132v); Vespers, Sin of Achan (fol. 133v); Compline, Stoning of Achan (fol. 134v).

OFFICE OF THE PASSION (fols. 135v–154v): Matins, preceded by initials, Punishment of Achan (fol. 136) and Joshua Stops the Sun (fol. 136v); each remaining hour preceded by 1 initial: Lauds, Ehud Presents a Gift to Eglon (fol. 142); Prime, Ehud Slays Eglon (fol. 144v); Terce, Jael Slays Sisera (fol. 146); Sext, Jephtha Sacrifices His Daughter (fol. 147v); None, Samson Slays a Lion (fol. 149); Vespers, Samson Slays the Philistines (fol. 150v); Compline, Foxes with Firebrands (fol. 153).

LITTLE OFFICE OF THE PASSION AND THE HOLY CROSS (fols. 155–167): Matins, preceded by 2 full-page miniatures, The Gates of Gaza (fol. 155) and Samson Betrayed by Delilah (fol. 155v), and 2 initials, Samson Taken Prisoner (fol. 156v) and Samson Blinded (fol.

157); initial, Lord Blessing preceding hymn, "Patris sapientia . . ." (fol. 157v). The following hours are preceded by 1 initial: Prime, Samson at the Mill (fol. 158v); Terce, Death of Samson (fol. 160); Sext, Elkanah and His Family (fol. 161v); None, Hannah Blessed by Eli, and borders with Holy Spirit, Lamb of the Apocalypse, Angels (fol. 163); Vespers, Presentation of Samuel in the Temple (fol. 164v). Compline, preceded by 2 initials, Samuel Called by the Lord, and borders with Justice and Fortitude presenting Visconti tilting helmets (fol. 166); Redeemer (fol. 166v).

PROVENANCE: Giangaleazzo Visconti, Filippo Maria Visconti, Cardinal Ludovico Calini (elevated 1766)? Giulio Cesare Rospigliosi-Pallavicini, Duke of Zagarolo (catalogue of 1851), Baron Horace Landau (acquired 1902), Baron Horace Finaly, *Comune* of Florence (bequest of 1945).

LITERATURE: Toesca, 1912, ed. 1966, 145f., figs. 266, 267; Mondolfo, 1949, 276–77; Pächt, 1950, 18; Toesca, 1951a, 855; idem, 1951b; Samek Ludovici, 1953, 212, 213, 221; Cipriani, 1959, 62f., pls. xxvii, xxviii, fig. 84; Cogliati Arano, 1970a, 407f., figs. 162–67; Meiss and Kirsch, 1972; Cadei, 1976, 18–102; idem, 1984, passim; Kirsch, 1981, passim; Bollati, 1987, 211–24, figs. 3, 7, 8, 14, 16.

EXHIBITED: Rome, 1953, no. 260; Milan, 1958, no. 236.

Milan, Biblioteca capitolare di Sant'Ambrogio
Lat. 6

Ambrosian Missal (Coronation Missal of Giangaleazzo Visconti)

395 by 265 mm, 7 + 318 folios
20 long lines
c. 1370, c. 1395, 1431, late 15th/early 16th century   Figs. 3, 4, 48, 93, 94, 96, 98

A collation of the Missal is not possible in its present binding. Although the illumination dates from the campaign of c. 1395, most of the text was apparently written in 1370. The last leaf of the original text (fol. 295) bears the colophon "Expletum anno domini MoCCCLXX XXIIII maii per Presbiterium Fatium de Castoldi, benefitiale Ecclesiae S. Euphemiae, Portae Romanae Mediolano." A gap between CXLVI and CLI in the red numeration added to the upper borders after the textual additions of 1395 indicates that 4 leaves were excised at this point. The Crucifixion leaf (fol. 156v, blank on the recto) between folios CXLVI and CLI, which is not numbered in the roman sequence, was probably inserted separately from the other additions.

1 full-page miniature, 1 miniature 14 lines high, 1 miniature 10 lines high, 13 historiated initials 5 or more lines high. Acanthus borders, sometimes enclosing Giangaleazzo's armorials, on all pages with miniatures or historiated initials. All illumination by Anovelo da Imbonate, except the Crucifixion (fol. 156v), which is by an associate.

Blank (fol. 1); Visconti genealogy (fols. 2–4); copy, in cursive script of the late 15th or early 16th century, of the letter of 10 September 1395 from Giorgio Azanelli to Andreolo Arese (fols. 4–5); Mass for the Victory of Parabiago (fols. 6–6v); blank (fol. 7); Coronation Mass (fols. 8–25v) preceded by a miniature 10 lines high showing Benesio Cumsinich and Giangaleazzo Visconti seated on a dais in front of Sant'Ambrogio in the presence of prelates, courtiers, armed knights, soldiers, and other spectators; initial 10 lines high showing the coronation of Giangaleazzo as Duke of Milan; borders on this folio with armorials, cheetahs, fruit trees, and other devices of Giangaleazzo (fol. 8). The following Masses are introduced by illuminated initials: Christmas Vigil, Annunciation to the Shepherds (fol. 16); Christmas, Nativity (fol. 28); Epiphany, Adoration of the Magi (fol. 46v); Mass for Giangaleazzo Visconti, Madonna of Mercy with Duke, Duchess, and Courtiers (fol. 176); Vigil of St. Martin, Obsequies of St. Martin (fol. 177); St. Martin, St. Martin Blessing (fol. 178); Vigil of St. Ambrose, Baptism of St. Augustine (fol. 193); St. Ambrose, St. Ambrose with Scourge and Crozier (fol. 198v); Commemoration of the Investiture of St. Ambrose, Investiture of St. Ambrose as Archbishop of Milan (fol. 200); Purification of the Virgin, Presentation of the Christ Child in the Temple (fol. 217); Mass for an Apostle, at the beginning of the Common of Saints, Pentecost (fol. 230); Mass for Male Martyrs, Male Saints (fol. 236). The Ordo of the Mass is preceded by an initial, Celebration of Mass (fol. 148); at the conclusion of the Preface to the Canon, a 14-line miniature, Lord in Majesty, signed in the lower border, above imperial and ducal shields: Hoc de Imbonate opus fecit Anovelus (fol. 153v); Canon preceded by full-page Crucifixion (fol. 156v) and initial, Elevation of the Host at Mass Celebrated by Two Saints, perhaps Philip and James, as in Lat. 757, fol. 329 (fol. 157).

The parchment of fols. 296–318 is thinner than that of the preceding folios. The contents are as follows: Ordo for the Coronation of the King of the Romans (fols. 296–298); additional masses (fols. 299–315); privilege granted to the Canons of Sant'Ambrogio by Sigismund, King of the Romans, dated on fol. 317, 5 November 1431 (fols. 316–17).

Provenance: Chapter Library, Sant'Ambrogio, Milan.

Literature: Mongeri, 1855, 533; Schlosser, 1895, 179; Toesca, 1912, ed. 1966, 148, figs. 274–76; D'Ancona, 1924, 23f.; D'Ancona, Aeschlimann, 1949, 9; Toesca, 1951a, 856; Baroni, Samek Ludovici, 1952, 39; Salmi, 1955b, 777; idem, 1956, 42; Cipriani, 1959, 52, pl. 52; Cogliati Arano, 1970a, 420f., figs. 345–56.

Exhibited: Zurich, 1948, no. 211; Paris, 1950, no. 88; Rome, 1953, no. 263; Milan, 1958, no. 95.

Paris, Bibliothèque nationale
Lat. 757

Franciscan Hours-Missal for the Use of Rome

265 by 207 mm, 1 + 450 + 1 folios
2 cols., 20 lines
c. 1380   Frontispiece; Figs. 9–19, 26, 27, 33, 34, 38, 42, 51, 52, 54–57, 95

Collation, based on catchwords and examination of the manuscript in its binding: 1^4 (1–3, cognate of 1 excised), 2^2 (4–5), 3^4 (6–9), 4^8 (10–17), 5^6 (18–23), 6^8–16^8 (24–111), 17^{12} (112–122, conjugate of 112 lacking), 19^8–32^8 (123–234), 33^6 (235–240), 34^8–59^8 (241–498), 60^2 (449–450).

Table of Contents (fols. 1–3v); arms of Julien Regin (fol. 4); Easter Tables, 1380–1520 (fols. 4v–5); Table of Lunar and Solar Conjunctions (fols. 6–9v); arms of Annet Regin (lower half of fol. 9v); Calendar (Franciscan), verses for Egyptian days, graded, written in black and red, with pink, red, and blue acanthus, set against burnished gold, in the upper, lower, and left margins (fols. 10v–22).

73 full-page miniatures. 135 historiated or otherwise illuminated initials 5 lines high at the beginning of all major texts, such as each of the canonical hours. Illuminated initials 1 or 2 lines high throughout the manuscript at the opening of lesser textual subdivisions, such as versicles and responses. All pages with initials 5 lines high are framed by acanthus arabesques of blue, green, red, and pink, often against burnished gold bands. Beginning with fol. 335, an emblematic knot and the monogram GV appear in many of these borders. Roman numerals of the 14th century in the center of the top margin of each recto, except on fols. 1–3 and 6–9.

DAILY VOTIVE OFFICES (fols. 25–56) illustrated with a full-page miniature preceding each office: Sunday Office of the Trinity, Lord above the Deep (fol. 24); Monday Office of the Dead, Creation of the Firmament (fol. 28); Tuesday Office of the Holy Spirit, Separation of Land from Water and Creation of Trees and Plants (fol. 37); Wednesday Office of All Saints, Creation of Heavenly Bodies (fol. 41); Thursday Office of the Sacrament, Creation of Birds and Fishes (fol. 45); Friday Office of the Holy Cross, Creation of Eve (fol. 49); Saturday Office of the Virgin Mary, Adam, Eve, and Other Animals Worshipping the Creator (fol. 53).

OFFICE OF THE VIRGIN (fols. 58–108v) with full-page miniatures preceding the canonical hours: Matins and Lauds, Christ Taken Prisoner (fol. 57v); Prime, Christ before Pilate (fol. 72v); Terce, Way to Calvary (fol. 76); Sext, Christ Nailed to the Cross (fol. 79); None, Crucifixion (fol. 82); Vespers, Descent from the Cross (fol. 85); Compline, Entombment (fol. 91).

SEVEN JOYS OF THE VIRGIN (fols. 110–112) preceded by full-page miniature: Giangaleazzo Visconti Worships the Madonna and Child (fol. 109v).

OFFICE OF THE DEAD (fols. 115v–146) preceded by full-page miniature: Obsequies of St. Martin (fol. 114v).

PENITENTIAL PSALMS (fols. 148–154v) preceded by full-page miniature, Procession with the Ark of the Covenant (fol. 147); LITANY (Franciscan, fols. 156–161) preceded by full-page miniature, Procession of St. Gregory (fol. 155).

OFFICE OF THE PASSION (fols. 163–184) preceded by full-page miniature: Last Judgment (fol. 162).

PASSION READINGS FROM THE FOUR GOSPELS (fols. 186–224) with a full-page author portrait preceding each reading: St. Matthew (fol. 185v); St. Mark (fol. 197v); St. Luke (fol. 206v); St. John (fol. 216v).

PRAYER TO ST. AUGUSTINE ("Dulcissime Yesu Christe . . . ," fols. 225–227) preceded by a full-page miniature: Baptism of St. Augustine (fol. 224v).

DAILY VOTIVE MASSES (fols. 230–261) with a full-page miniature preceding each mass: Sunday Mass for the Trinity, with a Franciscan *Confiteor*, Trinity (fol. 229v); Monday Mass of the Dead, Man of Sorrows (fol. 237); Tuesday Mass of the Holy Spirit, Dove of the Holy Spirit (fol. 241v); Wednesday Mass of All Saints, Coronation of the Virgin (fol.

245v); Thursday Mass of the Sacrament, Last Supper (fol. 250v); Friday Mass of the Holy Cross, Flagellation (fol. 254v); Saturday Mass of the Virgin Mary, Madonna of Mercy Adored by Giangaleazzo and Caterina Visconti and Courtiers (fol. 258).

ORDINARY OF THE MASS (fols. 263–282v) with two full-page miniatures: Elevation of the Host (fol. 262v); preceding the Canon of the Mass, Crucifixion (fol. 276v).

PROPER OF TIME AND PROPER OF SAINTS (fols. 284–366), with a full-page miniature preceding each mass: Christmas, Nativity (fol. 283v); St. Stephen, Stoning of St. Stephen (fol. 286v); St. John the Evangelist, Miracle of the Poisoned Chalice (fol. 289v); Circumcision, Circumcision of Christ (fol. 291v); Epiphany, Adoration of the Magi (fol. 293v); St. Anthony Abbot, Temptation of St. Anthony (fol. 296v); St. Agnes, Martyrdom of St. Agnes (fol. 298); Purification of the Virgin, Presentation of the Christ Child in the Temple (fol. 299v); Incarnation, Annunciation (fol. 302v); First Sunday in Lent, Temptation of Christ (fol. 305v); Second Sunday in Lent, Transfiguration (fol. 309); Third Sunday in Lent, Healing of the Mute Demoniac (fol. 312); Fourth Sunday in Lent, Feeding of the Multitude (fol. 315v); Fifth Sunday in Lent, Raising of Lazarus (fol. 318v); Passion Sunday, Entry into Jerusalem (fol. 322); Easter, Resurrection (fol. 325); St. George, St. George Slaying the Dragon (fol. 327v); Sts. Philip and James, Sts. Philip and James Officiating at Mass (fol. 329); Ascension, Ascension of Christ (fol. 331v); Pentecost, Descent of the Holy Spirit on the Apostles and the Virgin (fol. 334v); St. John the Baptist, Birth of St. John the Baptist (fol. 337v); Sts. Peter and Paul, Fall of Simon Magus (fol. 340v); St. Mary Magdalen, Magdalen Receives Communion from an Angel (fol. 343v); St. Lawrence, Martyrdom of St. Lawrence (fol. 347); Assumption of the Virgin, Assumption of the Virgin (fol. 349); Birth of the Virgin, Birth of the Virgin (fol. 351v); Invention of the Cross, Finding of the True Cross (fol. 355); St. Michael, St. Michael Defeats Satan (fol. 357v); St. Francis of Assisi, Stigmatization of St. Francis (fol. 360v); St. Catherine of Alexandria, St. Catherine Martyred on the Wheel (fol. 362v); St. Nicholas of Bari, St. Nicholas Giving Dowries (fol. 363v, Woman Holding Knot and Monogram on fol. 364); St. Thomas, Incredulity of St. Thomas (fol. 364v).

COMMON OF SAINTS (fols. 367v–383) with a full-page miniature preceding each common: Mass of the Vigil for an Apostle, Miraculous Draught of Fishes (fol. 367); Mass of a Martyr Bishop, Martyrdom of a Male Saint, possibly Blaise (fol. 369v); Mass of Many Martyrs, Beheading of Male Saints (fol. 372); Mass of a Confessor Bishop, Enthroned Bishop Saint (fol. 374v); Mass of a Confessor not a Bishop, St. Jerome Removes Thorn from Lion's Paw (fol. 377); Mass of Virgin Martyrs, St. Ursula and Eleven Followers (fol. 380).

OFFICE OF ST. JOHN THE BAPTIST (fols. 383v–396) with illuminated 5-line initials, some of them historiated, at the beginning of some of the hours: Matins, initial, with John the

Baptist Chasing a Locust in the Wilderness, and *bas-de-page;* bust of adult John the Baptist with a scroll inscribed "Ecce ag . . ." (fol. 383v); Prime, initial with bust of an elderly prophet holding an uninscribed scroll, looking upward, bust of woman (Virgin Mary?) in upper border (fol. 389); Terce (fol. 390); Sext (fol. 391); None (fol. 392); Vespers (fol. 393); Compline, initial with bust of John the Baptist holding a scroll inscribed "Ecce agnus dei . . ." (fol. 395).

OFFICE OF ST. NICHOLAS OF BARI (fols. 396v–410) with illuminated 5-line initials, some of them historiated, at the beginning of the hours: Matins (fol. 396v); Lauds, initial with head of a woman (fol. 401v); Prime (fol. 403); Terce, initial with a woman holding reddish-yellow ball (fol. 404); Sext (fol. 405v); None, initial with woman holding reddish-yellow ball (fol. 406v); Vespers, initial with gold monogram GV (fol. 407v); Compline, initial with woman holding reddish-yellow ball (fol. 409).

OFFICE OF ST. ANTHONY ABBOT (fols. 410v–424) with illuminated 5-line initials at the beginning of the hours: Matins (fol. 410v); Lauds (fol. 415); Prime (fol. 417); Terce (fol. 418); Sext (fol. 419v); Vespers (fol. 421v); Compline (fol. 423).

OFFICE OF ST. CATHERINE (fols. 424v–434) with illuminated 5-line initials at the beginning of the hours: Matins (fol. 424v); Lauds (fol. 427); Prime (fol. 428v); Terce (fol. 429); Sext (fol. 430); None (fol. 431); Vespers (fol. 432); Compline (fol. 433v).

OBSECRO TE AND OTHER PRAYERS (fols. 434v–439)

CONCLUSION OF MISSAL (fols. 440–450v) preceded by full-page miniature of the Baptism of Christ (fol. 439v); "Exorcismus salis et aque" (fol. 440); "Ordo ad catecuminum faciendum" (fol. 442); "Ordo ad incidendum capillum infantium" (fol. 447); "Benedictio fructuum arborum" (fol. 447v); "Benedictio agni pascalis," "Benedictio panis in ecclesia populo distribuendo") (fol. 448); "Benedictio casei et melis (*sic*) in Pasca," "Benedictio casei et ovorum," (fol. 448v); "Benedictio nove domus," "Benedictio incensi" (fol. 449); "Benedictio pere et baculi" (fol. 449v); "Benedictio vestimentorum" (fol. 450v; 6.5 cm at bottom of fol. 450 has been excised and replaced with blank parchment).

PROVENANCE: Giangaleazzo Visconti? Julien Regin; Annet Regin, apostolic protonotary and precentor of the Cathedral of Clermont-Ferrand, 1528–29; entered the French royal library between 1682 and 1707.

LITERATURE: Couderc, 1908, 19, pls. XLV–XLVI; Toesca, 1912, ed. 1966, 90–93, figs. 131–135; Leroquais, 1924, II, 361–63, pls. LXIX–LXXV; D'Ancona, 1925, 21, pl. XVI; Leroquais, 1927, I, 1–7, pls. VIII–XIII; Toesca, 1951a, 852; Salmi, 1955a, 868; Cipriani,

1959, 47, figs. 30–33, pls. VII–XI; Arslan, 1964, 33–45, figs. 35–39; Cogliati Arano, 1970a, 411–12, figs. 195–254; idem, 1970b; Treuherz, 1972, passim, figs. 2–6; Kirsch, 1981, 71–139; Sutton, 1982, 88–92; idem, 1983, 161; Zaccaria, 1983, 160f.

EXHIBITED: Paris, 1950, no. 104; Milan, 1958, no. 71, pl. XLIV; Paris, 1984, no. 83.

Paris, Bibliothèque nationale
Lat. 5888

Petrus de Castelletto, *Sermo in exsequiis Johannis Galeatii ducis Mediolani*

375 by 240 mm, 1 + 12 folios
48 long lines
1403   Figs. 30–32, 97, 103, 105

COLLATION: 1^6 (1–6), 2^6 (7–12).

Eulogy delivered by the Augustinian friar Petrus de Castelletto, of San Pietro in Ciel d'Oro, Pavia, at the funeral of Giangaleazzo Visconti, Duke of Milan, 20 October 1402, in the Cathedral of Milan (fols. 1–6v) preceded on fol. 1 by a half-page miniature, Giangaleazzo Visconti crowned by the Christ Child, who is seated in the Madonna's lap, in the presence of 12 personified virtues, 8 military angels carrying armorials of Giangaleazzo Visconti, and a host of cherubs and seraphs; initial with an Augustinian friar, probably Petrus de Castelletus, addressing other mourning Augustinians; Giangaleazzo's dove-with-sun device in upper and lower borders and, in all four borders, prophets holding scrolls extolling Giangaleazzo's virtues, inscribed alternately in red and blue, alternating with silver shields of Giangaleazzo, all within four-lobed burnished gold enclosures framed by triplet sprays of green, blue, pink, and gold tapered leaves. Genealogy of the Viscontis, composed by Petrus de Castelletus in 1403, as stated in the rubric at the top of fol. 7 (fols. 7–12v), each page containing six roundels arranged vertically, all, except the first roundel, framed by branches of oak leaves with golden acorns; each roundel except the first (Anchises Wedded to Venus by Jupiter, framed by roots, fol. 7) containing a profile portrait of a male member of the Visconti family, beginning with Aeneas (fol. 7) and concluding with Filippo Maria Visconti (fol. 12v). All the profile portraits are in grisaille, except that of Giangaleazzo Visconti (fol. 12v), which is in color. All the portraits are set against burnished gold. Each is identified by an inscribed name, in either red or blue ink, at the top of the roundel, and a descriptive *titulus*, in red or blue, on a scroll beneath each roundel.

Provenance: Library of the Dukes of Milan in the Castello of Pavia (inventory of 1426, no. 938); brought to the French royal library in the Château of Blois by Louis XII in 1499.

Literature: Delisle, 1868, I, 126, 131; Mazzatinti, 1886, 31–36; Toesca, 1910, 156; Zappa, 1910, 443–49; Durrieu, 1911, 377–90; Toesca, 1912, ed. 1966, 187f., figs. 374–76; D'Ancona, 1925, 50; Baroni, Samek Ludovici, 1952, 44f.; Pellegrin, 1955, 49, 281, A938; Salmi, 1955b, 80if.; Schilling, 1957, 67, 68, fig. 3; Longhi, in Millan, 1958, xxviii; Castelfranchi Vegas, 1966, 22f.; Matalon, 1966; Sellin, 1966; Pellegrin, 1969, 33; Longhi, 1973, 137f.; Castelfranchi Vegas, 1975, 95, 99, 101; Eisler, 1981, 11f.; Kirsch, 1981, 37–77.

Exhibited: Milan, 1958, no. 157, pls. lxiii–lxiv; Vienna, 1962, no. 165; Paris, 1984, no. 94, color pl. xvi.

Paris, Bibliothèque nationale
Smith-Lesouëf 22

Hours-Missal for the Use of Rome

160 by 120 mm, 375 + 3 folios
15 long lines
c. 1380, completed c. 1460
Sister manuscript of Lat. 757   Figs. 20, 22–24, 43–45, 49–50

Collation, based on catchwords and examination of manuscript in binding: 1^8 (1–8), 2^6 (9–14), 3^4 (15–18), 4^8–6^8 (19–42), 7^2 (43–44), 8^4 (45–48), 9^8 (49–56), 10^4–11^4 (57–64), 12^8–17^8 (65–112), 18^8 (113–119, conjugate of 114 lacking), 19^8–29^8 (120–208), 30^4–31^4 (209–216), 32^6 (217–222), 33^8–41^8 (223–294), 42^2 (295–296), 43^8–48^8 (297–344), 49^4 (345–348), 50^8–52^8 (349–372), 53^6 (373–378).

Easter Tables, 1380–1499 (fols. 1–2v); Calendar, graded, written in black and red, with red, pink, blue, green, and gold grape-leaf rinceaux in borders, sometimes enclosing an emblematic knot, the monogram GV, or acorns (fols. 3–14v); Table of Contents (on 4 of 7 unnumbered inserted leaves, of which the last 3 are blank).

21 full-page miniatures. Illuminated initials 5 lines high at the beginning of all major texts, such as each of the canonical hours. Illuminated initials 1 or 2 lines high throughout the manuscript at the opening of lesser textual subdivisions, such as versicles and

responses. All pages with initials 5 lines high are framed by red, pink, green, and blue grape-leaf rinceaux in all four borders, with gold staves in the lateral borders of all such pages completed in the 14th century. An emblematic knot and the monogram GV appear regularly in borders begun or entirely painted in the 14th century. Red and blue roman numerals of the 14th century in the center of the top margin of each recto; roman numeration continued, sometimes in purple and gold, in the 15th century. Roman numerals incorrect on fols. 116, 118, and 119. Where no other designation is given, the miniatures were painted entirely in the 14th century.

OFFICE OF THE VIRGIN (fols. 15v–69v) with a full-page miniature and a 5-line initial at the beginning of each of the hours, and half-page miniatures, all of the 15th century, at the end of Prime, Sext, and Vespers. Matins, Giangaleazzo Visconti Presented to the Virgin and Child by a Crowned Female Saint (probably Catherine of Alexandria), St. Anthony Abbot, and St. Christopher (fol. 15), Virgin and Child in initial (fol. 15v); Lauds, Flagellation (fol. 24), prophet in initial (fol. 24v); Prime, Christ before Pilate (fol. 34v), prophet, probably St. John the Baptist, in initial (fol. 35), Birago Master, half-page Mocking of Christ (fol. 38); Terce, Way to Calvary (fol. 38v), prophet in initial (fol. 39); Sext, Christ Nailed to the Cross (fol. 41v), prophet in initial (fol. 42), Belbello da Pavia, half-page Adoration of the Magi, (fol. 44v); None, Crucifixion, completed in the 15th century (fol. 45), 15th century, initial with a prophet (fol. 45v); Vespers, Descent from the Cross, completed in the 15th century (fol. 48v), Birago Master, Madonna and Child in initial (fol. 49), Annunciation to the Shepherds (fol. 56v); Compline, Entombment (fol. 57), prophet in initial (fol. 57v); PSALMS FOR THE OFFICE OF THE VIRGIN (fols. 61v–69v) preceded by two full-page miniatures and followed by a half-page miniature, all by the Birago Master: Harrowing of Hell (fol. 61), Resurrection (fol. 61v); Maries at the Tomb (fol. 62).

OFFICE OF THE VIRGIN FOR ADVENT (fols. 70–78v).

PRAYERS (fols. 79v–83v), beginning with O Intemerata, preceded by a full-page miniature by the Birago Master, Madonna of Humility (fol. 79).

SEVEN JOYS OF THE VIRGIN (fols. 84v–88v), preceded by a full-page Annunciation (fol. 84).

DAILY VOTIVE OFFICES (fols. 89v–118): Sunday Office of the Trinity, Birago Master, full-page Lord Admonishing Adam and Eve in Paradise (fol. 89), Birago Master, prophet in initial (fol. 89v); Monday Office of the Dead: Vespers, 15th century, skeleton in coffin in initial (fol. 92); Matins, 15th century, skull in initial (fol. 95); Lauds, 15th century, praying man in initial (fol. 98v); Terce, 15th century, King David in initial (fol. 103v);

Tuesday Office of the Holy Spirit, 14th century, Dove of the Holy Spirit in initial (fol. 104); Wednesday Office of All Saints, 15th century, Virgin and other saints in initial (fol. 106v); Thursday Office of the Holy Sacrament, 15th-century, Christ Blessing Sacraments in initial (fol. 109); Friday Office of the Holy Cross, 14th century, bearded prophet in initial, margins completed in the 15th century (fol. 112); Saturday Office of the Virgin Mary, prophet in initial (fol. 115).

INTROIT OF THE MASS (fols. 120–121v) preceded by Birago Master, full-page Last Supper (fol. 119v).

DAILY VOTIVE MASSES (fols. 122–151).

ORDINARY OF THE MASS (fols. 151v–178) preceded by a full-page Crucifixion, begun in the 14th century and completed in the 15th (fol. 168v).

PROPER OF TIME AND PROPER OF SAINTS (fols. 178v–212): Christmas (178v–182); Epiphany (fols. 182v–186); Easter (fols. 186v–188); Purification of the Virgin (fols. 188v–192); Annunciation (192v–196); Assumption of the Virgin (fols. 196v–198v); St. Anthony Abbot (fols. 199–202); St. Catherine of Alexandria (fols. 202v–204v); St. James Apostle (fols. 205–207); St. Mary Magdalen (fols. 207v–212) followed by Birago Master, half-page Christ in the House of Mary and Martha (fol. 212).

PRAYER OF ST. AUGUSTINE (Dulcissime Ihesu Christe . . . , fols. 214–217) preceded by Birago Master, full-page Baptism of St. Augustine (fol. 213).

PSALMS (fols. 217v–222v).

OFFICE OF THE DEAD (fols. 223v–264) preceded by a full-page miniature by the Birago Master, possibly begun in the 14th century, Funeral of a Nobleman (fol. 223, much rubbed, perhaps defaced, in area around the deceased, who wears a hooded red robe lined in white); skeleton in an initial, begun in the 14th century and completed in the 15th (fol. 224).

PENITENTIAL PSALMS (fols. 265–274v) preceded by an initial begun in the 14th century and completed in the 15th, David in the Water (fol. 265). LITANY (fols. 275–284).

PASSION READING FROM ST. MATTHEW (fols. 286–304v) preceded by Birago Master, full-page miniature of Lord and Lady Presented by Sts. Anthony Abbot and Catherine of Alexandria to the Man of Sorrows (fol. 285v); 15th-century, full-page Agony in the Garden (fol. 295); 14th-century, full-page Christ Taken Prisoner (fol. 296).

Unillustrated Passion readings: St. Mark (fols. 305–319v); St. Luke (fols. 320–334); St. John (fols. 334v–348).

Conclusion of the Missal (fols. 349–375): "Incipit ordo ad benedicendum aquam" preceded by a full-page miniature, begun in the 14th century and completed in the 15th, Baptism of Christ (fol. 348v); "In festo Purificationis" (fol. 354) followed by a full-page miniature by the Birago Master, Purification of the Virgin (fol. 359); "In die palmarum" (fol. 360); "Benedictio panis in ecclesia populo distribuendo, Benedictio agni et aliarum carnium" (fol. 372v); "Benedictio fructum novarum arborum" (fol. 373v); "Bendictio uve" (fol. 374); "Benedictio domus" (fol. 374v).

Provenance: Caterina Visconti? Bianca Maria Sforza? Smith-Lesouëf donation to the Bibliothèque nationale, Paris, 1913.

Literature: Leroquais, 1927, 1, 6f.; idem, 1943, 10–13, pls. vii–x; Alexander and de la Mare, 1969, 149; Cogliati Arano, 1970a, 410f., figs. 183–94; idem, 1970b; Kirsch, 1981, 71–139; Sutton, 1982, 92–94; idem, 1983, 161; Zaccaria, 1983, 160f.

Exhibited: Paris, 1984, no. 85.

GENEALOGY
The Viscontis

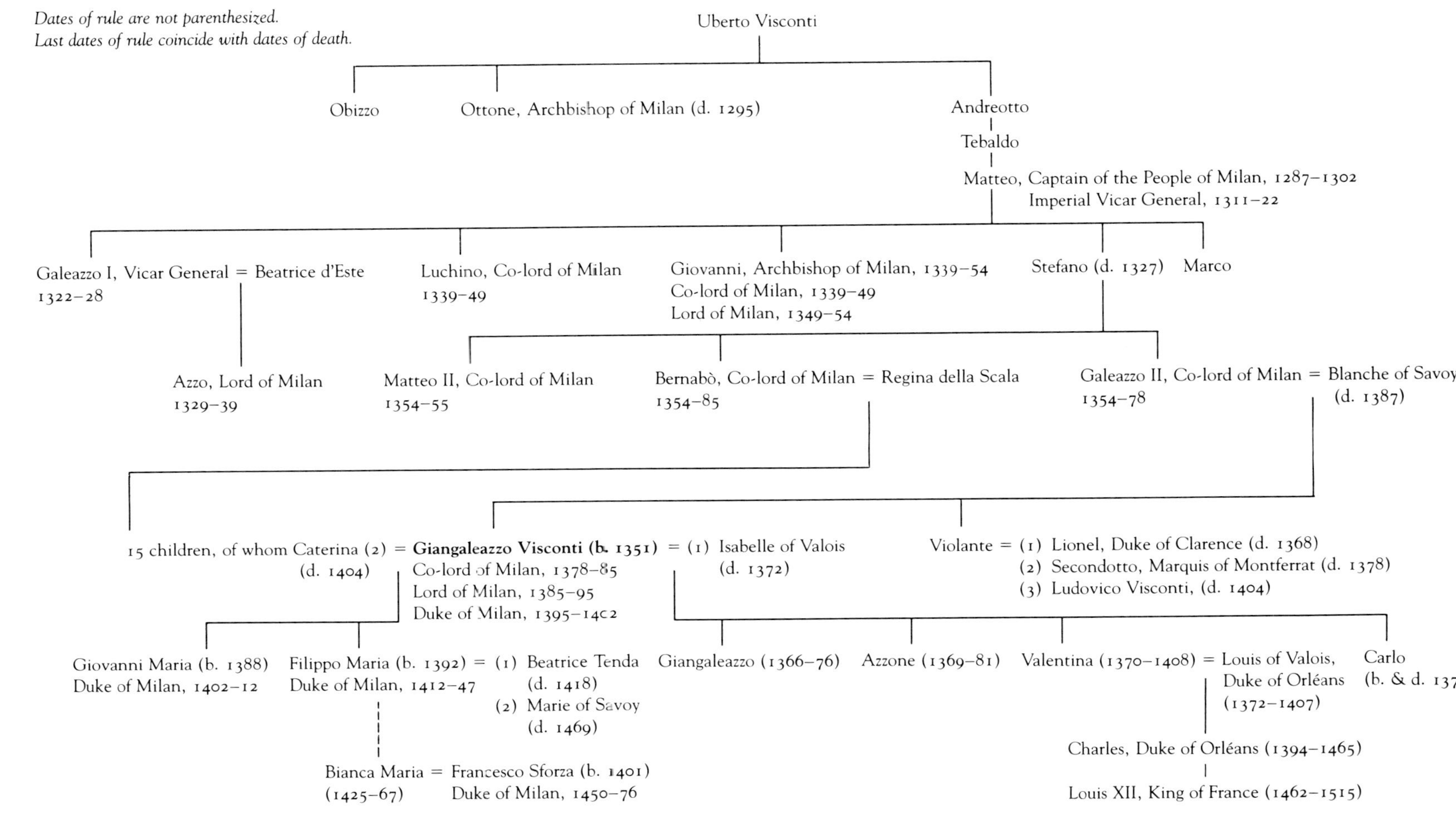

SELECTED BIBLIOGRAPHY

Abbreviations:

ASL   *Archivio storico lombardo*
RIS   *Rerum Italicarum Scriptores,* ed. L. Muratori, 1723–51; New Series, ed. G. Carducci, 1900–1917.

SOURCES EARLIER THAN 1600

Ambrose, Saint. *Hexameron,* ed. J. J. Savage (Fathers of the Church, 42). New York, 1961.
Annales mediolanensis, RIS, xvi, 642–839.
Annali della Fabbrica del Duomo di Milano dall'origine fino al presente, 6 vols. and appendixes (2 vols.). Milan, 1877–85.
Azario, P. *Liber gestorum in Lombardia,* in *RIS,* xvi, pt. 4, 291–423.
The Bestiary. See White.
Castelletto, P. de. *Sermo factus, & recitatus . . . in exsequiis quondam Illustrissimi Domini Ducis Mediolani . . . , RIS,* xvi, 1038–50.
Corio, B. *Storia di Milano,* ed. A. Morisi Guerra, 2 vols. Turin, 1978.
Decembrio, P. C. *Vita di Filippo Maria Visconti,* trans. and ed. E. Bartolini. Milan, 1983.
Fiamma, G. *Opusculum de rebus gestis ab Azone, Luchino, et Johanne Vicecomitibus ab anno MCCCXXVIII usque ad annum MCCCXLII, RIS,* xii, 997–1050.
Giovio, P. *Vita duodecim Vicecomitum Mediolani Principum.* Paris, 1549.
Gualla, J. *Sanctuarium Papie,* Pavia, 1505.
Morigi, P. *Il Duomo di Milano.* 1597.
Ordo, qui tentus fuit pro obsequio et associatione funeris . . . Illustrimi Principis et Excellentissimi Domini, D. Johannis Galeaz Vicecomitis, Ducis Mediolani, & c., RIS, xvi, 1029–36.
"Testamento di Bianca di Savoja vedova di Galeazzo Visconti." In L. Osio, *Documenti diplomatici tratti dagli Archivj Milanesi,* i, pt. ii, no. 192. Milan, 1865.
"Testamento del duca Giovanni Galeazzo Visconti." In L. Osio, *Documenti diplomatici tratti dagli Archivj Milanesi,* i, pt. ii, no. 223. Milan, 1865.
Vannozzo, F. di. *Le rime di Francesco di Vannozzo,* ed. A. Medin. Bologna, 1928.
Voragine, J. da. *Golden Legend,* ed. G. Ryan and H. Ripperger, 2 vols. New York, 1969.

OTHER WORKS

Alberzoni, M. P. "Insediamenti francescani in Milano (secolo XIII–XIV)." In *Il Francescanesimo in Lombardia: Storia e arte.* Milan, 1983.
Alexander, J. J. G., and A. C. de la Mare. *The Italian Manuscripts in the Library of Major J. R. Abbey.* London, 1969.
Arslan, E. "Aspetti della pittura lombarda nella seconda metà del Trecento." *Critica d'Arte,* xi, 1964, 33–45.
———. "Riflessioni sulla pittura gotica 'internazionale' in Lombardia nel tardo Trecento." *Arte lombarda,* viii, no. 2, 1963, 25–66.
Avril, F. *See* Paris, Bibliothèque nationale.
Baroni, C. "Scultura gotica." In *Storia di Milano,* v, 729–812. Milan, 1955.

————. *Scultura gotica lombarda.* Milan, 1944.

————, and S. Samek Ludovici. *La pittura lombarda del Quattrocento.* Messina and Florence, 1952.

Bartolini, E. *See* Decembrio.

Bellonci, M. "I dodici Cesari lombardi." In *I Visconti a Milano,* 7–121. Milan, 1977.

Beltrami, L. *Il castello di Milano.* Milan, 1894.

————. *Storia documentata della Certosa di Pavia.* Milan, 1896.

Berti Toesca, E. *Il Tacuinum sanitatis della Biblioteca Nazionale di Parigi.* Bergamo, 1937.

Bettini, S. *Le pitture di Giusto de' Menabuoi nel Battistero del Duomo di Padova.* Venice, 1960.

Bollati, M. "Giovannino e Salomone de Grassi." *Arte cristiana,* LXXV, 1987, 211–24.

Boulton, D'A. J. D. "Insignia of Power: The Use of Heraldic and Paraheraldic Devices by Italian Princes, c. 1350–c. 1500." In *Art and Politics in Late Medieval and Early Renaissance Italy: 1250–1500.* Notre Dame: University of Notre Dame, in press.

————. *The Knights of the Crown: The Monarchical Orders of Knighthood in Later Medieval Europe, 1325–1520.* Woodbridge (Suffolk), 1987.

Bueno de Mesquita, D. M. *Giangaleazzo Visconti, Duke of Milan (1351–1402)* Cambridge, 1941.

Cadei, A. *Belbello miniatore lombardo: Artisti del libro alla corte dei Visconti.* Rome, 1976.

————. "I capitelli più antichi del Duomo di Milano." In *Il Duomo di Milano,* ed. M. L. Gatti Perer, 2 vols., 1969, I, 77–88.

————. "Giovannino de Grassi nel Taccuino di Bergamo." *Critica d'arte,* XVII, 1970, 17–36.

————. *Studi di miniatura lombarda: Giovannino de Grassi, Belbello da Pavia.* Rome, 1984.

Castelfranchi Vegas, L. *International Gothic Art in Italy.* Leipzig, 1966.

————. "Il Libro d'Ore Bodmer di Michelino da Besozzo e i rapporti tra miniatura francese e miniatura lombarda agli inizi del Quattrocento." In *Etudes d'art français offertes à Charles Sterling,* ed. A. Châtelet and N. Reynaud, 91–103. Paris, 1975.

Cattaneo, E. "I momenti spirituali della costruzione del Duomo." In *Il Duomo di Milano,* ed. M. L. Gatti Perer, 2 vols., II, 53–72. Milan, 1969.

Chamberlin, E. R. *The Count of Virtue.* London, 1965.

Cipriani, R. Descriptions of Illuminated Manuscripts, in *Arte lombarda dai Visconti agli Sforza.* Milan, 1959.

————. *See also* Milan, 1958.

Cogliati Arano, L. Catalogue in Gengaro, M. L., and L. Cogliati Arano, *Miniature lombarde,* Milan, 1970.

————. "Due libri d'ore lombardi eseuiti verso il 1380." *Arte Lombarda,* no. 15, 1970, 37–44.

Cognasso, F. "L'egemonia di Milano nell'Italia settentrionale" and "Firenze contro Milano." In *Storia di Milano,* V, 521–40 and 541–47. Milan, 1955.

Couderc, C. *Album de portraits d'après les collections du département des manuscrits.* Paris, 1908.

Courcelle, P. *Recherches sur Saint Ambroise: "Vies" anciennes, culture, iconographie.* Paris, 1973.

D'Ancona, P. *La miniature italienne du Xe au XVIe siècle.* Paris, 1925.

D'Ancona, P., and E. Aeschlimann. *Dictionnaire des miniaturistes du moyen âge et de la renaissance dans les différentes contrées de l'Europe.* Milan, 1949.

Delaissé, L. M. J. "Remaniements dans quelques manuscrits de Jean de Berry." *Gazette des Beaux-Arts,* LXII, 1963, 123–46.

Delisle, L. *Le Cabinet des manuscrits de la Bibliothèque impériale,* 3 vols. Paris, 1868–91.

Dell'Acqua, G. A. "I Visconti e le arti." In *I Visconti a Milano,* 123–217. Milan, 1977.

Durrieu, P. "Michelino da Besozzo et les relations entre l'art italien et l'art français." *Mémoires de l'Académie des Inscriptions et Belles Lettres,* XXXVIII, 2, 1911, 377–90.

Eisler, C. *The Prayer Book of Michelino da Besozzo.* New York, 1981.

Galli, E. "Sulle origini araldiche della Biscia Viscontea," *ASL,* XLVI, 1919, 363–81.

Gilbert, C. "The Fresco by Giotto in Milan." *Arte lombarda,* nos. 47/48, 1977, 31–72.

Giulini, G. *Memorie spettanti alla storia, al governo ed alla descrizione della Città e Campagna di Milano,* 7 vols., vols. V and VI. Milan, 1854–57.

Hamburger, J. "The Rothschild Canticles: (Yale University, Beinecke Rare Books and Manuscripts Library, MS 404), Art and Mysticism in Flanders and the Rhinelands, circa 1330." Ph.D. diss., Yale University, 1987.

Hatfield, R. "The Compagnia de' Magi." *Journal of the Warburg and Courtauld Institutes*, XXXIII, 1970, 107–61.

Heimann, A. "Trinitas Creator Mundi," *Journal of the Warburg Institute*, II, 1938, 42–52.

Hill, G. F. *A Corpus of Italian Medals of the Renaissance before Cellini*, 2 vols. London, 1930.

Hofmann, H. *Die Heiligen Drei Könige* (Reinisches Archiv, 94). Bonn, 1975.

Jarry, E. *La vie politique de Louis de France, duc d' Orléans, 1372–1407*. Paris and Orléans, 1889.

Kirsch, E. W. "Belbello da Pavia, *Annunciation*," no. 20 (66–69), and "The Master of the Murano Gradual," no. 21 (70–74), in *Medieval and Renaissance Miniatures from the National Gallery of Art*, ed. G. Vikan. Washington, D.C., 1975.

———. "The Visconti Hours: The Patronage of Giangaleazzo Visconti and the Contribution of Giovannino dei Grassi." Ph.D. diss., Princeton University, 1981.

———. *See also* Meiss and Kirsch.

Krása, J. *Die Handschriften König Wenzels IV.* Vienna, 1971.

Leroquais, V. *Les Livres d'heures manuscrits de la Bibliothèque nationale*, 2 vols. and atlas. Paris, 1927; *Supplément*, Mâcon 1943.

———. *Les Psautiers manuscrits latins des Bibliothèques publiques de France*, 2 vols. Mâcon, 1940–41.

———. *Les Sacramentaires et missels manuscrits des bibliothèques publiques de France*, 4 vols. Paris, 1924.

Levi D'Ancona, M. *The Iconography of the Immaculate Conception in the Middle Ages and Early Renaissance* (Monographs on Archeology and Fine Arts, VII), 1957.

———. "The Rabbit Hutch and Political Allusions in the Visconti Hours." *Arte lombarda*, no. 50, 1978, 7–19.

Litta, P. *Famiglie celebri di Italia*, 16 vols. Milan, 1819–[1899?].

London, Sotheby's. *Hidden Friends: The Comites Latentes Collection of Illuminated Manuscripts* (exhibition catalogue), compiled by C. de Hamel, 1985.

Longhi, R. *Lavori in Valpadana dal Trecento al primo Cinquecento*. Florence, 1973.

Magenta, C. *I Visconti e gli Sforza nel Castello di Pavia*, 2 vols. Milan, 1883.

Mariani Canova, G. "Il recupero di un complesso librario dimenticato: I corali quattrocenteschi di S. Giorgio Maggiore a Venezia." *Arte veneta*, XXVII, 1973, 38–64.

Matalon, S. *Affreschi lombardi del Trecento*. Milan, 1963.

Mazzatinti, G. "Alcuni codici latini visconteosforzeschi della Biblioteca Nazionale di Parigi." *ASL*, XIII, 1886, 17–58.

Meiss, M. *French Painting in the Time of Jean de Berry: The Late Fourteenth Century and the Patronage of the Duke*, London, 1967; *The Boucicaut Master*, London, 1968; *The Limbourgs and Their Contemporaries*, New York, 1974.

———. *Painting in Florence and Siena after the Black Death*. Princeton, 1951.

———. "Ovum Struthionis: Symbol and Allusion in Piero della Francesca's Montefeltro Altarpiece." In *The Painter's Choice: Problems in the Interpretation of Renaissance Art*, 105–41. New York, 1976.

———, and E. W. Kirsch. *The Visconti Hours*. New York, 1972.

Mellini, G. L. *Altichiero e Jacopo Avanzi*. Milan, 1965.

Merlini, E. "Il trittico eburneo della Certosa di Pavia: Iconografia e committenza–Parte II." *Arte cristiana*, LXXIV, 1986, 139–54.

Milan, Palazzo Reale. *Arte lombarda dai Visconti agli Sforza*. Milan, 1958. (Manuscript entries by R. Cipriani.)

Mommsen, T. "Petrarch and the Decoration of the Sala Virorum Illustrium in Padua." *Art Bulletin*, XXXIV, 1952, 95–116.

Mondolfo, A. "La Biblioteca Landau-Finaly." In *Studi di bibliografia e di argomento romano in memoria di L. De Gregori*, ed. C. Arcamone Barletta, 265–85. Milan, 1949.

Mongeri, G., in F. D'Adda and G. Mongeri, "L'arte del minio nel ducato di Milano." *ASL*, 1885, XII, 330–56, 528–57, 759–96.

Muir, D. *A History of Milan under the Visconti.* London, 1924.

New Haven, Yale University. *Medieval and Renaissance Manuscripts at Yale* (*The Yale University Library Gazette*, LII, no. 4 1978).

New York, Pierpont Morgan Library. *Italian Manuscript Painting 1300–1550,* exhibition handlist, 1984–85.

Pacchioni, G. "Belbello da Pavia e Gerolamo da Cremona, miniatori." *L'arte,* XVIII, 1915, 241–52, 343–72.

Pächt, O. "Early Italian Nature Studies and the Early Calendar Landscape." *Journal of the Warburg and Courtauld Institutes,* XIII, 1950, 13–47.

Paris, Bibliothèque nationale. *Dix siècles d'enluminure italienne (VIᵉ–XVIᵉ siècles),* ed. F. Avril et al. Paris, 1984.

———. *Trésors des bibliothèques d'Italie.* Paris, 1950.

Pellegrin, E. *La Bibliothèque des Visconti et des Sforza, ducs de Milan au XVᵉ siècle.* Paris, 1955; *Supplément,* Florence, 1969.

Plummer, J. *Liturgical Manuscripts for the Mass and the Divine Office.* New York, 1964.

Ponzoni, C. *Le chiese di Milano.* 1930.

Ragusa, I. "The Egg Reopened." *Art Bulletin,* LIII, 1971, 435–43.

Riboldi, E., and G. Seregni, "Studii e ricerche per il repertorio diplomatico visconteo." *ASL,* XXXI, 1904, 204–17.

Robb, D. "The Iconography of the Annunciation in the Fourteenth and Fifteenth Centuries." *Art Bulletin,* XVIII, 1936, 480–526.

Romano, G. "Il primo matrimonio di Lucia Visconti e la rovina di Bernabò." *ASL,* XX, 1893, 585–611.

Salmi, M. *La miniatura italiana.* Milan, 1956.

———. "La pittura e la miniatura gotica in Lombardia." In *Storia di Milano,* Milan, V, 1955, 815–74; VI, 1955, 767–855.

Samek Ludovici, S. "L'alfabeto di Giovannino dei Grassi." *Linea grafica,* V, 1952, 117–22.

Samek Ludovici, S. "Belbello da Pavia." *Bollettino d'arte,* XXXVIII, 1953, 211–24.

———. *See also* Baroni and Samek Ludovici.

Salmon, P. *Les manuscrits liturgiques latins de la Bibliothèque Vaticane,* II (*Sacramentaires, Epistoliers, Evangéliaires, Graduels, Missels*) [Studi e Testi, 253], Biblioteca Apostolica Vaticana, 1969; IV (*Les Livres de lecture de l'office, Les Livres de l'office du chapitre, Les Livres d'heures*) [Studi e Testi, 267], Biblioteca Apostolica Vaticana, 1971.

Saxl, F. *Verzeichnis astrologischer und mythologischer illustrierter Handschriften des lateinischen Mittelalters,* II (*Die Handschriften der National-Bibliothek in Wien*), Heidelberg, 1927; III (with H. Meier, *Handschriften in englischen Bibliotheken*), London, 1953.

Schilling, R. "Ein Gebetbuch des Michelino da Besozzo." In *Münchner Jahrbuch der bildenden Kunst,* VIII, 1957, 65–80.

Schlosser, J. von. "Ein veronesisches Bilderbuch und die höfische Kunst des XIV. Jahrhunderts." *Jahrbuch der Kunsthistorische Sammlungen des allerhöchsten Kaiserhauses,* XVI, 1895, 144–230.

Schmidt, G. " 'Andreas Me Pinsit': Frühe Miniaturen von Nicolò di Giacomo und Andrea de' Bartoli in dem bologneser Offiziolo der Stiftsbibliothek Kremsmünster." *Wiener Jahrbuch für Kunstgeschichte,* XXVI, 1973, 57–73.

Schmitt, A. "Zur Wiederbelebung der Antike im Trecento." *Mitteilungen des Kunsthistorischen Institutes in Florenz,* XVIII, 1974, 167–218.

Seiler, P. "Das Grabmal des Azzo Visconti in San Gottardo in Mailand." In *Scultura e monumento sepolcrale del Tardo Medioevo a Roma e in Italia.* In press.

Sellin, D. "Michelino da Besozzo." Ph.D. diss., Bryn Mawr College, 1966.

Sevesi, P. M. "Il culto alla Concezione di Maria nella cappella Regio-Ducale di S. Gottardo e in S. Francesco di Milano." *Ambrosius,* XXX, 1954, 327–33.

Seznec, J. *The Survival of the Pagan Gods: The Mythological Tradition and Its Place in Renaissance Humanism and Art.* Princeton, 1972.

Stejskal, K. *European Art in the Fourteenth Century.* London, 1978.

Sutton, K. "The Original Patron of the Lombard Manuscript Latin 757 in the Bibliothèque Nationale, Paris." *Burlington Magazine,* CXXIV, 1982, 88–94.

———. Reply to Letter of M. Zaccaria. *Burlington Magazine*, cxxv, 1983, 161.

Toesca, P. "Michelino da Besozzo e Giovannino de' Grassi." *L'arte*, viii, 1905, 321–39.

———. "Le miniature dell'Elogio funebre di Gian Galeazzo Visconti." *Rassegna d'arte*, x, 1910, 156–59.

———. *La pittura e la miniatura nella Lombardia dai più antichi monumenti alla metà del Quattrocento*, 2d ed. Turin, 1966 (1st ed., Milan, 1912).

———. *Il Trecento.* Turin, 1951.

———. *L'ufiziolo visconteo Landau-Finaly.* Florence, 1951.

Treuherz, J. "The Border Decoration of Milanese Manuscripts 1350–1420." *Arte lombarda*, no. 36, 1972, 71–82.

Trexler, R. C. "The Magi Enter Florence: The Ubriachi of Florence and Venice." *Studies in Medieval and Renaissance History*, 1, 1978, 129–218.

———. "Triumph and Mourning in North Italian Magi Art." In *Art and Politics in Late Medieval and Early Renaissance Italy: 1250–1500.* Notre Dame: University of Notre Dame, in press.

I Visconti a Milano, with texts by M. Bellonci, G. A. Dell'Acqua, and C. Perogalli. Milan, 1977.

University of Glasgow, Library. *The Glory of the Page: Medieval and Renaissance Illuminated Manuscripts from the Glasgow University Library*, ed. N. Thorp. London, 1987.

Valeri, N. *L'Italia nell'età dei principati dal 1343 al 1516.* Verona, 1969.

Vienna, Kunsthistorisches Museum. *L'Art européen vers 1400.* Vienna, 1962.

Weiss, R. *The Renaissance Discovery of Classical Antiquity.* Oxford, 1969.

Welch, E. S. "Galeazzo Maria Sforza and the Castello di Pavia, 1469." *Art Bulletin*, lxxi, 1989, 352–75.

White, T. H., trans. and ed. *The Bestiary.* New York, 1960.

Wieck, R. S. *Time Sanctified: The Book of Hours in Medieval Art and Life.* New York, 1988.

Zaccaria, M. Letter to the Editor. *Burlington Magazine*, cxxv, 1983, 160f.

Zappa, G. "Michelino da Besozzo miniatore." *L'arte*, xiii, 1910, 443–49.

Zurich, Kunsthaus. *Kunstschätze der Lombardei, 500 vor Christus/1800 nach Christus.* Zurich, 1948–49.

INDEX

ILLUSTRATIONS

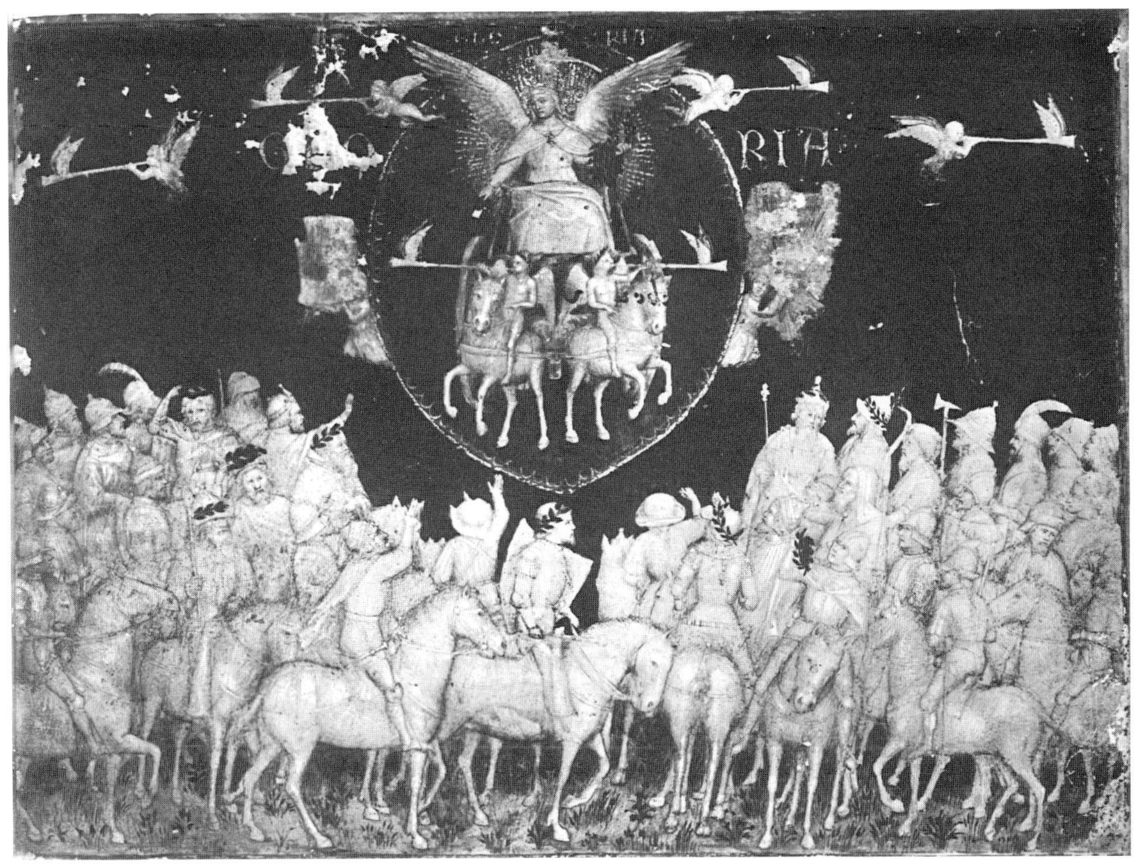

Fig. 1. Altichiero, c. 1380, Triumph of Fame. Paris, Bibl. nat., Lat. 6069 I, fol. 1

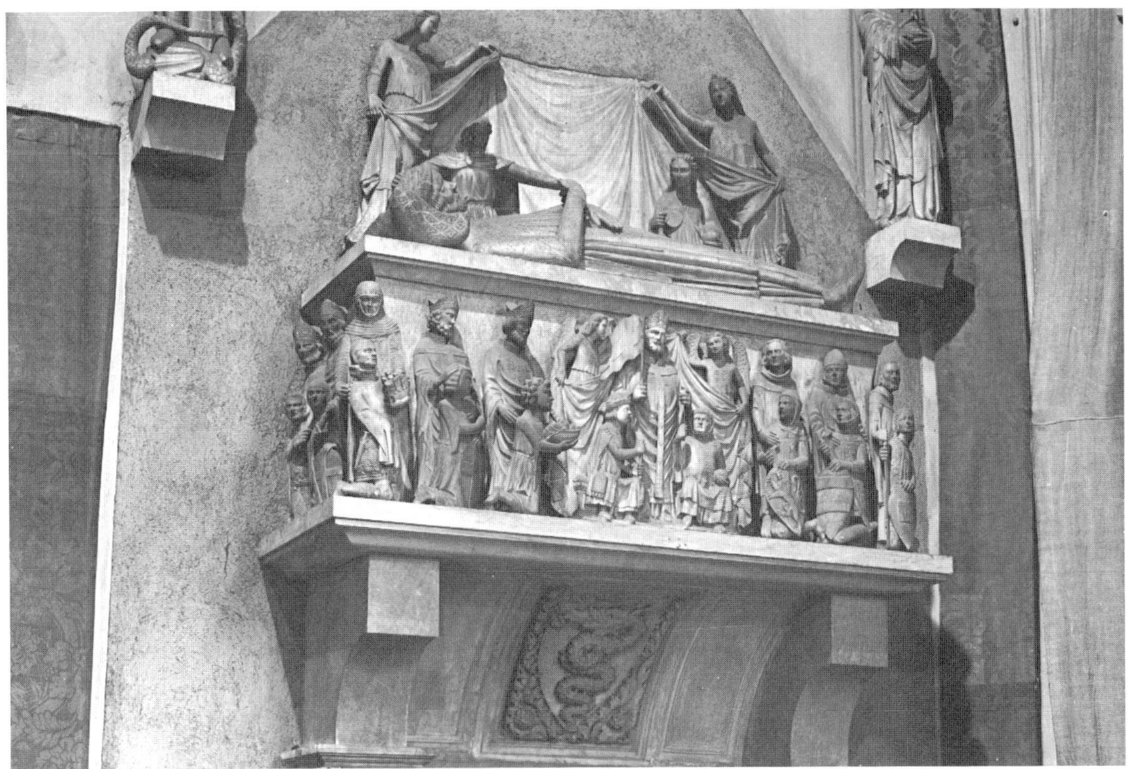

Fig. 2. Giovanni di Balduccio and assistants, c. 1342–46, Tomb of Azzo Visconti (detail). Milan, San Gottardo in Corte

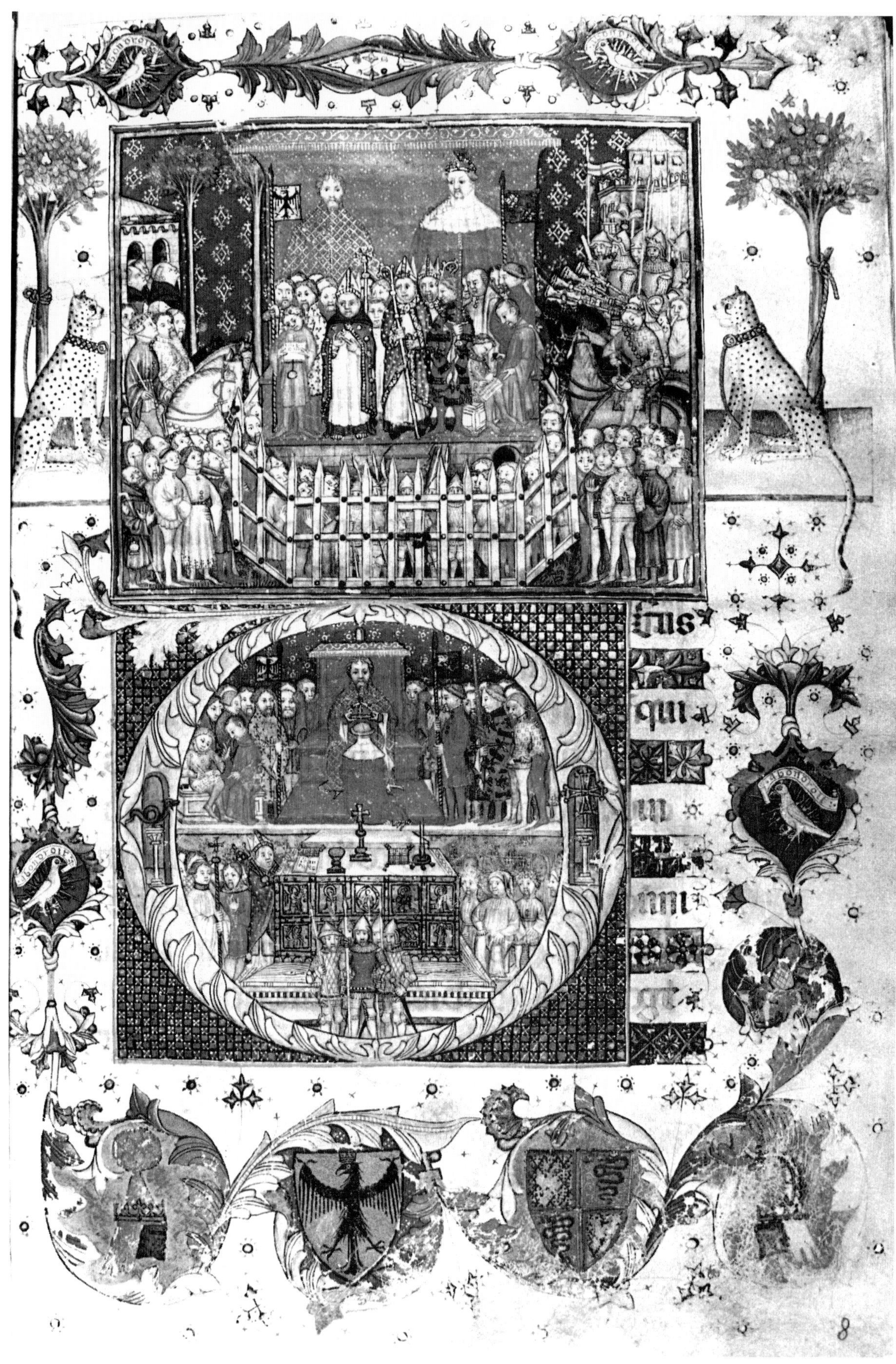

Fig. 3. Anovelo da Imbonate, c. 1395, Investiture of Giangaleazzo Visconti as Duke of Milan. Milan, Bibl. capitolare di Sant'Ambrogio, Lat. 6, fol. 8

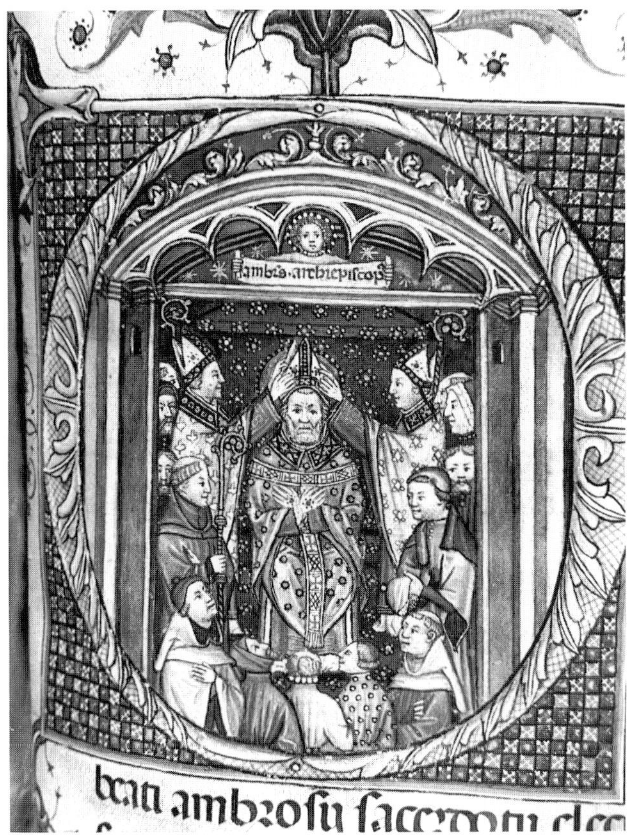

Fig. 4. Anovelo da Imbonate, c. 1395, Investiture of Saint Ambrose as Archbishop of Milan. Milan, Bibl. capitolare di Sant'Ambrogio, Lat. 6, fol. 200

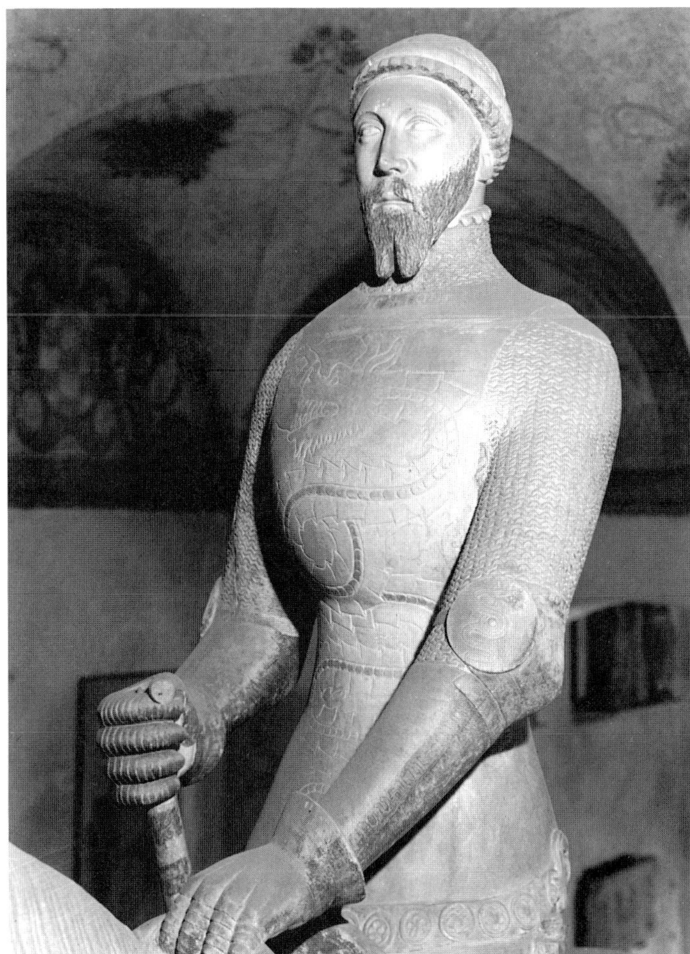

Fig. 5. Bonino da Campione, c. 1363, Bernabò Visconti (detail). Milan, Castello Sforzesco

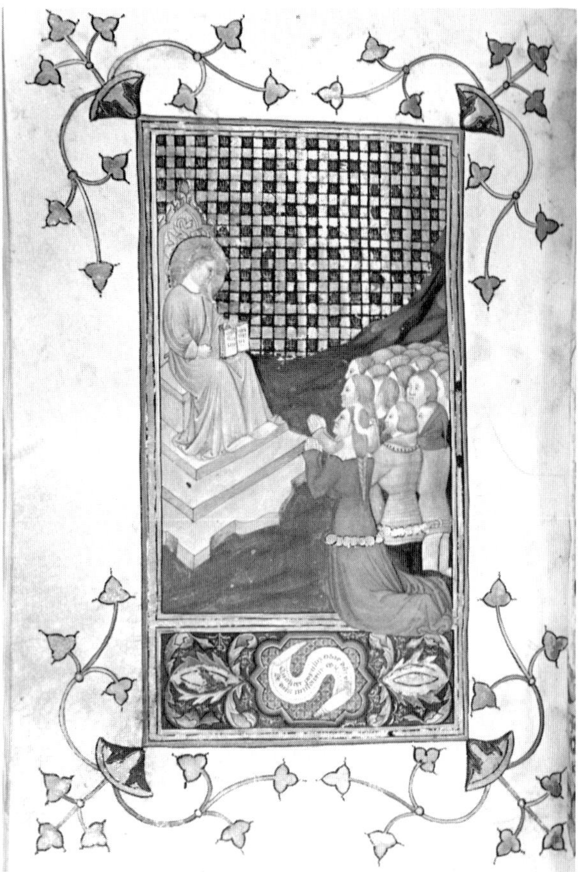

Fig. 6. Giovanni di Benedetto da Como, c. 1377–78, Blanche of Savoy and other nobles worship the enthroned Christ. Munich, Bayerische Staatsbibliothek, Cod. Lat. 23215, fol. 226v

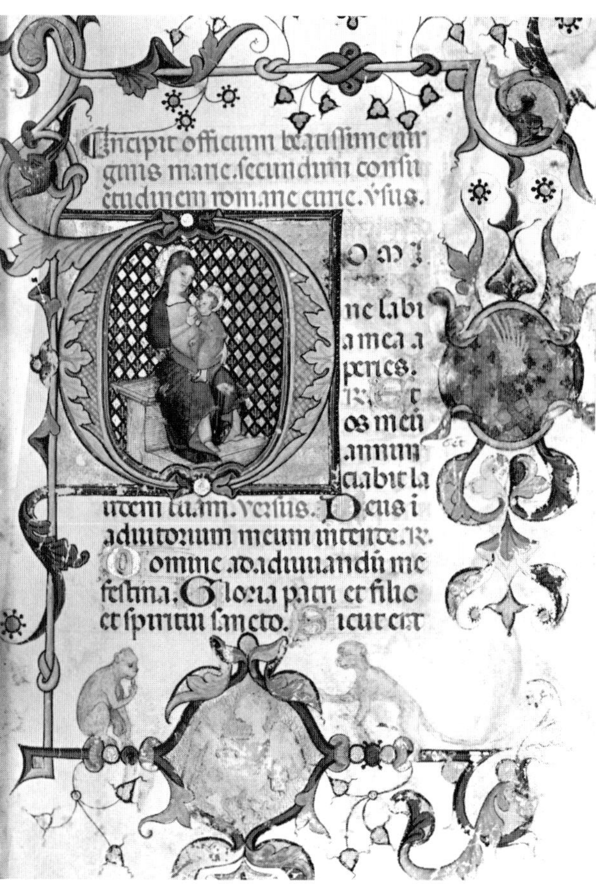

Fig. 7. Giovanni di Benedetto da Como, c. 1377–78, opening page of the Office of the Virgin. Munich, Bayerische Staatsbibliothek, Cod. Lat. 23215, fol. 9

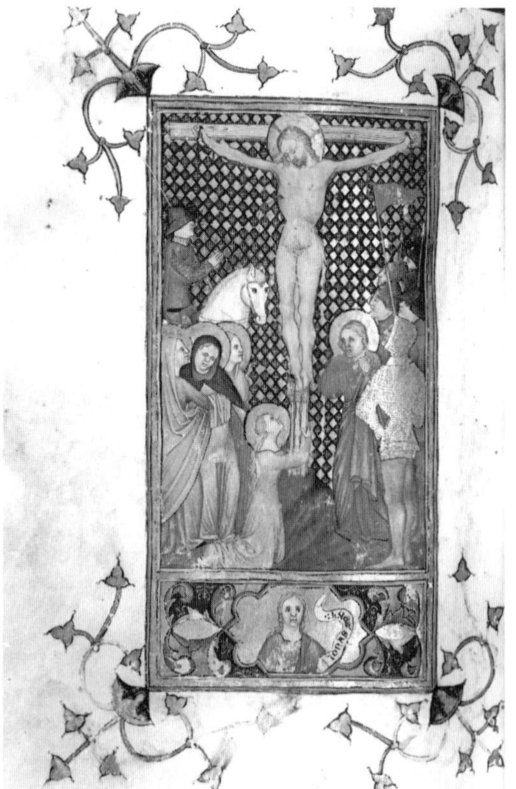

Fig. 8. Giovanni di Benedetto da Como, c. 1377–78, Crucifixion. Munich, Bayerische Staatsbibliothek, Cod. Lat. 23215, fol. 156v

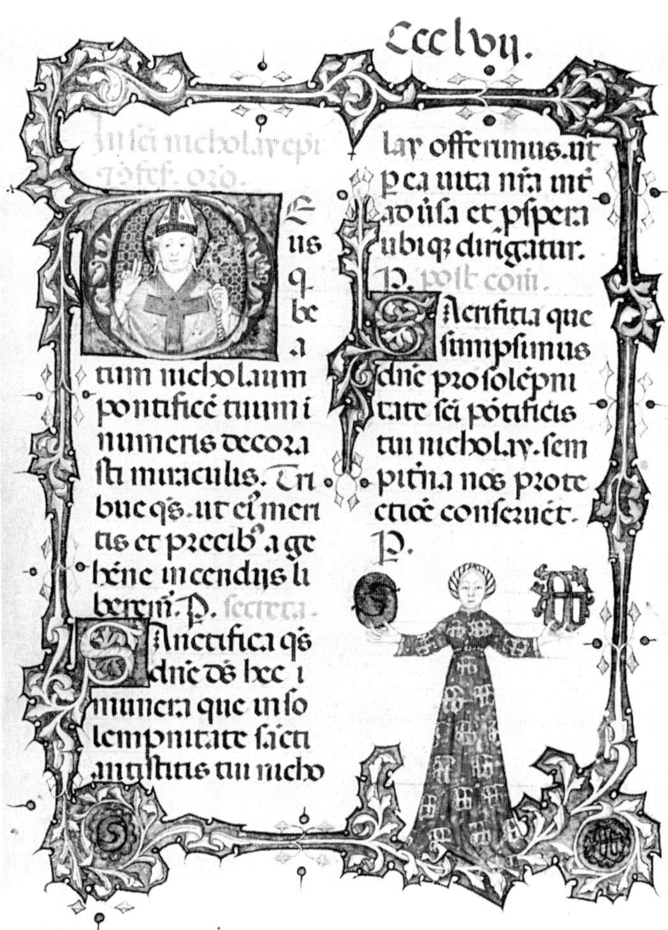

Fig. 9. Lombard, c. 1380, Mass of Saint Nicholas with heraldic woman. Paris, Bibl. nat., Lat. 757, fol. 364

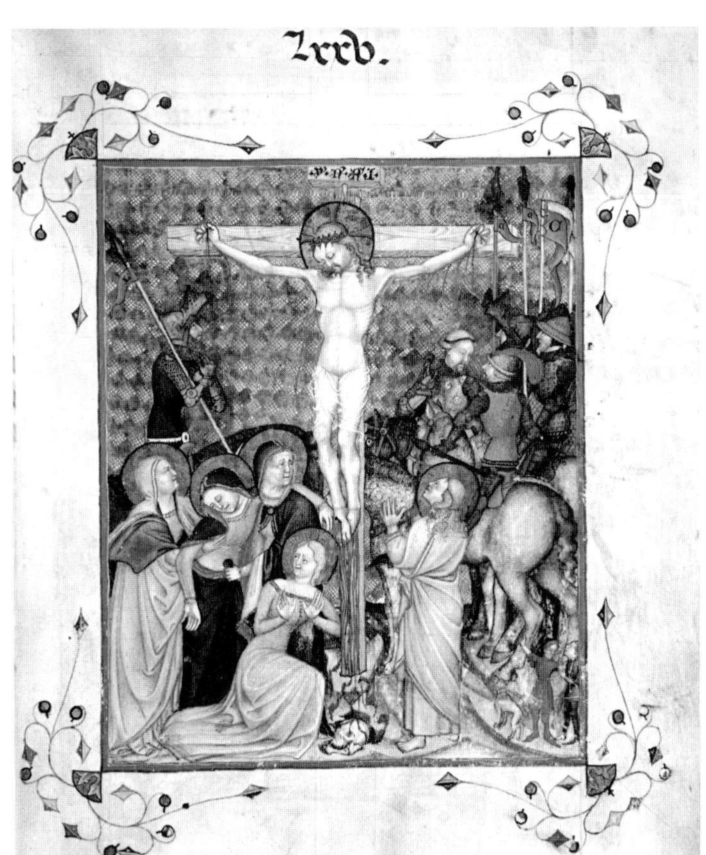

Fig. 10. Lombard, c. 1380, Crucifixion. Paris, Bibl. nat., Lat. 757, fol. 82

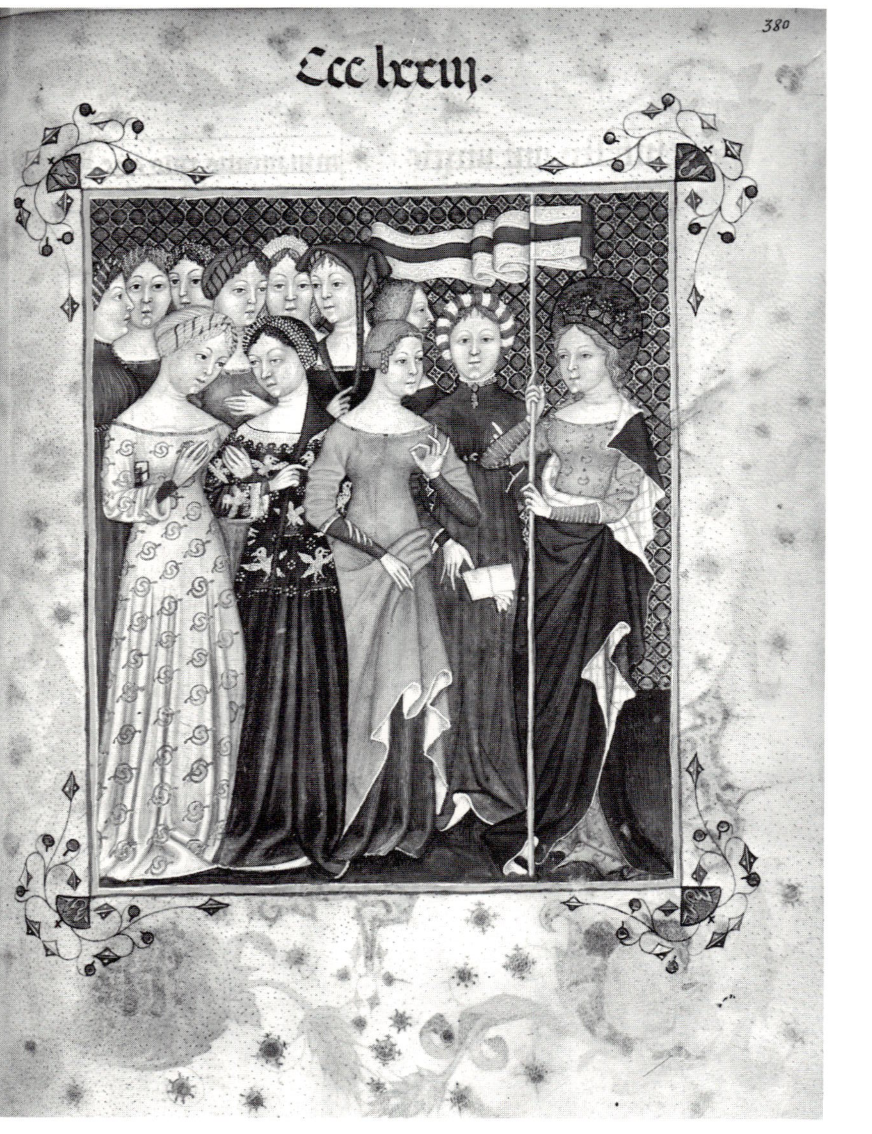

Fig. 11. Lombard, c. 1380, Saint Ursula and her companions, Paris, Bibl. nat., Lat. 757, fol. 380

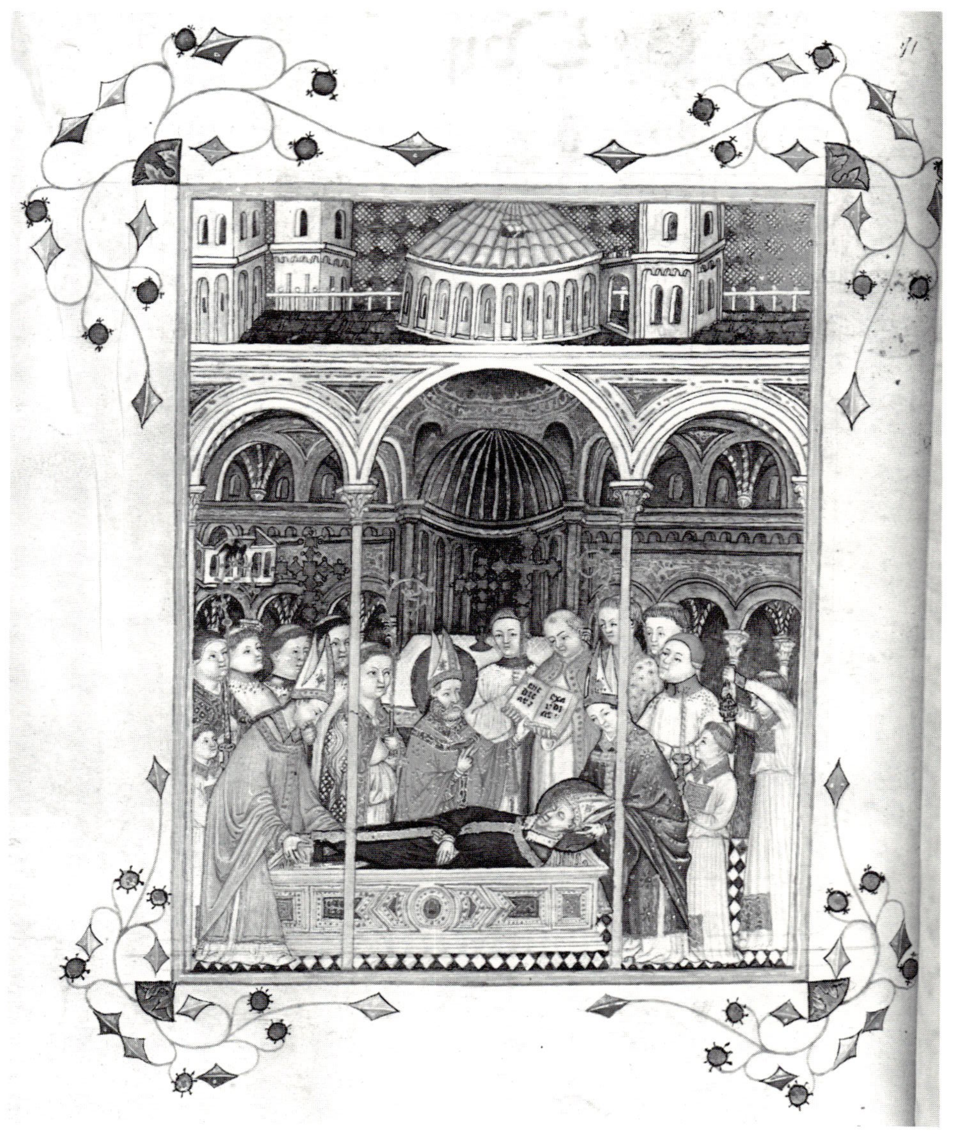

Fig. 12. Lombard, c. 1380, Funeral of Saint Martin. Paris, Bibl. nat., Lat. 757, fol. 114v

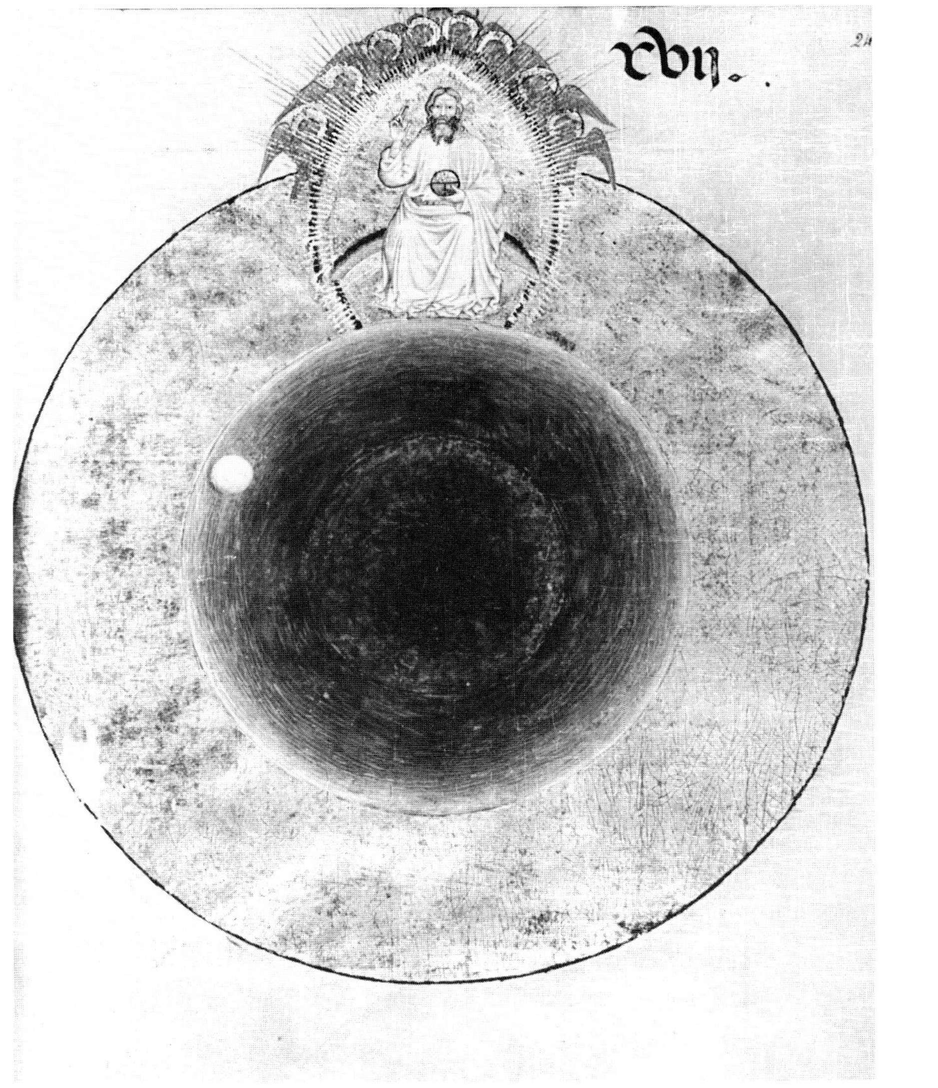

Fig. 13. Lombard, c. 1380, First Day of Creation. Paris, Bibl. nat., Lat. 757, fol. 24

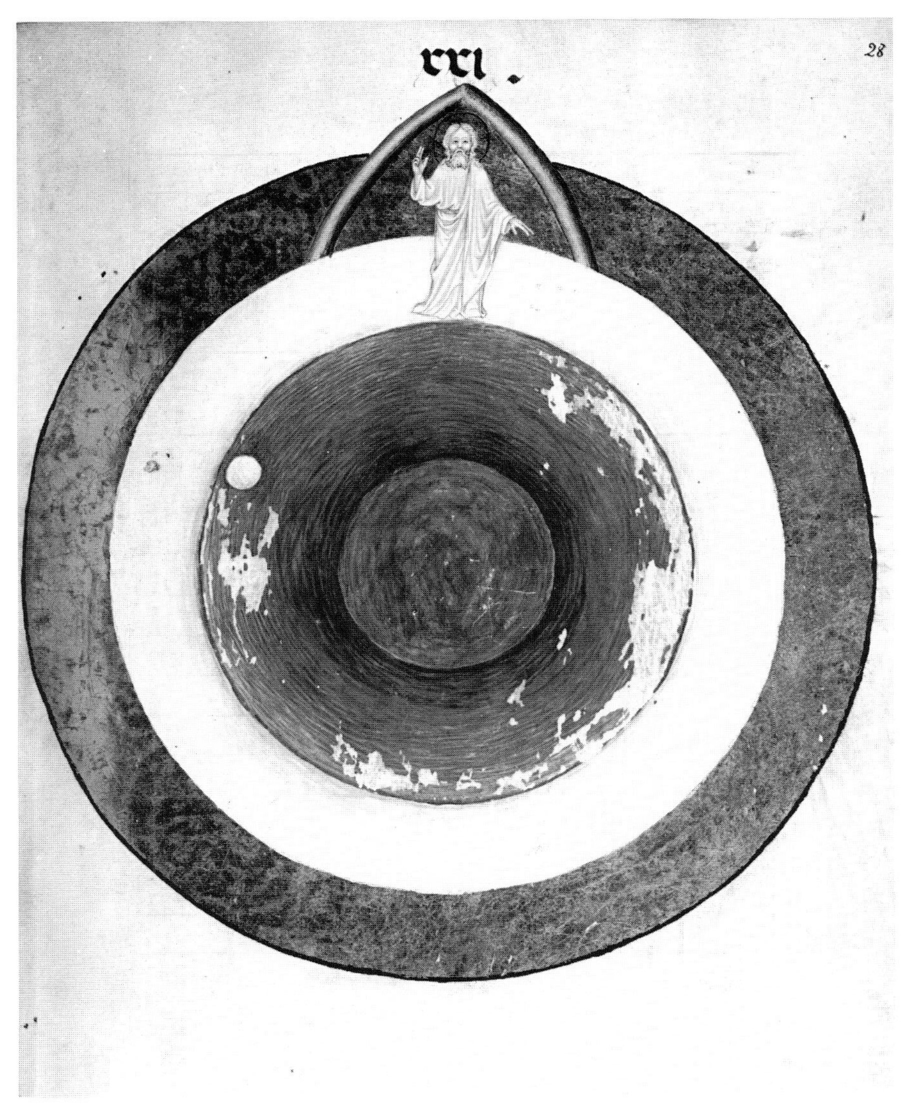

Fig. 14. Lombard, c. 1380, Creation of the Firmament. Paris, Bibl. nat., Lat. 757, fol. 28

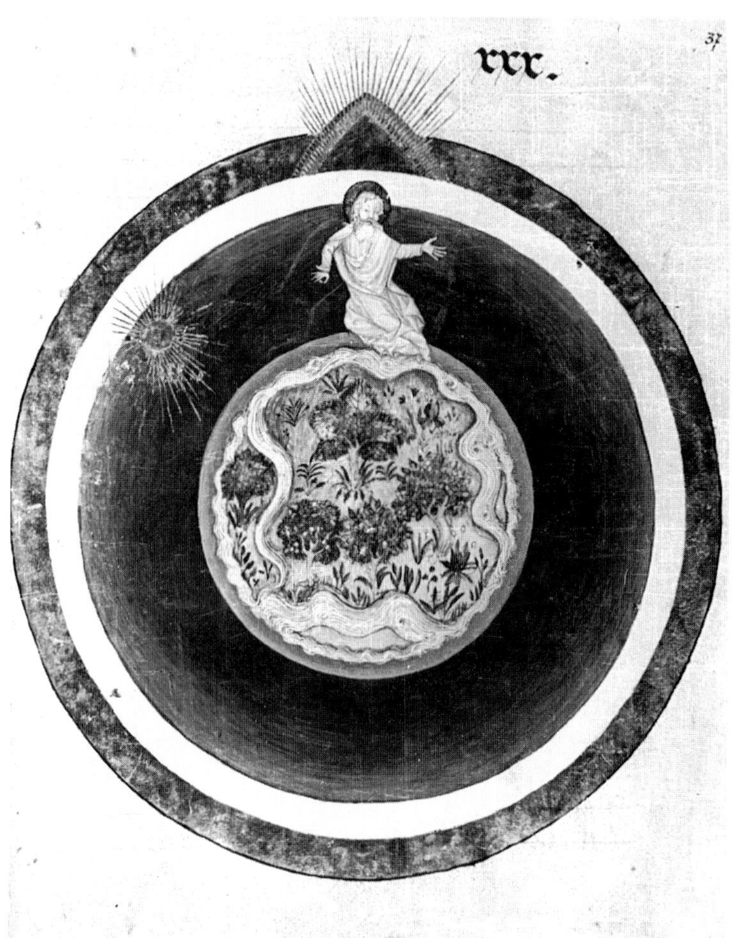

Fig. 15. Lombard, c. 1380, Separation of Land from Water, Creation of Trees and Plants. Paris, Bibl. nat., Lat. 757, fol. 37

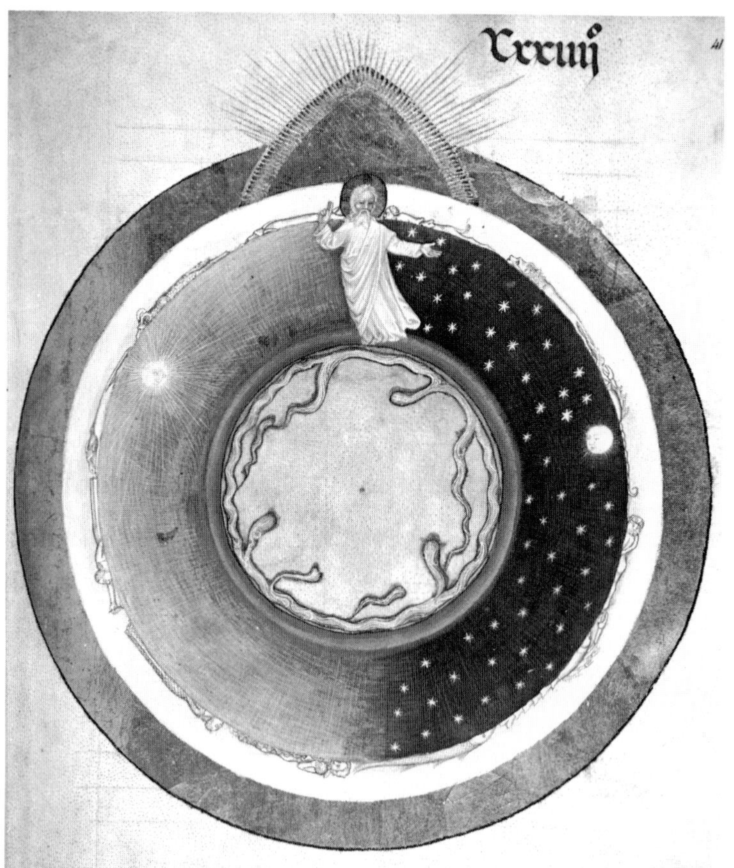

Fig. 16. Lombard, c. 1380, Creation of Sun, Moon, and Stars. Paris, Bibl. nat., Lat. 757, fol. 41

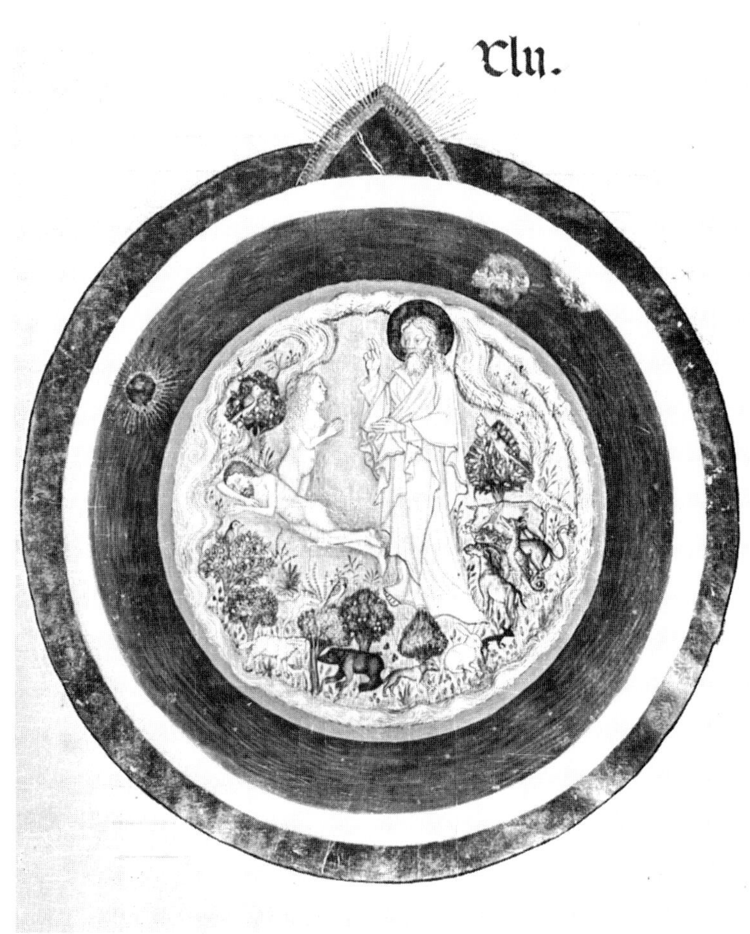

Fig. 17. Lombard, c. 1380, Creation of Eve. Paris, Bibl. nat., Lat. 757, fol. 49

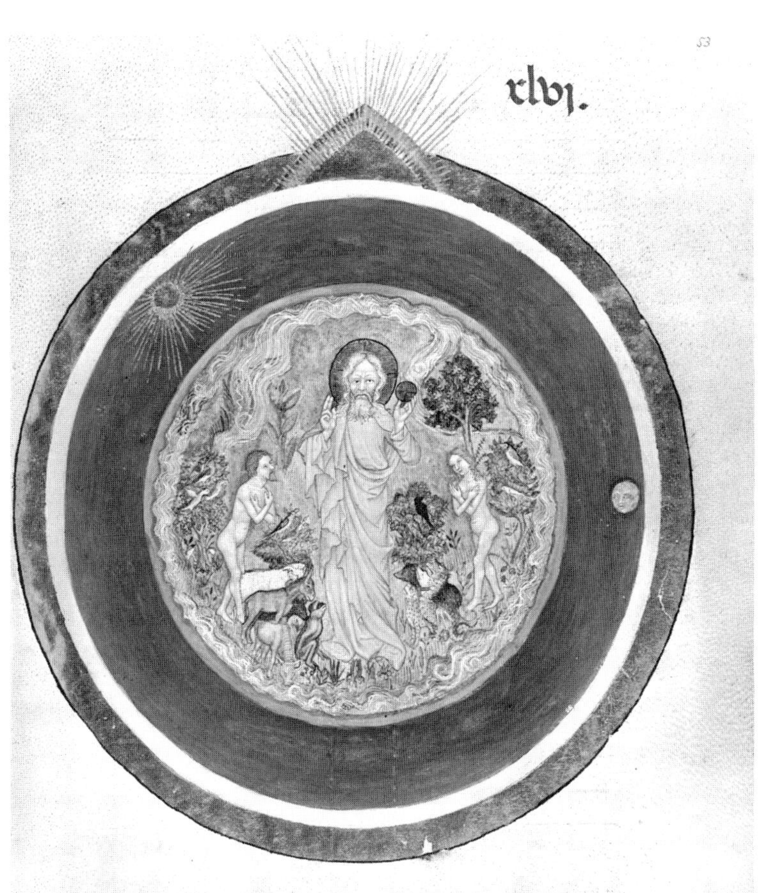

Fig. 18. Lombard, c. 1380, Adam, Eve, and other creatures worship the Creator. Paris, Bibl. nat., Lat. 757, fol. 53

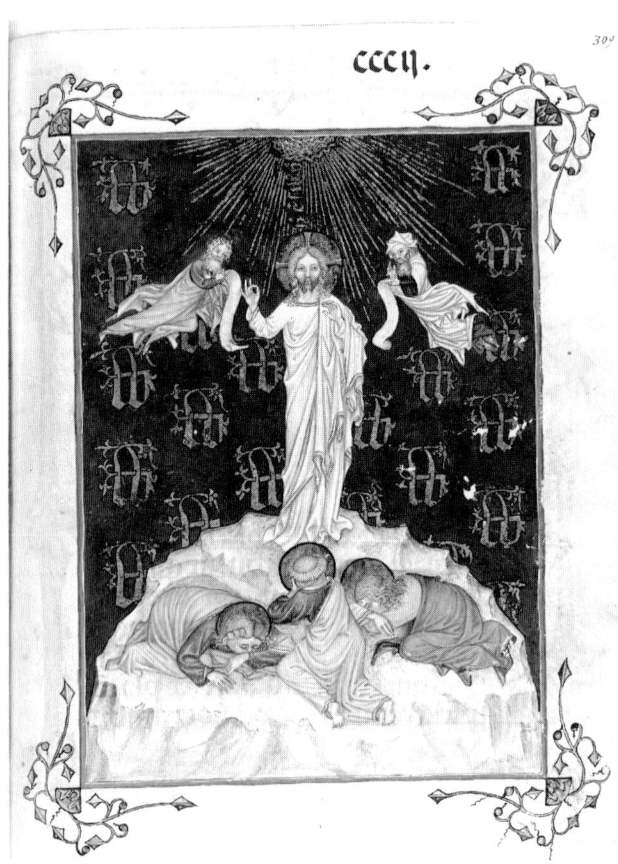

Fig. 19. Lombard, c. 1380, Transfiguration. Paris, Bibl. nat., Lat. 757, fol. 309

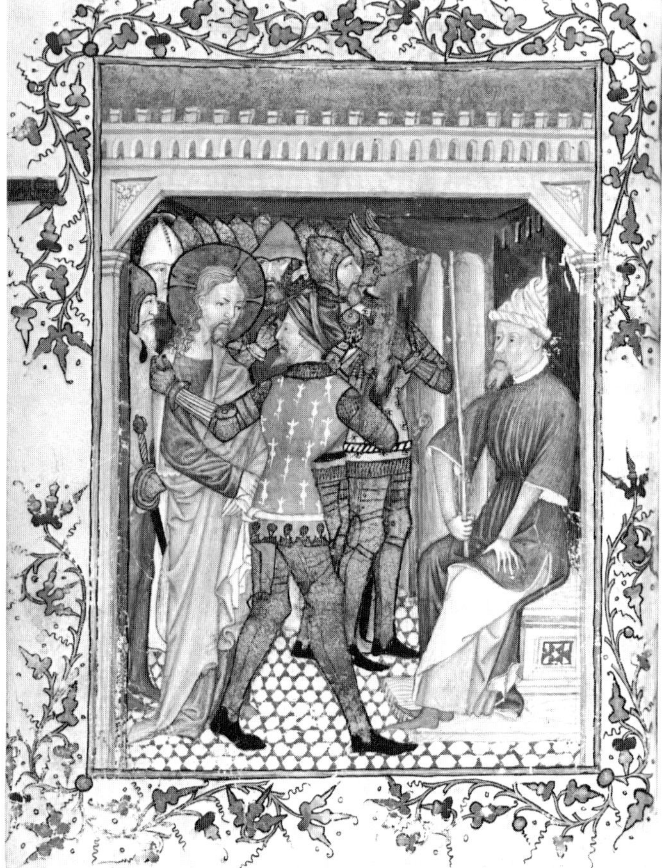

Fig. 20. Lombard, c. 1380, Christ before Pilate. Paris, Bibl. nat., Smith-Lesouëf 22, fol. 34v

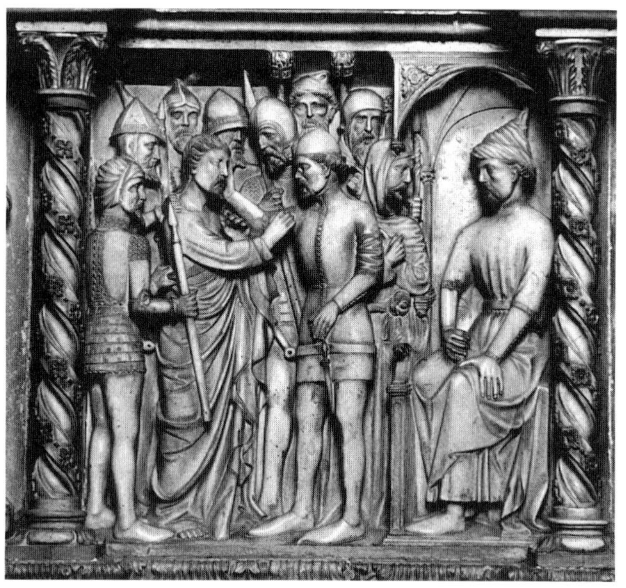

Fig. 21. Lombard, c. 1390, Christ before Pilate. Milan, Sant'Eustorgio, dossal (detail)

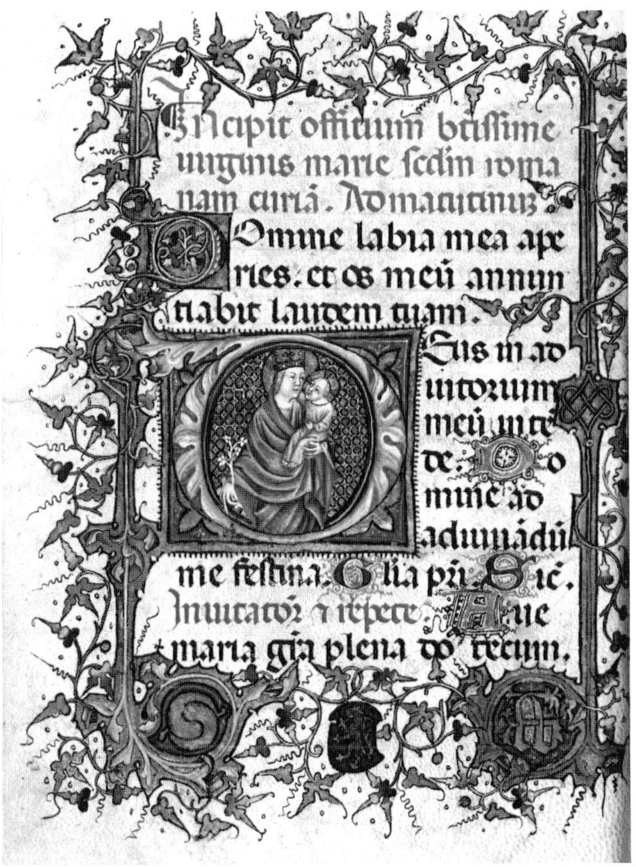

Fig. 22. Lombard, c. 1380, opening page of the Office of the Virgin. Paris, Bibl. nat., Smith-Lesouëf 22, fol. 15v

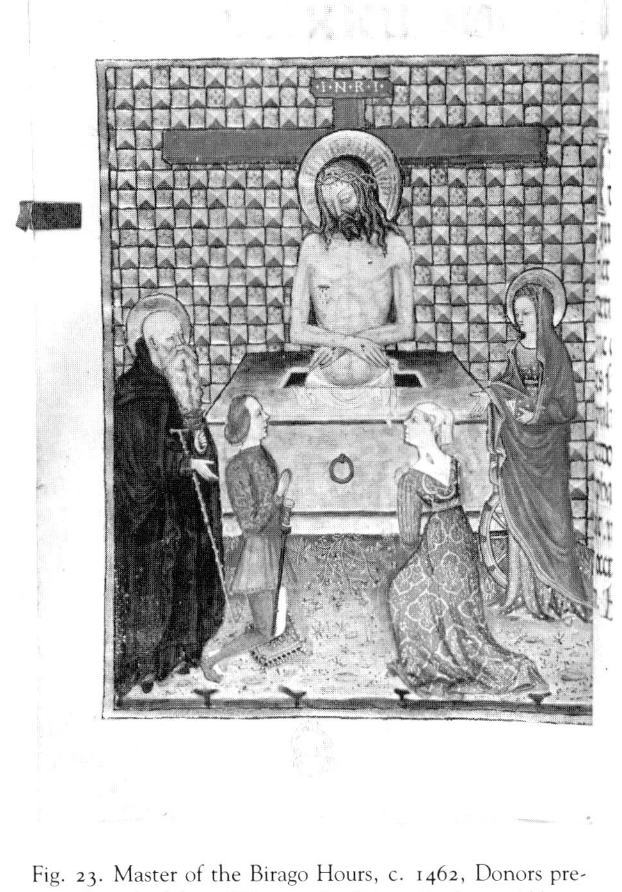

Fig. 23. Master of the Birago Hours, c. 1462, Donors presented to the Man of Sorrows by Saints Anthony Abbot and Catherine of Alexandria. Paris, Bibl. nat., Smith-Lesouëf 22, fol. 285v

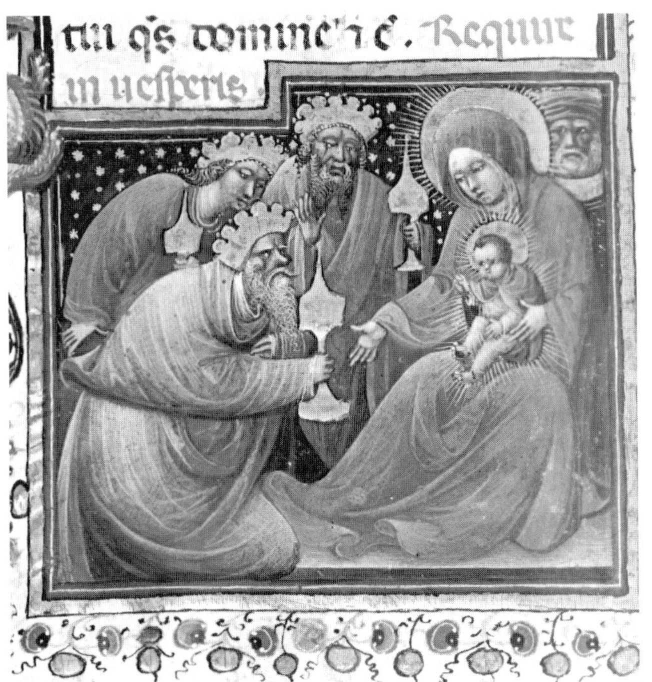

Fig. 24. Belbello da Pavia, c. 1462, Adoration of the Magi. Paris, Bibl. nat., Smith-Lesouëf 22, fol. 44v

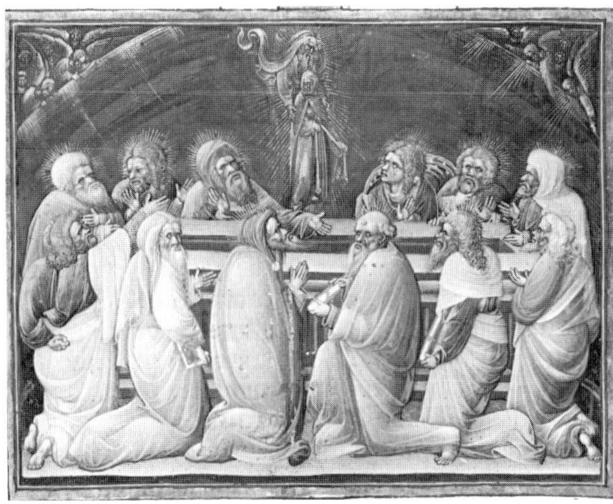

Fig. 25. Belbello da Pavia, c. 1460–62, Assumption of the Virgin. Mantua, Curia Vescovile, Missal of Barbara of Brandenburg, fol. 299

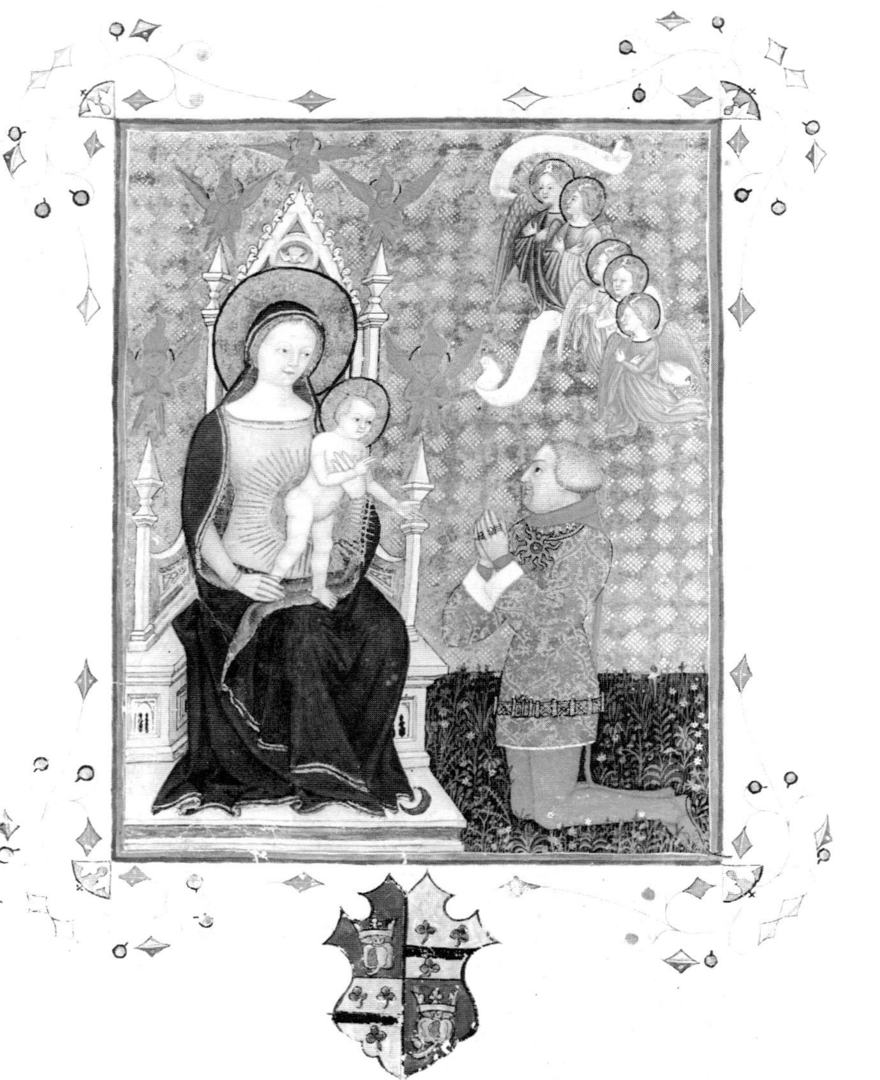

Fig. 26. Lombard, c. 1380, Giangaleazzo Visconti worships the Madonna and Child. Paris, Bibl. nat., Lat. 757, fol. 109v

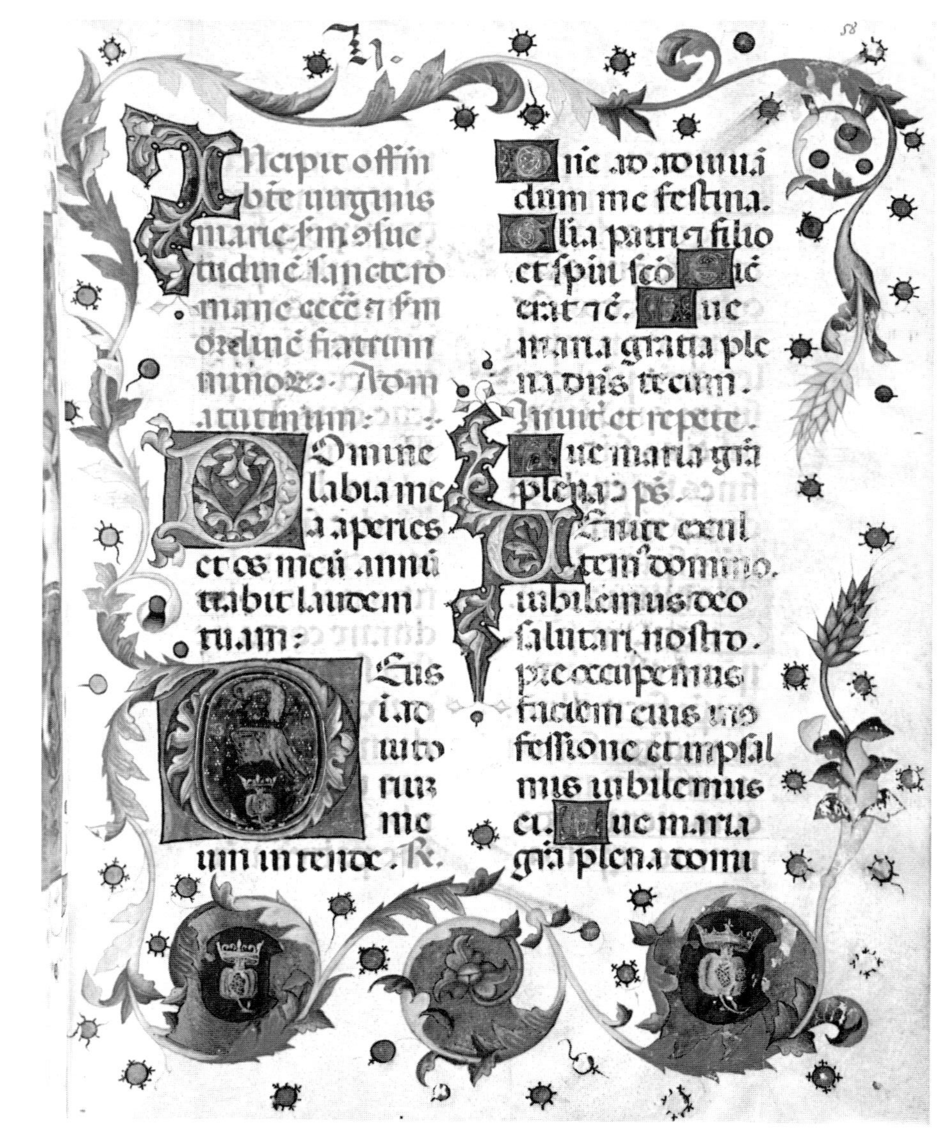

Fig. 27. Lombard, c. 1380, opening page of the Office of the Virgin. Paris, Bibl. nat., Lat. 757, fol. 58

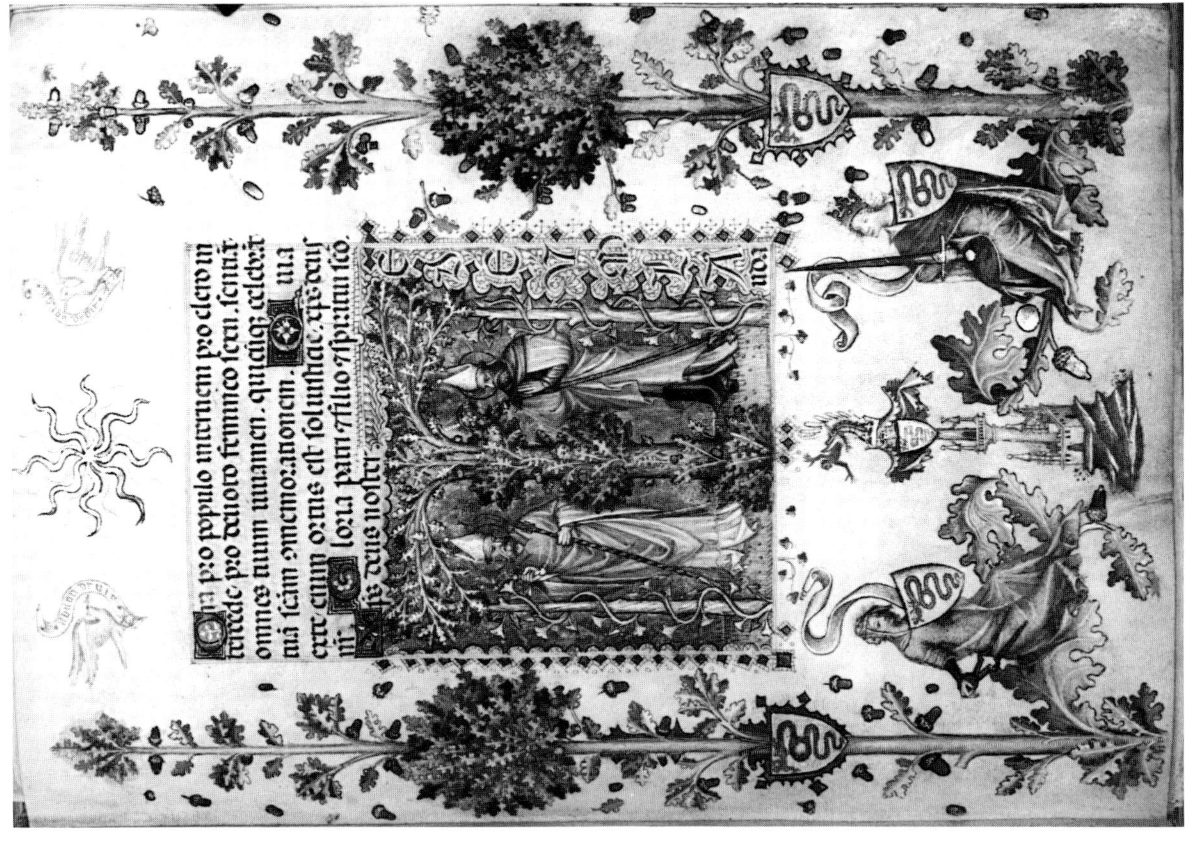

Fig. 29. Giovannino and Salomone dei Grassi, c. 1395, Saints Ambrose and Augustine. Florence, Bibl. naz., Landau-Finaly 22, fol. 17

Fig. 28. Lombard, c. 1400–1402, Woman Holding Visconti Armorials. Paris, Bibl. nat., Lat. 6340, fol. [II]v

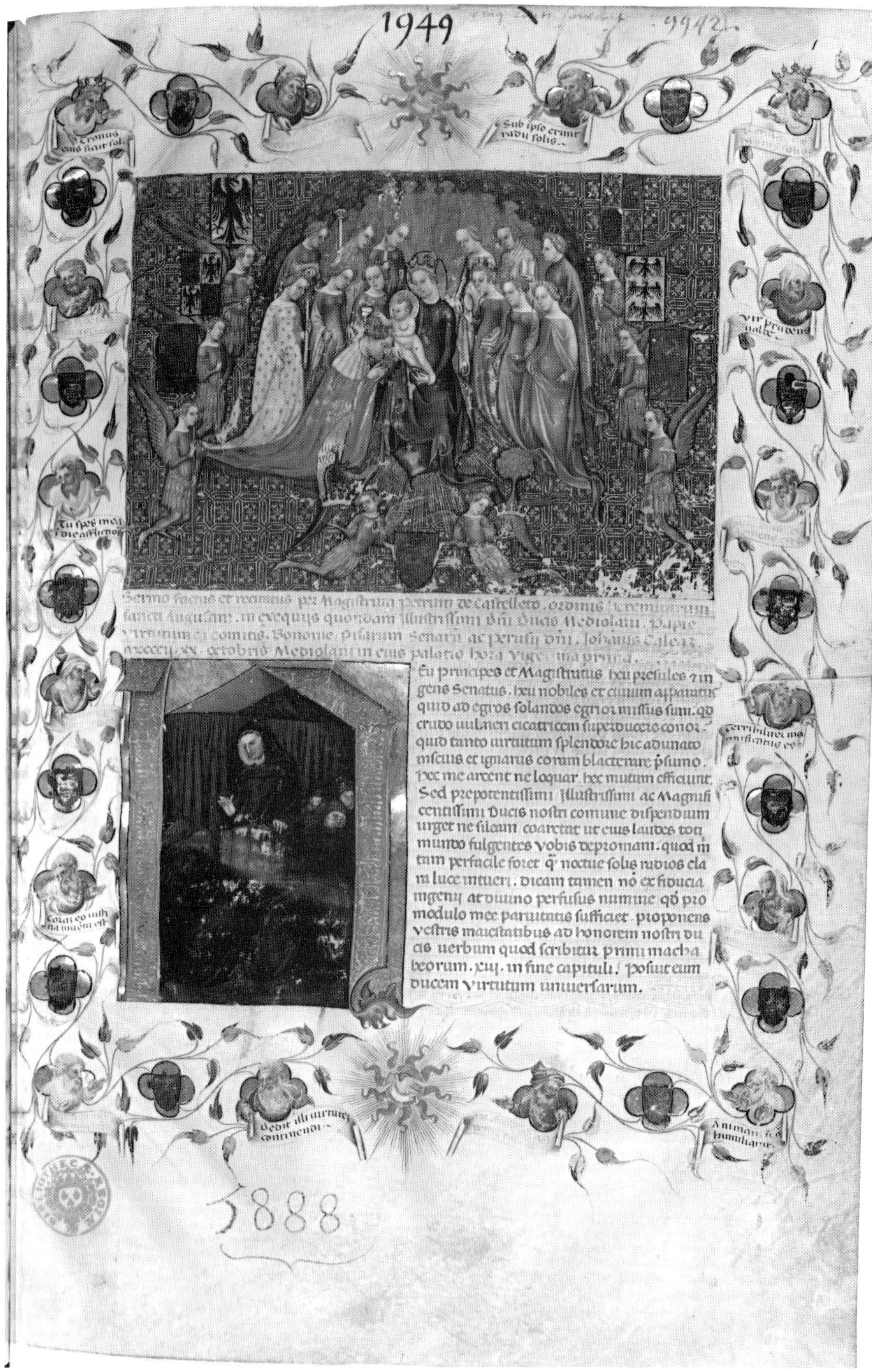

Fig. 30. Michelino da Besozzo, 1403, Coronation of Giangaleazzo in Heaven; Petrus de Castelletto addressing Augustinians. Paris, Bibl. nat., Lat. 5888, fol. 1

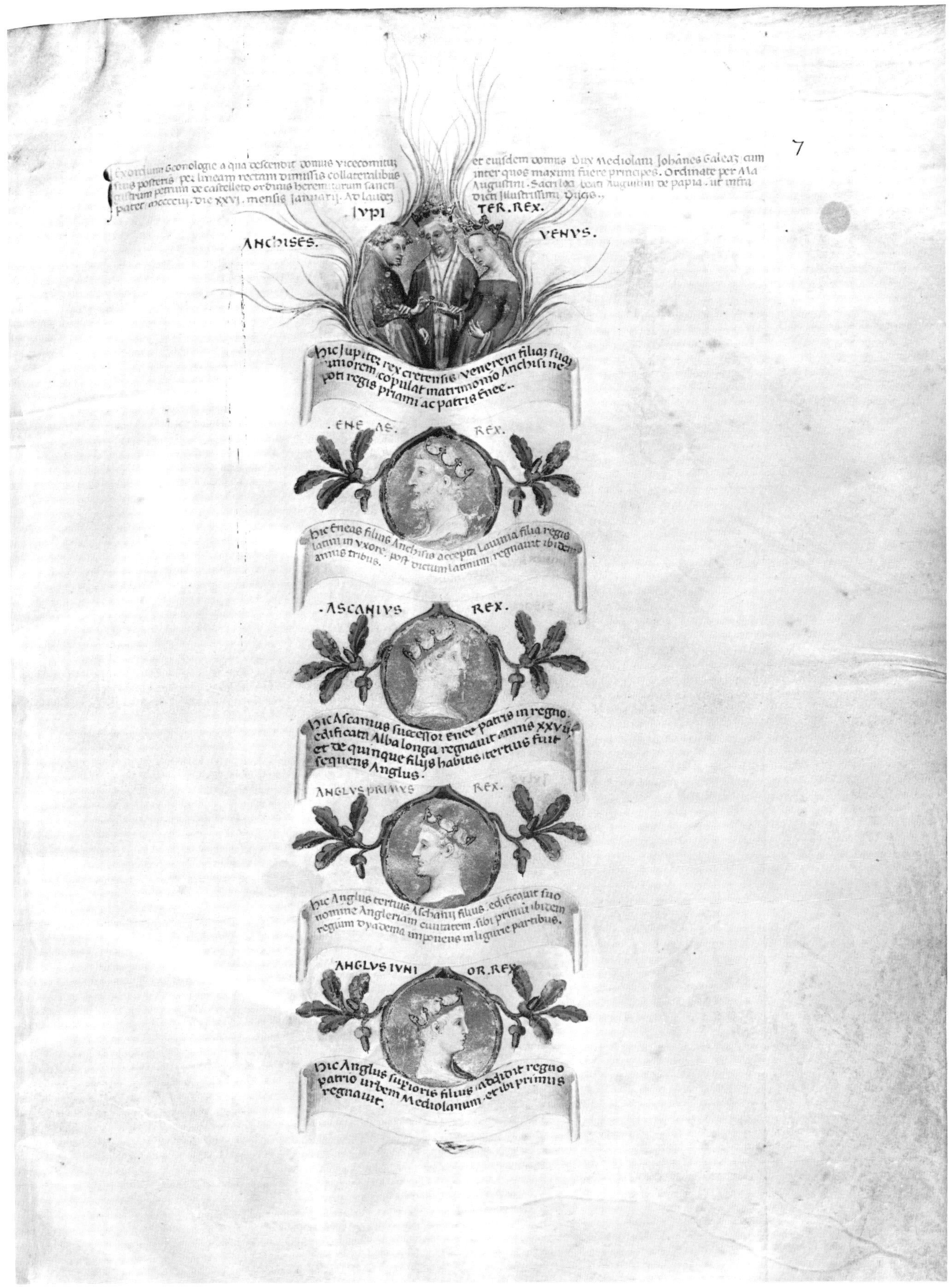

Fig. 31. Michelino da Besozzo, 1403, opening page of Visconti genealogy. Paris, Bibl. nat., Lat. 5888, fol. 7

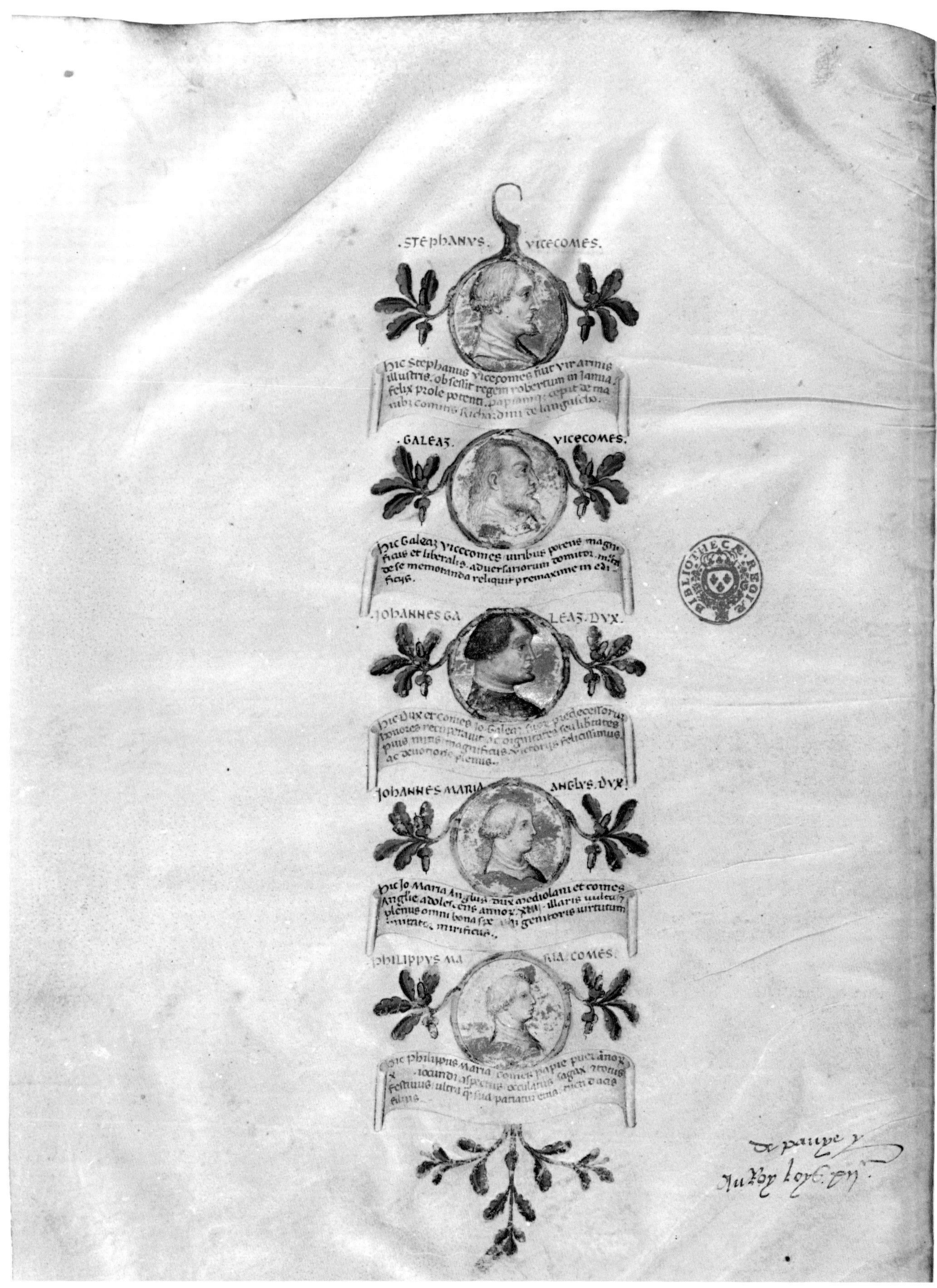

Fig. 32. Michelino da Besozzo, 1403, last page of Visconti genealogy. Paris, Bibl. nat., Lat. 5888, fol. 12v

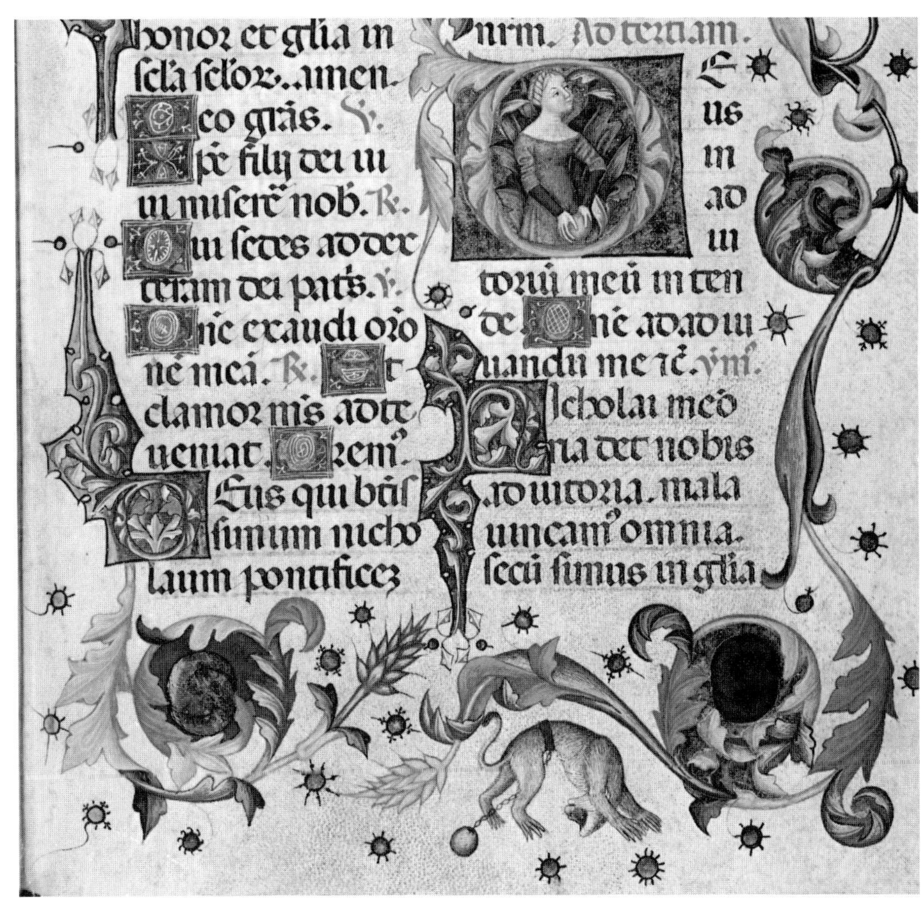

Fig. 33. Lombard, c. 1380, page from the Office of Saint Nicholas (detail). Paris, Bibl. nat., Lat. 757, fol. 404

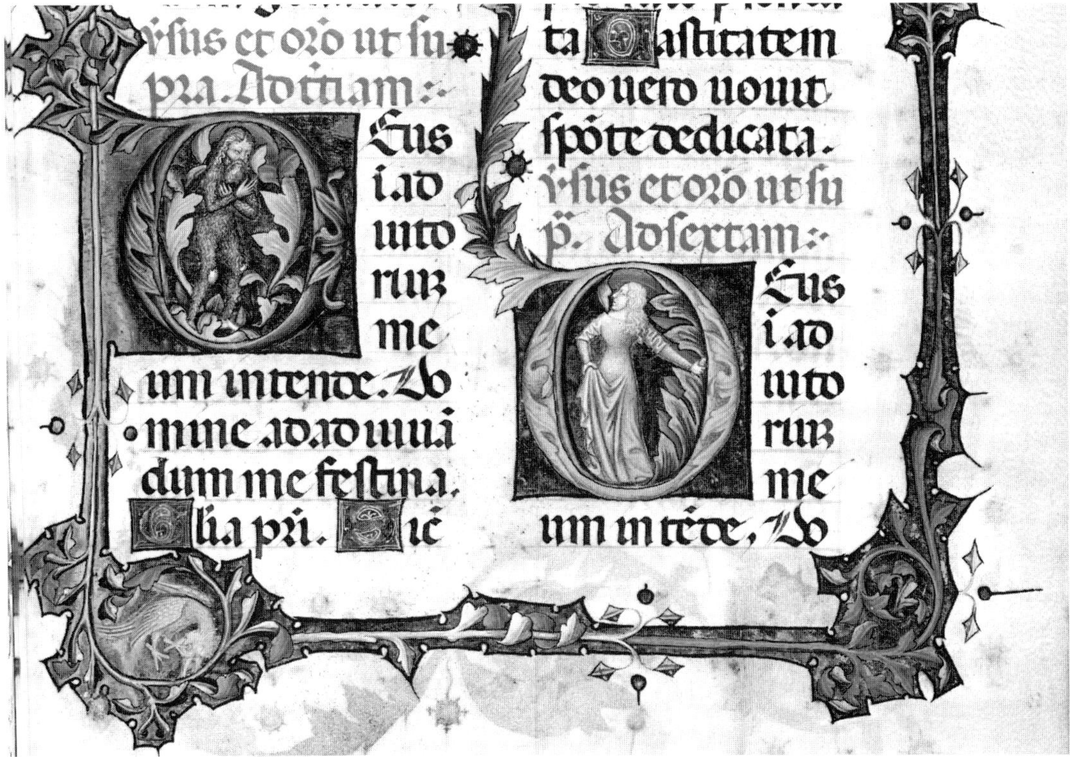

Fig. 34. Lombard, c. 1380, page from the Saturday Office of the Virgin Mary (detail). Paris, Bibl. nat., Lat. 757, fol. 55

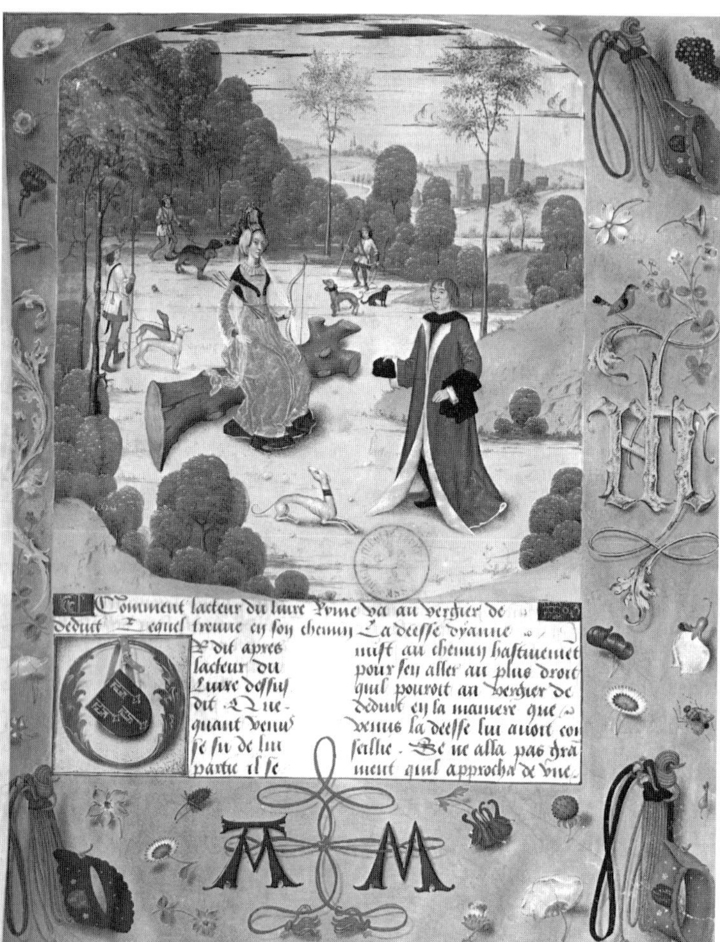

Fig. 35. French, fifteenth century, page with interlaced initials of Antoine Rollin and Marie d'Ailly. Paris, Bibl. nat., Fr. 9197, fol. 202

Fig. 36. Emblems of the Order of the Holy Spirit (from Boulton, 224, fig. 6.2; 237, fig. 6.5)

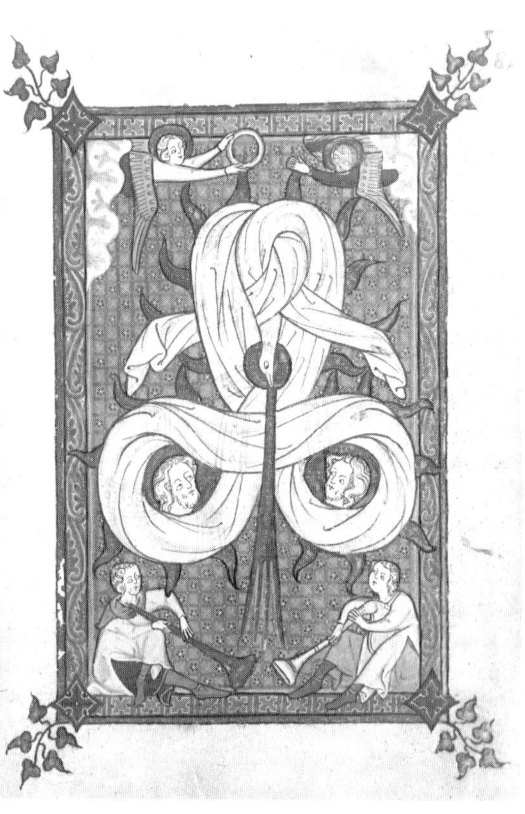

Fig. 37. Flemish, c. 1330, Trinity. New Haven, Yale University, Beinecke Lib., MS 404, fol. 84

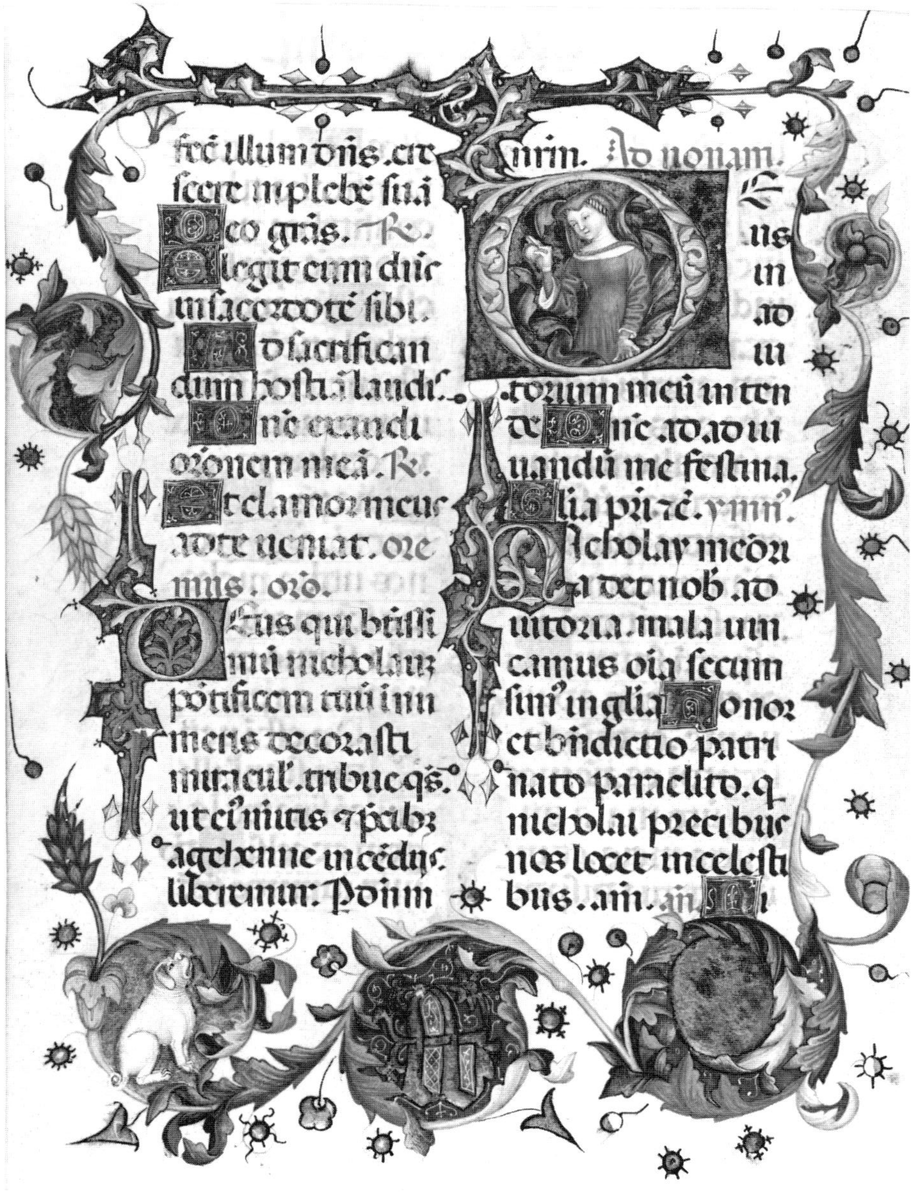

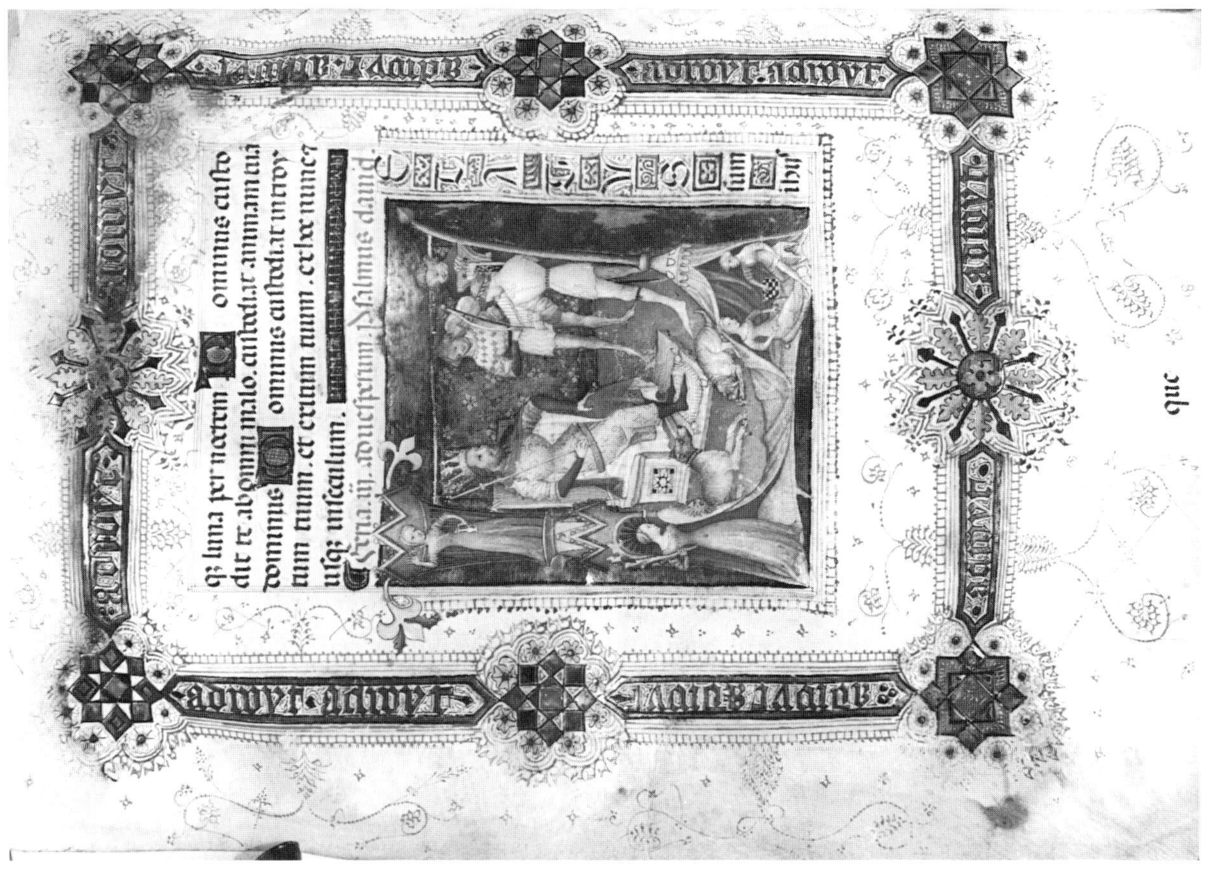

Fig. 39. Giovannino and Salomone dei Grassi, c. 1388–91, David and courtiers. Florence, Bibl. naz., Banco Rari 397, fol. 120v

Fig. 38. Lombard, c. 1380, page from the Office of Saint Nicholas. Paris, Bibl. nat., Lat. 757, fol. 406v

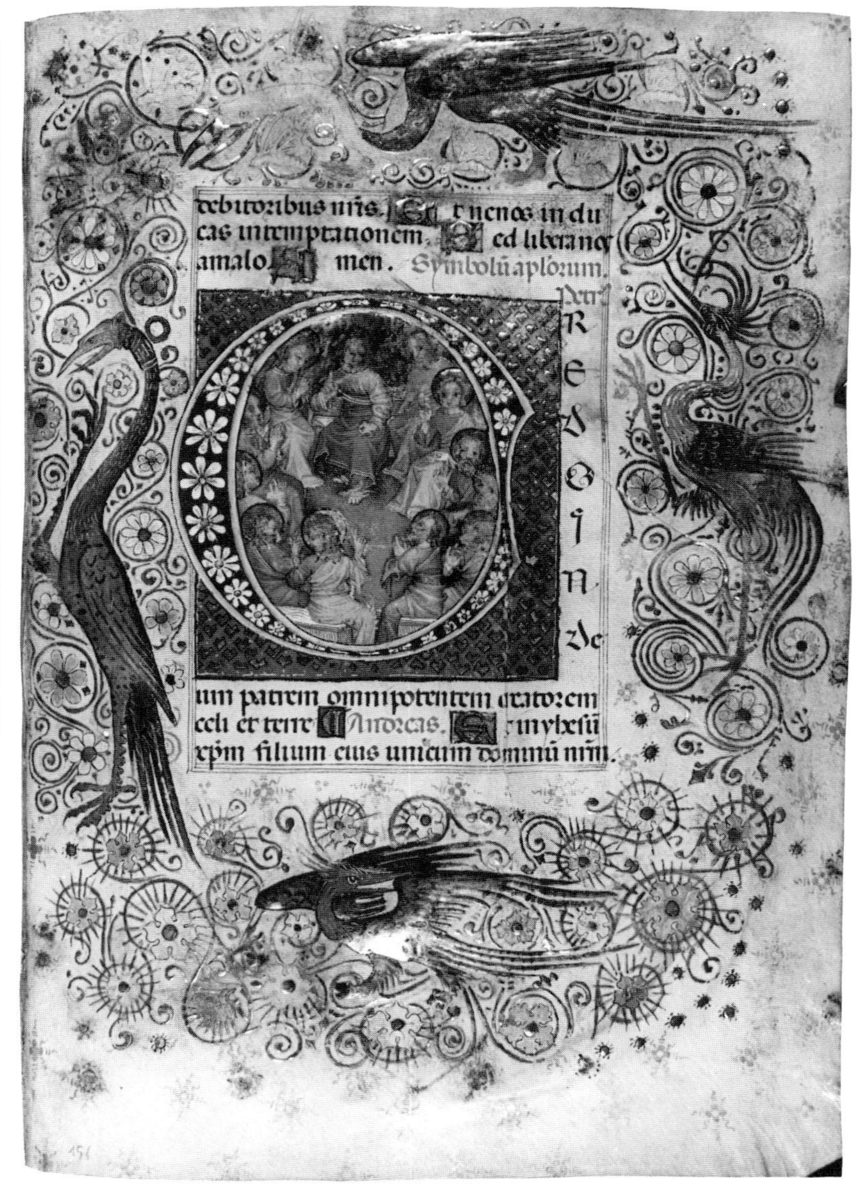

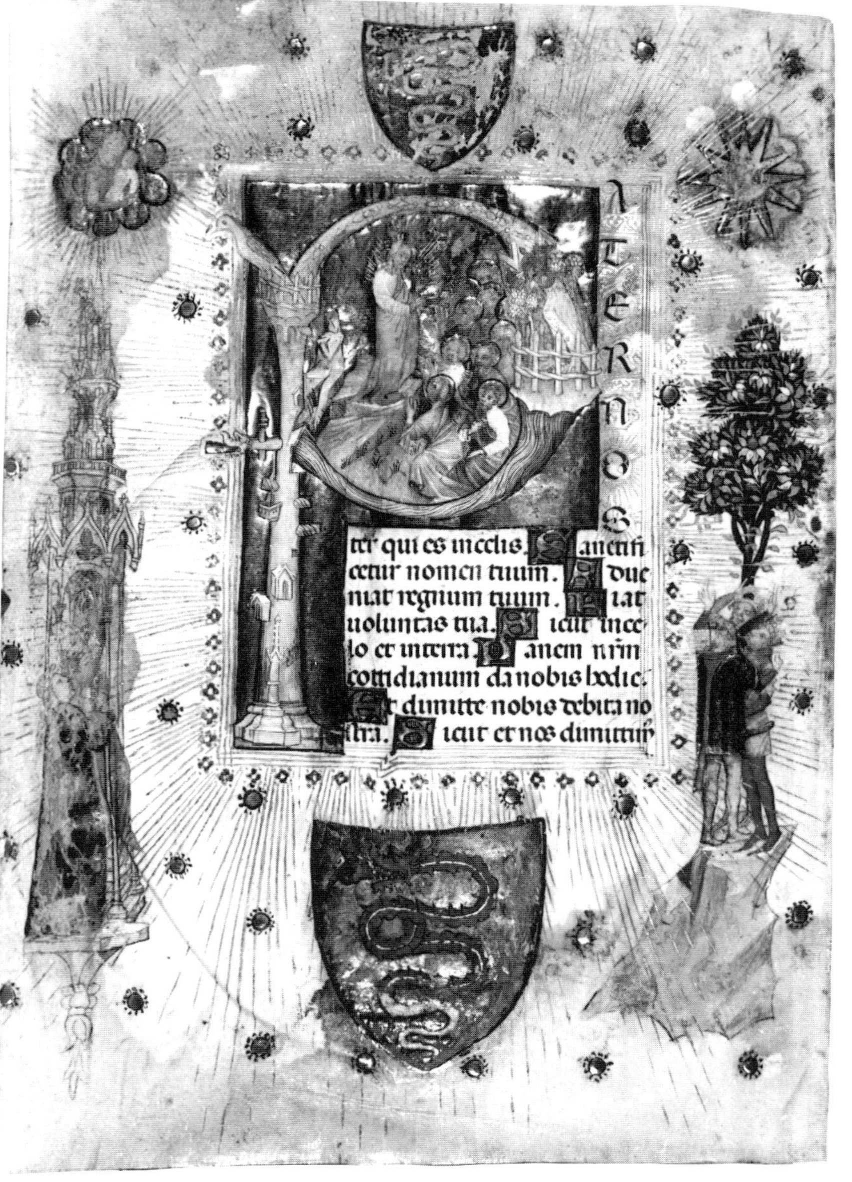

Fig. 40. Giovannino and Salomone dei Grassi, c. 1388–91, Sermon on the Mount; Apostles. Florence, Bibl. naz., Banco Rari 397, fols. 150v–151

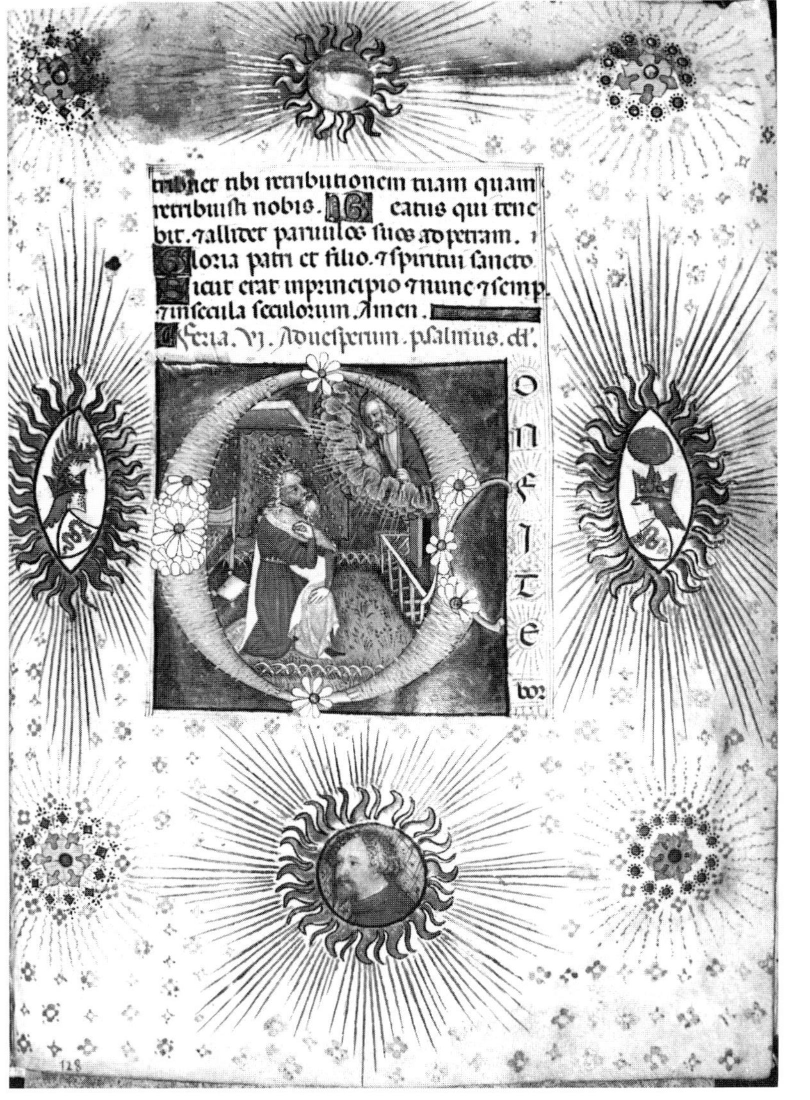

Fig. 41. Giovannino and Salomone dei Grassi, c. 1388–91, David addressed by the Lord, portrait of Giangaleazzo Visconti. Florence, Bibl. naz., Banco Rari 397, fol. 128

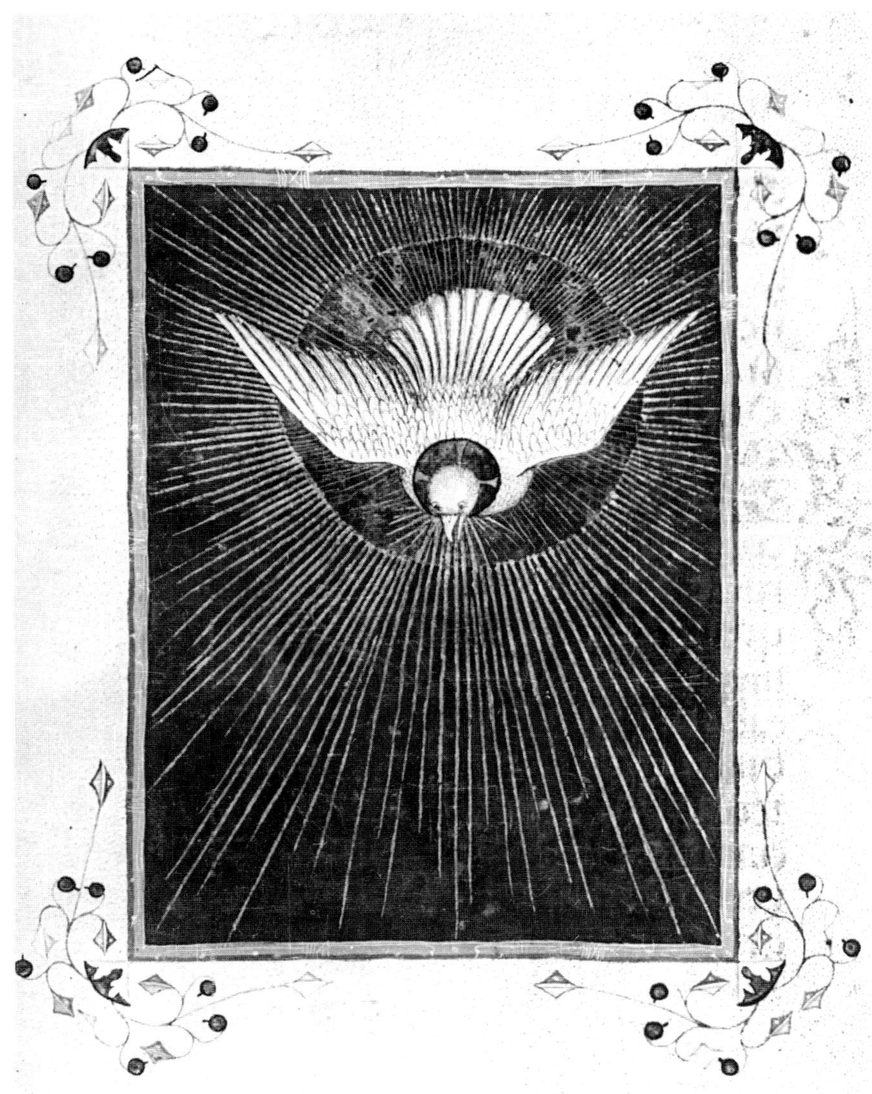

Fig. 42. Lombard, c 1380, Dove of the Holy Spirit. Paris, Bibl. nat., Lat. 757, fol. 241v

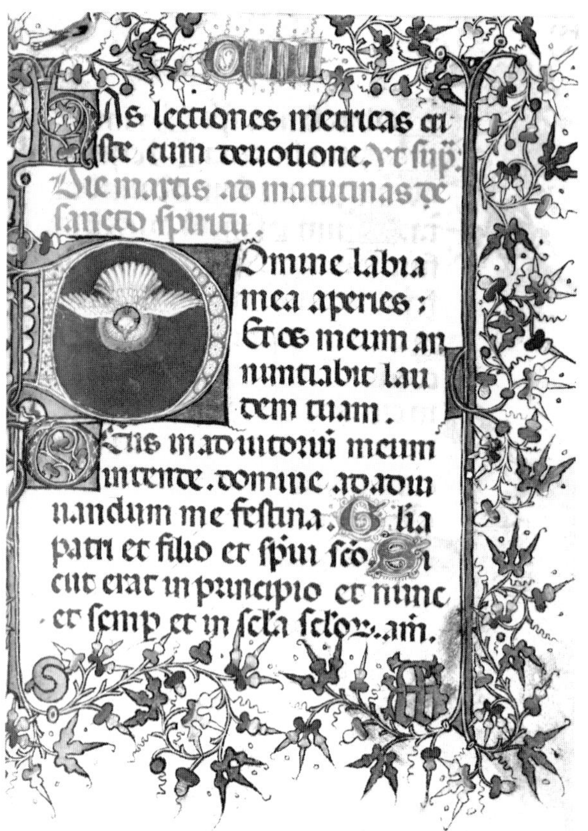

Fig. 43. Lombard, c. 1380, opening page of the Tuesday Office of the Holy Spirit. Paris, Bibl. nat., Smith-Lesouëf 22, fol. 104

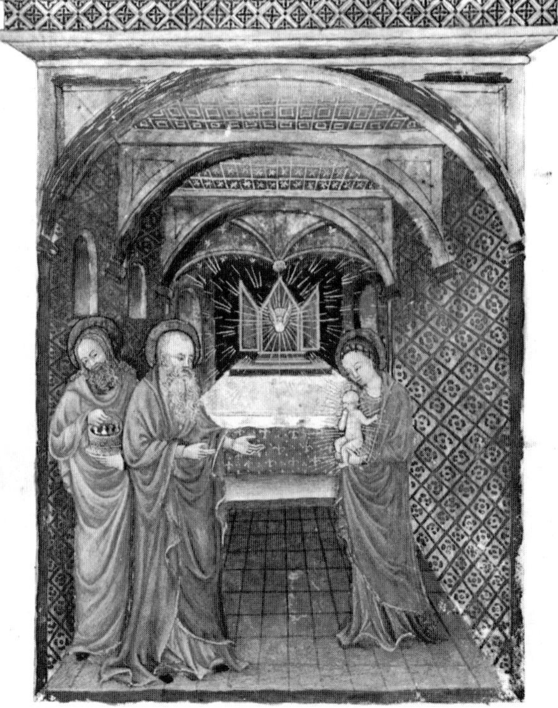

Fig. 44. Master of the Birago Hours, c. 1462, Purification of the Virgin. Paris, Bibl. nat., Smith-Lesouëf 22, fol. 359

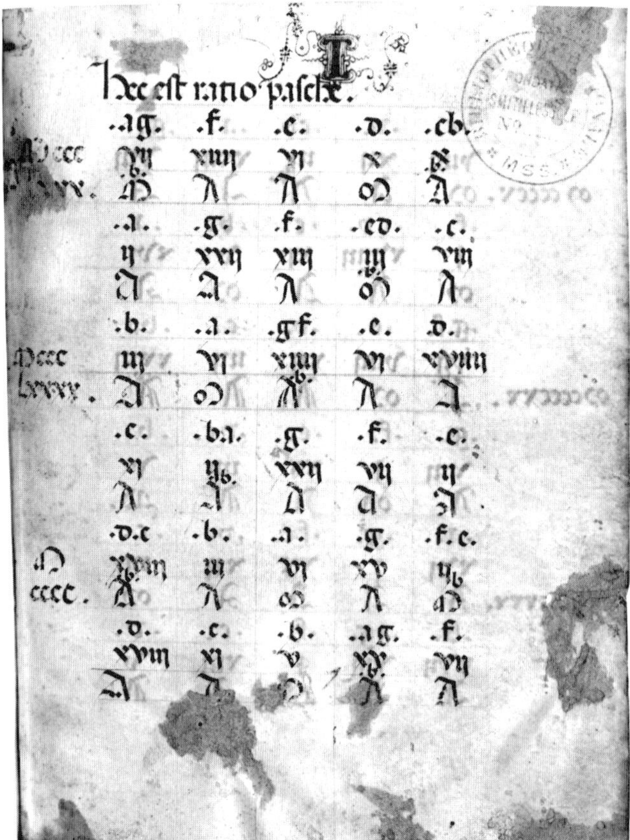

Fig. 45. Lombard, c. 1380, Easter Table. Paris, Bibl. nat., Smith-Lesouëf 22, fol. 1

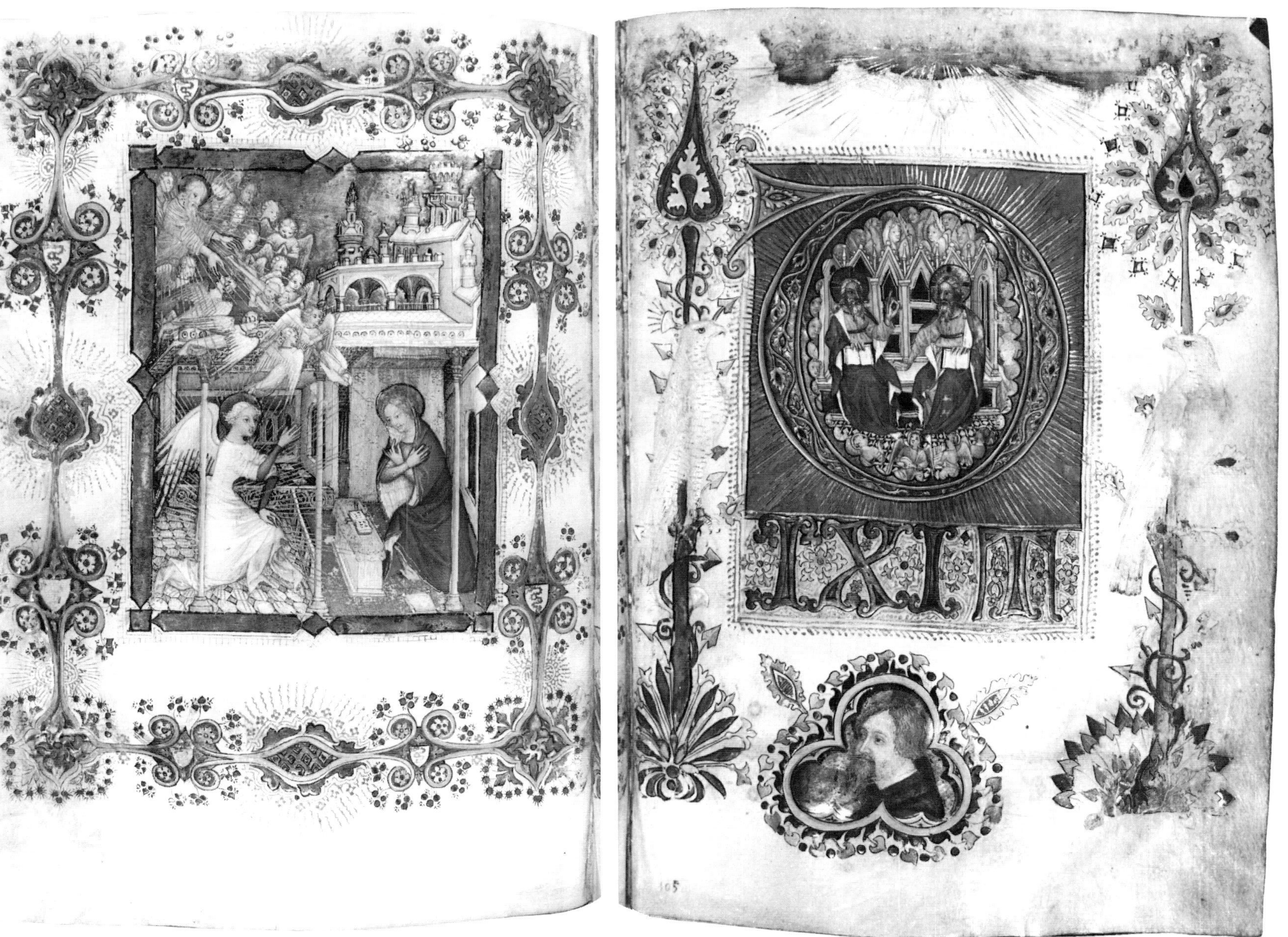

Fig. 46. Giovannino (and Salomone?) dei Grassi, c. 1388–91, Annunciation; Trinity, portrait of Giangaleazzo Visconti. Florence, Bibl. naz., Banco Rari 397, fols. 104v–105

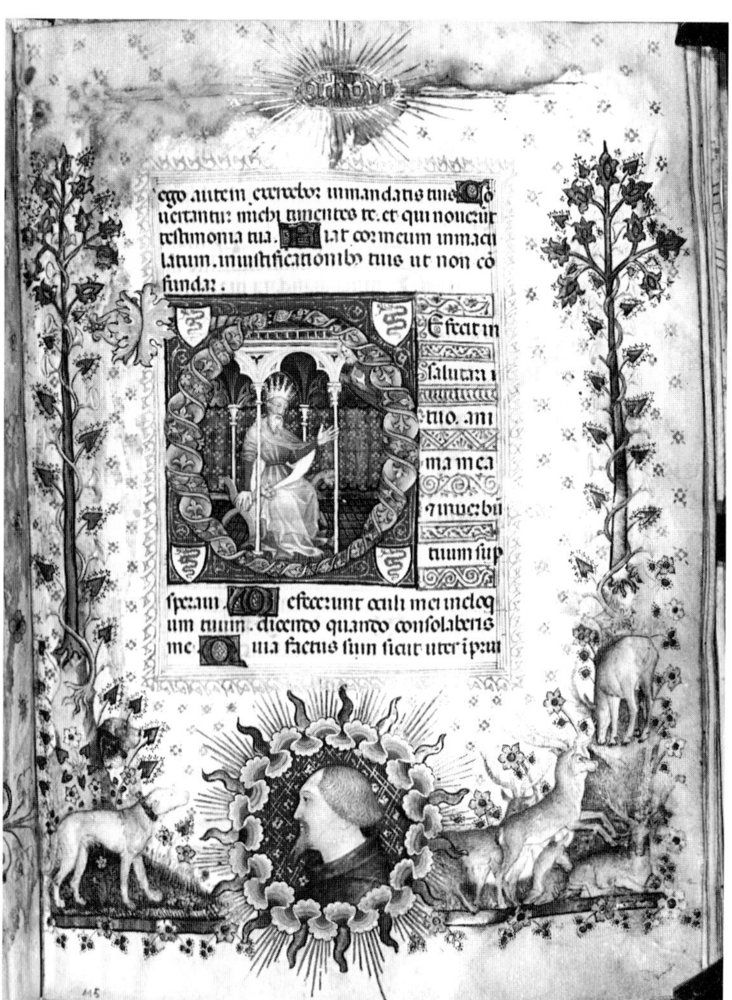

Fig. 47. Giovannino dei Grassi, c. 1388–91, David and the Lord, portrait of Giangaleazzo Visconti. Florence, Bibl. naz., Banco Rari 397, fol. 115

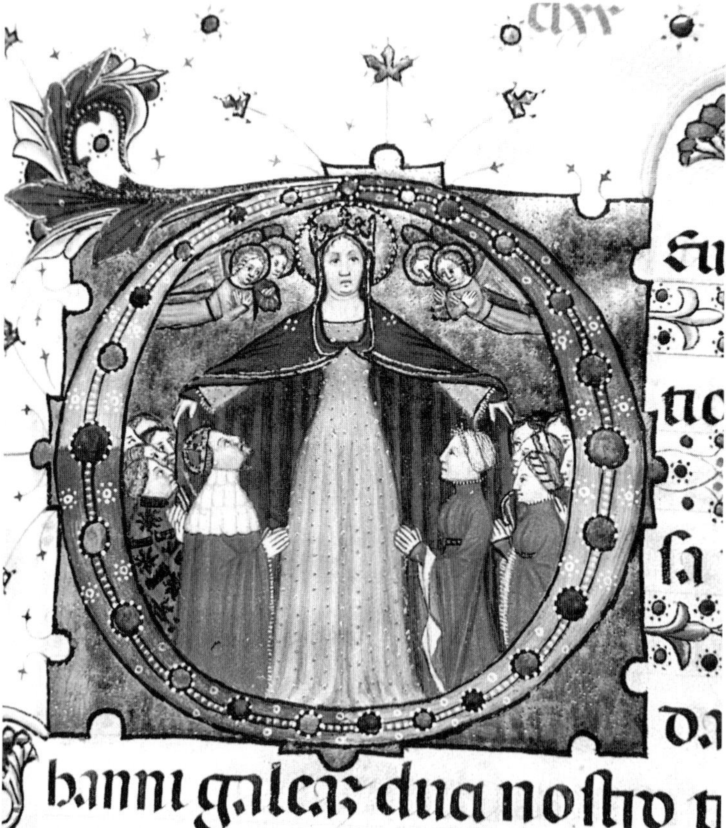

Fig. 48. Anovelo da Imbonate, c. 1395, Giangaleazzo and Caterina Visconti with courtiers worship the Madonna of Mercy. Milan, Bibl. capitolare di Sant'Ambrogio, Lat. 6, fol. 176

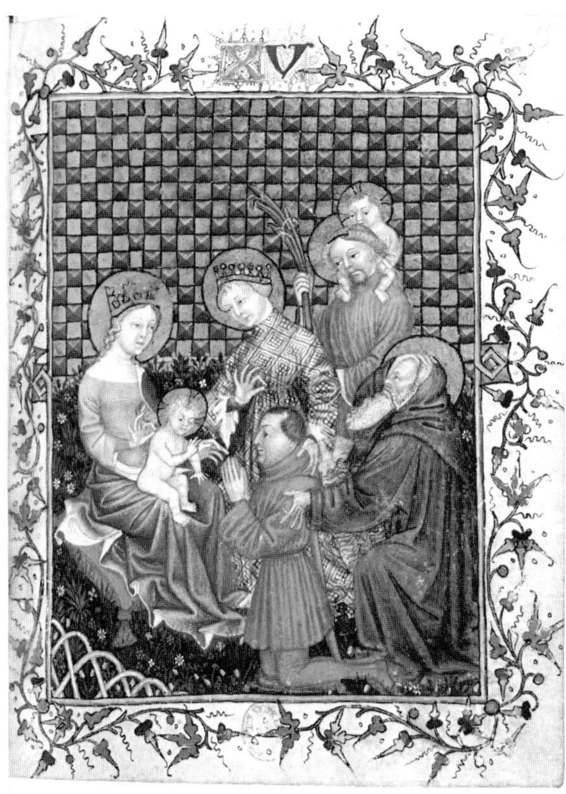

Fig. 49. Lombard, c. 1380, Giangaleazzo Visconti presented to the Madonna and Child by a crowned female saint (Catherine?), Saint Christopher, and a hermit saint (Anthony Abbot?). Paris, Bibl. nat., Smith-Lesouëf 22, fol. 15

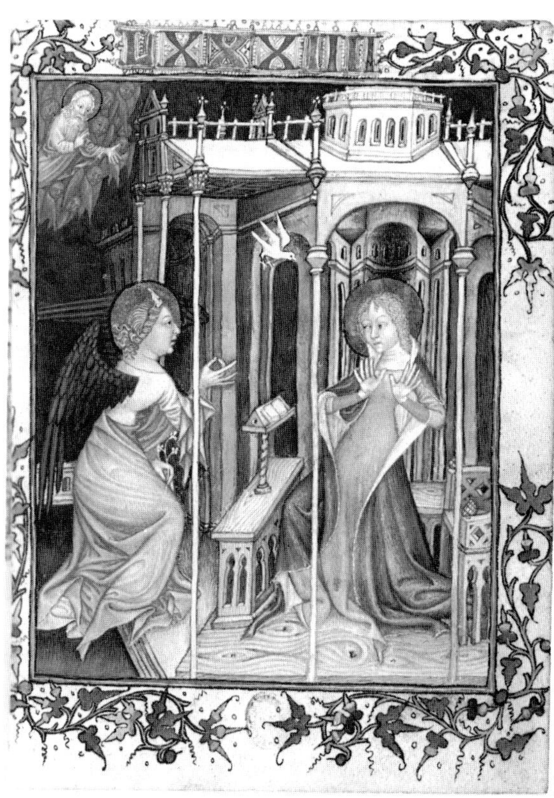

Fig. 50. Lombard, c. 1380, Annunciation. Paris, Bibl. nat., Smith-Lesouëf 22, fol. 84

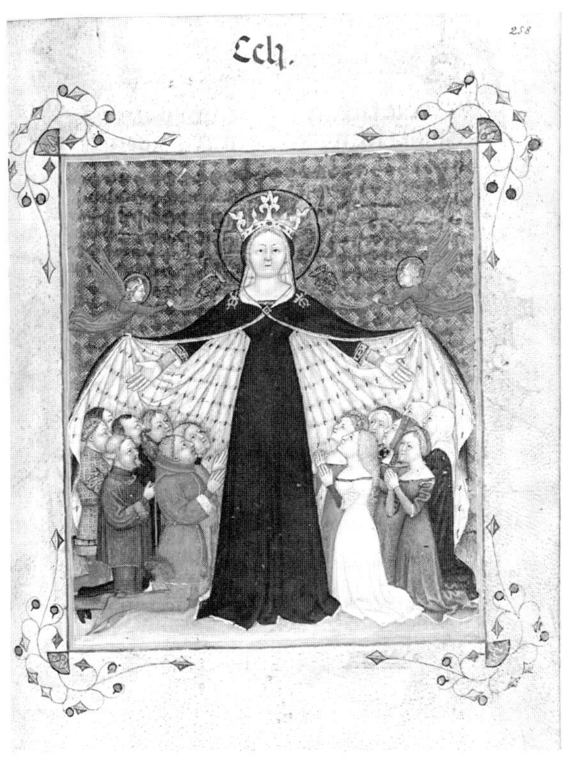

Fig. 51. Lombard, c. 1380, Giangaleazzo and Caterina Visconti with courtiers worship the Madonna of Mercy. Paris, Bibl. nat., Lat. 757, fol. 258

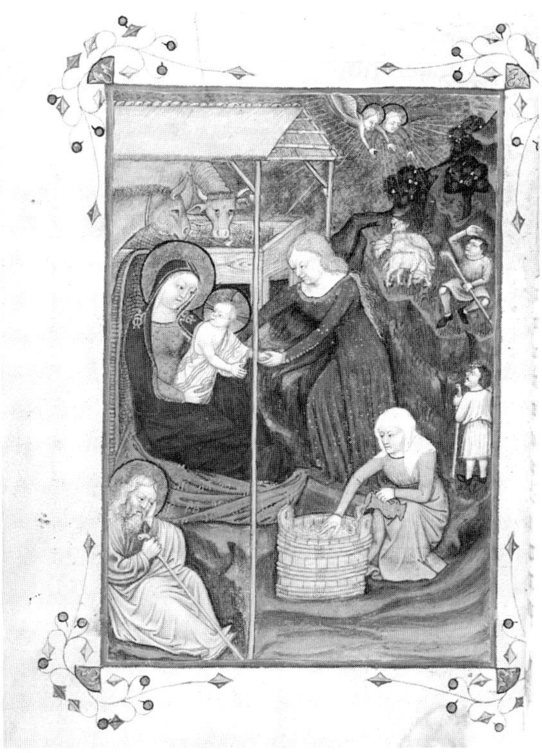

Fig. 52. Lombard, c. 1380, Nativity. Paris, Bibl. nat., Lat. 757, fol. 283v

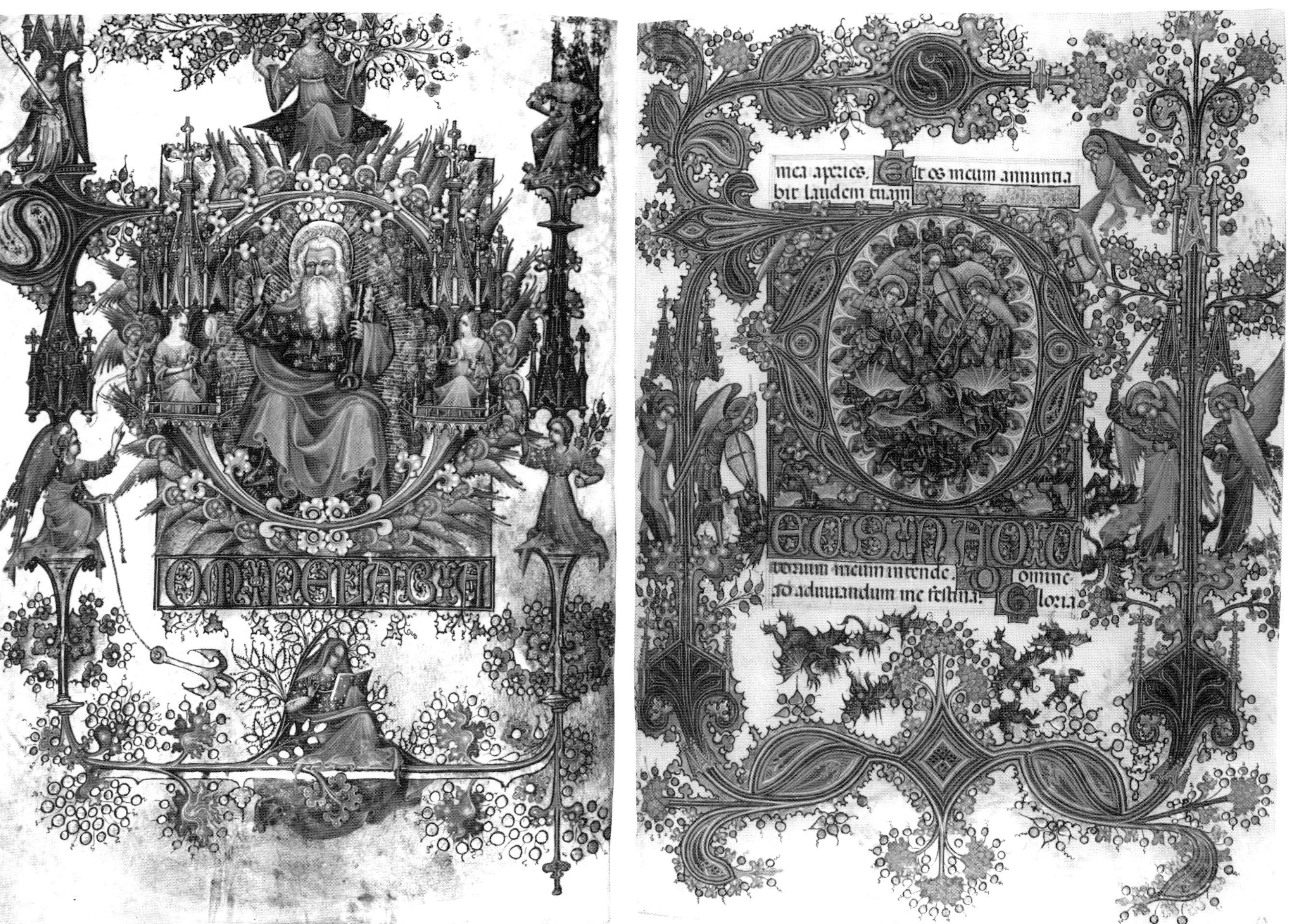

Fig. 53. Belbello da Pavia (on a dei Grassi design), c. 1427, Celestial Court and Fall of the Rebel Angels. Florence, Bibl. naz., Landau-Finaly, fols. 11v–12

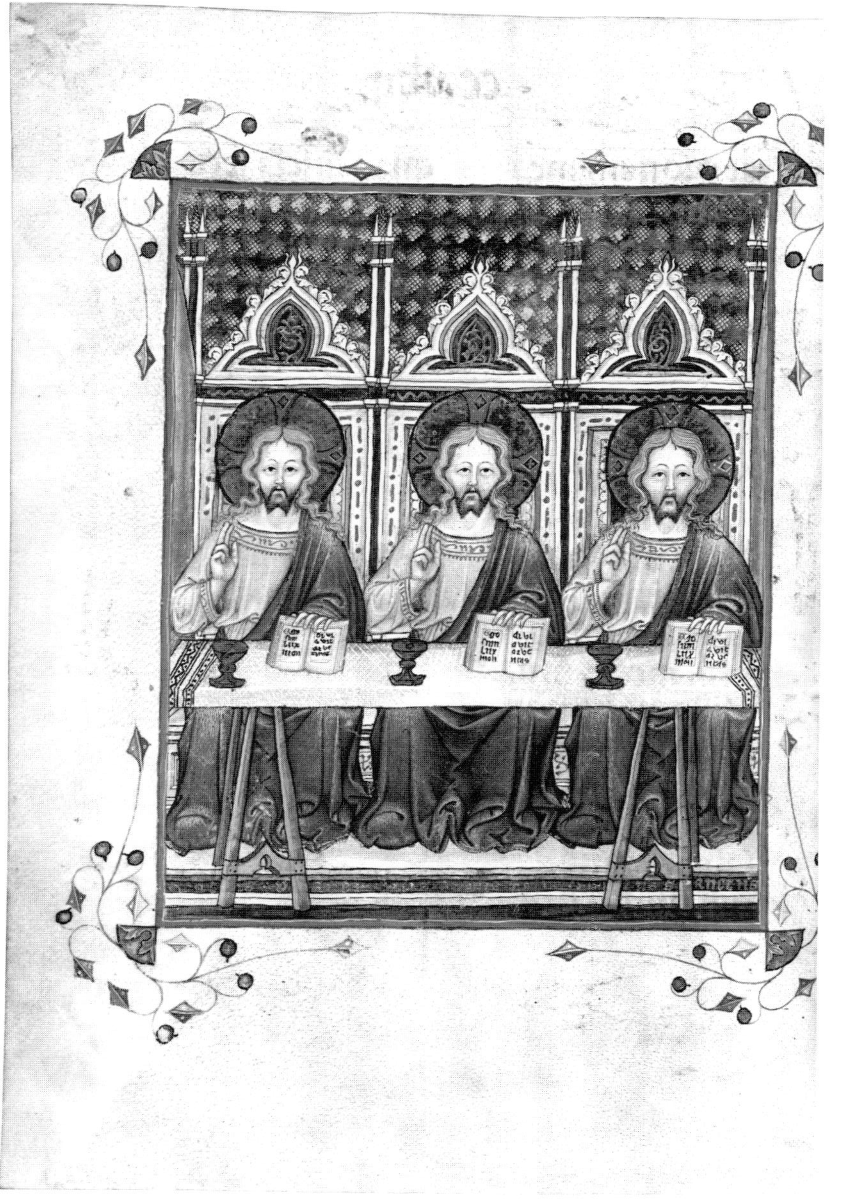

Fig. 54. Lombard, c. 1380, Trinity. Paris, Bibl. nat., Lat. 757, fol. 229v

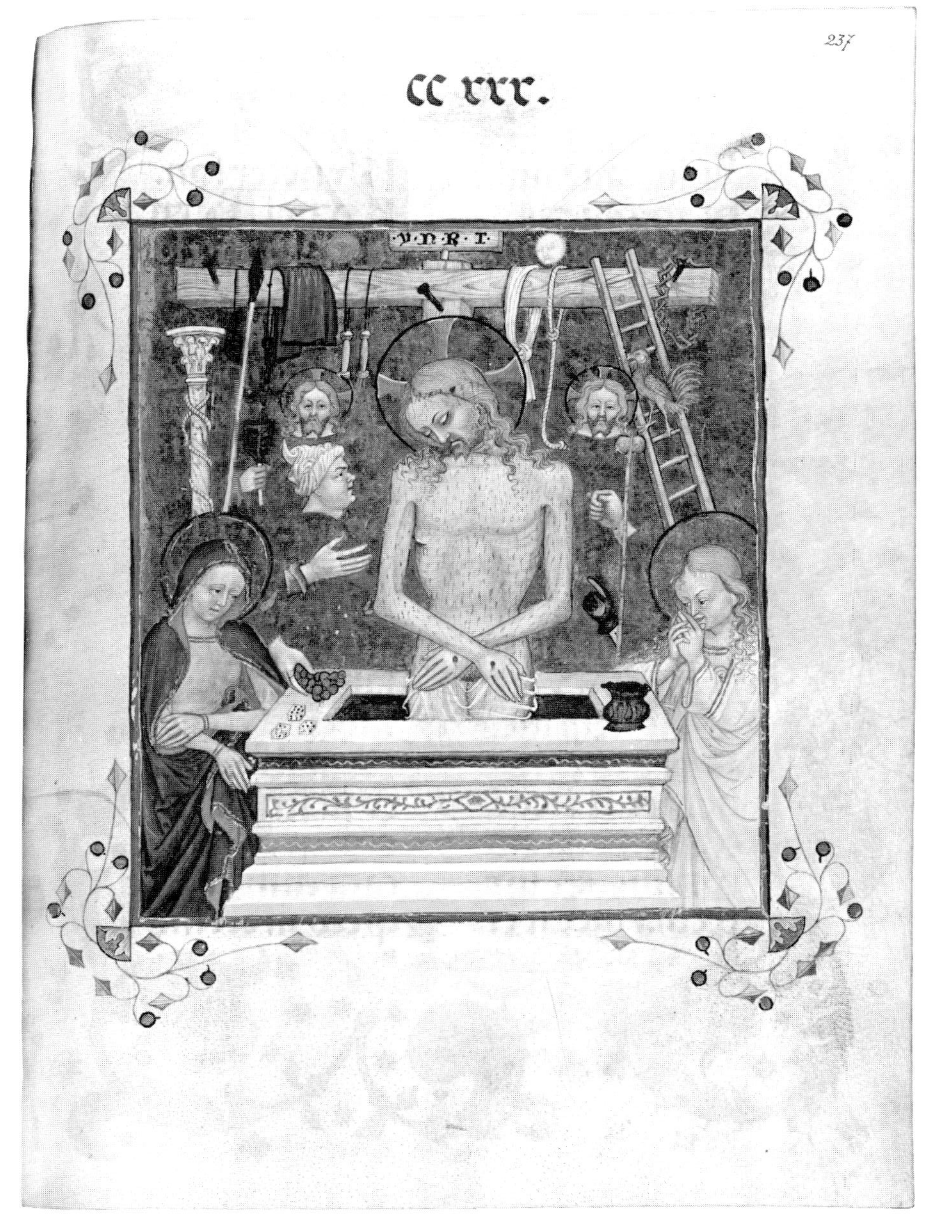

Fig. 55. Lombard, c. 1380, Man of Sorrows. Paris, Bibl. nat., Lat. 757, fol. 237

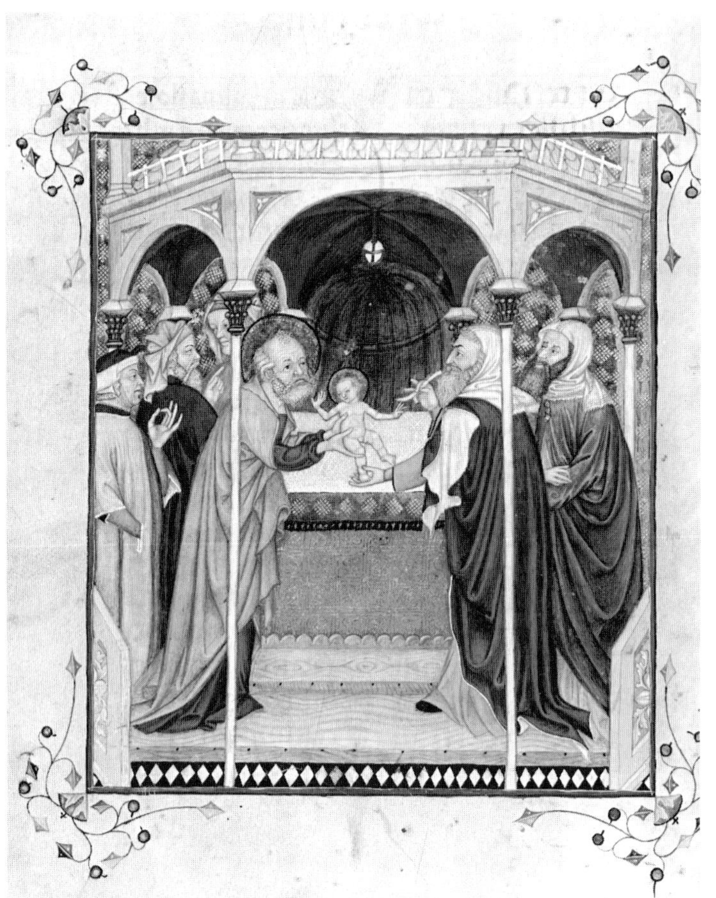

Fig. 56. Lombard, c. 1380, Circumcision of Christ. Paris, Bibl. nat., Lat. 757, fol. 291v

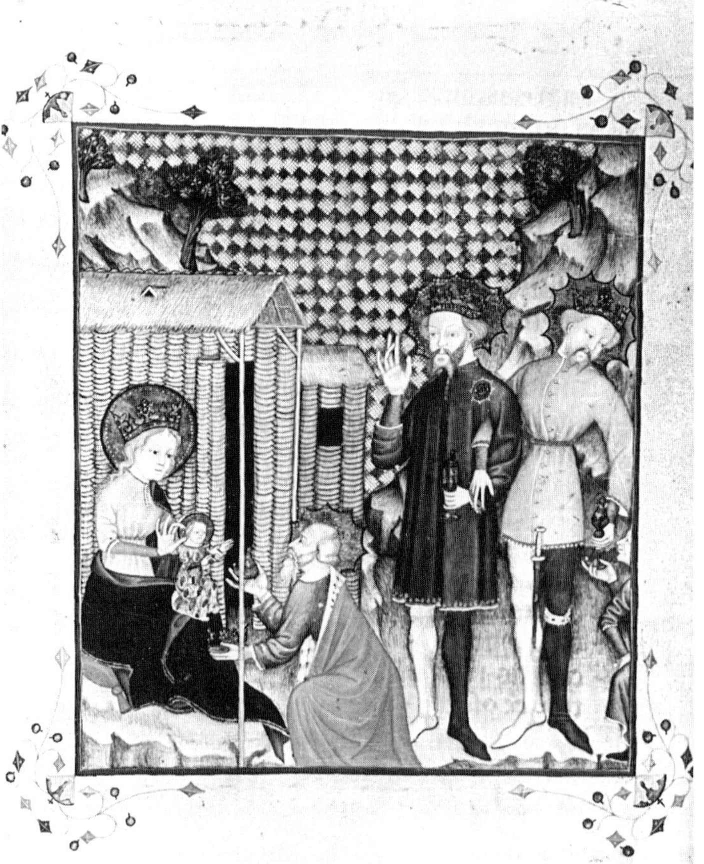

Fig. 57. Lombard, c. 1380, Adoration of the Magi. Paris, Bibl. nat., Lat. 757, fol. 293v

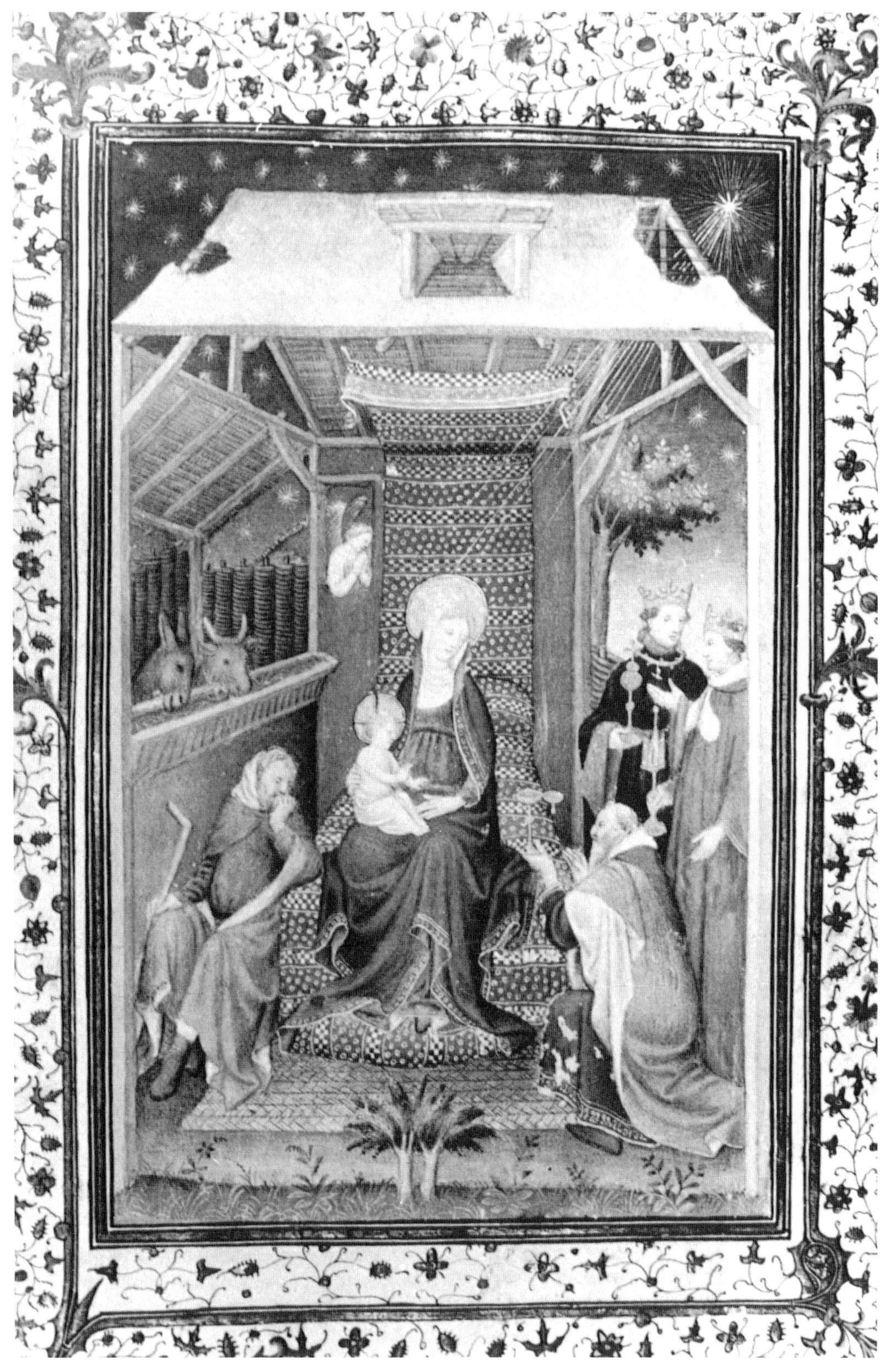

Fig. 58. Boucicaut Master, 1405–8, Adoration of the Magi. Musée Jacquemart-André, MS 2, fol. 83v

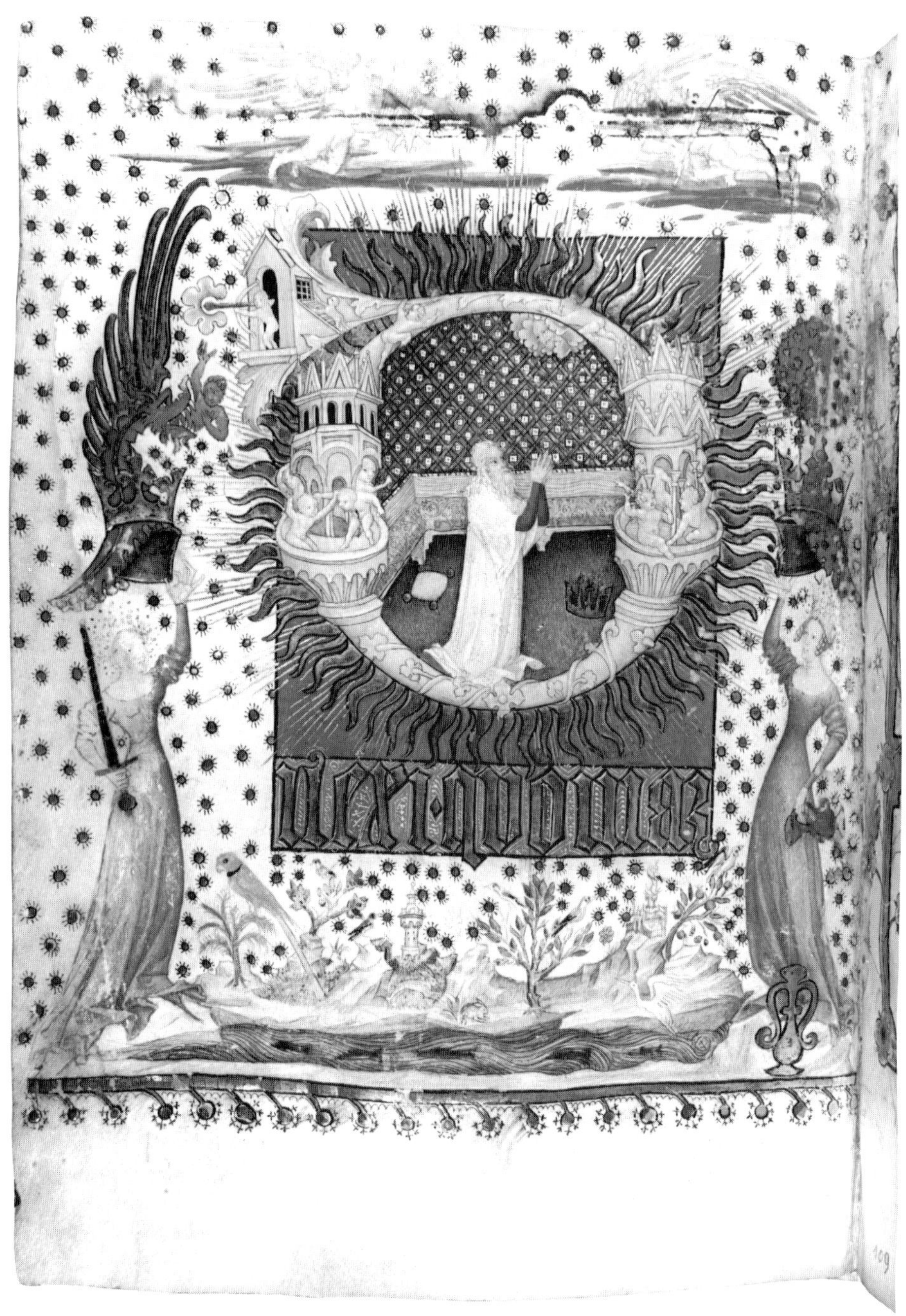

Fig. 59. Giovannino and Salomone dei Grassi, c. 1389–91, David in prayer; Justice and Temperance in margins. Florence, Bibl. naz., Banco Rari 397, fol. 108v

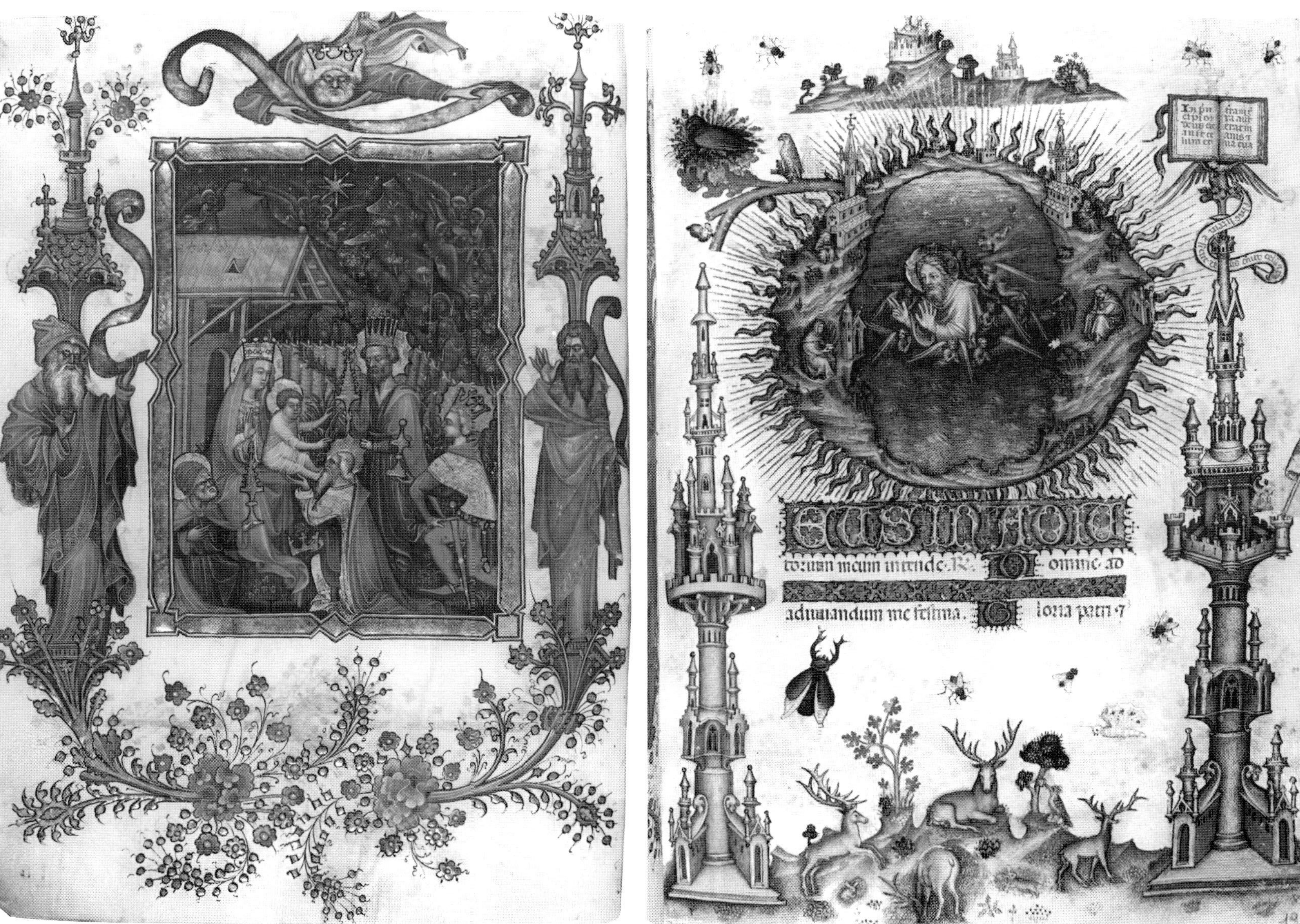

Fig. 60. Belbello da Pavia (on a dei Grassi design), c. 1427, Adoration of the Magi; Giovannino and Salomone dei Grassi, c. 1395, Creation of Heaven and Earth. Florence, Bibl. naz., Landau-Finaly 22, fols. 18v–19

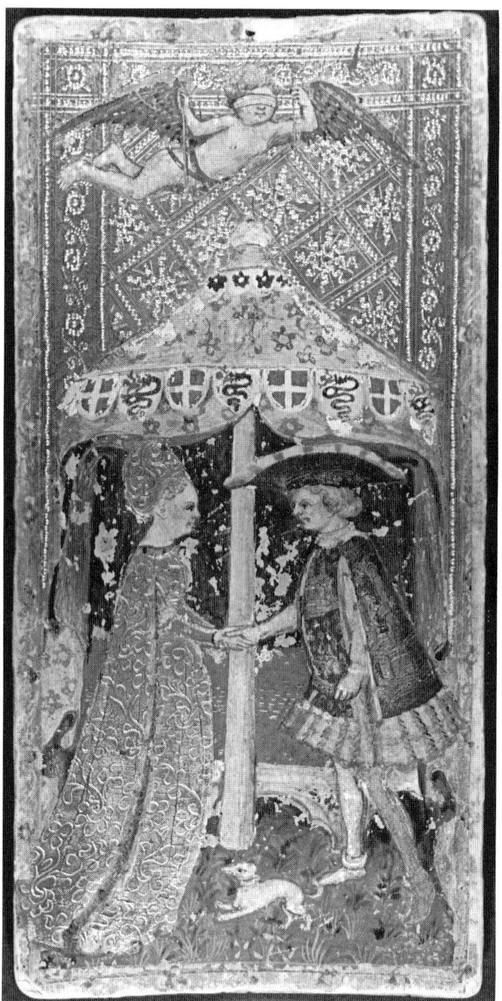

Fig. 61. North Italy, second quarter of the fifteenth century, tarot card with Filippo Maria Visconti and Marie of Savoy. New Haven, Yale University, Beinecke Lib., Cary Collection of Playing Cards, No. ITA 109

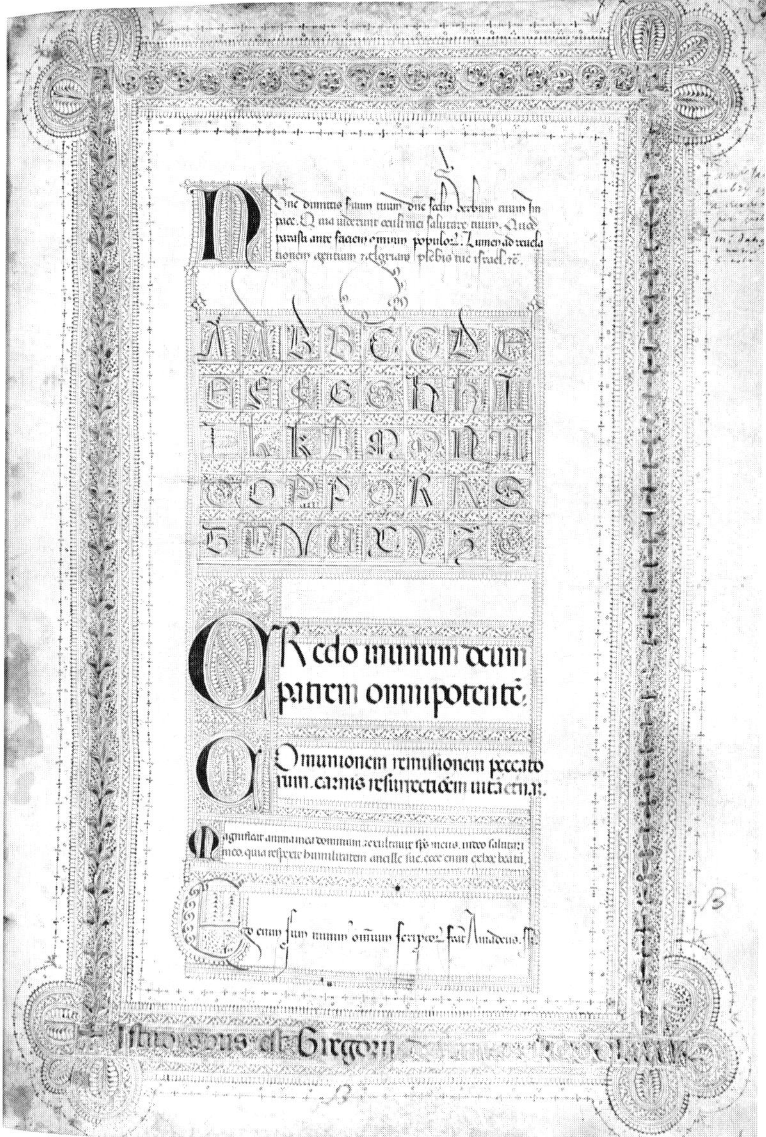

Fig. 62. Frater Amadeus, 1385, specimen page of writing. Glasgow University Lib., Hunterian MS 374, fol. 1

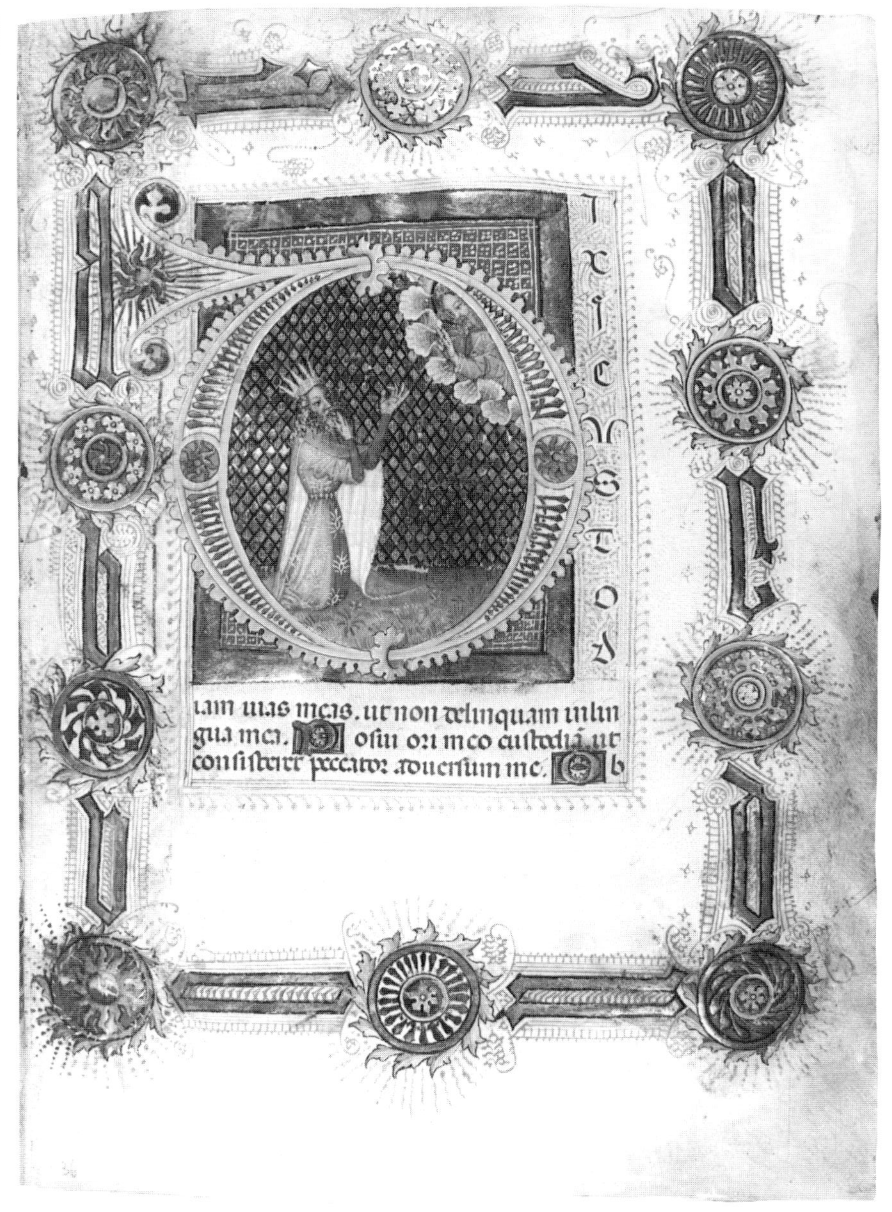

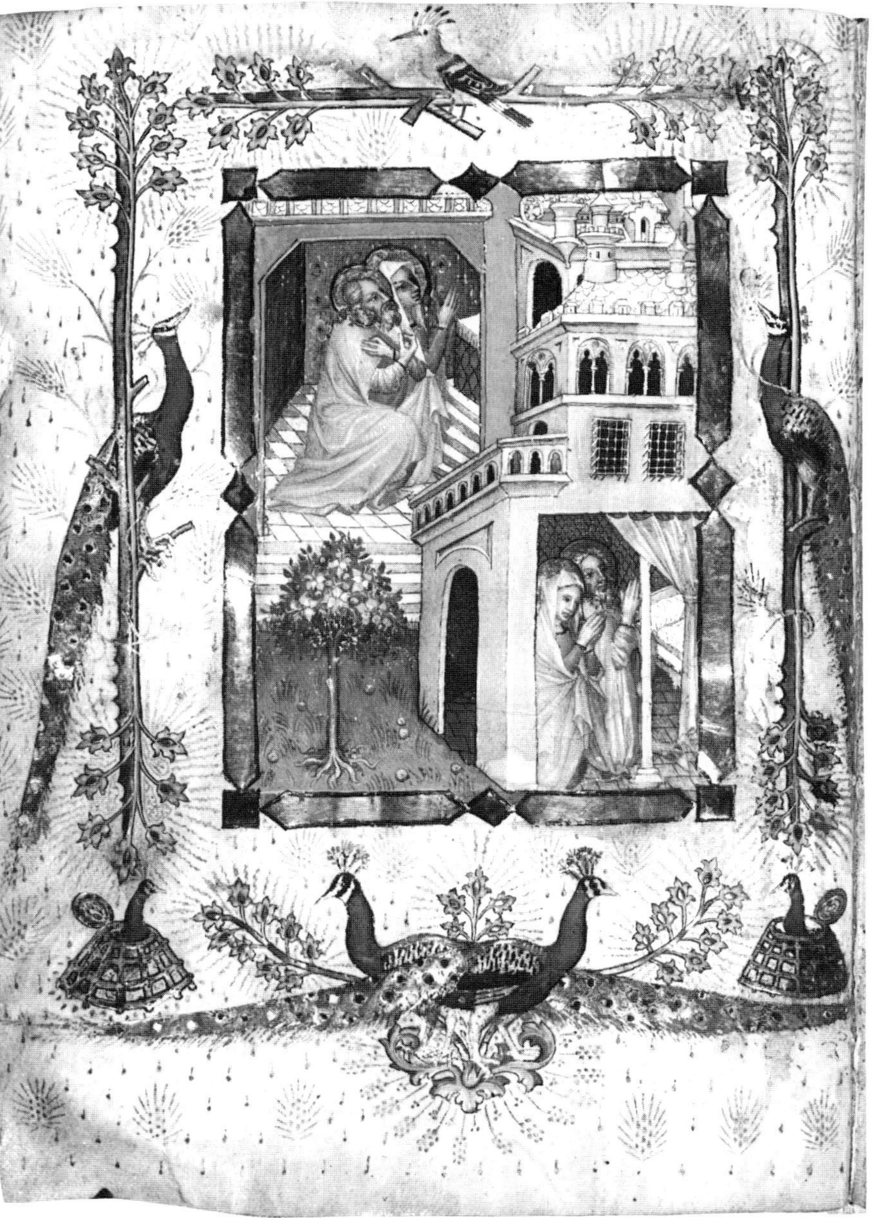

Fig. 63. Giovannino dei Grassi (and assistant?), c. 1388–91, Anna and Joachim give thanks; David pointing to his mouth. Florence, Bibl. naz., Banco Rari 397, fols. 35v–36

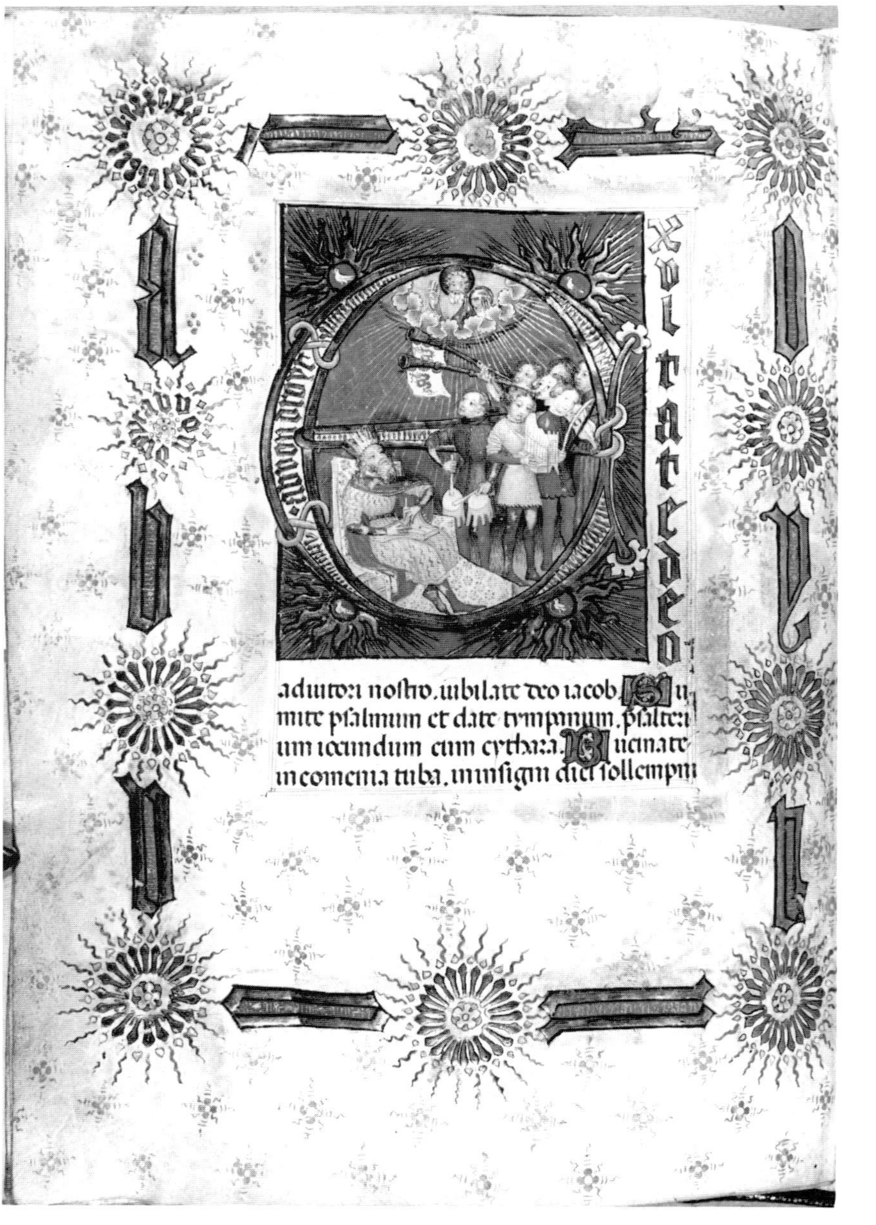

Fig. 64. Giovannino dei Grassi, c. 1388–91, David and courtiers playing musical instruments. Florence, Bibl. naz., Banco Rari 397, fol. 76v

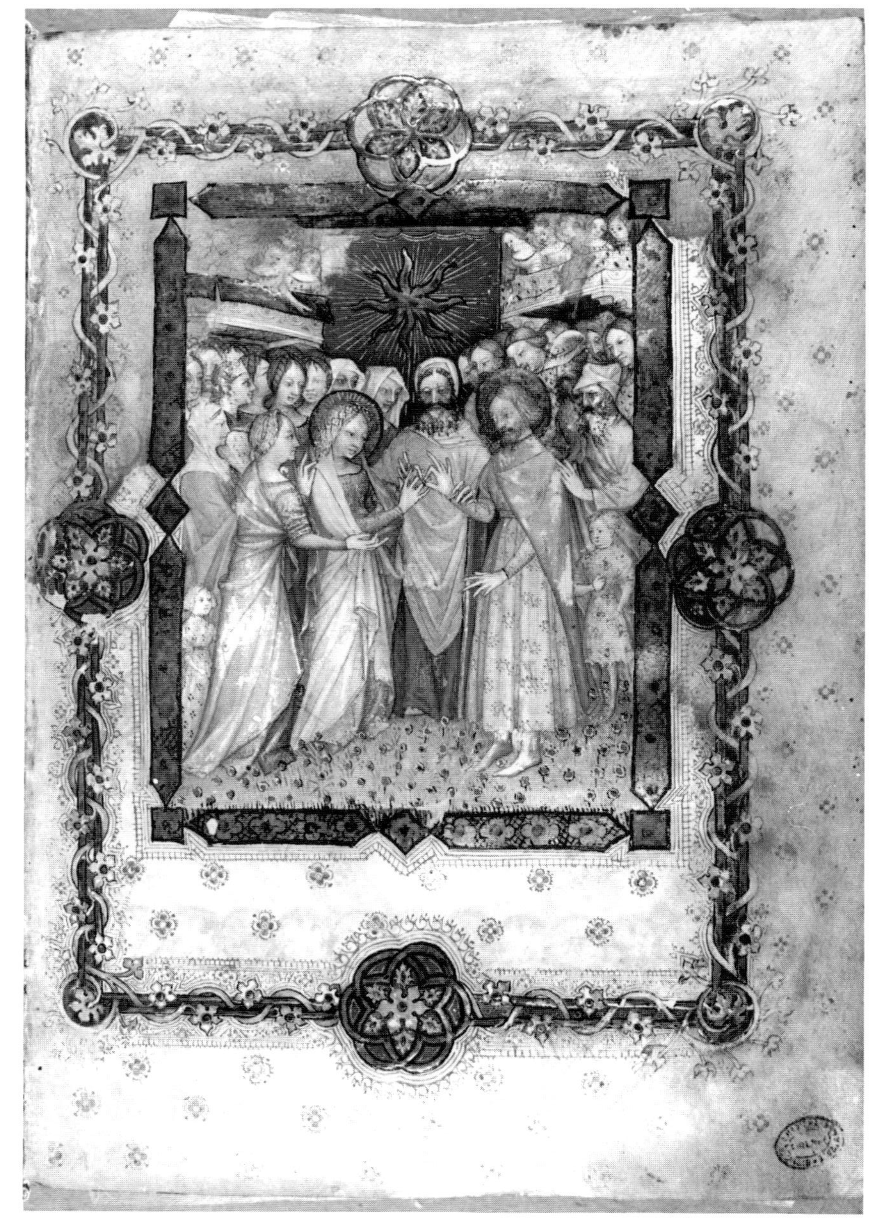

Fig. 65. Giovannino dei Grassi, c. 1388–91, Marriage of Anna and Joachim. Florence, Bibl. naz., Banco Rari 397, fol. 1

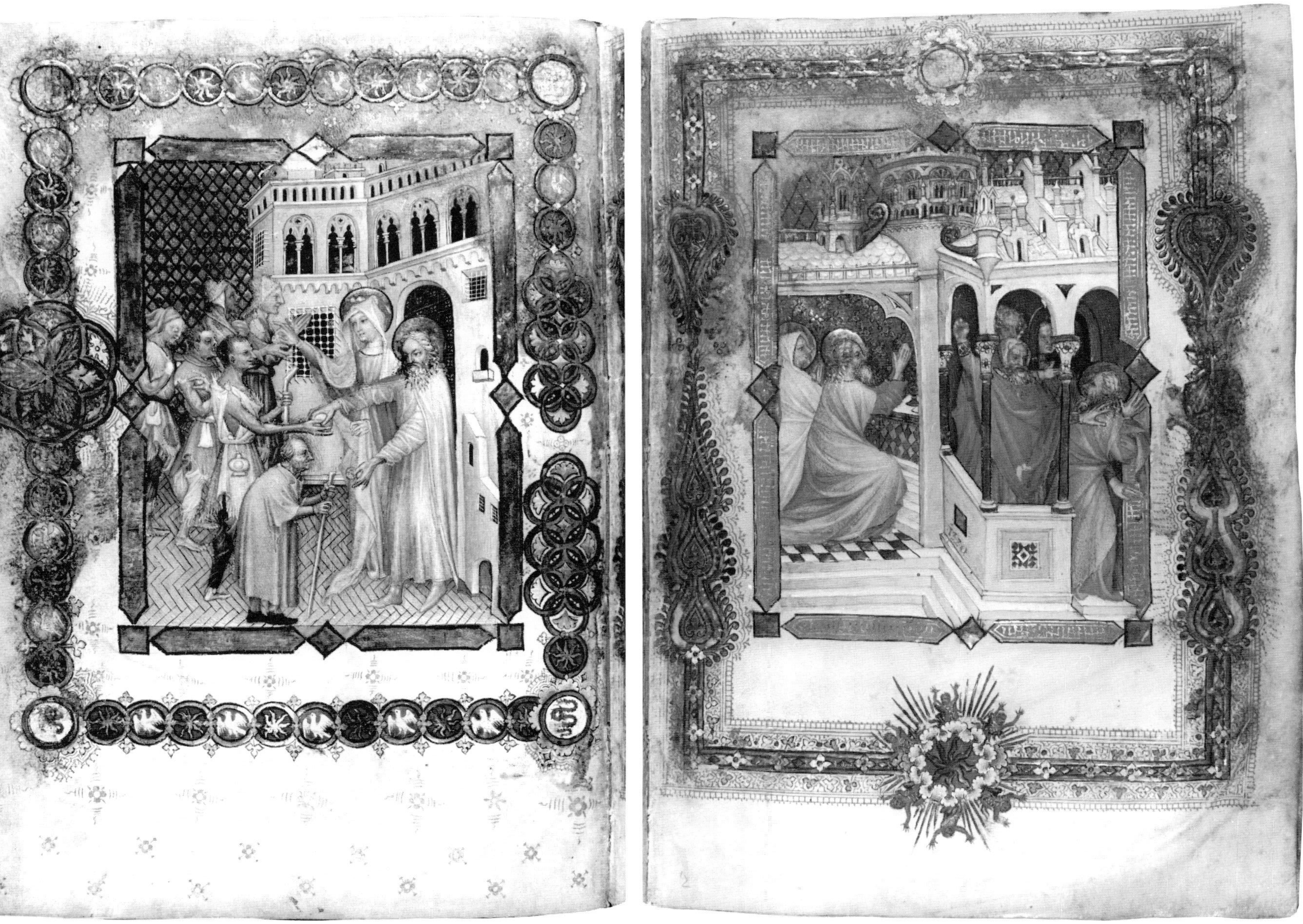

Fig. 66. Giovannino dei Grassi, c. 1388–91, Charity of Anna and Joachim; Prayer of Anna and Joachim, Expulsion of Joachim from the Temple.
Florence, Bibl. naz., Banco Rari 397, fols. 1v–2

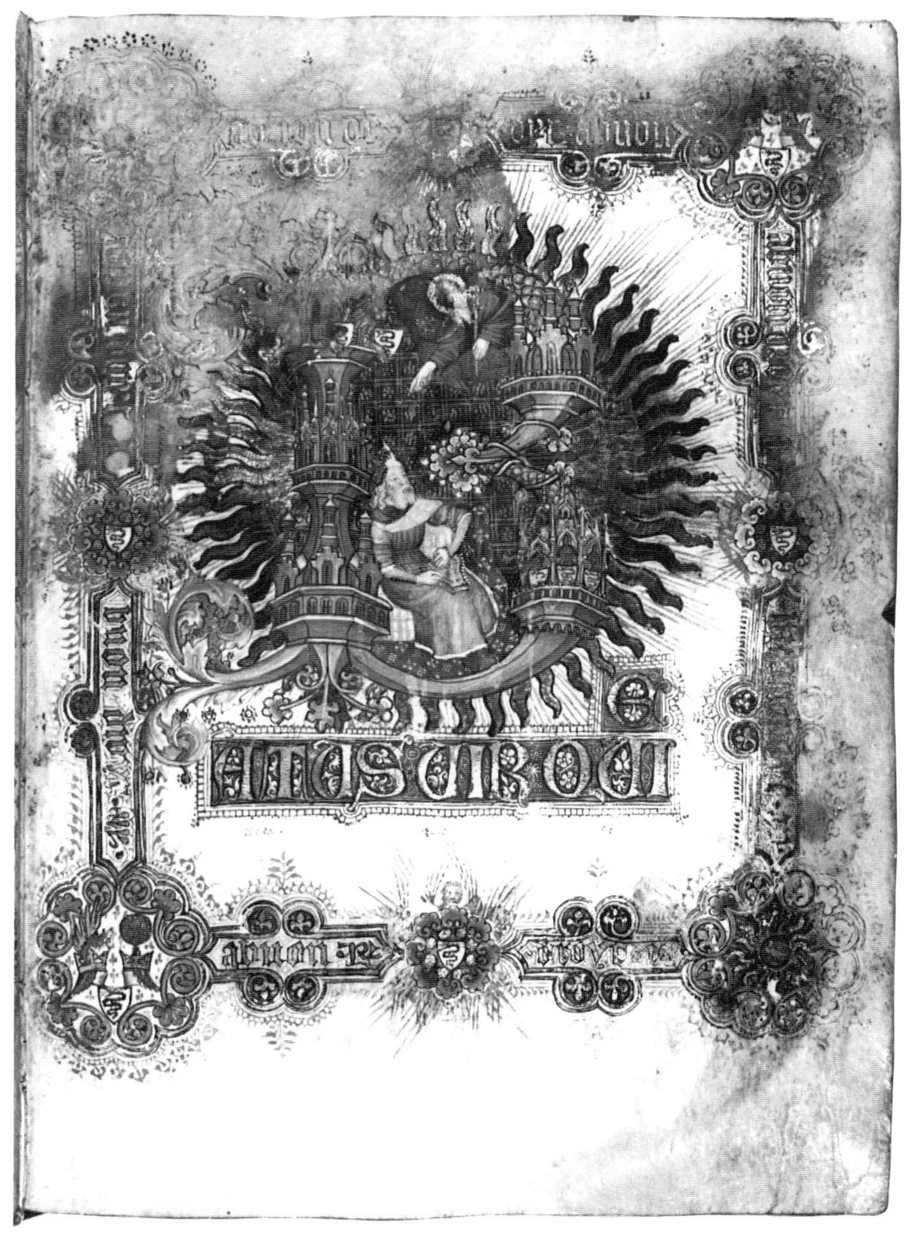

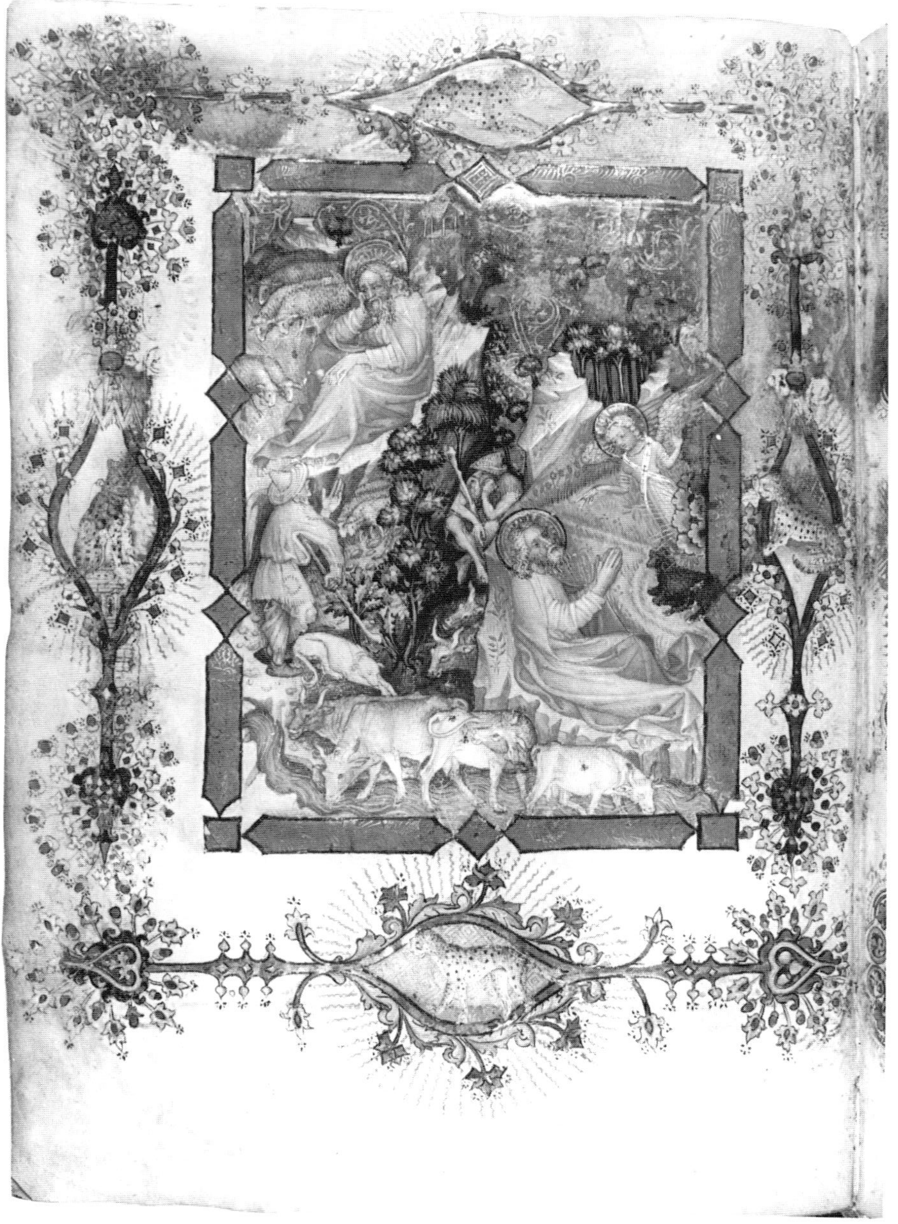

Fig. 67. Giovannino dei Grassi, c. 1388–91, Joachim in the Wilderness, Annunciation to Joachim; David playing psaltery. Florence, Bibl. naz., Banco Rari 397, fols. 2v–3

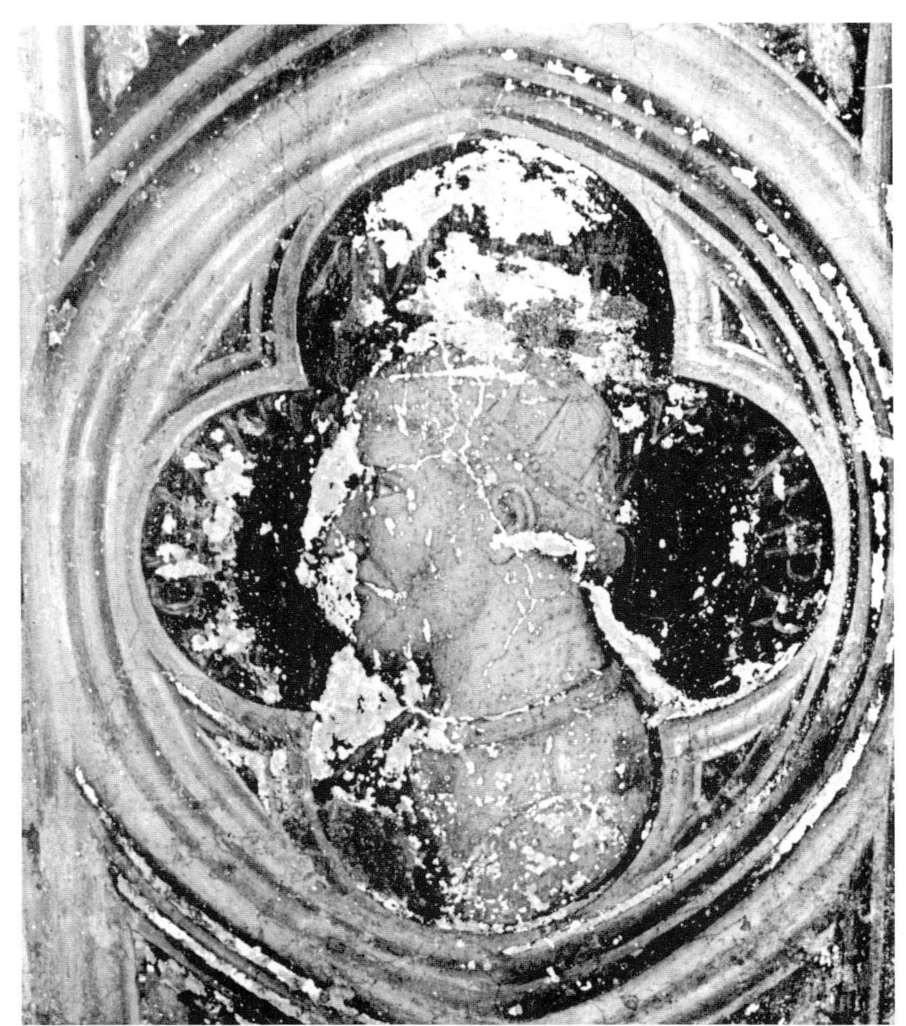

Fig. 68. Cristoforo de' Predis, c. 1477, Galeazzo Maria Sforza as David. London, Wallace Collection, M342

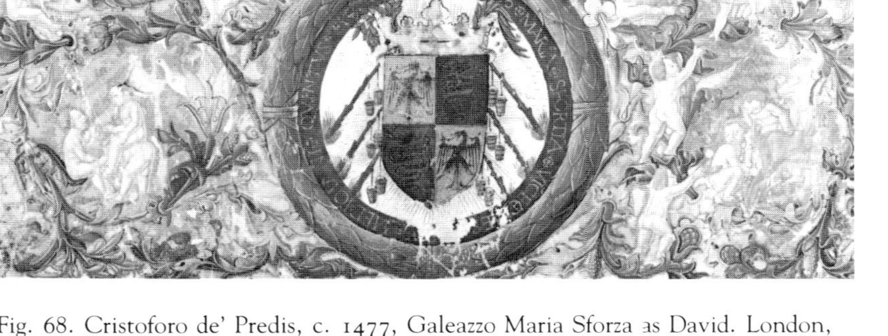

Fig. 69. Altichiero, 1360s, bust of Emperor Aurelian. Verona, Museo di Castelvecchio

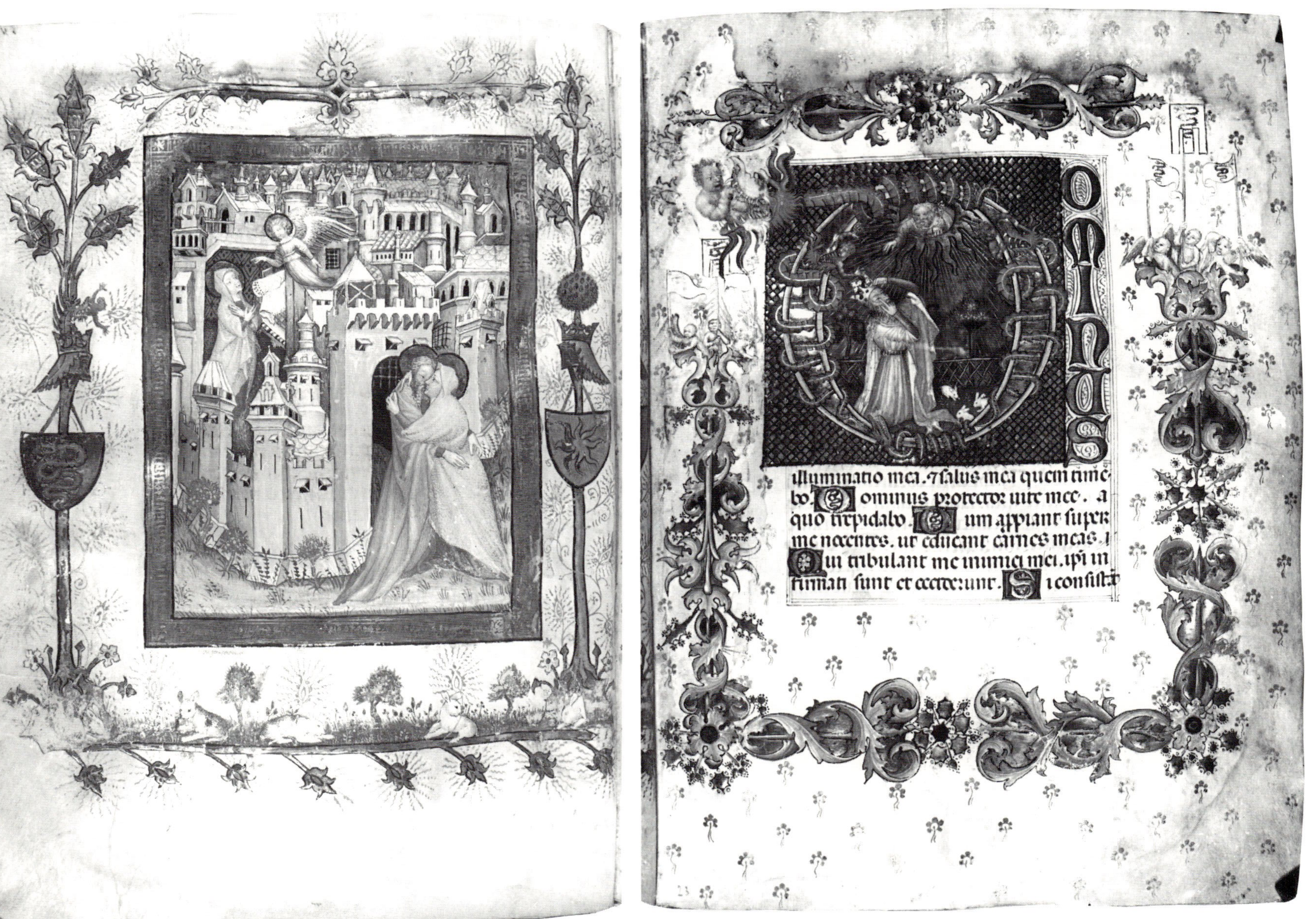

Fig. 70. Giovannino dei Grassi, c. 1388–91, Annunciation to Anna, Meeting at the Golden Gate; David pointing to his eye. Florence, Bibl. naz., Banco Rari 397, fols. 22v–23

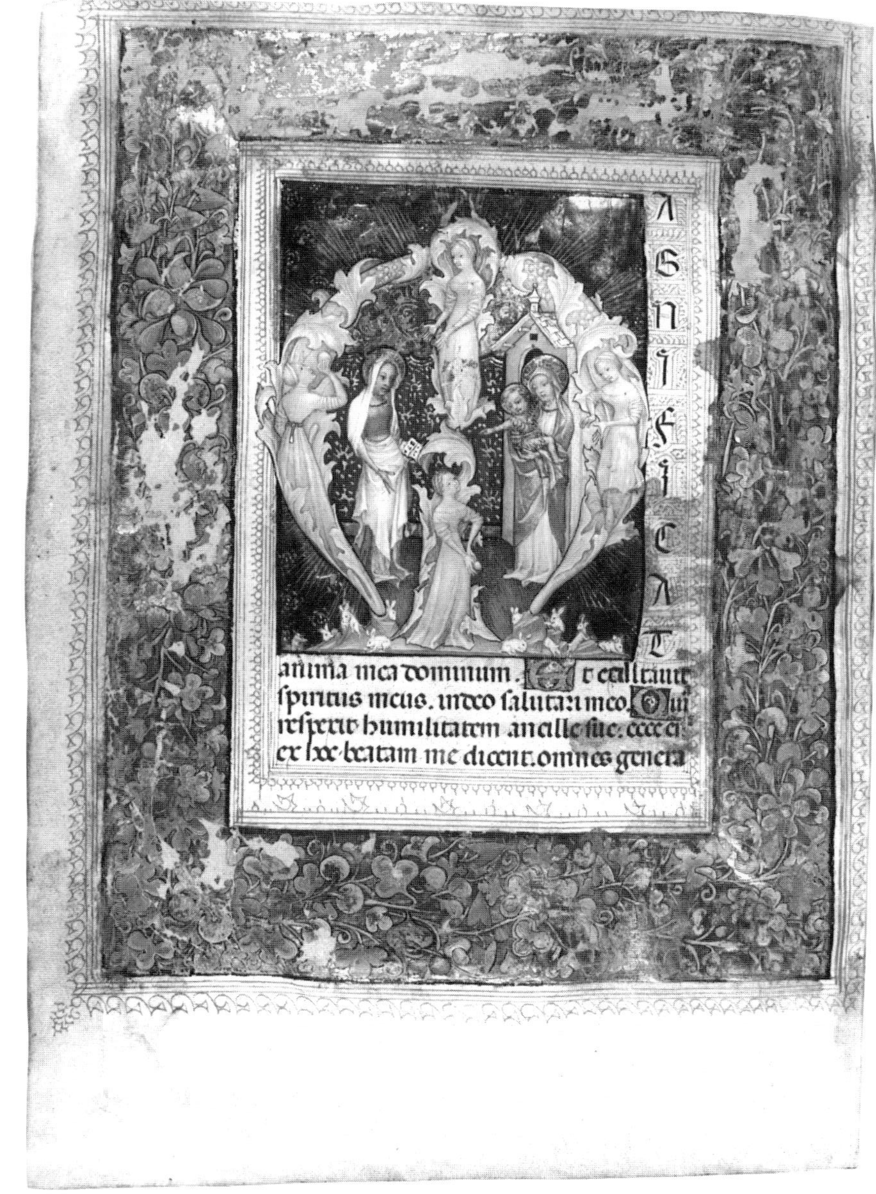

Fig. 71. Giovannino dei Grassi (and assistant?), c. 1388–91, David in prayer. Florence, Bibl. naz., Banco Rari 397, fol. 124v

Fig. 72. Giovannino dei Grassi (borders by Salomone dei Grassi?), c. 1388–91, Virgin Mary with Saints Elizabeth and John the Baptist. Florence, Bibl. naz., Banco Rari 397, fol. 147v

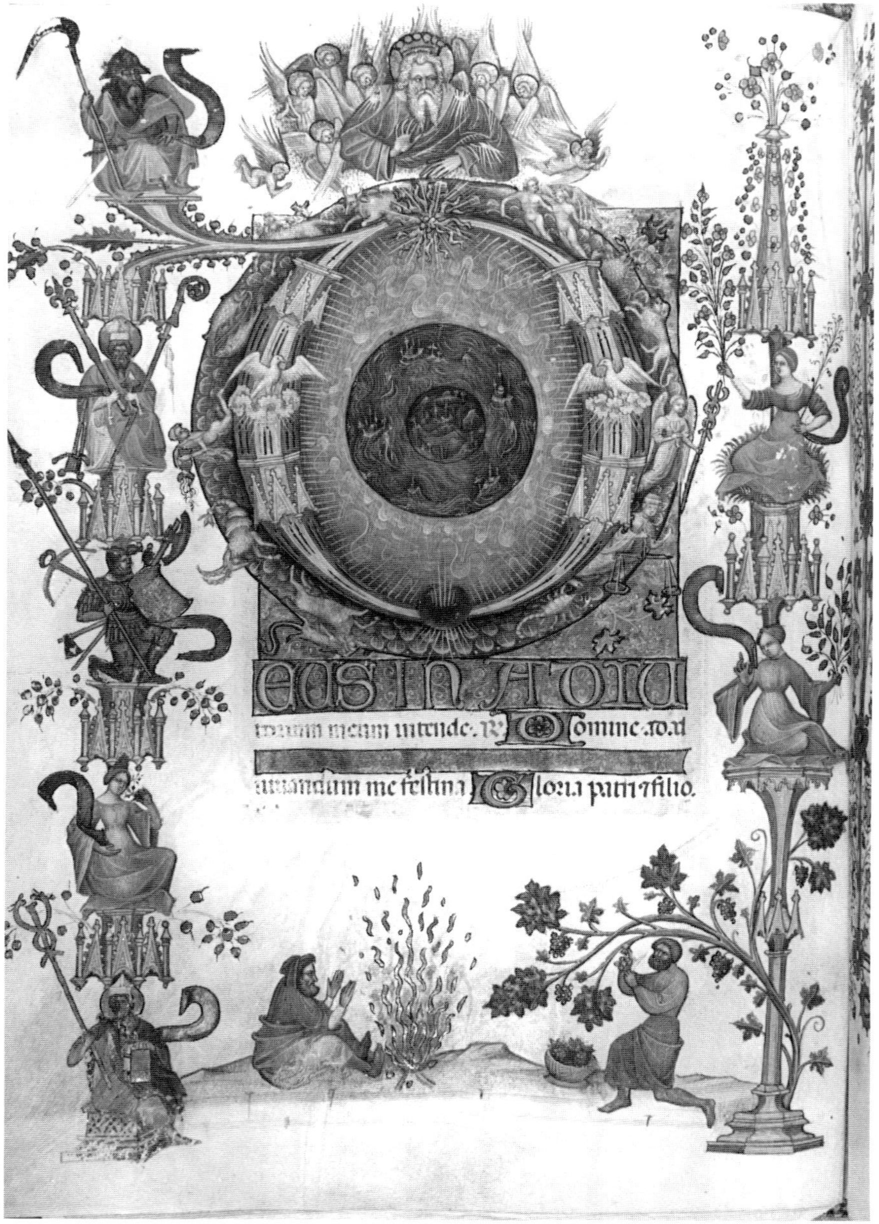

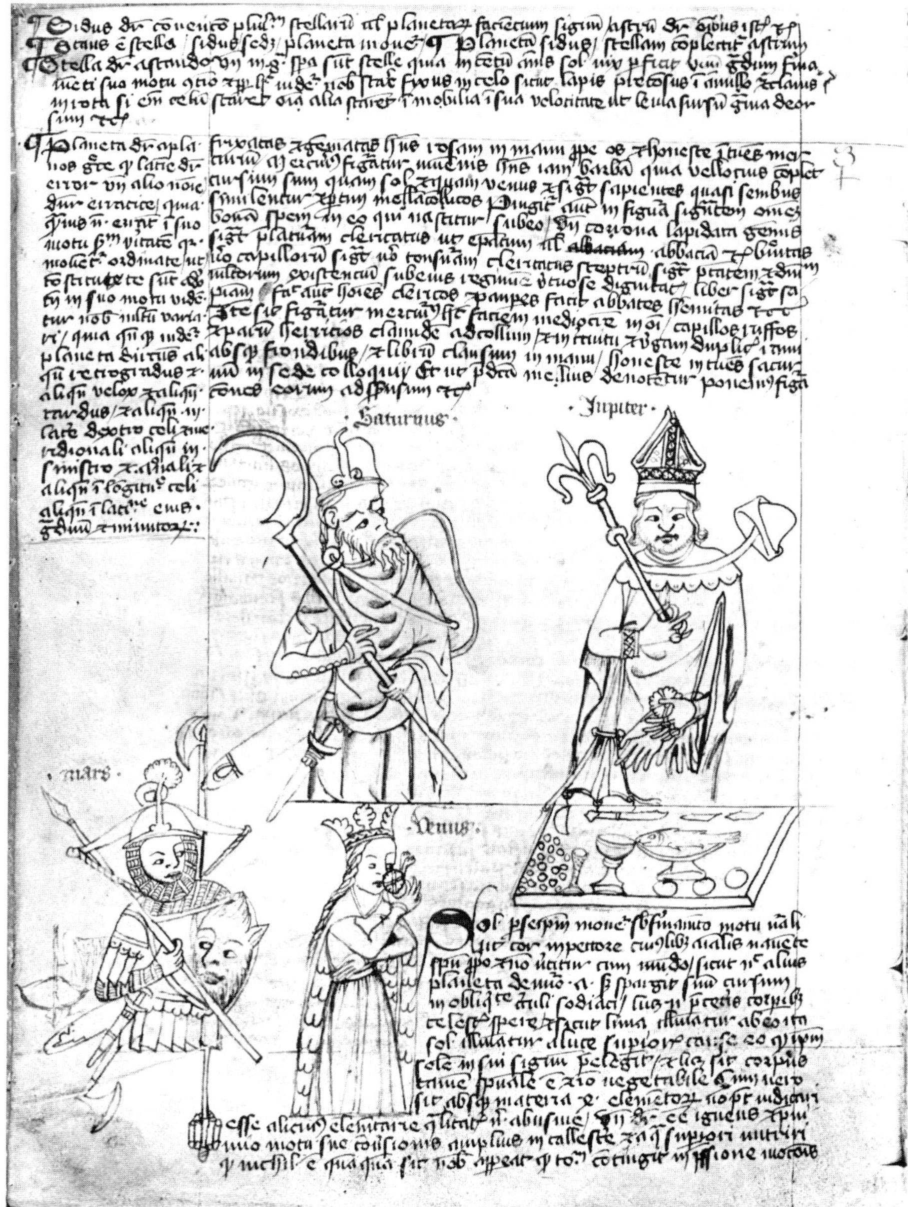

Fig. 73. Belbello da Pavia (on a design of Giovannino dei Grassi), c. 1427, Creation of Sun, Moon, and Stars. Florence, Bibl. naz., Landau-Finaly 22, fol. 37v

Fig. 74. Textbook illustrator, fourteenth century, Saturn, Jupiter, Mars, and Venus. Vienna, Österreichische Nationalbibliothek, Cod. 2378, fol. 12v

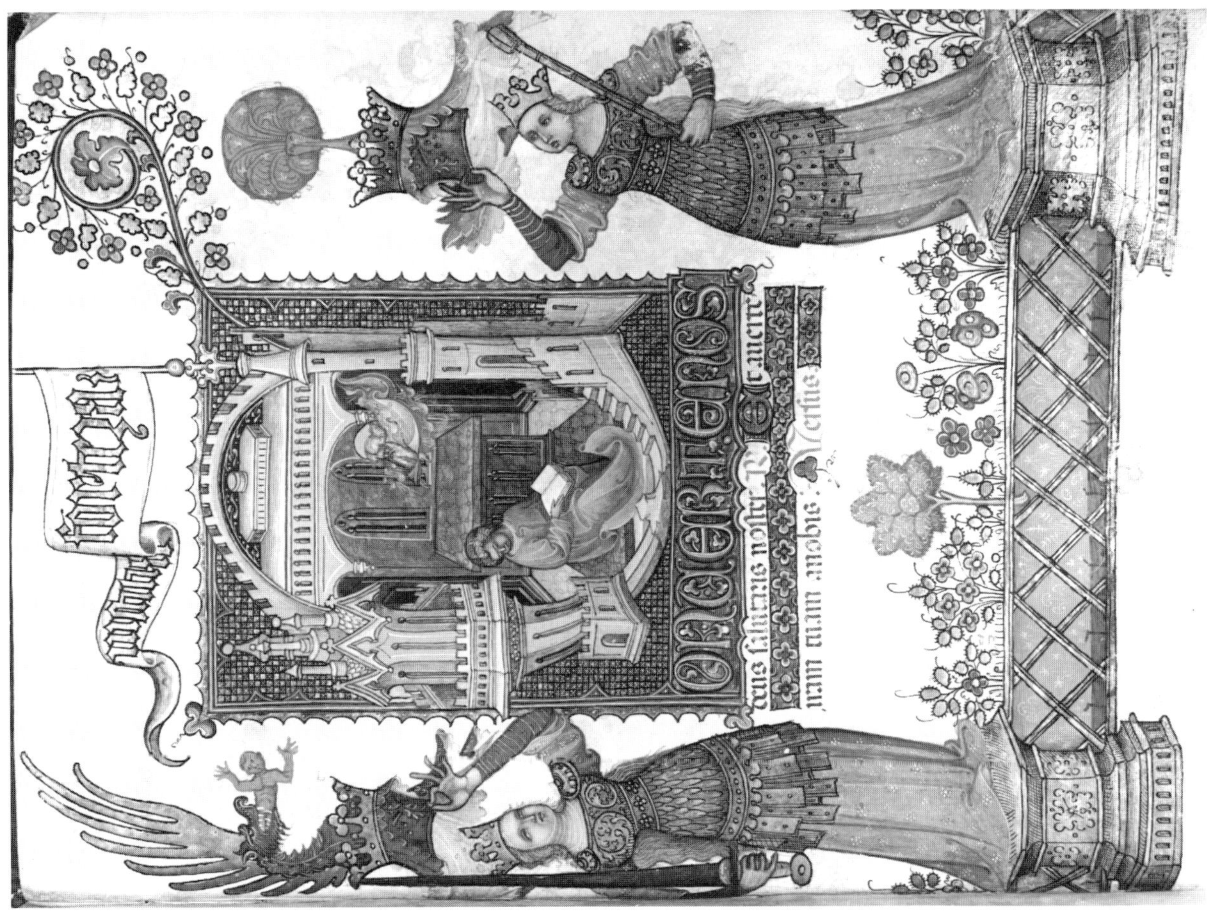

Fig. 76. Belbello da Pavia, c. 1427, Samuel called by the Lord; Justice and Fortitude in margins. Florence, Bibl. naz., Landau-Finaly 22, fol. 166

Fig. 75. Salomone dei Grassi, c. 1395, Separation of Firmament from Water. Florence, Bibl. naz., Landau-Finaly 22, fol. 26

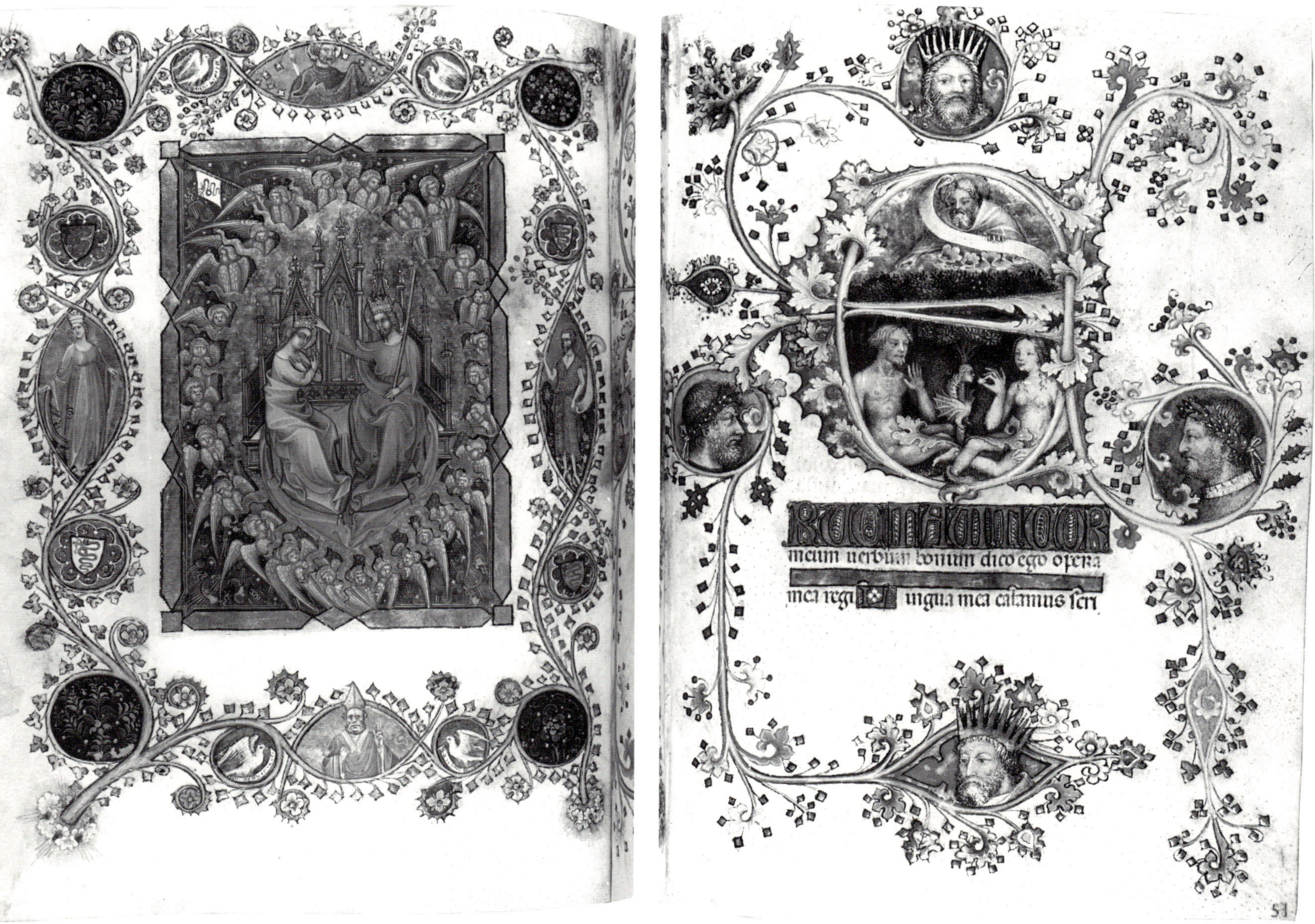

Fig. 77. Belbello da Pavia, c. 1427, Coronation of the Virgin; Giovannino and Salomone dei Grassi, c. 1395, Sin of Adam and Eve. Florence, Bibl. naz., Landau-Finaly 22, fols. 50v–51

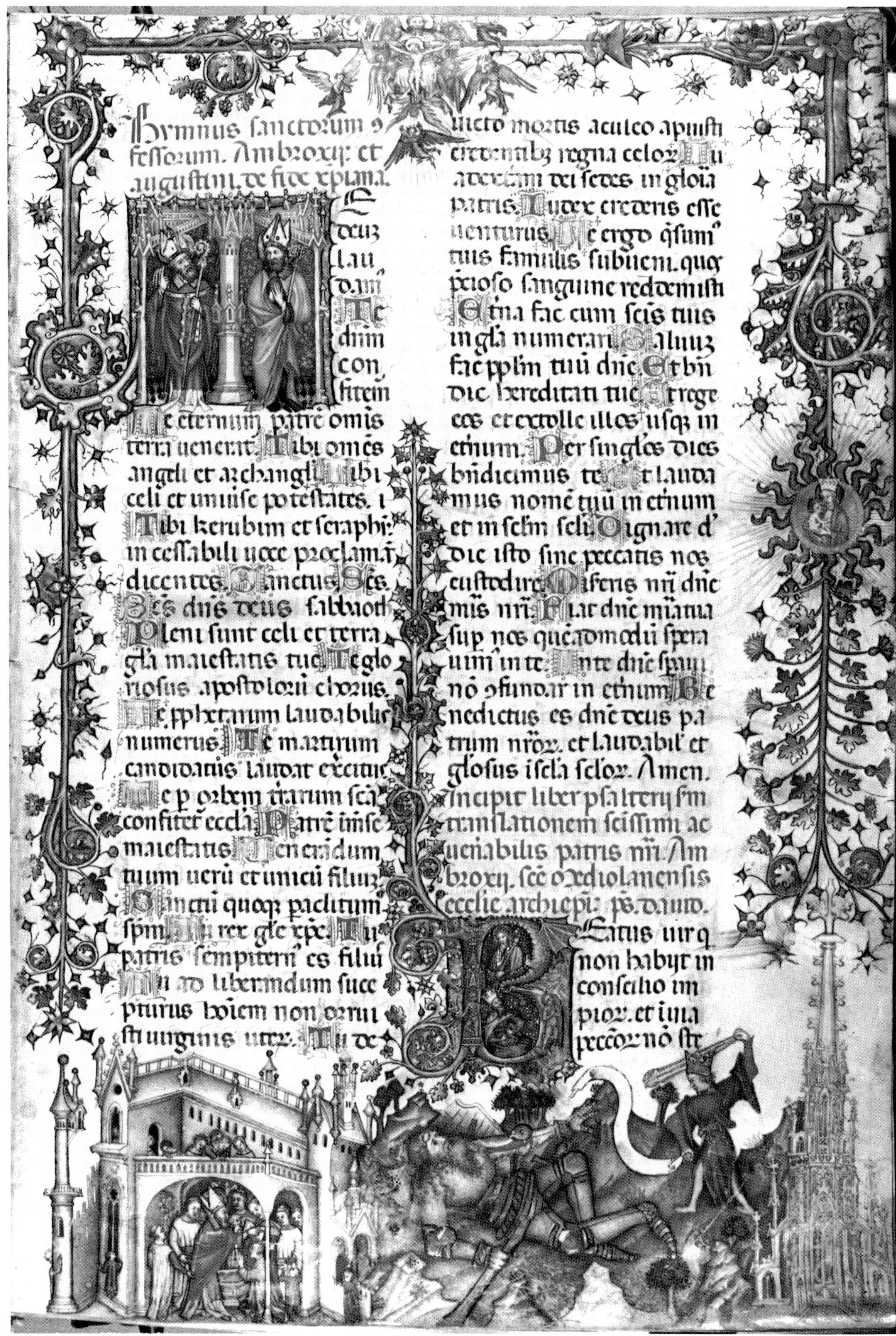

Fig. 78. Salomone dei Grassi, 1396–98, opening page of the Beroldo. Milan, Bibl. Trivulziana, Lat. 2262, fol. 1

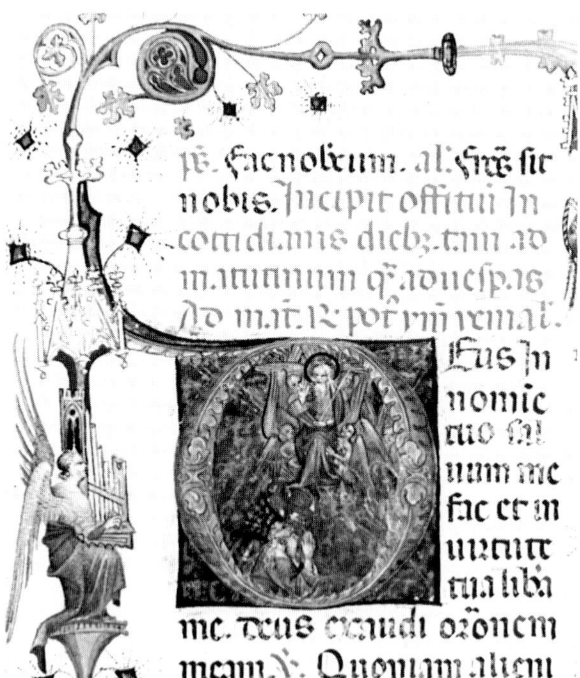

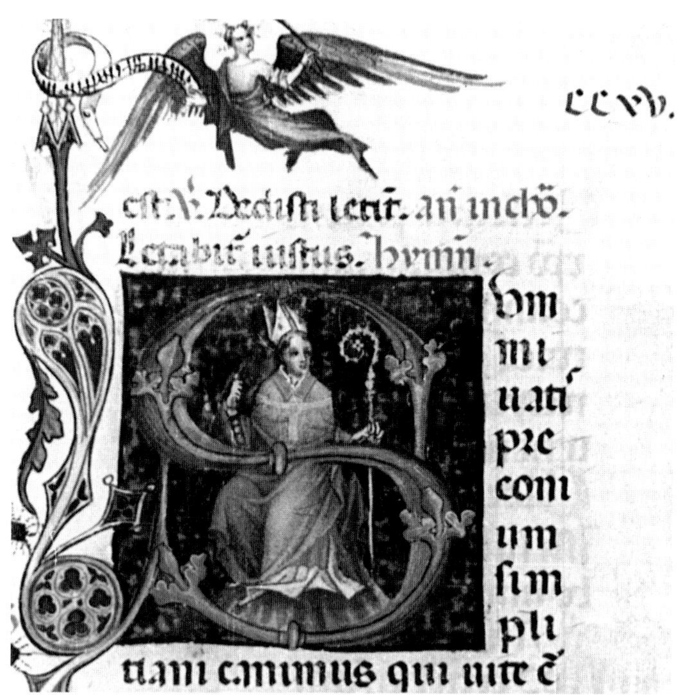

Fig. 79. Salomone dei Grassi, 1396–98, David in prayer, music-making angel in margin. Milan, Bibl. Trivulziana, Lat. 2262, fol. 255

Fig. 80. Salomone dei Grassi, 1396–98, Saint Ambrose. Milan, Bibl. Trivulziana, Lat. 2262, fol. 215

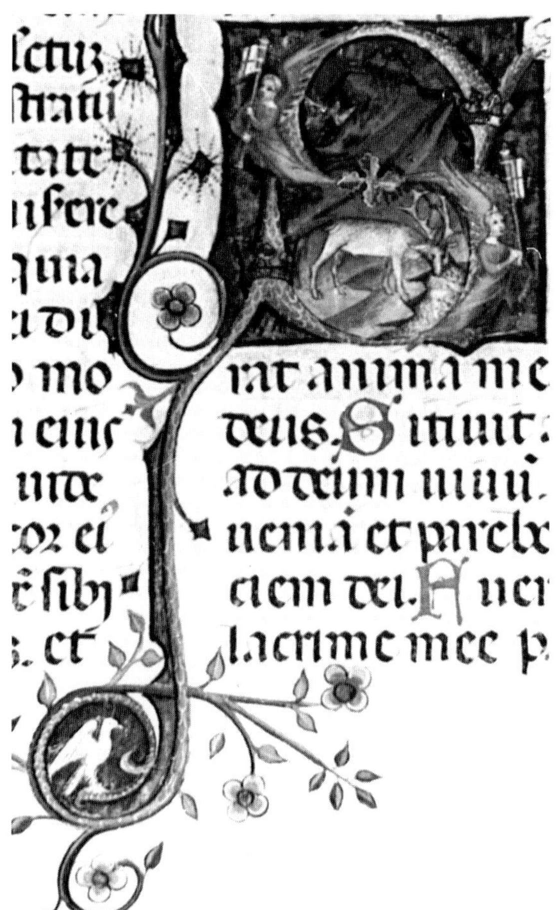

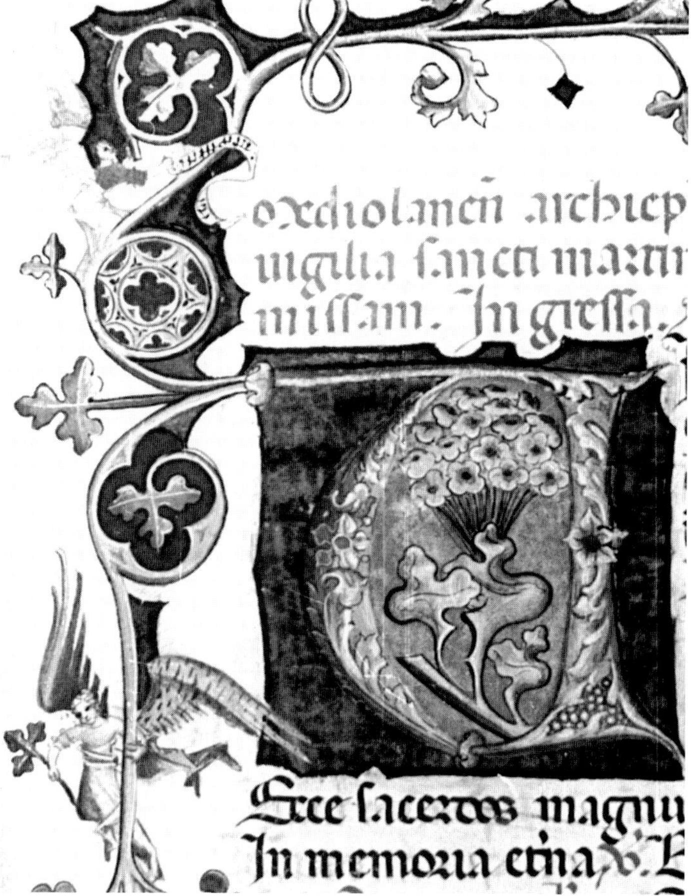

Fig. 81. Salomone dei Grassi, 1396–98, hind drinking; dove in border. Milan, Bibl. Trivulziana, Lat. 2262, fol. 14v

Fig. 82. Salomone dei Grassi, 1396–98, nosegay; angel in border. Milan, Bibl. Trivulziana, Lat. 2262, fol. 59

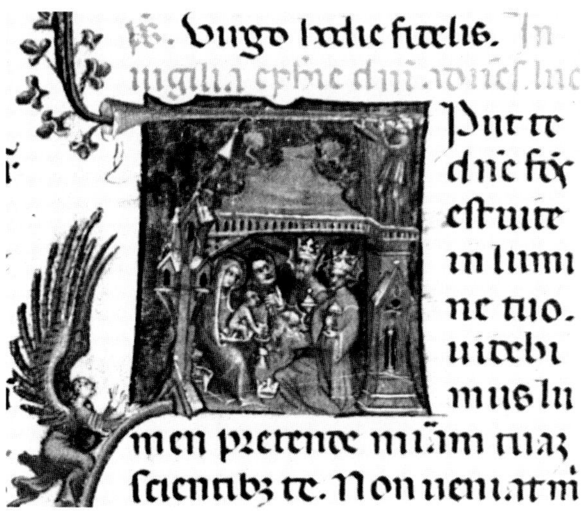

Fig. 83. Salomone dei Grassi, 1396–98, Adoration of the Magi. Milan, Bibl. Trivulziana, Lat. 2262, fol. 99v

Fig. 84. Salomone dei Grassi, 1396–98, angel with scroll. Milan, Bibl. Trivulziana, Lat. 2262, fol. 5

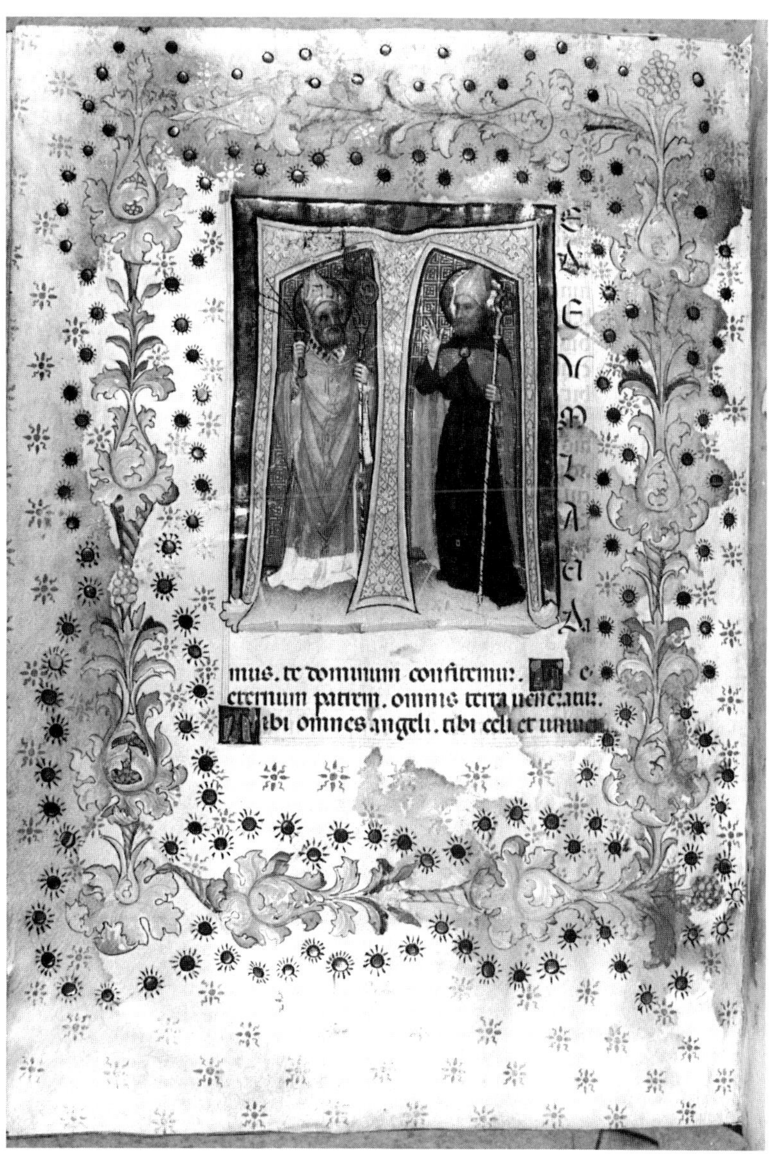

Fig. 85. Salomone dei Grassi, c. 1395, Saints Ambrose and Augustine. Florence, Bibl. naz., Banco Rari 397, fol. 148v

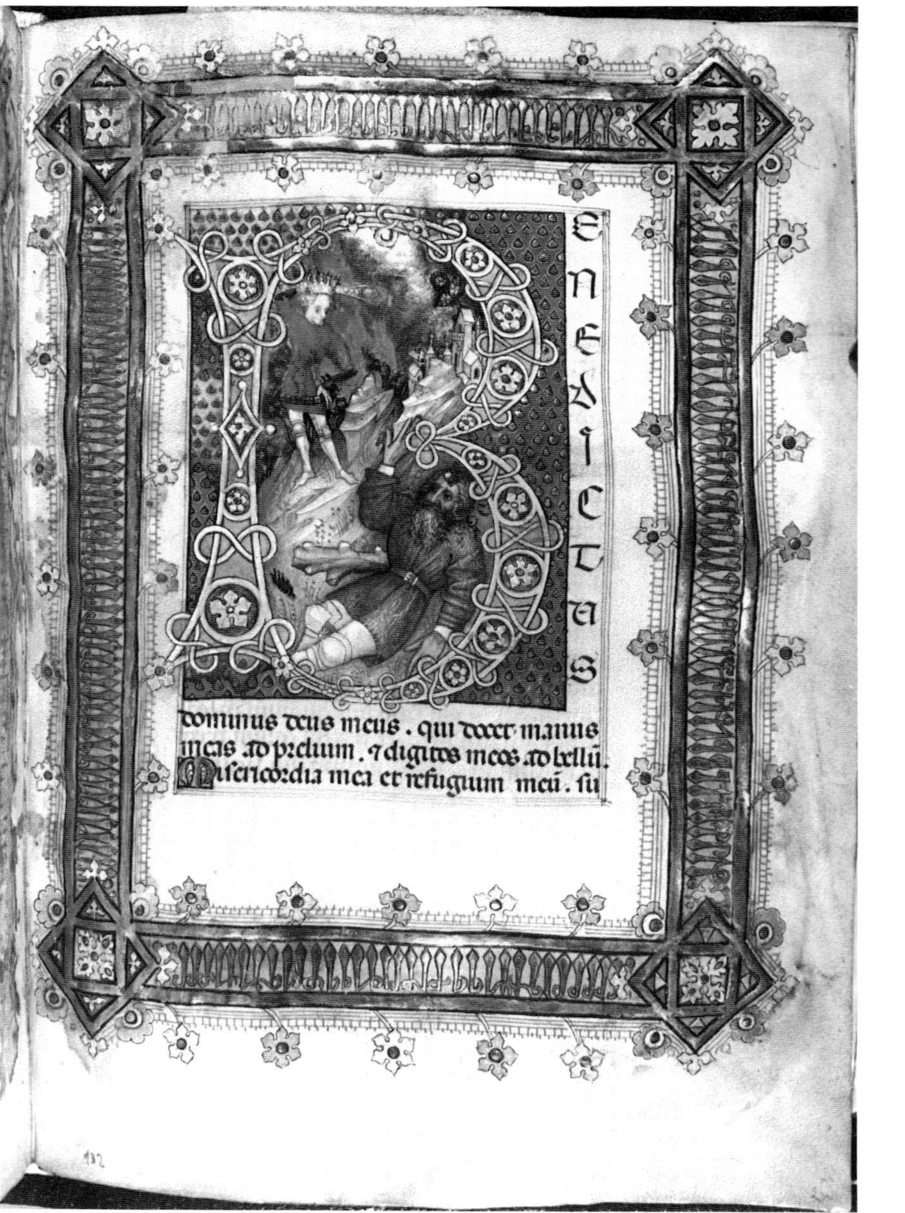

Fig. 86. Giovannino and Salomone dei Grassi, c. 1388–91, David and Goliath. Florence, Bibl. naz., Banco Rari 397, fol. 132

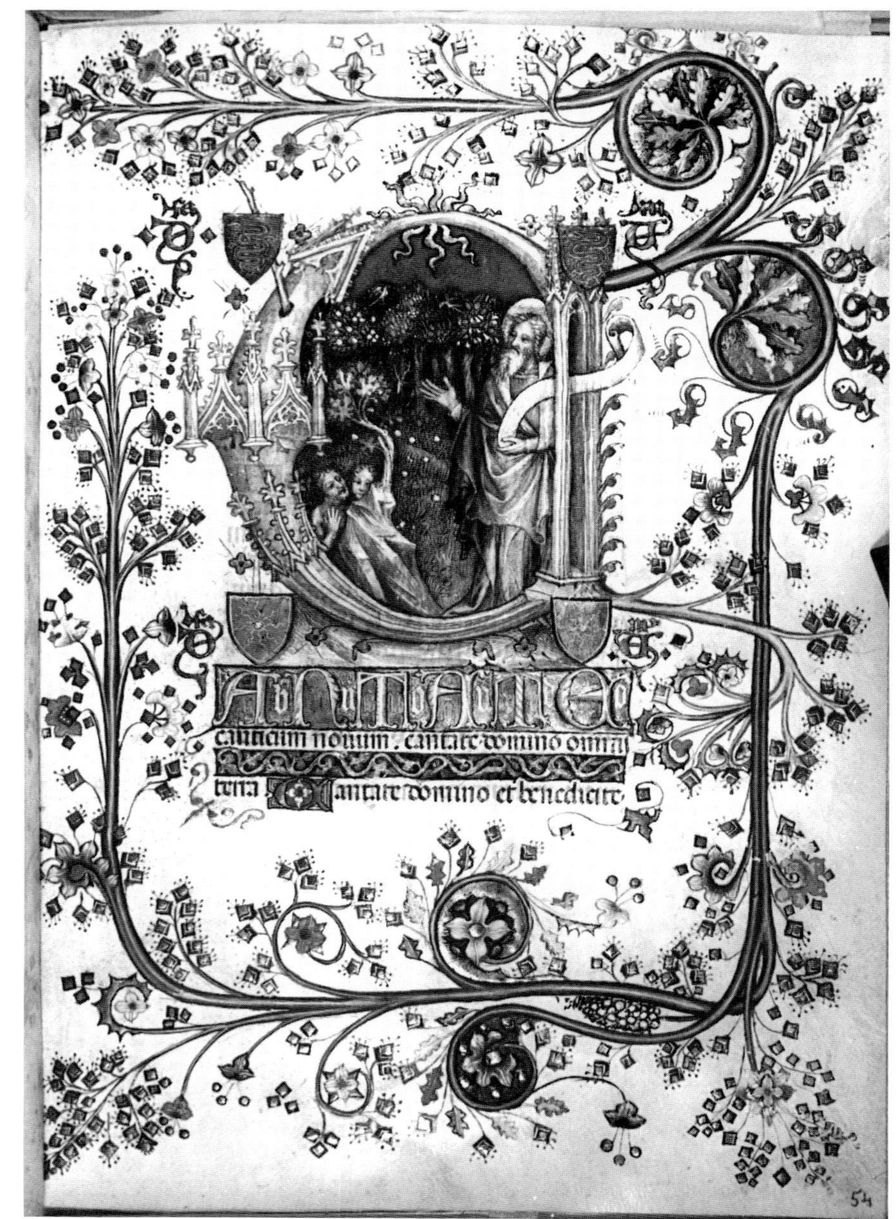

Fig. 87. Giovannino and Salomone dei Grassi, c. 1395, Adam and Eve reproached by the Lord. Florence, Bibl. naz., Landau-Finaly 22, fol. 54

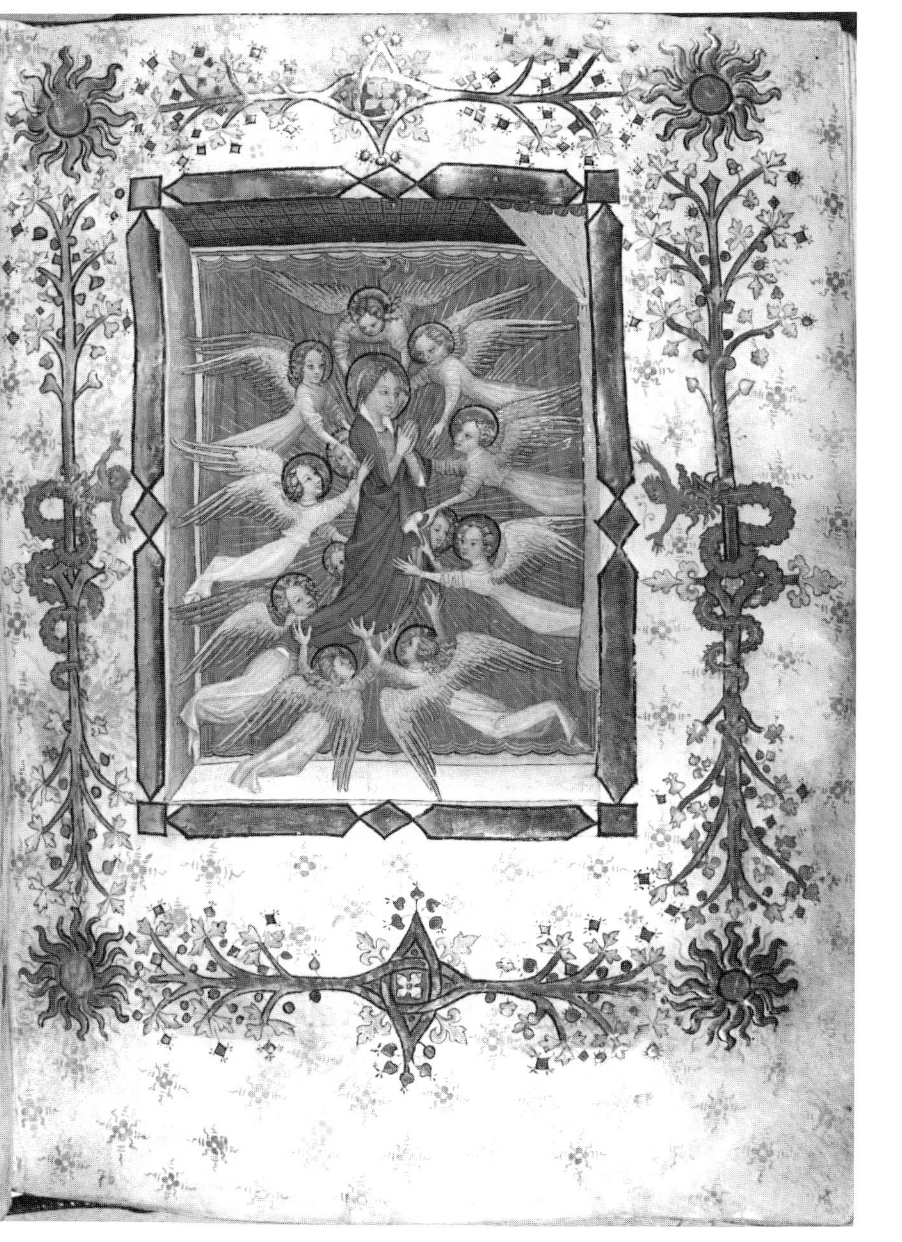

Fig. 88. Assistant of Giovannino dei Grassi, c. 1388–91. Virgin visited by angels in the Temple. Florence, Bibl. naz., Banco Rari 397, fol. 76

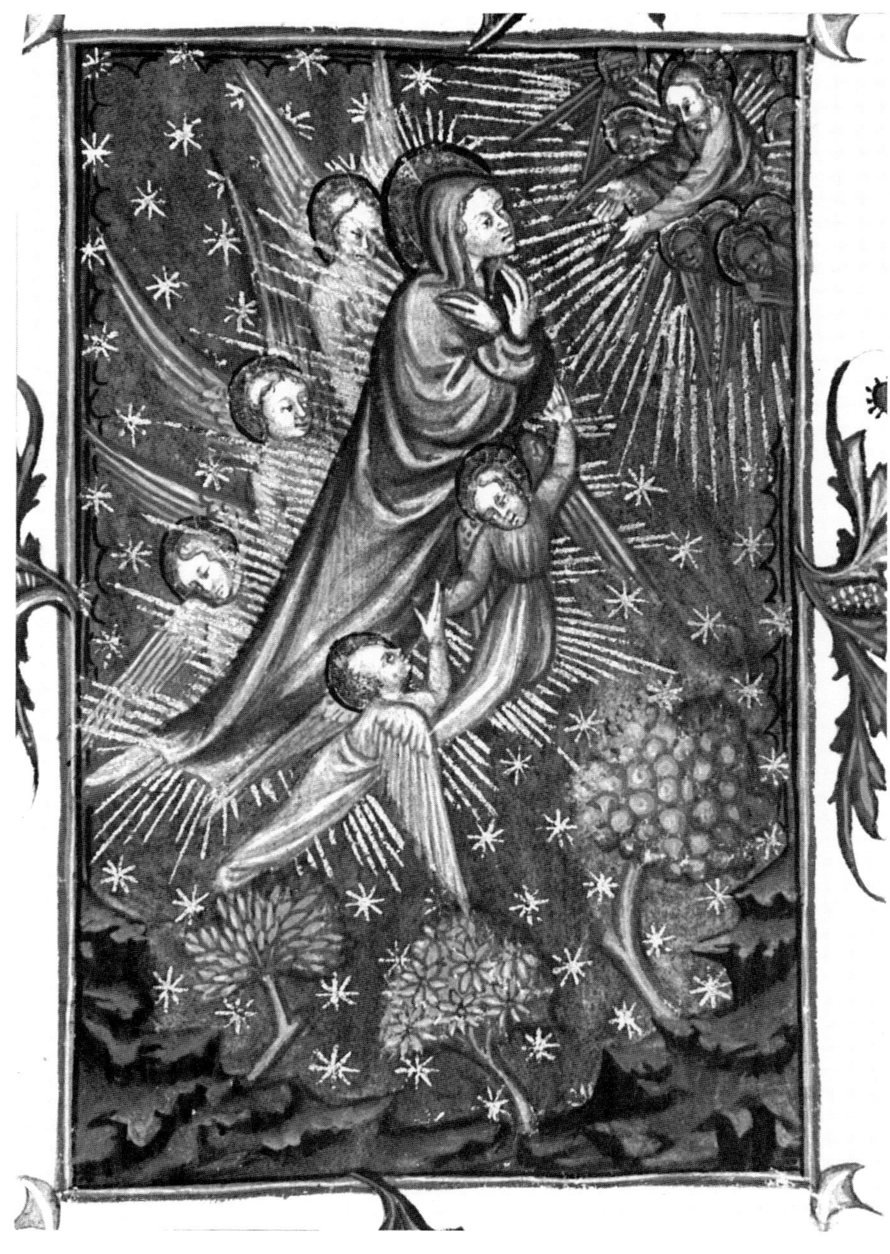

Fig. 89. Lombard, 1380s. Assumption of the Virgin. Modena, Bibl. Estense, Lat. 842, fol. 232

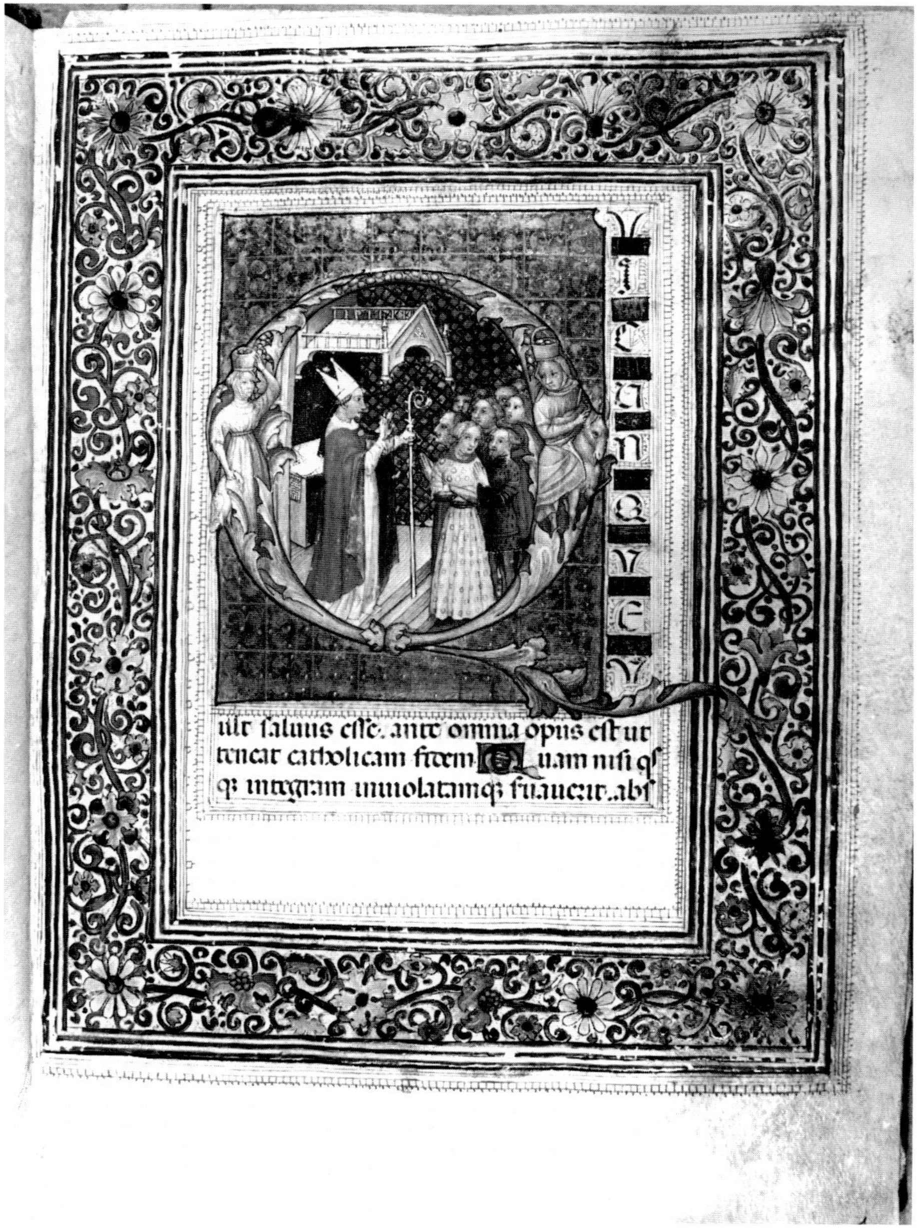

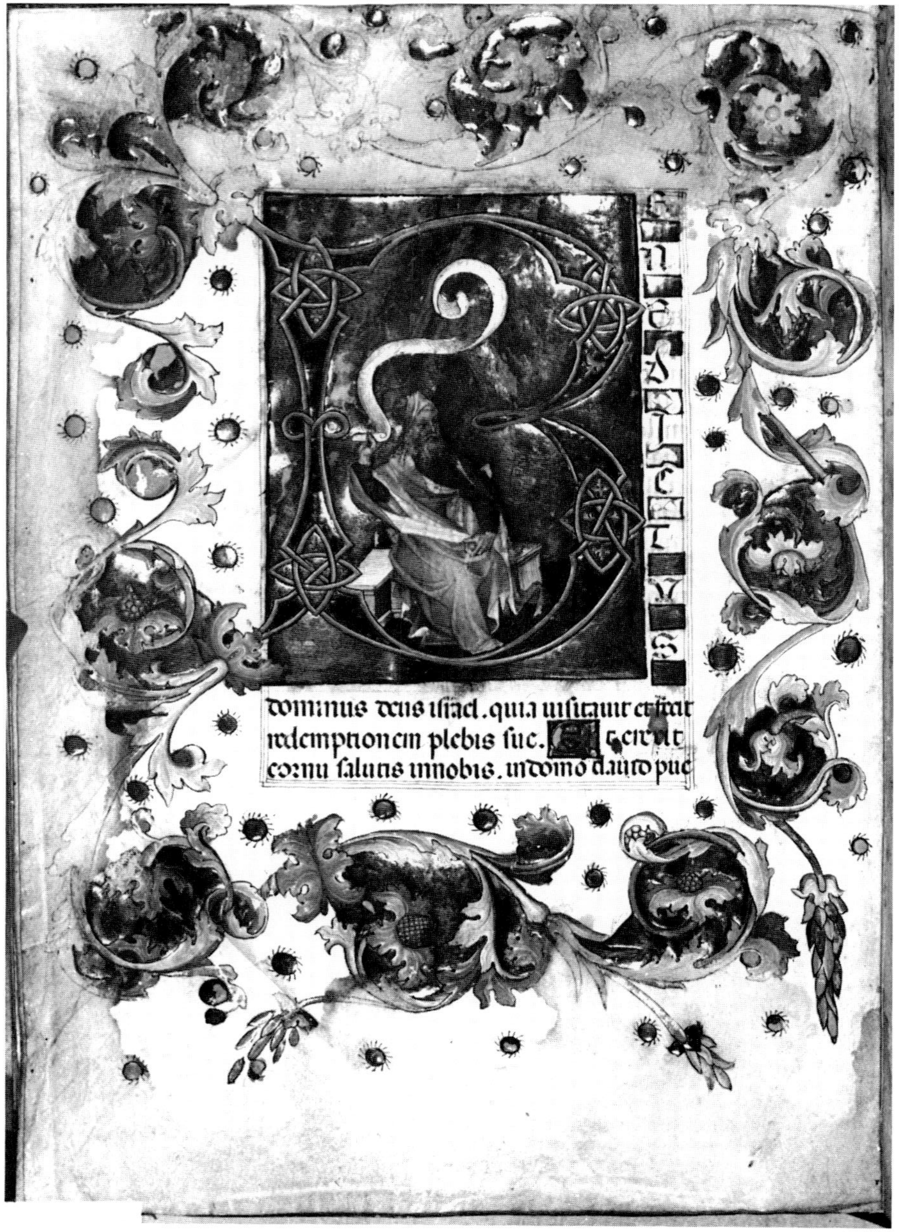

Fig. 91. Salomone dei Grassi, c. 1388–91, Zachariah. Florence, Bibl. naz., Banco Rari 397, fol. 146v

Fig. 90. Salomone dei Grassi, c. 1395, Bishop addresses the faithful; gold punching behind initial by Belbello da Pavia, c. 1427. Florence, Bibl. naz., Landau-Finaly 22, fol. 1

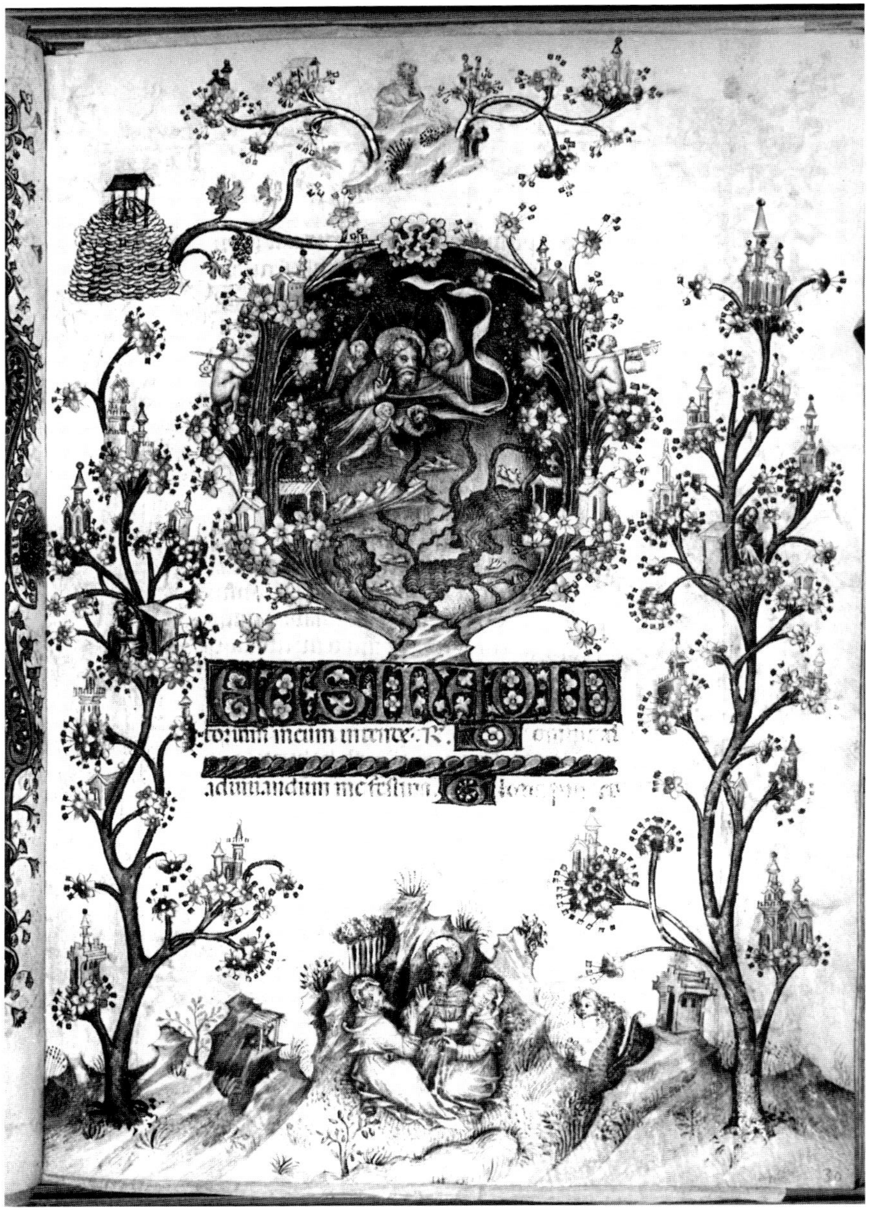

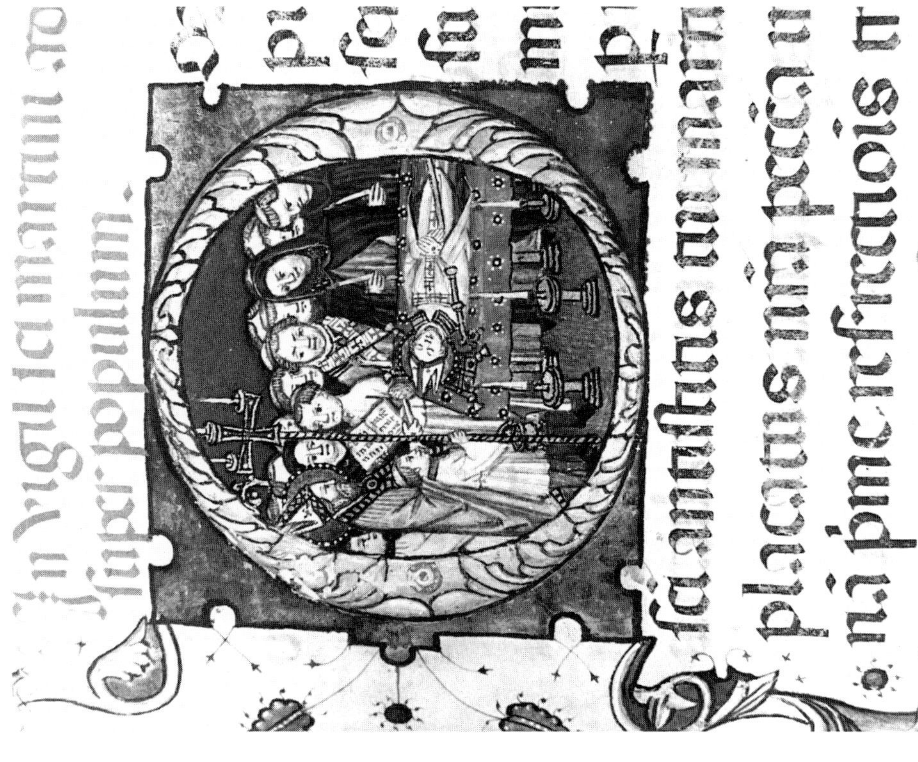

Fig. 93. Anovelo da Imbonate, c. 1395. Funeral of Saint Martin. Milan, Bibl. capitolare di Sant'Ambrogio, Lat. 6, fol. 177

Fig. 92. Giovannino and Salomone dei Grassi, c. 1395, Separation of Land from Water. Florence, Bibl. naz., Landau-Finaly 22, fol. 30

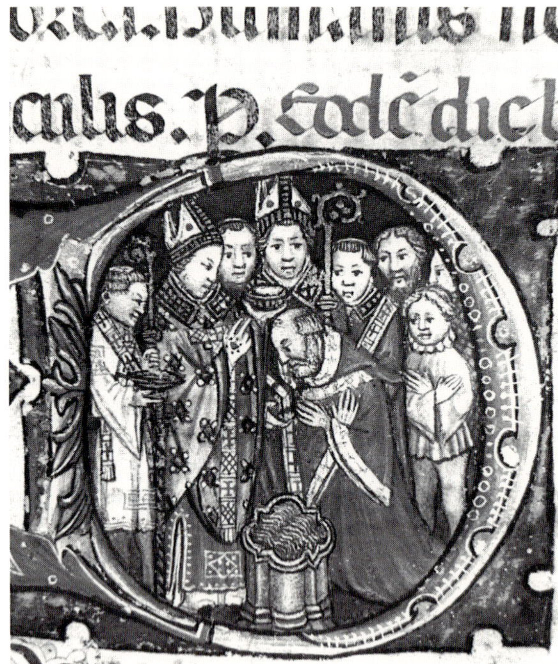

Fig. 94. Anovelo da Imbonate, c. 1395, Baptism of Saint Augustine. Milan, Bibl. capitolare di Sant'Ambrogio, Lat. 6, fol. 193

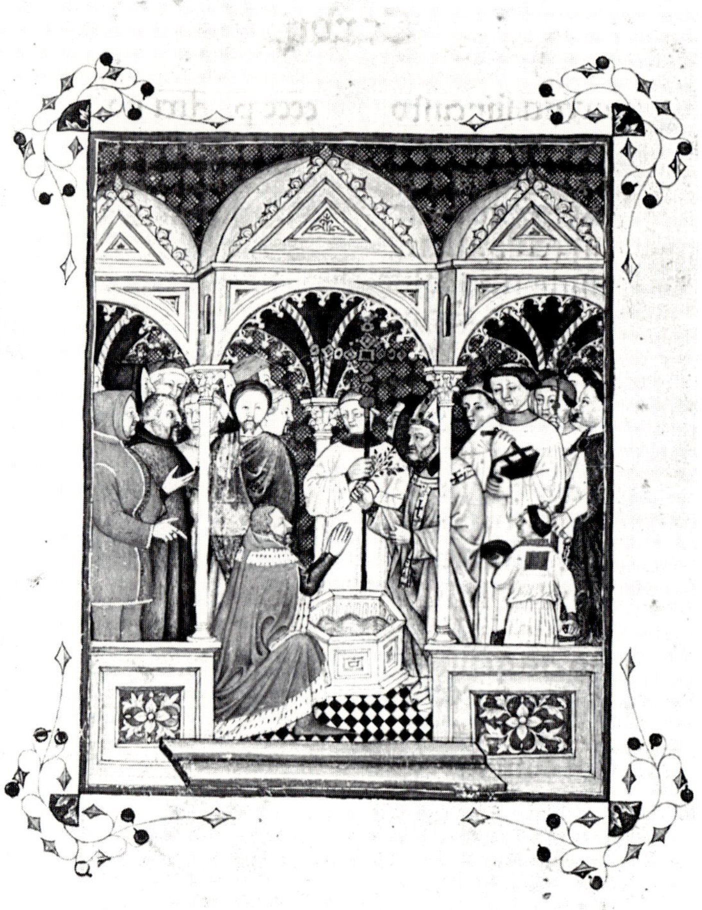

Fig. 95. Lombard, c. 1380, Baptism of Saint Augustine. Paris, Bibl. nat., Lat. 757, fol. 224v

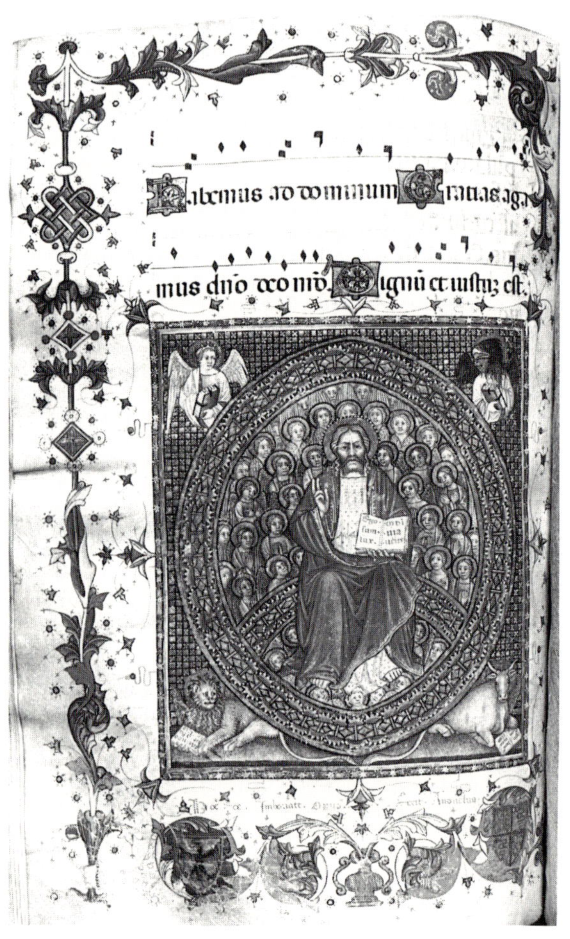

Fig. 96. Anovelo da Imbonate, c. 1395, Christ in Majesty. Milan, Bibl. capitolare di Sant'Ambrogio, Lat. 6, fol. 153v

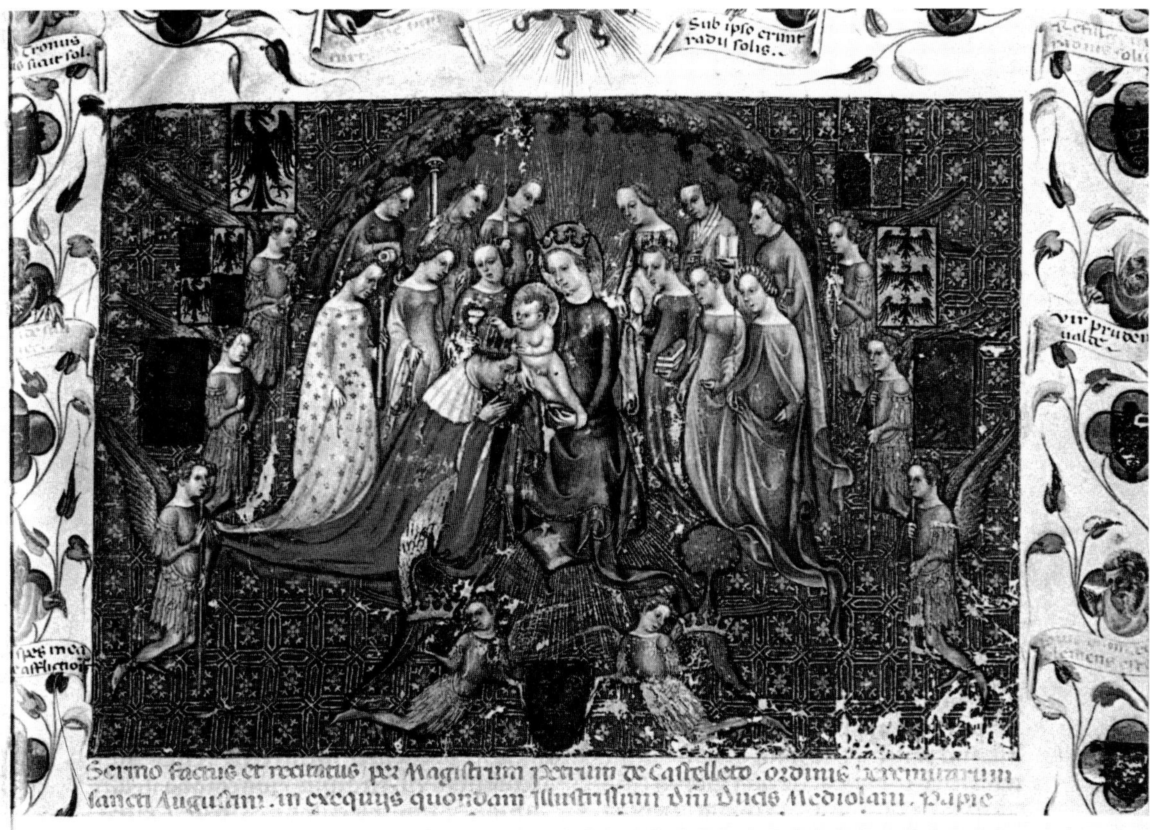

Fig. 97. Detail of Figure 30

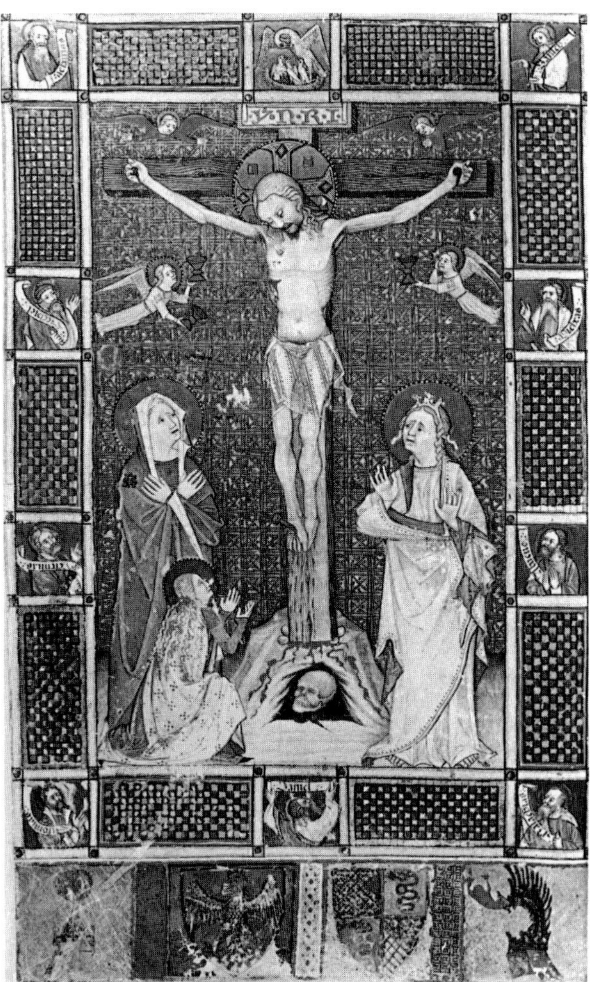

Fig. 98. Associate of Anovelo da Imbonate, c. 1395, Crucifixion. Milan, Bibl. capitolare di Sant'Ambrogio, Lat. 6, fol. 156v

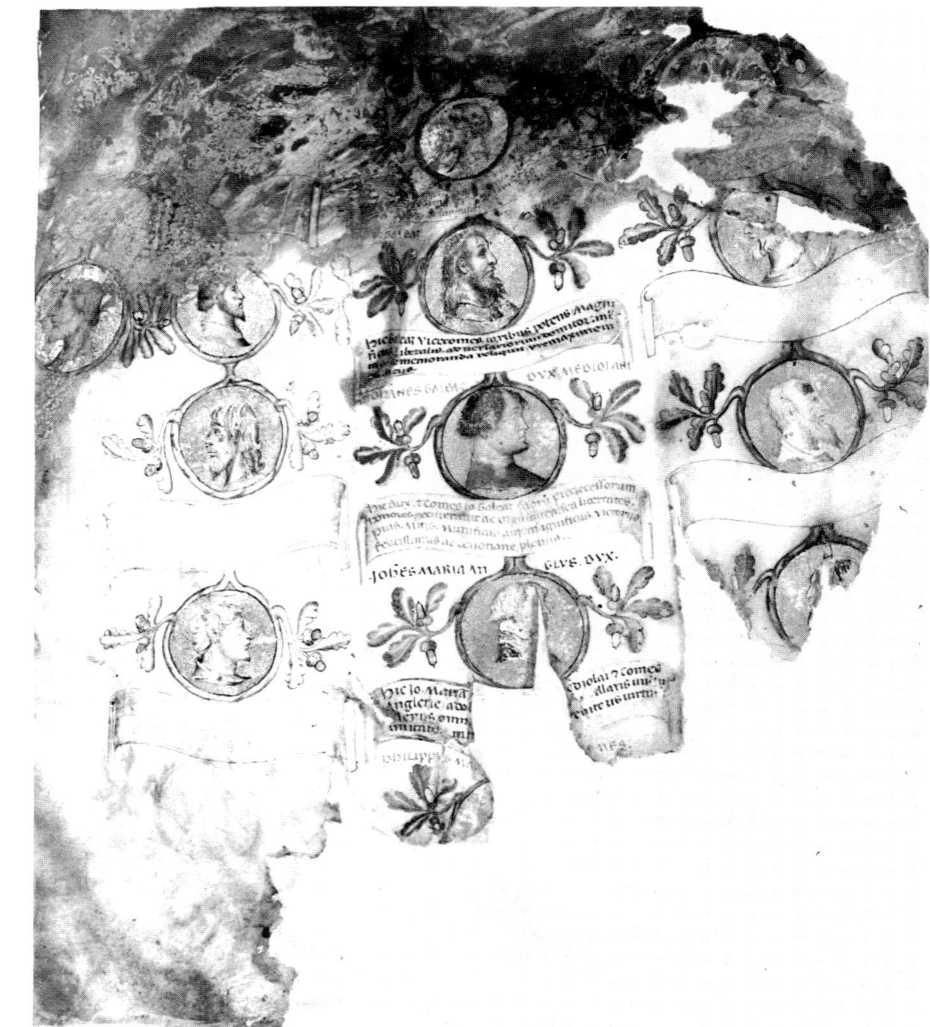

Fig. 99. Bologna, fourteenth century, Tree of Consanguinity. Vatican, Bibl. Vat., Pal. Lat. 629, fol. 260v

Fig. 100. Style of Michelino da Besozzo, page from a Visconti genealogy. London, Brit. Lib., Add. 26814, fol. 8

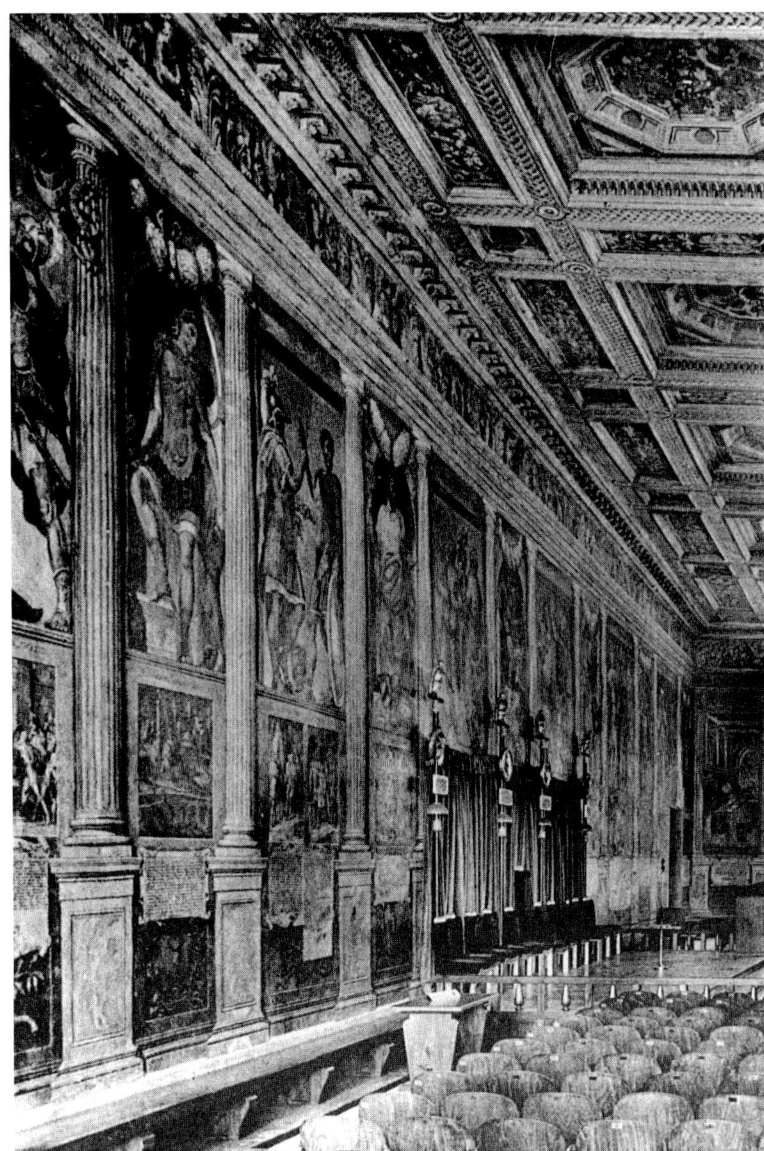

Fig. 101. Paduan painter, c. 1540. Padua, Carrara Palace, Sala Virorum Illustrium (detail)

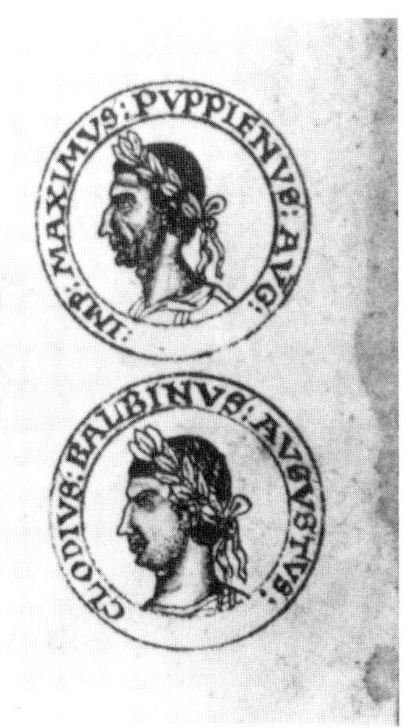

Fig. 102. Giovanni Mansionario, c. 1320, Emperors Pupienus and Balbinus. Vatican, Bibl. Vat., Chig. I.VII.259, fol. 13

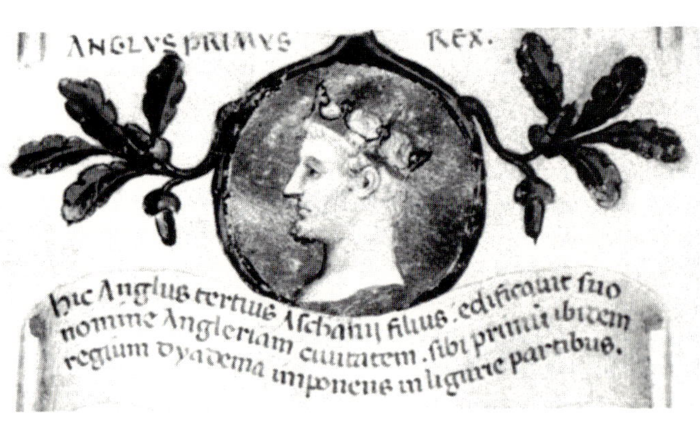

Fig. 103. Detail of Figure 31

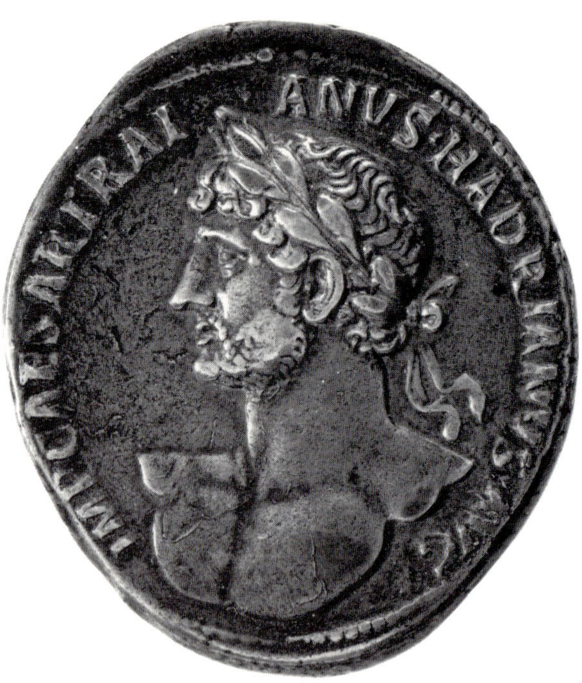

Fig. 104. Eight-denarius piece of Emperor Hadrian,
119. London, British Museum

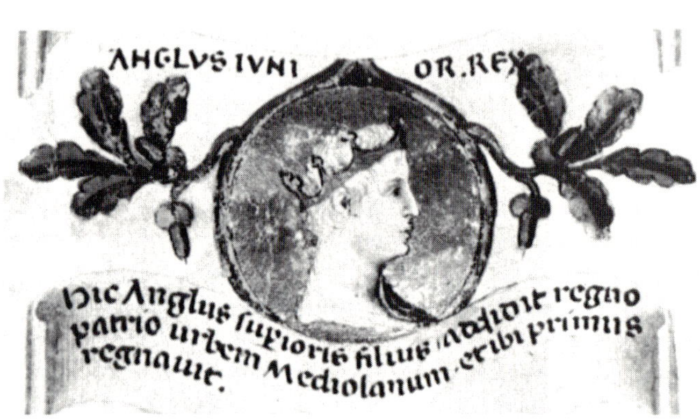

Fig. 105. Detail of Figure 31

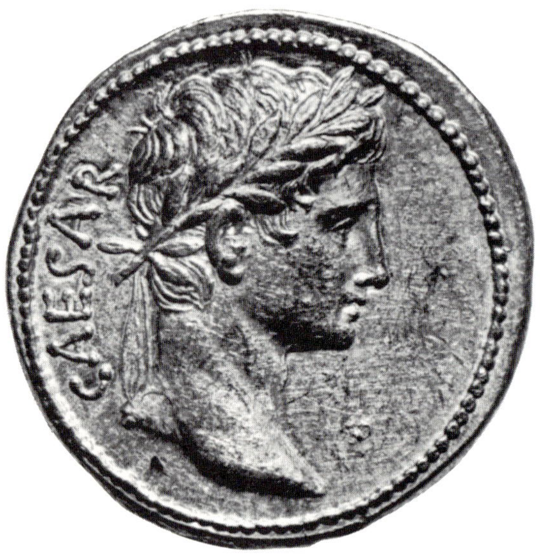

Fig. 106. Aureus of Augustus, c. 20 B.C. Milan,
private collection

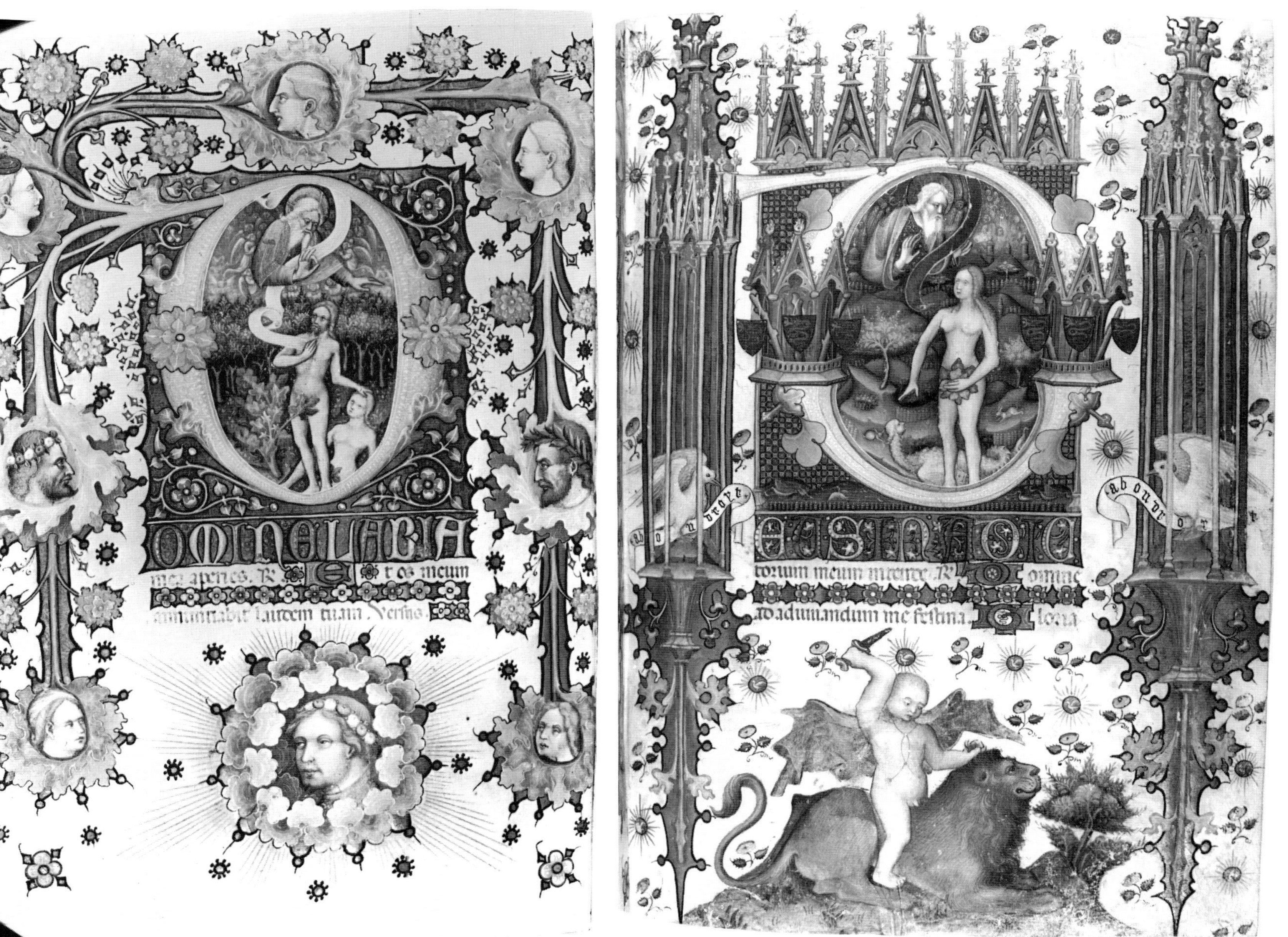

Fig. 107. Associate of Belbello da Pavia, c. 1427, Transference of Blame; Visconti genealogy in the border of LF 57v. Florence, Bibl. naz., Landau-Finaly 22, fols. 57v–58